T0093529

Heterogenous Computational Intelligence in Internet of Things

We have seen a sharp increase in the development of data transfer techniques in the networking industry over the past few years. We can see that the photos are assisting clinicians in detecting infection in patients even in the current COVID-19 pandemic condition. With the aid of ML/AI, medical imaging, such as lung X-rays for COVID-19 infection, is crucial in the early detection of many diseases. We also learned that in the COVID-19 scenario, both wired and wireless networking are improved for data transfer but have network congestion. An intriguing concept that has the ability to reduce spectrum congestion and continuously offer new network services is providing wireless network virtualization. The degree of virtualization and resource sharing varies between the paradigms. Each paradigm has both technical and non-technical issues that need to be handled before wireless virtualization becomes a common technology. For wireless network virtualization to be successful, these issues need careful design and evaluation. Future wireless network architecture must adhere to a number of Quality of Service (QoS) requirements. Virtualization has been extended to wireless networks as well as conventional ones. By enabling multitenancy and tailored services with a wider range of carrier frequencies, it improves efficiency and utilization. In the IoT environment, wireless users are heterogeneous, and the network state is dynamic, making network control problems extremely difficult to solve as dimensionality and computational complexity keep rising quickly.

Deep Reinforcement Learning (DRL) has been developed by the use of Deep Neural Networks (DNNs) as a potential approach to solve high-dimensional and continuous control issues effectively. Deep Reinforcement Learning techniques provide great potential in IoT, edge and SDN scenarios and are used in heterogeneous networks for IoT-based management on the QoS required by each Software Defined Network (SDN) service. While DRL has shown great potential to solve emerging problems in complex wireless network virtualization, there are still domain-specific challenges that require further study, including the design of adequate DNN architectures with 5G network optimization issues, resource discovery and allocation, developing intelligent mechanisms that allow the automated and dynamic management of the virtual communications established in the SDNs which is considered as research perspective.

Heterogenous Computational Intelligence in Internet of Things

Edited by
Pawan Singh
Prateek Singhal
Pramod Kumar Mishra
Avimanyou K. Vatsa

CRC Press
Taylor & Francis Group
Boca Raton London New York

CRC Press is an imprint of the
Taylor & Francis Group, an **informa** business

Cover image credit: Shutterstock

First edition published 2024
by CRC Press
2385 Executive Center Drive, Suite 320, Boca Raton, FL, 33431

and by CRC Press
4 Park Square, Milton Park, Abingdon, Oxon, OX14 4RN

CRC Press is an imprint of Taylor & Francis Group, LLC

© 2024 selection and editorial matter, Pawan Singh, Prateek Singhal, Pramod Kumar Mishra and Avimanyou K. Vatsa; individual chapters, the contributors

Reasonable efforts have been made to publish reliable data and information, but the author and publisher cannot assume responsibility for the validity of all materials or the consequences of their use. The authors and publishers have attempted to trace the copyright holders of all material reproduced in this publication and apologize to copyright holders if permission to publish in this form has not been obtained. If any copyright material has not been acknowledged please write and let us know so we may rectify in any future reprint.

Except as permitted under U.S. Copyright Law, no part of this book may be reprinted, reproduced, transmitted, or utilized in any form by any electronic, mechanical, or other means, now known or hereafter invented, including photocopying, microfilming, and recording, or in any information storage or retrieval system, without written permission from the publishers.

For permission to photocopy or use material electronically from this work, access www.copyright.com or contact the Copyright Clearance Center, Inc. (CCC), 222 Rosewood Drive, Danvers, MA 01923, 978-750-8400. For works that are not available on CCC please contact mpkbookspermissions@tandf.co.uk

Trademark notice: Product or corporate names may be trademarks or registered trademarks and are used only for identification and explanation without intent to infringe.

ISBN: 978-1-032-42637-2 (hbk)
ISBN: 978-1-032-42639-6 (pbk)
ISBN: 978-1-003-36360-6 (ebk)

DOI: 10.1201/9781003363606

Typeset in Times
by SPi Technologies India Pvt Ltd (Straive)

Contents

Acknowledgment

We express our heartfelt gratitude to CRC Press (Taylor & Francis Group) and the editorial team for their guidance and support during the completion of this book. We are sincerely grateful to reviewers for their suggestions and illuminating views for each book chapter presented here in *Heterogenous Computational Intelligence in Internet of Things*.

About the Editors

Dr. Pawan Singh is an Associate Professor in the Department of Computer Science & Engineering, Amity School of Engineering and Technology, Amity University Uttar Pradesh, Lucknow, India. He has completed Ph.D. degree in Computer Science from Magadh University, Gaya. He has more than fifteen years of experience in research and teaching. He has published several research articles in SCI/SCIE/Scopus journals and conferences of high repute. He has also authored various books. He has various National and international patents and some are granted. He holds contributions in IEEE, Elsevier, etc. repute journals. He is also a reviewer in various reputed journals. His current areas of interest include Computer Networks, Parallel Processing and Internet of Things.

Mr. Prateek Singhal is an Assistant Professor in the Department of Computer Engineering & Applications at GLA University, Mathura. He is pursuing a Ph.D. degree in Medical Imaging from the Maharishi University of Information Technology, Lucknow, India and has more than four years of experience in research and teaching and has published several research articles in SCI/SCIE/Scopus journals and conferences of high repute. He has also authored a book on Cloud Computing and also an edited book for Taylor & Francis. He has various national and international patents and some have been granted. He has made contributions to journals published by a variety of reputed publishers, including IEEE, Elsevier, Springer, and others. He has also been a reviewer in various reputed journals. He is also on the team of the research advisory member in his present institute. His current areas of interest include Image Processing, Medical Imaging, Human Computation Interface, Neuro-Computing, Internet of Things and Signal Processing.

Dr. Pramod Kumar Mishra is working as a Head and Professor in the Department of Computer Science & Engineering at Banaras Hindu University, Varanasi. He has completed Ph.D. degree on A study of efficient shortest path algorithms for serial and parallel computers from APS University, Rewa, India. He has more than Thirty years of experience in research and teaching. He has received various Awards and fellowships from the good repute organizations. He has also received various grants from national and international government

bodies/Agency. He has published several research articles in SCI/SCIE/Scopus journals and conferences of high repute. He has also authored a book on Cloud Computing.
He has various National and international patents and some are granted. He holds
contributions in IEEE, Elsevier, etc. reputed journal. He is in the team of the research
advisory member in his present institute. His current areas of interest include AI
and Machine Learning Algorithms, Data Analytics, Parallel Computing, High-
Performance Clusters, Algorithm Engineering (AE), High-Performance AE, Parallel
Computation, and Computational complexity.

Dr. Avimanyou K. Vatsa is working as an assistant professor in the department of computer science, Fairleigh
Dickinson University – Teaneck. He also worked as
an assistant professor at West Texas A&M University,
a teaching & research assistant at the University of
Missouri, Columbia, and an assistant professor for more
than ten years in several engineering colleges and a university in India. Also, he worked as a software engineer
in the industry. He always motivates and inspires stu-
dents with a statement: "Nothing is impossible, just put your hard work and sincere
effort persistently toward your goal.

List of Contributors

M. Abinaya
SRMIST
Kattankulathur, India

Anwar Ahamed Ansari
Bansal Institute of Science & Technology
Bhopal, India

Taeesh Azal Assadi
B.M.S. College of Engineering
Bengaluru, India

Anirudh Banerjee
Amity University
Lucknow, India

Prayas Banerjee
Sister Nivedita University
Kolkata, India

Pavan Bhatt
VPMP Polytechnic
Gandhinagar, India

Shuva Biswas
Sister Nivedita University
Kolkata, India

M. H. Chaithra
REVA University
Bengaluru, India

Nabendu Chaki
University of Calcutta
Kolkata, India

Sonali R. Chavan
Sant Gadge Baba Amravati University
Amravati, India

Preeti Choudhury
Sister Nivedita University
Kolkata, West Bengal

Soma Datta
Sister Nivedita University,
Kolkata, India

Tanmoy Debnath
B.M.S. College of Engineering
Bengaluru, India

Shivani Dubey
Greater Noida Institute of Technology
Greater Noida, India

Shashwat Gupta
Amity University (U.P) Lucknow
    Campus
Lucknow, India

Fariha Haroon
Kalindi College, University of Delhi
New Delhi, India

Bramah Hazela
Amity University (U.P) Lucknow
    Campus
Lucknow, India

Rajalaxmi Hegde
NMAM Institute of Technology
Deralakatte, India

Sandeepkumar Hegde
NMAM Institute of Technology
Deralakatte, India

N. M. Jyothi
Koneru Lakshmaiah Education
    Foundation
Guntur, India

Anjali Kakarla
Koneru Lakshmaiah Education Foundation
Vaddeswaram, Guntur, India

M. Kalpana
SRMIST
Kattankulathur, India

A. Karthikeyan
PSG College of Technology
Coimbatore, India

Pradeep Kumar
Amity University (U.P) Lucknow
    Campus
Lucknow, India

B. K. Rajya Lakshmi
Hyderabad Institute of Technology and
    Management
Hyderabad, India

Sushobhan Majumdar
Jadavpur University
Kolkata, India

V. Nithyapriyaa
PSG College of Technology
Coimbatore, India

Shubh Oswal
B.M.S. College of Engineering
Bengaluru, India

Tejaswini Pamidimukkala
Koneru Lakshmaiah Education
    Foundation
Vaddeswaram, Guntur, India

Divyang Pandya
LDRP Institute of Technology &
    Research
Gandhinagar, India

B. Parthiban
PSG College of Technology
Coimbatore, India

A. Pavani
Koneru Lakshmaiah Education
    Foundation
Guntur, India

S. Pavithra Shri
PSG College of Technology
Coimbatore, India

S. Prabakeran
SRMIST
Kattankulathur, India

T. Pragatheeswaran
PSG College of Technology
Coimbatore, India

Nafisur Rahman
School of Engineering Sciences and
    Technology, Jamia Hamdard
New Delhi, India

S. P. Rajamohana
Pondicherry University
Pondicherry, India

Sheenu Rizvi
Amity University
Lucknow, India

Vipulkumar Rokad
KSV University
Gandhinagar, India

Subir Kumar Roy
VLSI Systems Research Group, IIIT
    Bangalore
Bangalore, India

Tonny Saha
Sister Nivedita University
Kolkata, West Bengal

Ajay Kumar Sahu
Greater Noida Institute of
    Technology
Greater Noida, India

P. Saleem Akram
Koneru Lakshmaiah Education
    Foundation
Vaddeswaram, Guntur, India

Yatish Sekaran
B.M.S. College of Engineering
Bengaluru, India

Nipun Sharma
Presidency University
Bangalore, India

Swati Sharma
Presidency University
Bangalore, India

Swati Sherekar
Sant Gadge Baba Amravati University
Amravati, India

Rashmi Singh
Bansal Institute of Science &
 Technology
Bhopal, India

Shikha Singh
Amity University (U.P) Lucknow Campus
Lucknow, India

Vikas Singhal
Greater Noida Institute of Technology
Greater Noida, India

Garima Srivastava
Amity University (U.P) Lucknow Campus
Lucknow, India

Sai Dileep Suvvari
B.M.S. College of Engineering
Bengaluru, India

Husna Tabassum
HKBK College of Engineering
Bengaluru, India

Kashish Thakur
Sister Nivedita University
Kolkata, India

V. B. Tharmentheran
PSG College of Technology
Coimbatore, India

Chiriki Usha
Dadi institute of Engineering and
 Technology
Visakhapatnam, India

Lavanya Veeranki
Koneru Lakshmaiah Education
 Foundation
Vaddeswaram, Guntur, India

Shaik Mohammed Waseem
VLSI Systems Research Group, IIIT
 Bangalore
Bangalore, India

1 Human-Interacted Computation System
A State of the Art in Music

Nipun Sharma and Swati Sharma

Presidency University, Bangalore, India

1.1 INTRODUCTION

The COVID-19 global pandemic has led to dramatic shifts in the paradigm of teaching and learning. The emergence of online, interactive and automated teaching methodologies has been remarkable. The majority of the teaching and learning involves human interactions which are complemented with advanced teaching aids such as 3-D animations and smartboards. However, some of the self-paced learning systems are now completely automated, operate on the user's input and supplying recommendations as output. These intelligent recommender systems cater to a wide variety of skill sets such as imaging, photography, painting, web design, software coding, game development and music. Machine learning and artificial intelligence each play an important role in the design of state-of-the-art recommender systems for learning and mastering a skill. Given that the majority of students now acquire their skills from the internet, the online space is thronged with all sorts of teaching applications for users of all ages and levels of ability.

This chapter holistically covers a complete design procedure for designing a human interacted computational system for music recommendations. The presentation of the state of the art is organized in such a way that it builds the understanding from the bottom up. In Section 1.1 a typical Human Interacted Computation System for Music Domain is introduced with three primary stages of execution. Section 1.2 discusses the aspects and complexities of Music Information Retrieval. Section 1.3 discusses the components and technologies used in Music Recognition and Classification. Section 1.4 discusses the final block of the system that is the Music Recommendation. It discusses an array of recommender techniques that can be implemented based upon the case requirement.

1.1.1 HUMAN INTERACTED COMPUTATION SYSTEMS

Human-Computer Interaction is an integral component of the system's design. The usability of the system determines its quality. The focus for research has shifted from traditional system design to the development of interactive, intelligent, natural, adaptive, self-correcting systems [1]. The system design of the Human Interacted

DOI: 10.1201/9781003363606-1

computation system utilizes virtual reality, augmented reality, geotagging, user-preference database analysis and the extensive use of Artificial Neural Networks for predictions and recommendation purposes. The most important domain that has risen in the development of the systems is remote self-paced learning systems. One very specific area of such computational systems is the recommendation systems. These need to be computationally fast, accurate and intelligent. They require a good amount of human interaction as an input for behavioural analysis and to produce tangible output as results of classification problem or recommendations.

Even in the most primitive format, a computer is a human-interacted computational system governed by two key primary objectives of functionality and usability [2]. From the very beginning, the success of the machine depends not on the complexity but on its usability; even the most advanced machines serve no purpose if they are not usable. Another important parameter of success of such machines is the ability to provide a user-friendly for computer interaction. The modes of input devices may have changed for traditional keyboards and pointing devices to VR glasses and smart wearables, but none of this would be successful and meaningful if it adds complications and hinders user adoption [2]. The usage success of the HCI is purely a subjective affair and it depends on the domain and context in which the system is designed; however, the optimal balance between the functionality and usage of the system overall affects the success, no matter the context [3, 4]. In order to increase the success rate and efficiency of such HCI computers, many techniques, such as ubiquitous computing and artificial intelligence, are deployed into system design [5].

1.1.2 APPLICATION OF HUMAN INTERACTED COMPUTER SYSTEMS IN MUSIC

It is said that music is the food for soul, and so a good and robust Recommendation System for Music has a daunting task at hand. The task of designing a successful Music Recognition and Recommendation system involves a multi-layered series of tasks at different stages, that include music notes analysis and synthesizing them for the recommendation system, audio note representation, models used to analyse these recognition tasks and the prediction of recommendations based on user input [6, 7].

1.2 MUSIC INFORMATION RETRIEVAL

This section introduces the complexities involved in music information retrieval. In contrast to other domains, populating and creating a meaningful dataset for music recommendation is far more complicated. Music is a multi-faceted and multi-modal form of art. Computational Music Information retrieval is a tedious task, based on extracting features and creating data ready for models by using one or multiple categories of music perception. Music perception is paradoxical, in that is it depends upon various parameters which may not even be related to the music itself. For example, the psychological effect cannot be ignored when you are designing intelligent human interacted systems for Music. Figure 1.1 shows vividity of music information which is embedded in various parameters, all of which are equally important in designing a complete human interacted music recommendation system. The key information is hidden in the music content. This tells us about the tangible and

FIGURE 1.1 Block diagram of a human interacted computation system for the music domain.

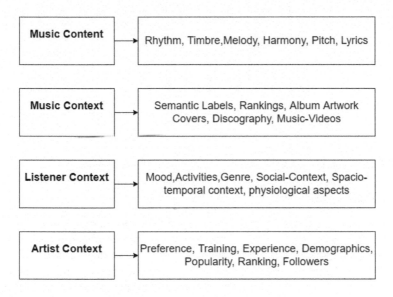

FIGURE 1.2 Categories and metadata in various music modalities.

constant parameters of music: rhythm, pitch, harmony, melody and lyrics. This functional aspect of a musical piece is constant and will not change once a piece of music is composed. The second category is music context, which can be thought of as the additional informational metadata that helps in the segmentation of music when all the other features fail to cluster. These features include album artwork, discography, semantic labels and rankings etc. The third category is the listener's context, which is very dynamic and causes the recommender systems to flex their computational power. It includes mood activities and psychological aspects, which are changing continuously. The final category is the artist context. Although this may seem like static informational metadata, its information is also prone to change as it includes social media parameters such as followers, demographics, popularity, rankings etc. These may also change with the addition of the new music content and changes in the artists' preferences over time (Figure 1.2).

1.3 MUSIC RECOGNITION AND CLASSIFICATION

The second block of the complete system illustrated in Figure 1.3 is the music recognition and classification. This is the most resource extensive block of the entire system in terms of computational power and exploratory data analysis.

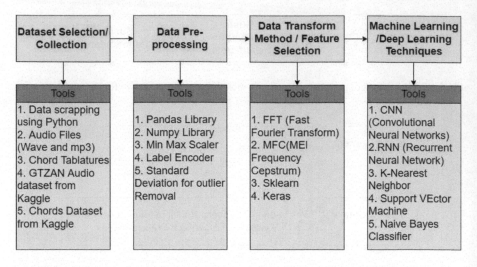

FIGURE 1.3   Various blocks of music recognition and classification stage.

1.3.1 DATA COLLECTION

Data Collection, or repository population, is the first step for any system employing machine learning. In the context of human interacted music recommendation systems, data availability is made possible by utilizing the online datasets repositories primarily or collecting samples of music clips by either playing the instruments or clipping existing recordings. One of the most popular datasets for music genre classification is the GTZAN dataset, available in Kaggle. This is a dataset of 30 seconds of 1000 sound clippings. These sound clippings are classified into nine different genres: Rock, Pop, Jazz, Disco, Classical, Hip-Hop, Country, Metal and Blues [8]. Another interesting dataset for guitar chords classification is available in Kaggle by the name of Major VS Minor guitar chords for determining the guitar tonality. Finally, populating custom datasets for custom system designs are practiced.

1.3.2 DATA PRE-PROCESSING

Data Pre-processing is the second step in the classification and recognition-based tasks as shown in Figure 1.3. The process primarily involves presenting the input data into a recognizable format for the machines to learn from. This step involves a lot of techniques that transform non-numerical data into a numerical form. It also involves the arrangement of data into tabular formats for prediction purposes. A wide array of Python modules are used to accomplish this. These include pandas, NumPy, min-max scalar, label encoding techniques, outlier removals and addressing NaN (Not a Numeral) values.

1.3.3 DATA TRANSFORMATION

After the selection of the dataset, especially in the case of music, transforming the data into a usable numerical format is a daunting task again. We have two options to convert the audio/music data into a frequency domain and we need to make a conscious decision to choose one technique over the other depending on the particular scenario. The next section discusses the two transform techniques.

- FFT

The most popular method of converting a signal from time domain to frequency domain is the Fourier transform. The frequency domain values of the time domain signal is obtained by performing a simple mathematical formula, as given in Equation (1.1), on the time domain signal.

$$x[k] = \sum_{n=0}^{N-1} x[n] e^{-j2\pi kn/N} \qquad (1.1)$$

However, Fast Fourier Transform (FFT) is a frequency transformation algorithm, which carries out the conversion linearly. Although it is versatile, it is not the best choice for the music signals as heard by the humans as they hear the sound logarithmic scale. This fact is confirmed by the harmonics in the musical notes. A musical note, let us say, A-Note has a frequency of 110Hz in the first octave but A-Note appears after integral multiples of 110Hz featuring in different octaves. The presence of harmonics in the music signals reiterates the logarithmic nature of the music rather than the linear. To address this issue another logarithmic or non-linear technique to transform the time domain signal to frequency is utilized, which is the Mel Frequency Cepstrum (MEL).

- MEL

As discussed, the non-linear or logarithmic analysis of the frequency spectrum is done by a technique called the Mel Frequency Cepstrum, an algorithm that essentially converts a linear frequency scale into a logarithmic scale creating coefficients in such a way that the humans can relate to it as a real-world sound or music. The mathematical formula for Mel Transform is given in Equation (1.2).

$$\text{Mel}(f) = 2595 \ \log 10 \left(1 + \frac{f}{700} \right) \qquad (1.2)$$

It can be clearly inferred that using MEL to generate input values that are needed to be provided for Machine Learning Algorithms to train the models is a more optimal option. The comparison of performances of FFT and MEL shows that the Accuracy of MEL is almost 4% higher than FFT on the MLP on GTZAN dataset [9].

1.3.4 DATA MODELLING

The final stage of any Recommender System is machine learning. In contrast to any other data analysis scenarios, machine learning in context to music recognition and recommendation is performed by certain tried-and-tested algorithms. At present, this is a relatively new area of research and a lot of experimentation is being carried out to evaluate the effectiveness of various available machine learning or deep learning techniques. This experimentation is limited by the extensive resource consumption of the music-based data. The computational requirements of such data is large and requires sophisticated hardware with GPUs and high-end processors. A review of the few tested techniques in building Recommender Systems is presented in this section.

- Convolutional Neural Networks (CNN)
  Neural Networks are multi-layered networks essentially consisting of an input layer, a hidden layer and an output layer. Convolutional Neural Networks (also known as Covnets) are extremely popular for image classification problems. Convolutional Neural Networks (CNN) consists of convolutional layers that consists of filters. These filters are scanned over the entire input array to generate a filtered array which is passed on to the next layer. Multiple layers participate in the Covnets, including the input layer, the convolutional layer, the activation function layer, the pool layer and the output layer.

  Customization in Covnets is done by altering the activation function like tanh, RELU, Leaky RELU, sigmoid etc. Some parametric tune at pooling layer by selecting either the max-pooling and average pooling.
- Recurrent Neural Networks (RNN)
  Recurrent Neural Networks have become one of the preferred choices for the deep learning technique for music recognition and recommendation. This is primarily attributed to its feedback mechanism incorporation, which is a crucial aspect of recommender-based systems. The change of user preference over time can only be precisely measured if it has a feedback of user activity fed back to the system. As shown in Figure 1.4 Error MSE keeps the system's efficiency at an optimal level. RNN is a sequential deep learning algorithm which is characterized by looping between the layers. (This is what is known as feedback.) As all the other deep learning algorithms take into account the current state of the input, the presence of the memory module or the previous outputs makes it a good choice for music recommendation. The option of hyperparameter tuning options in RNN also gives it an edge over other techniques.
- K-Nearest Neighbours (KNN)
  k-Nearest Neighbour is a supervised machine learning algorithm which is used for both regression and classification problems. The idea behind kNN is a very simple and straightforward one. kNN algorithm works on a basic assumption that similar data points are spatially close. The k in kNN algorithm refers to the number of neighbours considered in predicting the label of a new data point. kNN algorithm will allocate a label to a data point based on the majority vote of its nearest neighbours. Thus, if a data point is to be assigned a label, the nearest neighbours are identified and a majority vote is taken. K being the hyperparameter of kNN algorithm, as the value of k is changed, the predicted label may also change. With the help of hyperparameter tuning, the optimum value of k is determined and this is subsequently

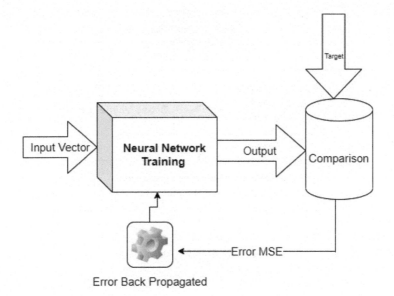

FIGURE 1.4 Recurrent neural network.

used to predict unlabelled data points. kNN can be computationally expensive in terms of both time and storage. kNN is sensitive to the scale of data as it relies on computing the distances. For features with a higher scale, the calculated distances can be very high and might produce poor results. It is thus advised to scale the data before running the KNN.
- Support Vector Machine (SVM) (Figure 1.5)
- Naïve Bayes
  Naive Bayes is a machine learning algorithm which is widely used for classification problems. Naïve Bayes has demonstrated higher efficiencies and accuracy in text classification such as spam detection, document segregation etc. This classifier is based on the simple concept of Bayes' theorem. The characteristics contributing in making the Naïve Bayes algorithm a popular choice for classification is its computational efficiency and its prediction of posterior probability. Apart from the incremental learning approach that this classifier follows, it is also robust to noise and missing values in the dataset. The usage of Naïve Bayes algorithm in Music Information Retrieval (MIR) has gained the attention and focus of researchers over the last few years. The essence of music lies in its emotion which, in addition to other factors, is reflected in the lyrics of the song. Exploiting Naïve Bayes Classifier for MIR primarily involves classifying the lyrics of the song to identify its emotion, and subsequently its genre. The Naïve Bayes Classifier's performance is tested and proven by varied researches in text classification. Taken as a whole, the Naïve Bayes classifier is an excellent choice for music recognition and retrieval if based entirely on the lyrics. As the words of the lyrics are independent of each other with equal weights Naïve Bayes classification algorithm is a very good fit for MIR (Figure 1.6).

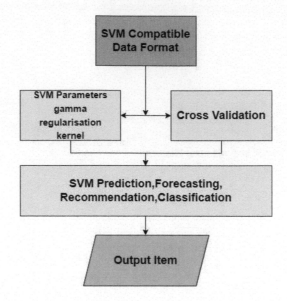

FIGURE 1.5   Support Vector Machine.

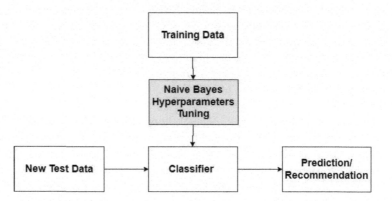

FIGURE 1.6   Naïve Bayes-based classifier system.

1.4 RECOMMENDATION TECHNIQUES

The evolution of recommended systems is inspired from various problem statements. The state of the art in the music domain is primarily governed by cold start problem, automatic playlist continuation and evaluation parameters selection to measure its efficiency. A systematic review of machine learning state of the art specifically for guitar playing and learning is discussed in [10]. This discusses the evolution of recommender systems from merely being typecasted as content based and collaborative filtering to highly customized and adaptive ones.

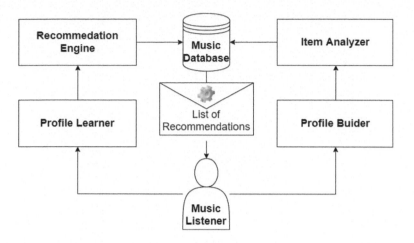

FIGURE 1.7 Content based recommendation system.

1.4.1 CONTENT-BASED RECOMMENDATION TECHNIQUES

Content-based (CB) recommendation techniques recommend music on the basis of preferred listened content [11]. Fundamentally, a CB recommender system performs the following two tasks: 1) It analyses the metadata of the content listened to by the user and finds common attributes to store in the user profile so that a match in the database of the music can be made. 2) It takes the common attributes as features and finds highly probable matches known as recommendations form the common pool of music. However, to find recommendation a CB recommender system generally employs two techniques. The most popular technique is to use machine learning models on the set of features and the other techniques is to find similarities heuristically (Figure 1.7).

1.4.2 COLLABORATIVE FILTERING-BASED RECOMMENDATION TECHNIQUES

Collaborative filtering is a community-driven recommendation system, where a listener is recommended music based on the choices of the people in his community [12]. It may be noteworthy that the quality of the recommendation will depend on the participation of the listener in the right community. There are two types of collaborative filtering: user-based and item based. There are many methods to compute the similarity between the users of the community and it's important to maintain a high level of similarity accuracy for accurate recommendation [13] (Figure 1.8).

1.4.3 CONTEXT-AWARENESS-BASED RECOMMENDATION TECHNIQUES

The notion behind the Context-awareness-based Recommendation System (CARS) is that an item is not merely an item and a user is not merely just a user. The perception of the experience creates a context and sentiments play an important part in this. Therefore, a CARS exerts all of its prowess in context formation and extraction as

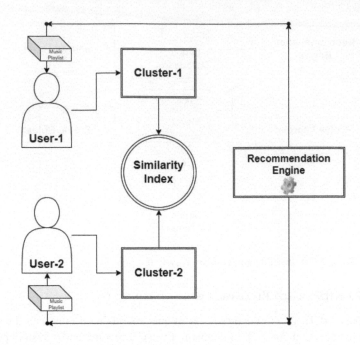

FIGURE 1.8   Collaborative filtering based recommendation system.

shown in Figure 1.9 The music recommender system has primarily four areas from where the context is extracted i.e. music content, listener context, music context and artist context. An important definition of CARS states that it is characterized by the situation of the entity [14, 15]. A wide array of applications have propped up as in mobile scenarios [16] and tourism industry [17].

1.4.4   COMPUTATIONAL INTELLIGENCE-BASED RECOMMENDATION TECHNIQUES

Computational Intelligence techniques include Artificial Neural Networks, Fuzzy Linguistic Modelling, Evolutionary Computing, Swarm Intelligence, Artificial Immune Systems and Bayesian Techniques as shown in Figure 1.8. Many Recommender Systems implement a probabilistic method such as Bayesian classifier for construction [18]. A combination of both CB and CF approaches is also constructed on top of a hierarchical Bayesian network [19]. ANNs are mappings of biological brain and these interconnections of nodes with assigned weights on links can be used to model a recommender system. A TV recommender system inspired by ANN utilizes back propagation NN [20]. An ANN-based movie recommender system is proposed in [21] which trains the filtering part by ANN. Designing of a RS encounters both stochastic and non-stochastic uncertainty. Stochastic search techniques use Genetic Algorithm (GA) [22]. A GA-based K-means clustering is used to make a shopping recommendation system to obtain an optimal similarity function [23]. On the other hand, Fuzzy Set theory takes care of the non-stochastic uncertainty; it performs well in handling imprecise information, ambiguity in the data and situations and gradualness of preference profile (Figure 1.10) [24].

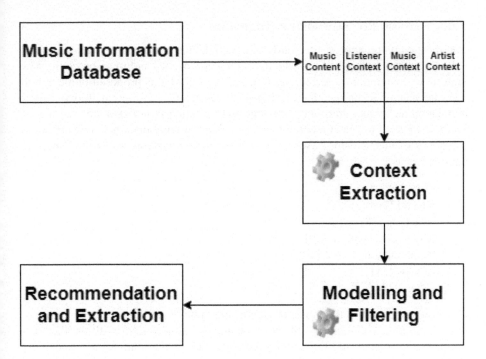

FIGURE 1.9 Context awareness-based recommendation system.

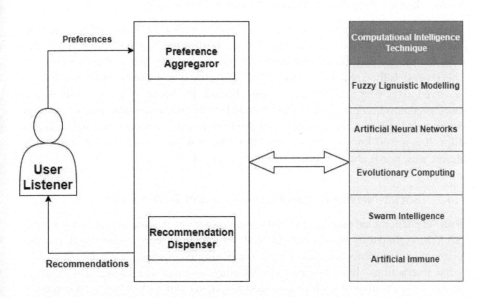

FIGURE 1.10 Computational intelligence-based recommendation system.

1.4.5 HYBRID RECOMMENDATION TECHNIQUES

The most common approach towards achieving higher performance in any process is to eliminate the drawbacks of the traditional approaches and to embrace the new features of contemporary techniques [25, 26]. This is what is proposed in the hybrid recommendation technique that combines the best features of more than two recommendation techniques into one. Although hybridization is not as simple as it may seem as we need to select a common anchor point of combination. There are seven categories of mechanisms based on which the hybrid systems are built. These are enumerated as:

- weighted [26]
- mixed [27]
- switching [28]
- feature combination [29]
- feature augmentation [30]
- cascade [31]
- meta-level [32]

However, in context to the music recommender systems the most common practice is to combine a collaborative filtering recommendation system with another recommendation system to eliminate the glitches such as the cold-start or scalability problem. In Figure 1.9, the collaborative filtering is hybridized with content-based filtering based on selected features such as the interest and ratings to generate and predict recommendations from the tagged music database (Figure 1.11).

1.4.6 KNOWLEDGE-BASED RECOMMENDATION TECHNIQUES

The knowledge-based recommendation systems use the knowledge, preferences and constraints of the items consumed by the user [33]. It then scribbles that knowledge with the background knowledge base with the preferences list and constraints list. This process is then able to generate a list of identified items and constraints that can be served to the user as recommendations. Knowledge-based systems mostly deploy case-based reasoning to retrieve the relationship between items and needs. Ontology is a knowledge-based representation method for domain concepts and their relationships. It is a well-known method to address the semantic similarity between items, preferences, needs and constraints (Figure 1.12) [34].

1.4.7 SOCIAL-NETWORK-BASED RECOMMENDATION TECHNIQUES

With the phenomenal growth of social networking tools, the Social Network Analysis (SNA) has found a strong foothold in the development of recommender systems. The recommender systems are increasingly facilitating engagement by users. It enables social interactions, hash tagging, commenting, sharing and liking. The word of mouth creates a trust in such recommender systems and a more engaged content is more likely to be recommended [31]. This positive correlation between the music

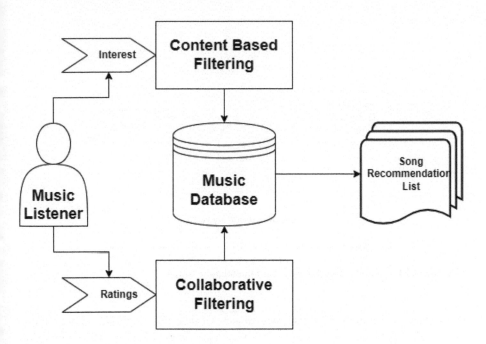

FIGURE 1.11 Hybrid recommendation system.

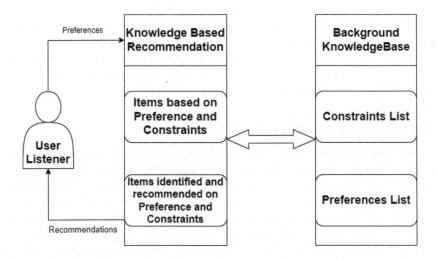

FIGURE 1.12 Knowledge based recommendation system.

listener or user and trust is also proven by some experiments [35]. The trust metric based on social media analysis is being improved consistently [36]. Assigning a tangible numerical value to the trust is a primary objective, which is being addressed also [37]. The relationship between the local trust matrix and the global trust matrix

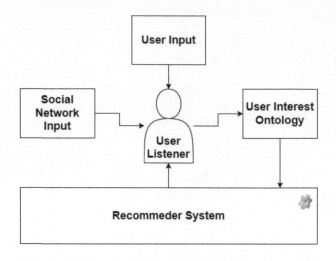

FIGURE 1.13   Social network based recommendation system.

is also being explored [38]. Other mechanisms of incorporating SNA such as social bookmarks [39], social media tags [40], physical context [41], and the relationship amongst the co-authors [42] are also being explored. However, the model presented in [43] explores the collaborative approach of incorporating the social networks in the recommender systems. To avoid the over-emphasized user similarity problem, the SNA is integrated with trust-based recommendation architecture to maintain an optimum level of prediction accuracy [44]. Figure 1.13 illustrates the impact of social media input as an ingredient along with user input to form the user interest ontology. This user interest ontology is responsible to recommendations, which is clearly influenced by the social network input.

1.4.8 GROUP RECOMMENDATION TECHNIQUES

Group recommendation systems (GRS) disburse recommendations based on users' preference clusters which include a group of users, though these users may not be aware or they may not have interacted with one another physically or on social platforms [45, 46]. Another nomenclature for GRS is e-group activity recommender, and this has found applications in numerous fields such as movies, dancing, browsing the internet and travelling. The aggregation of members in a group is accomplished by many techniques such as social choice theory etc. Average strategy [47] uses applications based on social media. Least misery strategy [48, 49] is used in a system known as Polylens, which is an example of a group recommender system. A variant of average without misery is used in MusicFX and Voting mechanism [50] is used for creating a Facebook-based application called GROUPFUN. In a provision for the replication and copying of choices of members is given. An application specifically targeting ski resort suggestions implements synchronous conversational systems As shown in Figure 1.14 feedback is gathered in preference aggregator and final candidate items are generated.

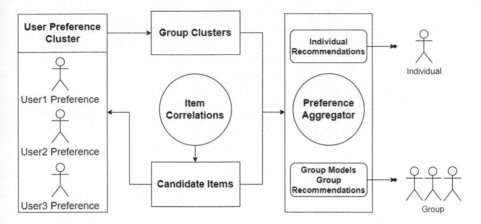

FIGURE 1.14   Group recommendation system

1.5   CONCLUSION AND FUTURE TRENDS

This chapter presents a comprehensive study of the Human-interacted Computational system development form the perspective of music recognition, classification and recommendation. Although this field of research is progressing quickly, yet we have organized the developmental framework of designing a music-based recognition and recommender system by presenting the options of deep learning methods for machine learning. Section 1.4 of the chapter presents a comprehensive discussions of recommender systems for this domain with graphical block diagrams for better comprehension. The state of the art is quickly changing in this domain, but keeping a track of the chronological development can assist in designing more optimized solutions, algorithms and systems.

REFERENCES

[1] J. Nielsen, *Usability Engineering*, vol. 1. Morgan Kaufmann, 1993.

[2] J. Wiley, "Human Computer Interaction: Developing Effective Organizational Information Systems Dov Te'eni Jane Carey Ping Zhang with a Foreword by Izak Benbasat".

[3] F. Karray, F. Karray, M. Alemzadeh, J. A. Saleh, and M. N. Arab, "Human-computer interaction: Overview on state of the art tutorials view project multiple cooperative swarms clustering view project human-computer interaction: overview on state of the art," 2008. [Online]. Available: https://www.researchgate.net/publication/266145394

[4] H. Purwins, B. Li, T. Virtanen, J. Schlüter, S. Y. Chang, and T. Sainath, "Deep learning for audio signal processing," *IEEE Journal on Selected Topics in Signal Processing*, vol. 13, no. 2, pp. 206–219, May 2019. doi: 10.1109/JSTSP.2019.2908700.

[5] M. Schedl, "Deep learning in music recommendation systems," *Frontiers in Applied Mathematics and Statistics*, vol. 5, Aug. 29, 2019. doi: 10.3389/fams.2019.00044.

[6] C. C. S. Liem, ACM Special Interest Group on Multimedia, Association for Computing Machinery, ACM Digital Library, and J. ACM International Conference on Multimedia 20th: 2012: Nara, *MIRUM'12 : the proceedings of the second International ACM Workshop on Music Information Retrieval with User-Centered and Multimodal Strategies*: November 2, 2012, Nara, Japan.

[7] G. Chettiar, K. Selvakumar, and G. S. Chettiar Kalaivani, n.d. "Music genre classification techniques a machine learning based intelligent model for an autonomous vehicle system for data selection on board View project Music Genre Classification Techniques." [Online]. Available: https://www.researchgate.net/publication/356377974

[8] N. Sharma and S. Sharma, "A systematic review of machine learning state of the art in guitar playing and learning," 2022. doi: 10.1729/Journal.31664.

[9] M. J. Pazzani and D. Billsus, "LNCS 4321 - Content-based recommendation systems."

[10] M. Deshpande and G. Karypis, "Item-based top-n recommendation algorithms," 2003. [Online]. Available: http://www.cs.umn.edu/

[11] B. Sarwar, G. Karypis, J. Konstan, and J. Riedl, "Item-based collaborative filtering recommendation algorithms."

[12] A. K. Dey, G. D. Abowd, and D. Salber, "A conceptual framework and a toolkit for supporting the rapid prototyping of context-aware applications," *Human Computer Interaction*, vol. 16, no. 2–4, pp. 97–166, 2001. doi: 10.1207/S15327051HCI16234_02.

[13] K. Verbert et al., "Context-aware recommender systems for learning: A survey and future challenges," *IEEE Transactions on Learning Technologies*, vol. 5, no. 4. pp. 318–335, 2012. doi: 10.1109/TLT.2012.11.

[14] W. Woerndl, M. Brocco, and R. Eigner, "Context-aware recommender Systems in Mobile Scenarios." [Online]. Available: http://www.igi-global.com

[15] S. Staab and H. Werthner, "Intelligent systems for tourism," *IEEE Intelligent Systems*, vol. 17, no. 6, pp. 53–66, 2002. doi: 10.1109/MIS.2002.1134362.

[16] *Recommender Systems Handbook*. Springer US, 2011. doi: 10.1007/978-0-387-85820-3.

[17] K. Yu, V. Tresp, and S. Yu, "A nonparametric hierarchical Bayesian framework for information filtering."

[18] S. H. Hsu, M.-H. Wen, H.-C. Lin, C.-C. Lee, and C.-H. Lee, "LNCS 4471 - AIMED- A personalized TV recommendation system," 2007.

[19] C. Christakou, S. Vrettos, and A. Stafylopatis, "A hybrid movie recommender system based on neural networks," 2007. [Online]. Available: www.worldscientific.com

[20] K. Jae Kim and H. Ahn, "A recommender system using GA K-means clustering in an online shopping market," *Expert Systems with Applications*, vol. 34, no. 2, pp. 1200–1209, Feb. 2008. doi: 10.1016/j.eswa.2006.12.025.

[21] J. Bobadilla, F. Ortega, A. Hernando, and J. Alcalá, "Improving collaborative filtering recommender system results and performance using genetic algorithms," *Knowledge-Based Systems*, vol. 24, no. 8, pp. 1310–1316, Dec. 2011. doi: 10.1016/j.knosys.2011.06.005.

[22] A. Zenebe and A. F. Norcio, "Representation, similarity measures and aggregation methods using fuzzy sets for content-based recommender systems," *Fuzzy Sets and Systems*, vol. 160, no. 1, pp. 76–94, Jan. 2009. doi: 10.1016/j.fss.2008.03.017.

[23] R. Burke, "Hybrid web recommender systems," in *Lecture Notes in Computer Science (including subseries Lecture Notes in Artificial Intelligence and Lecture Notes in Bioinformatics)*, vol. 4321 LNCS, 2007, pp. 377–408. doi: 10.1007/978-3-540-72079-9_12.

[24] B. Mobasher, X. Jin, and Y. Zhou, "Semantically enhanced collaborative filtering on the web."

[25] B. Smyth and P. Cotter, "Personalized electronic program guides for digital TV AI magazine volume 22 number 2 (2001) (© AAAI)," *Smyth and Cotter*, 2000. [Online]. Available: www.replaytv.com

[26] D. Billsus and M. J. Pazzani, n.d. "User modeling for adaptive news access."

[27] D. C. Wilson, B. Smyth, and D. O'Sullivan, "Sparsity reduction in collaborative recommendation: a case-based approach," 2003. [Online]. Available: http://smi.ucd.ie

[28] D. Wilson and B. Smyth, n.d. "Preserving recommender accuracy and diversity in sparse datasets." [Online]. Available: www.aaai.org

[29] R. Burke, "Hybrid recommender systems: Survey and experiments †." n.d. [Online]. Available: http://www.personalogic.aol.com/go/gradschools/

[30] M. J. Pazzani, "A framework for collaborative, content-based and demographic filtering." n.d. [Online]. Available: http://www.ics.uci.edu/~pazzani/

[31] S. Bouraga, I. Jureta, S. Faulkner, and C. Herssens, "Knowledge-based recommendation systems: A survey," *International Journal of Intelligent Information Technologies*, vol. 10, no. 2, pp. 1–19, Jan. 2014. doi: 10.4018/ijiit.2014040101.

[32] S. E. Middleton, D. de Roure, and N. R. Shadbolt, "Ontology-based recommender systems," in *Handbook on Ontologies*, Springer Berlin Heidelberg, 2009, pp. 779–796. doi: 10.1007/978-3-540-92673-3_35.

[33] C.-N. Ziegler and G. Lausen, n.d. "Analyzing correlation between trust and user similarity in online communities." [Online]. Available: http://www.epinions.com

[34] P. Massa and P. Avesani, n.d. "Trust-aware collaborative filtering for recommender systems."

[35] J. A. Golbeck, "Computing and applying trust in web-based social networks," 2005.

[36] C.-S. Hwang and Y.-P. Chen, "Using trust in collaborative filtering recommendation."

[37] K. Shiratsuchi, S. Yoshii, and M. Furukawa, "Finding unknown interests utilizing the wisdom of crowds in a social bookmark service," 2006. [Online]. Available: http://b.hatena.ne.jp

[38] W. Woerndl and G. Groh, "Utilizing physical and social context to improve recommender systems," Apr. 2008, pp. 123–128. doi: 10.1109/wi-iatw.2007.123.

[39] H. Ma, T. C. Zhou, M. R. Lyu, and I. King, "Improving recommender systems by incorporating social contextual information," *ACM Transactions on Information Systems*, vol. 29, no. 2, Apr. 2011. doi: 10.1145/1961209.1961212.

[40] S. Y. Hwang, C. P. Wei, and Y. F. Liao, "Coauthorship networks and academic literature recommendation," *Electronic Commerce Research and Applications*, vol. 9, no. 4, pp. 323–334, Jul. 2010. doi: 10.1016/j.elerap.2010.01.001.

[41] J. Palau, M. Montaner, B. López, and J. Lluís De La Rosa, "Collaboration analysis in recommender systems using social networks."

[42] B. Smyth, "Trust in recommender systems," 2005.

[43] A. Jameson and B. Smyth, "Recommendation to groups."

[44] I. Garcia and L. Sebastia, "A negotiation framework for heterogeneous group recommendation," *Expert Systems with Applications*, vol. 41, no. 4 PART 1, pp. 1245–1261, 2014. doi: 10.1016/j.eswa.2013.07.111.

[45] L. Quijano-Sanchez, J. A. Recio-Garcia, B. Diaz-Agudo, and G. Jimenez-Diaz, "Social factors in group recommender systems," *ACM Transactions on Intelligent Systems and Technology*, vol. 4, no. 1, Jan. 2013. doi: 10.1145/2414425.2414433.

[46] W. Pnnz et al., "PolyLens: A recommender system for groups of users."

[47] J. Masthoff, "Group modeling: Selecting a sequence of television items to suit a group of viewers," *User Modelling and User-Adapted Interaction*, vol. 14, no. 1, pp. 37–85, 2004. doi: 10.1023/B:USER.0000010138.79319.fd.

[48] G. Popescu, "LNCS 8029 - Group recommender systems as a voting problem," 2013.

[49] A. Jameson, S. Baldes, and T. Kleinbauer, "Two methods for enhancing mutual awareness in a group recommender system."

[50] K. McCarthy, M. Salamó, L. Coyle, L. McGinty, B. Smyth, and P. Nixon, "CATS: A synchronous approach to collaborative group recommendation." [Online]. Available: www.aaai.org

2 Heterogeneous Computing of Multi-Agent Deep Reinforcement Learning on Edge Devices for Internet of Things

Shaik Mohammed Waseem and Subir Kumar Roy

VLSI Systems Research Group, IIIT Bangalore, Bangalore, India

2.1 INTRODUCTION

Internet of Things (IoT), as the name suggests, is an internet of embedded systems, or computing devices, that enables the concurrent execution of tasks and the transmission and reception of sensory and computational data through their interconnection [1–3]. Edge devices, classified either as an entry device or an exit device to a network, are responsible for the computation or the control of the data required at the boundary of a particular network. When end devices in a network are capable of performing and computing an Artificial Intelligence (AI)-based task, they are generally referred to as Intelligent Edge (IE) devices [4]. Heterogeneous computing (HC), when introduced at the edge of the network, can influence the scalability of futuristic requirements driven by data computations and processing, which are usually involved in the execution of complex artificial intelligence-based algorithms. Through HC one can aim to use different hardware platforms that differ in various aspects such as technology node, structure etc., to collectively achieve a greater overall performance. Heterogeneous computing also allows the handling of diverse and fragmented data in an efficient manner by way of proper scheduling [4, 5]. Typically, HC systems consist of different types of computational units – Central Processing Unit (CPU), Field Programmable Gate Array (FPGA), Application Specific Integrated Circuit (ASIC), Graphics Processing Unit (GPU), Digital Signal Processor units (DSP) etc. [5]. All these advantages make the heterogeneous way of computing a more interesting and beneficial way to demonstrate intelligent decision-making at the edge of an IoT. This work combines the aspects of Edge Computing, IoT, Artificial Intelligence and Heterogeneous Computing and demonstrates its advantages by way of executing

DOI: 10.1201/9781003363606-2

a collaborative task by agents through Multi-Agent Deep Reinforcement Learning (MADRL) for the box push application. An agent in the context of MADRL refers to an entity that takes required actions in an environment subject to the observations it receives from the environment. The proposed approach uses the Avnet Ultra 96 v2 Embedded Platform, consisting of a Xilinx Zynq Ultrascale+ System on Chip (SoC). It has several ARM processor cores and the FPGA fabric to demonstrate heterogeneous computing by way of proposing a novel hardware architecture for the MADRL algorithm using on-chip memory.

MADRL, as is suggested by the name, is the combination of Reinforcement Learning and Deep Neural Networks in a multi-agent environmental setting. Reinforcement Learning is a Machine Learning (ML) method in which an agent tries to maximize a long-term numerical notion (generally referred to as the reward) through repetitive interactions (generally by taking an action in a state) with the environment [6, 7]. At each time interval, the agent is not provided with any information about which action it needs to take from the set of actions pertaining to the current state. The agent over the due course of time (after several trials/episodes) learns to take optimal actions in the environment. Such mapping of actions with the states in an optimal way is often referred to as a policy [6]. Reinforcement learning, or Deep Reinforcement Learning, when seen from the perspective of control-theoretic framework, offers algorithms which are powerful enough to design or search for an optimal controller for those systems that have uncertain or stochastic dynamics [8]. Reinforcement Learning algorithms, such as the Proximal Policy Optimization (PPO), Trust Region Policy Optimization (TRPO) and Deep Deterministic Policy Gradient (DDPG), have proven to be more beneficial when compared to traditional control systems algorithms such as Proportional, Integral and Derivative (PID) in high-fidelity simulation environments [9].

Multi-Agent Reinforcement Learning (MARL) differs from a single-agent system, where the underlying environment's dynamics are influenced by the joint actions or multiple actions which increases the inherent uncertainty in the environment. Further, the curse of dimensionality worsens as an exponential increase is seen in state-action space with an increase in the number of agents. Yet the advantages that comes with MARL, or MADRL, especially with human-like co-operative or collaborative social environment-based learning that often is part of sharing experiences between agents (instantaneous or episodic information), makes it worth studying and implementing to solve those problems that were often deemed to be difficult to resolve in a single-agent setup or traditional methods [10, 11]. The effect of action taken by an agent in the environment, when it depends on the action taken by other agents, necessitates co-ordination, co-operation or collaboration between agents to achieve an intended goal (or objective). Some of the common advantages that come with MARL include: i). better performance can be achieved with agents having similar tasks as their learning is faster by virtue of sharing knowledge; ii) with MARL, a decentralized task can be realized using parallel computation; iii) scalability can be done at ease by way of increasing the number of agents; and iv) it allows robustness in a system (failed agents can be replaced by successful agents) [12]. These advantages and benefits often come with impending challenges, at both, algorithmic and implementation level.

The exponential growth in the usage of connected devices that generates tens or hundreds of Zetta Bytes (ZB) of data every year across the globe (International Data Corporation has estimated a 42 billion IoT devices by 2025, capable of generating roughly 80 ZB data) has necessitated huge processing (computations), along with energy efficiency [13]. With increase in technologies deploying artificial intelligence as a service, or as a product, for Internet of Things (IoT) devices has made it necessary for the research community to study the edge-computing paradigm and explore the possibilities it offers to solve real-life problems. FPGAs as edge devices offer advantages in terms of: i). consistent throughput to the huge number of service requests from varied IoT device sensors; ii). temporal and spatial parallelism for executing/accelerating algorithms that demand high concurrency and data dependency; and iii). better (lower) power consumption statistics when compared to off-the-shelf GPUs [14–16]. With recent available data on computational requirement of nearly 29000 Central Processing Unit (CPU) cores and tens of Graphics Processing Units (GPUs) for training the robots for automation tasks using Reinforcement Learning (RL) algorithms, like the Rubik's cube from OpenAI; and 6000 CPU cores, along with multiple GPUs, for training in-hand manipulation tasks (or learning dexterity tasks) also from OpenAI, further highlights the extent to which FPGAs can be of use with the ever-increasing computational demands along with lower energy requirements [17, 18].

Our Contribution (Key Highlights):

- The novel hardware architecture for heterogeneous computing of Multi-Agent Deep Reinforcement Learning has been proposed for a collaborative task while targeting the design and implementation for Avnet Ultra96 v2 FPGA embedded board.
- Results presented as part of the work show an acceleration factor of 127x for the design architecture as compared to a software-based implementation using an off-the-shelf Intel i3-8130U CPU.
- The resource utilization and power statistics provided and discussed as part of the results further highlight the viability of the proposed FPGA-based hardware architecture to be deployed at the edge of network.
- Detailed discussion about the collaborative task in a Multi-Agent environment, along with the state-action graphs has been illustrated with the help of Matlab/Simulink models.
- An introduction for Internet of Things (IoT), Intelligent Edge, Heterogeneous Computing, Multi Agent Deep Reinforcement Learning has been presented.
- A short literature survey has been presented to discuss previous works in the direction of reinforcement learning, Multi-Agent, FPGA and edge domains.

The chapter presents a short literature survey, in the context of the edge computing paradigm, FPGA and Reinforcement Learning in Section 2.2. Details about important considerations and understanding with respect to Actor-Critic framework, Proximal Policy Optimization algorithm, Multi-Agent Deep Reinforcement learning along with the Matlab/Simulink-based implementations for a benchmark problem of two robots pushing a box is discussed in Section 2.3. Section 2.4 discusses the actual novel hardware architecture built to implement MADRL in a heterogeneous computing platform based on off the shelf FPGA boards. Section 2.5 presents results along with detailed discussion. Section 2.6 concludes the work.

2.2 THE STATE-OF-THE-ART

Shi et al., in [19], elaborately discussed the challenges and opportunities as part of data processing at the edge of the network, while also presenting a lucid definition of edge computing and case studies that help to understand the concept in detail. C. Xu et al., in [20], discussed a network-assisted computing model by presenting a case study of mobile interactive computer vision applications (three in number) while using FPGA as an edge-based compute offloading platform. The advantages in terms of response time and energy efficiency when compared with off-shelf CPU cores and Cloud-based offloading were highlighted in the work. With an aim of increasing system performance, T. Gomes et al., in [21], proposed FPGA-based edge device architecture by using FPGAs (SoC) for off-loading computer-intensive tasks along with discussion on IoT-ARM communication stack.

Furthermore, a survey by M. G. S. Murshed et al. [22] comprehensively discusses about the techniques of training and deploying Machine Learning (ML) models at the edge of the network. Specific ML architectures designed exclusively for resource-constrained edge computing devices were also discussed elaborately along with an outline of challenges and future directions about edge-based ML devices. Further, the authors in [23] provided a review of techniques involving the execution of ML models on hardware (that generally have low performances in IoT paradigm) by terming it as "Internet of Conscious Things" and discussed the state-of-the-art ML developments with respect to IoT devices. In [24], C. Hao et al. presented a DNN-FPGA methodology using both top-down and bottom-up approaches to discuss the IoT intelligence on embedded FPGAs. The authors demonstrated their approach with the FPGA platform (PYNQ-Z1) for an object detection task. Further, the need of local embedded processing near the sensor instead at the cloud is well discussed in [25] by V Sze et al., while highlighting the limitations, challenges and advantages that come with it as part of hardware for machine learning.

S M Waseem et al., in [26], proposed a novel hardware architecture for edge devices based on the Simple Reinforcement Learning algorithm and compared its hardware implementation with Q- learning algorithm-based implementation. An elaborated discussion related to reinforcement learning algorithms and their applications in the context of both single and multiple agents was also presented. In [27], S Shao et al. explored robotic control applications using FPGA-based Reinforcement Learning accelerators implementing the Trust Region Policy Optimization (TRPO) algorithm. In the reported work, Humanoid (A MuJoCo robotic locomotion benchmark) was used for evaluation with implementation targeted for Stratix-V FPGA with reported speed up of almost 20x against conventional CPU and 4.65x when compared with Tesla GPU (C2070).

A heterogeneous platform (CPU-FPGA)-based proximal policy optimization accelerator was proposed by Y Meng et al. in [28], where the authors accelerated the considered algorithm by implementing a systolic-array based architecture along with a novel memory-blocked data layout and enabling the data stream access in both forward and backward propagations. Xilinx Alveo U200 was reportedly used as an FPGA and MuJoCo benchmark (OpenAI Gym) Humanoid and Hopper were considered for the experimental purposes by the authors. Further, S M Waseem et al. in [29] proposed an FPGA-based hardware architecture for Proximal Policy Optimization and discussed its use in agricultural technology. Avnet Ultra 96 v2 Embedded FPGA Platform was used by the authors for demonstration and Xilinx PYNQ framework for validation. An FPGA-based platform for a state-of-the-art Deep Reinforcement Learning algorithm called Asynchronous Advantage Actor-Critic (generally termed 'A3C') was presented in [30]. The authors demonstrated the advantages of the platform which they called 'FA3C' (implemented on Xilinx VCU1525 FPGA board), in terms of performance and energy efficiency in comparison with NVIDIA Tesla P100 GPU for six Atari 2600 games (Pong, Breakout, Space Invaders, Seaquest, Qbert and Beam Rider).

2.3   MULTI-AGENT DEEP REINFORCEMENT LEARNING – BOX PUSH COLLABORATIVE TASK

Agent in this work is defined as an entity which mainly comprises of two Deep Neural Networks (DNNs), namely 'Critic' and 'Actor', and attributes a higher degree of autonomy in taking actions for a particular observation. Hence, collaborative Multi-Agent Deep Reinforcement Learning in this work suggests multiple agents coming together to perform a task collaboratively with different rewards or pay-offs assigned to each of the agent while carrying out training depending on a considered or chosen algorithm – here the Proximal Policy Optimization (PPO) algorithm as shown in Figure 2.1 with the help of a flowchart [31–34]. In an Actor-Critic framework, or setup, the actor DNN is responsible for learning which best action should to be taken for a particular observation (from the environment) – this is also referred to as policy. While, the role of the critic DNN is to learn evaluating the actor DNN, which also highlights whether or not the action taken by actor DNN has led the environment to a better state, by analysing the reward received from the environment and thereby providing feedback to the actor DNN, in order to carry out optimization, or improve its policy. In simpler words, the critic DNN acts as a critic/teacher for the associated actor/student model. Authors in [35] demonstrate the effectiveness of a Multi-Agent Proximal Policy Optimization (MAPPO) algorithm in terms of performance with comparison to its multi-agent counterpart algorithms (off-policy) using a single GPU desktop computer for benchmark multi-agent environments like Starcraft and Hanabi challenge without any algorithmic modifications (domain-specific).

The Multi-Agent environment considered for evaluating the novel hardware architecture discussed in the following sections of this chapter is of two agents working in collaboration to move an object. The two agents are trained in a frictionless two-dimensional surface with elements being represented as circles. A target object represented as Box or Object 'C' has a radius of 2 m, while robots 'A' and 'B' are represented with relatively smaller circles of radii 1 m each, as shown in Figure 2.2. While all the elements have mass and obey Newton's laws of motion, the goal of

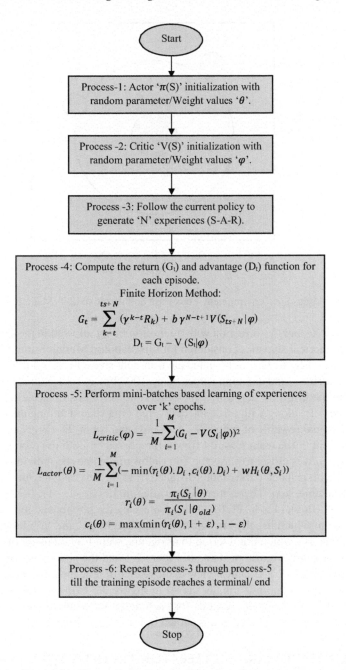

FIGURE 2.1   Proximal policy optimization algorithm flowchart.

robot's 'A' and 'B' is to collaboratively push the box or object 'C' outside a circular ring with radius 8 m by way of force being applied through collision. Contact forces (between boundaries of the environment elements are modelled as spring mass damper systems). While the total energy of the system is conserved, the elements can

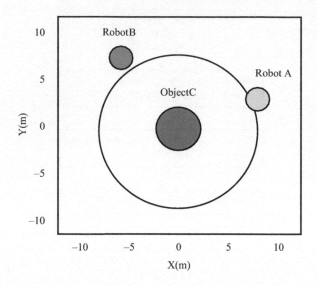

FIGURE 2.2 Multi-agent environment – box push collaborative task (Matlab/Simulink).

move only in 'X' and 'Y' direction with no motion being allowed in the third dimension. Few numerical statistics considered for this standard Matlab/Simulink environment [36], are –12m to 12m of bounded environment space in 'X' and 'Y' directions with spring stiffness and damping values being 100 N/m and 0.1 N/m/s, respectively. Action from the last time step with same observations for positions and velocities of robots 'A' and 'B' along with box 'object C' are being shared among agents.

The individual rewards of robot 'A' (Areward) and robot 'B' (Breward) are modelled as the sum of the team reward (Treward) received by both the robots as the box or object 'C' moves closer towards the 8 m radius circle and the individual penalties of the robot with respect to the robot's distance from the box and magnitude of action from the last time step. There are 9 action magnitudes {(–1, –1), (–1, 0), (–1, 1), (0, –1), (0, 0), (0, 1), (1, –1), (1, 0), (1, 1)} from which a possible action can be chosen by an agent which usually are forces (N) applied in 'X' and 'Y' directions. The robots 'A' and 'B', which are referred to as agents, were trained using the Proximal Policy Optimization Algorithm stated in Figure 2.1 and the state-action graphs have been plotted to provide a graphical view to the reader of how the multi-agent environment set up works in simulation, as shown in Figure 2.3 (a). The training progress was analysed by the episodic rewards for each agent individually along with other parametric data as necessitated and is shown in Figure 2.3 (b) and (c).

2.4   FPGA HARDWARE ACCELERATOR ARCHITECTURE – MULTI-AGENT DEEP REINFORCEMENT LEARNING

a) *MADRL Application (Host System) – FPGA Fabric*

Embedded FPGA (Xilinx) boards generally host different types of memories in their hierarchies such as DDR (Dual-Data Rate), BRAM (Block Random Access Memory)

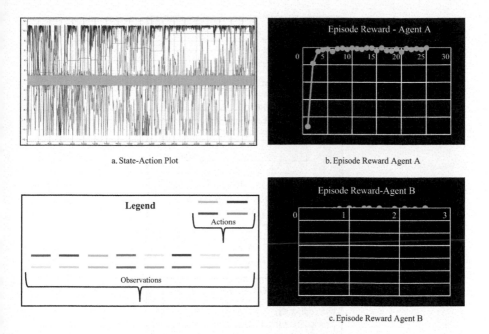

a. State-Action Plot   b. Episode Reward Agent A

c. Episode Reward Agent B

FIGURE 2.3 State-action plots for multi-agent box push collaborative task (Matlab/Simulink).

and UltraRAM etc. BRAM has been available as integral part of FPGA fabric for many Xilinx-based FPGAs and is fast by orders of magnitude in comparison to DDR [37]. The authors of this work have extensively focused on the advantages the BRAMs (on FPGA fabric memory) and FPGA Logic blocks could provide in the design of Multi-Agent Deep Reinforcement Learning hardware architecture as part of heterogeneous computing. The design and architecture novelty presented in this work as part of edge-based data computation and its access further highlights the intrinsic heterogeneous – FPGA design, implementation and validation skills and intended advantages they bring with it.

The Multi-Agent Deep Reinforcement Learning application when executed as part of host system as shown in Figure 2.4 along with the necessary processing system, memory and drivers gets executed in conjunction with FPGA fabric-based Reinforcement Learning Accelerator (designed as part of this work and discussed in following sections of this chapter). The sensors and actuators that gets interfaced with the Embedded FPGA board considered are driven by the respective drivers (mostly provided by the manufacturer, as part of the product's software).

b) *Multi-Agent Reinforcement Learning Accelerator (FPGA Fabric – PL)*

As discussed in the earlier sections, each agent comprises mainly two neural networks/function approximators called 'Critic' and 'Actor'. The critic deep neural network configuration considered for the Programmable Logic (PL) side implementation is 16×12×12×1 (16 neurons in input layer, 12 neurons in hidden layer-1, 12 neurons

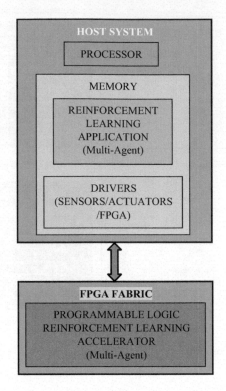

FIGURE 2.4   Heterogeneous computing – the multi-agent deep reinforcement learning application execution (PS-PL).

in hidden layer-2 and 1 neuron in output layer). The actor deep neural network configuration is 16×20×20×9 (16 neurons in input layer, 20 neurons in hidden layer-1, 20 neurons in hidden layer-2 and 9 neurons in output layer along with a 'Softmax' layer). The implementation was done for two agents 'Agent A' and 'Agent B' in line with the experimental simulation of box push environment–collaborative task discussed in Section 2.3 of this chapter. The 'Critic' and 'Actor' networks DNN configuration is the same for both agents. The sensor observations or states of the environment are provided as inputs to both the DNNs of an agent along with the individual reward for each agent while 'action' data is collected for the respective state/observation. Further, the calculation of loss, training of neural networks and updating of weights/parameters is all carried out as per the algorithm discussed in the previous section using a flowchart. The entire computational and intermediate data storage part of agent A, B and the reinforcement learning algorithmic are rendered on FPGA fabric, as shown in Figure 2.5 along with direction of data flow. For the observations received from the environment being run as an application in the processing system, the responsible single precision floating point (FP32)-based computations and intermediate storages are all off-loaded to the PL side of the system.

The architecture was realized using single precision floating point FP32-based standard Xilinx IPs involving adder implemented with only DSP48 primitives, multiplier with a maximum of DSP48 primitive, the operation involving division,

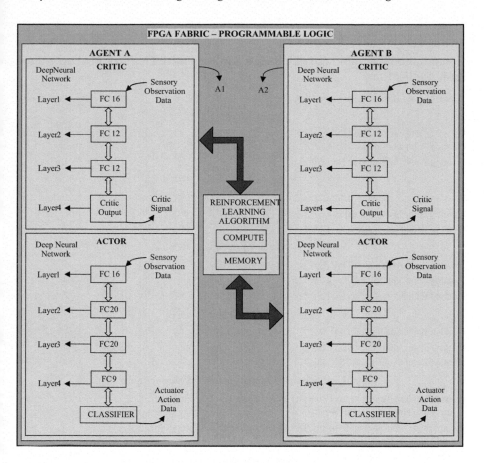

FIGURE 2.5 Multi agent deep reinforcement learning programmable logic implementation.

extension, truncation and comparator with no DSP primitive and exponential involving only DSP48 primitive [38], as shown in Table 2.1. Table 2.1 provides the information on the type and number of different computational and memory units used to realize this work of Multi-Agent Deep Reinforcement Learning for the said application of box push. The type of realization of each computational unit, about the usage of DSP in an FPGA is also mentioned to provide the implementation details at higher level.

Memory units (both Random Access Memory (RAM) and Read Only Memory (ROM)) used during the design were of different sizes, different address and data width and especially of different types such as 'Block' memory or 'Distributed' memory. These memories were especially used to realize the data storage pertaining to Weights, Bias, Loss, Input, Output etc., while implementing the hardware architecture as discussed in the above sections. Additional computational units used in the design include DSP 48 Multiplier, DSP Add/Subtract, DSP 48 Multiply Accumulate, DSP 48 Multiply Add, Control-Bus-AXI-S as part of the Multi-Agent Reinforcement Learning Algorithm.

TABLE 2.1

Computational and Memory Units Used in the Entire Design – MADRL – Box Push Application

Type of Computational/Memory Unit	Number of Units used
Agent A (Actor)	
Floating Point Adder (Full DSP 32)	6
Floating Point Multiplier (Max DSP 32)	10
Floating Point Comparator (No DSP 32)	2
Agent A (Critic)	
Floating Point Adder (Full DSP 32)	6
Floating Point Multiplier (Max DSP 32)	6
Floating Point Comparator (No DSP 32)	2
Agent B (Actor)	
Floating Point Adder (Full DSP 32)	6
Floating Point Multiplier (Max DSP 32)	10
Floating Point Comparator (No DSP 32)	2
Agent B (Critic)	
Floating Point Adder (Full DSP 32)	6
Floating Point Multiplier (Max DSP 32)	6
Floating Point Comparator (No DSP 32)	2
Additional – Overall Computational and Memory units	
RAM – Random Access Memory units (For Weights/Bias/(Loss- Input/ Output/Weight/Bias)/Input/Output)	47
Variable size – Variable Style (Block/Distributed) – Variable Address Width	
ROM – Read only memory	14
Control-Bus-AXI-S	1
DSP 48 Multiplier	2
DSP Add/Subtract	1
DSP 48 Multiply Accumulate	1
DSP 48 Multiply Add	1
Floating Point Adder (Full DSP 32)	2
Floating Point Multiplier (Max DSP 32)	4
Floating Point Comparator (No DSP 32)	2
Floating Point Truncation (No DSP)	2
Floating Point Extension (No DSP)	2
Floating Point Division (No DSP)	2

c) *FPGA implementation of MADRL Hardware Architecture (PS-PL interface)*

The observation or sensory information from the environment is provided to the accelerator hardware through ARM (Advanced RISC Machines) – AMBA (Advanced Microcontroller Bus Architecture) AXI (Advanced Extensible Interface) interface. Dedicated on-chip memory blocks (DOCMB) in the form of BRAM (Block Random

Access Memory) were used as part of hardware design for data storages with respect to sensor/observation data, Agent's reward, Agent's loss, Agent's discounted future reward and Agent's action. All the BRAM blocks were controlled by an instantiated Xilinx's dedicated BRAM controller which, in turn, form an AXI interconnect-based communication with Processing System as part of Zynq Ultrascale + MPSoC (ZU3EG) device as shown in Figure 2.6. Xilinx Vivado HLS 2019.2 was used to design the entire hardware architecture, with Xilinx Vivado 2019.2 being used to synthesize, run implementation and write bit stream. The experimental setup involves Ultra96 v2 embedded platform [39], being connected to the computer system using USB port as shown in Figure 2.7. The validation of hardware architecture on FPGA fabric was carried out with the help of Xilinx's PYNQ framework [40], with MMIO (Memory mapped Input–Output)-based data read/write by using Jupyter notebook as graphical user application interface on a booted Linux operating system with the help of an external memory card.

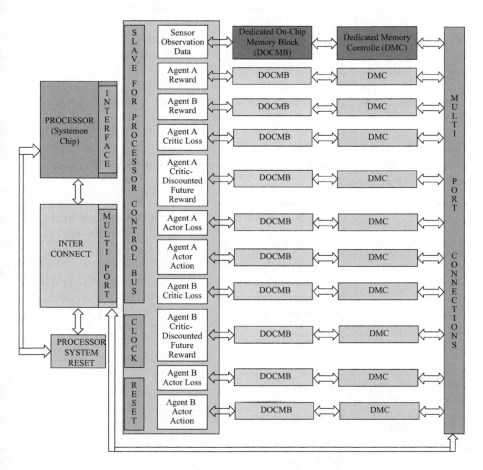

FIGURE 2.6   FPGA implementation of MADRL hardware architecture.

FIGURE 2.7   Experimental setup of Avnet Ultra96 v2 embedded platform.

2.5 RESULTS AND DISCUSSION

For the FPGA-based hardware architecture designed and targeted for Avnet Ultra96 v2 Embedded platform (Xilinx – ZU3EG – Zynq ultrascale + MPSoC) [41], discussed in Section 2.4 of this chapter, when compared with the Intel i3-8130U CPU-based implementation for the same application of collaborative box pushing task, with the same configuration of Actor-Critic deep neural network configuration as part of agent framework yielded acceleration factor of 127x as illustrated in Table 2.2 and Figure 2.8. The FPGA hardware architecture is capable of processing

TABLE 2.2

Comparison of FPGA based MADRL Heterogeneous Hardware Execution with CPU Only Execution

Parameter	This Work (FPGA based Hardware Architecture)	CPU Only Execution (Performed by authors of this paper)
Hardware Platform	Avnet Ultra 96v2 Embedded board – Xilinx ZU3EG	Intel i3-8130U CPU
Application	Collaborative Box Pushing Task	Collaborative Box Pushing Task
Algorithm	Proximal Policy Optimization (PPO) – Multi Agent set up	Proximal Policy Optimization (PPO) – Multi Agent set up
Agent Framework	Actor – Critic	Actor – Critic
Critic Deep Neural Network Configuration	16×12×12×1	16×12×12×1
Actor Deep Neural Network Configuration	16×20×20×9	16×20×20×9
Number of Agents	2	2
Learning Rate	0.0001	0.0001
Number of Episodes	25	25
Execution Time	39302110671997070 atto second	5 seconds
Acceleration factor	127x CPU only execution	–

Acceleration Factor (Time)

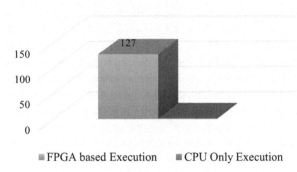

- FPGA based Execution   ■ CPU Only Execution

FIGURE 2.8   Acceleration factor FPGA based execution vs CPU only execution.

TABLE 2.3
Resource Utilization of MADRL Heterogeneous Hardware Architecture

Type of Resource	Utilization
LUT	31762
LUTRAM	5402
FF	33704
BRAM	37
DSP	54
BUFG	2

102 million samples per second and utilizes lower resources as reported in Table 2.3 in comparison to the implementations stated in literature by authors in their work for different applications executed using a multi-agent Proximal Policy Optimization algorithm. A number of them have been discussed in Section 2.2 of this chapter as part of the state-of the art. The power statistics which are low, further highlight the efficiency and ability of the proposed heterogeneous hardware architecture to be used as an accelerator for Multi-Agent Deep Reinforcement Learning as part of edge device-based deployment with the majority of the power (1.771 W) of the total power reported (2.687 W) being associated with the processing system, which is part of Zynq ultrascale + MPSoC, architecture thereby highlighting the lower stats for other resources, as shown in Table 2.4.

TABLE 2.4
Power statistics of MADRL Heterogeneous Hardware Architecture

Dynamic (2.366 W)						Static (0.321 W)		Total (W)
Clocks(W)	Signals(W)	Logic(W)	BRAM(W)	DSP(W)	PS(W)	PS (W)	PL (W)	
0.082	0.165	0.280	0.037	0.031	1.771	0.102	0.219	2.687

2.6 CONCLUSION

The proposed FPGA-based heterogeneous hardware architecture for Multi-Agent Deep Reinforcement Learning (MADRL) is principally designed to take advantage of the on-chip memory available as part of the FPGA fabric and reduce the effort of data access from off-chip memory, thereby increasing the acceleration factor to a greater extent. The main focus behind the architectural design was to allow the computations and processing to happen at the edge of the network. The disadvantage with this type of implementation is evident in the increased dependency on the availability of on-chip memory, which thereby makes it harder to execute very large deep neural networks. The authors of this chapter are also investigating the possibilities for a FPGA-based hardware accelerator to enhance computer vision as a part of edge processing, in order to support the larger goal of autonomous robot/robots which would be capable of detecting an infected plant/plants in a greenhouse environment and spraying chemicals on it, all directed from the remote setting of the authors' host institute in a further advance in edge-based agriculture technology.

ACKNOWLEDGEMENT

The authors would like to express their sincere gratitude for IIITB and Machine Intelligence and Robotics Centre (Government of Karnataka) for supporting this work.

DATA AVAILABILITY

All data generated or analysed during this study are included in this published article.

REFERENCES

[1] H.F. Atlam, R.J. Walters, G.B. Wills. Fog computing and the internet of things: A review. *Big Data Cogn. Comput.*, 2, 10, 2018. https://doi.org/10.3390/bdcc2020010
[2] Fog Computing and the Internet of Things: Extend the Cloud to Where the Things Are. n.d. https://www.cisco.com/c/dam/en_us/solutions/trends/iot/docs/computing-overview.pdf
[3] B. Di Martino, M. Rak, M. Ficco, A. Esposito, S.A. Maisto, S. Nacchia. Internet of Things reference architectures, security and interoperability: A survey, *Internet of Things*, 1–2, 99–112, 2018. https://doi.org/10.1016/j.iot.2018.08.008.
[4] Xiaofei Wang, Yiwen Han, Victor Leung, Dusit Niyato, Xueqiang Yan, Xu Chen. *Edge AI: Convergence of edge computing and artificial intelligence*, 2020. https://doi.org/10.1007/978-981-15-6186-3.
[5] J. Lee, G. Jo, W. Jung, H. Kim, J. Kim, Y.-J. Lee, J. Park. Chapter 2 – SnuCL: A unified OpenCL framework for heterogeneous clusters. In Hamid Sarbazi-Azad (Ed.), *Emerging Trends in Computer Science and Applied Computing*, Advances in GPU Research and Practice, Morgan Kaufmann, 23–55, 2017. https://doi.org/10.1016/B978-0-12-803738-6.00002-1.
[6] Richard S. Sutton and Andrew G. Barto. 2018. *Reinforcement Learning: An Introduction*. A Bradford Book, Cambridge, MA, USA.
[7] Csaba Szepesvari. *Algorithms for Reinforcement Learning – Synthesis lectures on Artificial Intelligence and Machine Learning*, Morgan and Claypool Publishers, San Rafael, CA, 2010.

[8] Lucian Buşoniu, Tim de Bruin, Domagoj Tolić, Jens Kober, Ivana Palunko. Reinforcement learning for control: Performance, stability, and deep approximators, *Annual Reviews in Control*, 46, 8–28, 2018. ISSN 1367-5788. https://doi.org/10.1016/j.arcontrol.2018.09.005

[9] William Koch, Renato Mancuso, Richard West, Azer Bestavros. 2019. Reinforcement learning for UAV attitude control. ACM Trans. Cyber-Phys. Syst. 3, 2, Article 22 (April 2019), 21 pages. https://doi.org/10.1145/3301273

[10] Annie Wong, Thomas Bäck, Anna V. Kononova, Aske Plaat. *Multiagent deep reinforcement learning: Challenges and directions towards human-like approaches*. CoRR/abs/2106.15691, arXiv:2106.15691v1, 2021.

[11] Ming Tan. Multi-agent reinforcement learning: Independent vs. cooperative agents. In *Proceedings of the Tenth International Conference on Machine Learning*, 330–337, Morgan Kaufmann, 1993.

[12] L. Busoniu, R. Babuska, B. De Schutter. A comprehensive survey of multiagent reinforcement. In *IEEE Transactions on Systems, Man, and Cybernetics, Part C (Applications and Reviews)*, vol. 38, no. 2, pp. 156–172, March 2008. https://doi.org/10.1109/TSMCC.2007.913919

[13] Edge to Core and the Internet of Things: Internet of Things and data placement, Dell technologies Information hub. https://infohub.delltechnologies.com/. Accessed 3rd September, 2022.

[14] Saman Biookaghazadeh, Ming Zhao, Fengbo Ren. Are FPGAs suitable for edge computing? In *HotEdge'18 USENIX Workshop on Hot Topics in Edge Computing*, Boston, USA, 2018. (https://www.usenix.org/system/files/conference/hotedge18/hotedge18-papers-biookaghazadeh.pdf)

[15] S.M. Waseem, A. Venkata Suraj, S.K. Roy. Accelerating the activation function selection for hybrid deep neural networks – FPGA implementation. In *2021 IEEE Region 10 Symposium (TENSYMP)*, 1–7, 2021. doi: 10.1109/TENSYMP52854.2021.9551000.

[16] M. Chiang, T. Zhang. Fog and IoT: An overview of research opportunities. *IEEE Internet of Things Journal*, 3(6), 854–864, 2016.

[17] OpenAI, Ilge Akkaya, Marcin Andrychowicz, Maciek Chociej, Mateusz Litwin, Bob McGrew, Arthur Petron, Alex Paino, Matthias Plappert, Glenn Powell, Raphael Ribas, Jonas Schneider, Nikolas Tezak, Jerry Tworek, Peter Welinder, Lilian Weng, Qiming Yuan, Wojciech Zaremba, Lei Zhang. Solving Rubik's cube with a robot hand. [arXiv:1910.07113v1], CoRR/abs/1910.07113, 2019.

[18] OpenAI, Marcin Andrychowicz, Bowen Baker, Maciek Chociej, Rafal Jozefowicz, Bob McGrew, Jakub Pachocki, Arthur Petron, Matthias Plappert, Glenn Powell, Alex Ray, Jonas Schneider, Szymon Sidor, Josh Tobin, Peter Welinder, Lilian Weng, Wojciech Zaremba. Learning dexterous in-hand manipulation. [arXiv:1808.00177v5], CoRR/abs/1808.00177, 2019.

[19] W. Shi, J. Cao, Q. Zhang, Y. Li, L. Xu. Edge computing: Vision and challenges. *IEEE Internet of Things Journal*, 3(5), 637–646, October 2016.

[20] C. Xu et al. The case for FPGA-based edge computing. *IEEE Transactions on Mobile Computing*. https://doi.org/10.1109/TMC.2020.3041781.

[21] T. Gomes, S. Pinto, T. Gomes, A. Tavares, J. Cabral. Towards an FPGA-based edge device for the Internet of Things. *2015 IEEE 20th Conference on Emerging Technologies & Factory Automation (ETFA)*, 1–4, 2015. https://doi.org/10.1109/ETFA.2015.7301601

[22] M.G. Sarwar Murshed, Christopher Murphy, Daqing Hou, Nazar Khan, Ganesh Ananthanarayanan, and Faraz Hussain. 2021. Machine learning at the network edge: A survey. *ACM Comput. Surv.* 54, 8, Article 170 (November 2022), 37 pages. https://doi.org/10.1145/3469029

[23] M. Merenda, C. Porcaro, D. Iero Edge machine learning for AI-enabled IoT devices: A review. *Sensors*, 20, 2533, 2020. https://doi.org/10.3390/s20092533

[24] Cong Hao, Xiaofan Zhang, Yuhong Li, Sitao Huang, Jinjun Xiong, Kyle Rupnow, Wen-Mei Hwu, and Deming Chen. FPGA/DNN Co-Design: An Efficient Design Methodology for IoT Intelligence on the Edge. In *Proceedings of the 56th Annual Design Automation Conference 2019 (DAC '19)*. Association for Computing Machinery, New York, NY, USA, Article 206, 1–6, 2019. https://doi.org/10.1145/3316781.3317829

[25] V. Sze, Y. -H. Chen, J. Emer, A. Suleiman, Z. Zhang. Hardware for machine learning: Challenges and opportunities. *2017 IEEE Custom Integrated Circuits Conference (CICC)*, 1–8, 2017. https://doi.org/10.1109/CICC.2017.7993626

[26] Shaik Mohammed Waseem, Subir Kumar Roy. Hardware realization of reinforcement learning algorithms for edge devices. In *VLSI and Hardware Implementations Using Modern Machine Learning Methods*, 1st Edition, CRC Press, Taylor and Francis, 2021. https://doi.org/10.1201/9781003201038-12

[27] S. Shao et al. Towards hardware accelerated reinforcement learning for application- specific robotic control. *2018 IEEE 29th International Conference on Application- specific Systems*, Architectures and Processors (ASAP), 1–8, 2018. https://doi.org/10.1109/ASAP. 2018.8445099.

[28] Y. Meng, S. Kuppannagari, V. Prasanna. Accelerating Proximal policy optimization on CPU-FPGA heterogeneous platforms. In *2020 IEEE 28th Annual International Symposium on Field-Programmable Custom Computing Machines (FCCM)*, 19–27, 2020. https://doi.org/10.1109/FCCM48280.2020.00012.

[29] S.M. Waseem, S.K. Roy. FPGA implementation of proximal policy optimization algorithm for Edge devices with application to agriculture technology. *J Ambient Intell Human Comput*, 2022. https://doi.org/10.1007/s12652-022-04117-z

[30] Hyungmin Cho, Pyeongseok Oh, Jiyoung Park, Wookeun Jung, Jaejin Lee. FA3C: FPGA-accelerated deep reinforcement learning. In *Proceedings of the Twenty-Fourth International Conference on Architectural Support for Programming Languages and Operating Systems (ASPLOS '19)*. Association for Computing Machinery, New York, NY, USA, 499–513, 2019. https://doi.org/10.1145/3297858.3304058

[31] Proximal Policy Optimization Agents – Mathworks (Matlab) Support/Help Documentation, n.d. https://www.mathworks.com/help/reinforcement-learning/ug/ppo-agents.html

[32] John Schulman, Filip Wolski, Prafulla Dhariwal, Alec Radford, Oleg Klimov. *Proximal policy optimization algorithms*. ArXiv:1707.06347 [Cs], July 19, 2017.

[33] Volodymyr Mnih, Adrià Puigdomènech Badia, Mehdi Mirza, Alex Graves, Timothy P. Lillicrap, Tim Harley, David Silver, Koray Kavukcuoglu. Asynchronous methods for deep reinforcement learning. ArXiv:1602.01783 [Cs], February 4, 2016.

[34] John Schulman, Philipp Moritz, Sergey Levine, Michael Jordan, Pieter Abbeel. High-dimensional continuous control using generalized advantage estimation. ArXiv:1506. 02438 [Cs], October 20, 2018.

[35] Yu Chao, Akash Velu, Eugene Vinitsky, Yu Wang, Alexandre Bayen, Yi Wu. The surprising effectiveness of PPO in cooperative, multi-agent games. arXiv:2103.01955v2, 2021.

[36] Train Multiple Agents to Perform Collaborative Task n.d. https://www.mathworks.com/help/reinforcement-learning/ug/train-2-agents-to-collaborate.html

[37] K. Huang, M. Gungor, S. Ioannidis, M. Leeser. Optimizing use of different types of memory for FPGAs in high performance computing. In *2020 IEEE High Performance Extreme Computing Conference (HPEC)*, 1–7, 2020. https://doi.org/10.1109/HPEC43674.2020. 9286144.

[38] Xilinx Vivado Design Suite User Guide, High-Level Synthesis, UG902 (v2020.1) May 4, 2021.

[39] Avnet Ultra96 v2 Embedded Platform. n.d. https://www.avnet.com/wps/portal/us/products/new-product-introductions/npi/aes-ultra96-v2/

[40] Xilinx PYNQ Framework - Open source project from Xilinx. n.d. http://www.pynq.io/

[41] Xilinx Zynq UltraScale+ MPSoC Data Sheet: Overview DS891 (v1.9) May 26, 2021. Product Specification. https://www.xilinx.com/support/documentation/data_sheets/ds891-zynq-ultrascale-plus-overview.pdf

3 Spectral Analysis of Speech Signal for Psychiatric Health Assessment and Prediction

Optimized Using Various Kernels of Support Vector Classifiers

N. M. Jyothi

Koneru Lakshmaiah Education Foundation, Guntur, India

B. K. Rajya Lakshmi

Hyderabad Institute of Technology and Management, Hyderabad, India

Husna Tabassum

HKBK College of Engineering, Bengaluru, India

Chiriki Usha

Dadi institute of Engineering and Technology, Visakhapatnam, India

M. H. Chaithra

REVA University, Bengaluru, India

A. Pavani

Koneru Lakshmaiah Education Foundation, Guntur, India

DOI: 10.1201/9781003363606-3

3.1 INTRODUCTION

In the current research, the preliminary screening of the psychiatric health of a person is carried out using the features of speech sound signal. The current work is carried out using Support Vector Machine (SVM) and its various kernels. It is the most popular and powerful machine learning (ML) algorithm preferred for classification and prediction as it provides very high accuracy with lower time complexity. The kernels of SVM optimize the performance and can classify the data with higher dimensions and solve complex problems smoothly.

Support Vector Classifier kernels – ANOVA kernel, NuSvc kernel, sigmoid kernel, poly kernel and radial basis function (rbf) kernels are applied in order to predict the classification. The speech signal of a person obtained is classified into three classes on the basis of measures of such acoustic features as Mentally Healthy (Class value 1), Needs further counseling (Class value 2), Consult immediately (Class value 2).

This is a novel model, as the literature study reveals little work has been carried out using a speech signal for psychological health prediction and assessment. The application of different SVM kernels for speech signal classification is the first of its kind. Another unique aspect of this model is that the experiment is carried out using a speech dataset which is built using real-time data collected at the public psychiatric heath centre and obtained directly by the patient. It eliminates the traditional assessment methods.

The major challenge faced in the research work is the extraction of required speech features and the elimination of noise from the signal and building training dataset. As the dataset is built afresh, prior knowledge of feature behavior is less known and this proved to be quite challenging. The features are complex and non-linear in nature. Hence, SVM kernels with a non-linear nature are chosen as each kernel is unique in its performance. ANOVA, sigmoid, poly, rbf, and NuSVC kernels are very powerful kernels of an SV classifier and hence the model is trained and tested on all the kernels to obtain very high accuracy. The average of the accuracies of all kernels is considered as the final accuracy of the model in order to consider the performance of all the kernels in classification and prediction. The results of prediction are more realistic than the assessment made by the model matched with the psychologist's report. This can be used as an assistant to the work of counselors or psychologists as a preliminary screening model which saves time for both mental health workers and subjects who want to be assessed. The predicted classification worked with an overall rate of 93.2% accuracy, which is higher than observed in the existing models.

3.2 LITERATURE SURVEY

Firstly, the literature survey is conducted to capture the role of speech in psychological health and the following observations were obtained by the earlier research work done in psychology. Speech and psychological health have been linked for more than three decades, according to research conducted by psychologists all across the world. Speech is the gateway to the mind; it is the indicator of the mind. And we express all of our sentiments and emotions by speaking or doing. The intended speech stimulates the muscular movement of the vocal chords by transmitting the neural signal to the speaker's brain which, in turn, produces speech [1]. Speech captures tones, emotions, rhythms, and a range of other signals in addition to content. As a result, the creation and expansion of speech corpora for people with mental diseases is becoming increasingly important [2]. Disturbances in speech flow, such as halting or voice fluctuations, are the most typical manifestations of psychological alterations that impede a person's capacity to monitor any component of speech production according to their own desire. Anything that disturbs normal brain activities, such as psychological processes like depression or anxiety, are illustrations of processes that can elicit cognitive or psychological symptoms, also including communication difficulty [3]. As a result, in order to address the underlying psychiatric condition, the patient must consult a mental health expert. A psychogenic speech disorder is a speech disorder produced by changes in the psychological processes. Speech disorders, especially those linked with psychomotor sluggishness, muted affect, alogia (lack of conversation due to psychological problem), and poor speech content are common in a number of severe mental ailments such as unipolar depression, schizophrenia, and bipolar disorders. The researchers examined and tested natural speech from 52 individuals with mental diseases such as unipolar, and/or bipolar schizophrenia-affected disorders, as well as 30 psychologically healthy people, focusing on the formation of speech ("alogia"), the modulation ("impaired acoustic pattern"), and the quality ("decreased quality of speech"). According to the findings, subjects with mental illness had longer pauses with very little speaking and put more effort into speech production [4]. Speech impairments, variations and low-quality speech are typical in Severe Mental Illness (SMI) patients suffering from bipolar, depression, and schizophrenia [5]. Improved computerized technology has led to better assessment of speech impairments with greater reliability and higher approximation compared with manual diagnostic assessment [6]. Speech variability and content changes have also been observed in several clinical psychological examinations [7]. In various researches, higher cognitive load has been associated with low-quality speech formation in schizophrenic patients [8]. Some psychosocial factors have been linked to cognitive issues like concentration and information processing content delivery, and linguistic proficiency, all of which influence to speech variability [9].

The next survey is conducted to know the latest methodologies applied by the earlier researchers in assessing psychological health. Authors attempted to build a ML model which can predict psychiatric disorders in adolescents in Sweden using Random Forest, XG Boost and achieved 73.9% accuracy [10]. A thorough literature survey of applications of ML on mental health assessment is made and a discussion of how there is a lot of scope for work to be executed in mental health assessment using ML techniques. A survey of 54 of the latest research papers was conducted and authors justified that there is a lot of potential and scope for ML-enabled applications in the area of mental health. Machine learning (ML) techniques can assist AI in identifying learning patterns of human behavior in identifying symptoms and progression of mental illness and also discuss how ML models can be used to detect, diagnose and treat mental illness problems [11]. A study conducted on 75 research publications between the years 2013 and 2018 to assess the quality of data collected and model selection on mental health. Authors used data collected from social media to model and understand mental well-being and the health outcome for patients. Quantitative techniques are applied to predict the presence of specific mental illness among subjects [12]. Prediction of stress, anxiety and depression were made on both employed and unemployed people using ML techniques such as Random Forest, decision tree and Naive Bayes and K-nearest neighbor. Data was collected using patient-based questionnaires and an average accuracy of 79% prediction was obtained [13]. Mental health assessment among 60 children is carried out to diagnose attention deficit and pervasive development disorders using ML techniques. Ten features, including age, pregnancy complication, family history, results of IQ tests and so on, are considered. Averaged One- Dependence Estimator, K*, Functional Trees and Logical Analysis of Data tree were used to predict the psychological disorders and obtained accuracy of 80% [14]. During the period of the COVID-19 outbreak, a study on psychological issues like stress, suicidal tendencies, depression etc., in healthcare workers is conducted. The research aimed to detect and predict psychological disorders during the pandemic period among healthcare workers. They obtained multimodal neuro-physiological parameters from ECG, EEG, EMG, EDA, heartbeat and respiration rate. They applied statistical and ML techniques and obtained satisfactory results [15]. Authors did a survey of the most recent 28 research articles on mental health and observed that the potential of ML algorithms continue along with the growing scope for AI in mental healthcare. The study conducted for the early detection of mental illness using a combined method of ML algorithms and neural networks. Data was collected using a survey and achieved 82% accuracy [16]. Autism disorder in 102 adolescents is investigated considering the data of clinical history, communication, intellectual and motor disabilities. A predictive model using ML and AI is built. An average accuracy score of 75% is obtained [17]. The prediction of mental illness is made by collecting huge information produced by humans through daily activities. The use of social media, smartphones, and web applications generate a huge volume of data. By applying data mining, hidden patterns are explored and association among attributes also is found out. ML algorithms such as Random Forest and decision tree is used for the classification of mental illness and general attributes such as education, income, age, sleep pattern, diabetes, gender, lifestyle etc used and obtained 83.3% accuracy of prediction [18]. Investigation of anxiety disorders among adults, both male and female, is conducted using clinical data. A decision model is developed using ML classifiers like Random Forest, decision tree, XG Boost and obtained an average score of 85% accuracy [19].

The role of ML and big data applications in mental health and its recent trends is studied and an exhaustive survey is conducted. It is observed that nearly 300 research articles focused on the application of ML in mental health and various ML algorithms are utilized for classification, prediction, detection and clinical decision-making. ML techniques, including Support Vector Machines, continue to be the future of mental health applications [20]. A research study found out that one-fifth of all students studying in higher education in Malaysia suffered from anxiety, depression and other psychological problems. The authors collected data from the students and prepared their own datasets and applied ML algorithms like Random Forest, Logistic Regression, Decision Tree and Neural Network and obtained accurate results [21]. The psychological vulnerabilities of IT employees to anxiety, depression etc., due to their work pressures is studied by the authors. A dataset collected through question-naires is used on the ML model to predict whether or not the employee needs psycho-logical counseling. Logistic Regression, KNN, Decision Tree, Random Forest, Bagging algorithms were all used and a maximum accuracy of 81.7% is obtained [22].

3.2.1 RESEARCH GAP

The literature survey and its study clearly reveal that psychological health assess-ment using the latest technology is still in its infancy and there is a lot of scope for increased research in this field. It also means that little work has happened using the speech as the input factor for psychological health assessment even though speech is formed directly from the mental process and its acoustic features carries hidden aspects of the mind. There exists a gap in the reality and assessment. It is also clear that Machine Learning continues to be a promising field (alongside AI) in diagnos-ing psychological problems. Recent and most of the approaches used in psychiatric assessment depend mainly on data obtained by intermediary reports or as given by the care takers, which are subjective with cognitive constraints like the recall of past events etc., Hence, there is an alarming need of objective assessment where the data is obtained live based on the current conditions of the person. This research work fills the gap of earlier research, by using speech signals obtained directly by the person through spectral analysis. From the spectrogram of the speech, hidden features are extracted. The hidden features of the speech sound reveal the psychi-atric health of a person. The acoustic features of a psychologically healthy per-son differs in people who are psychologically damaged, like person suffering from trauma, depression, schizophrenia etc., The speech audio features vary from person to person based on the time interval between each word utterance, the volume of the sound, and the speed of the speech. Loudness represents the energy level of the speech. These features throw light on the psychological health of a person. One more interesting point noted from the literature survey is almost all the research made use of their own built dataset collected from survey or questionnaires built by themselves as psychological factors are very complex and depend on various parameters and ready dataset may not be suitable for their specific case study of research.

3.2.2 NOVELTY OF THE MODEL

The method adopted in the current research is the first of its kind. Spectral analysis of speech is carried out to assess the psychological health by extracting features. Live speech is acquired directly from the patient without the intervention of inter-mediate reports or persons. The dataset is built from live speech recording of people visiting public psychological and counseling health centre. The acoustic features, such as loudness, pause counts and speed of the speech, are obtained and used for building a training dataset along with personal data. The model is built, trained and tested using various kernels of Support Vectors in order to optimize the classifica-tion and obtain high accuracy. The literature survey clearly reveals this method is not followed in earlier works by other authors. The accuracy obtained in the current research, at 93.2%, is higher than the already existing models. The current model also compared with other ML algorithms like decision tree, Random Forest, Naïve Bayes Classifiers, K-nearest and all the kernels of SVM. But SVM kernel accuracy is much higher than rest of the algorithms. Hence, this research is a novel model to predict and assess the psychological health of a person using speech signal and no work is carried out using various kernels of support vector classifiers. The classification and prediction matched with the psychiatrist's opinion.

3.3 PROPOSED METHODOLOGY

The steps involved in spectral analysis of speech signal are shown in Figure 3.1.

3.3.1 ACQUIRING SPEECH FILE

The model building consists of the analysis of speech sound signal in audacity. In the first step speech signal of a mentally healthy person is considered (chosen with no previous or current psychiatric problem) to get the benchmark values of pause count, pace and loudness in the speech. These values help in building an initial training dataset with Mentally_ Healthy class labels. These values are used as thresholds to label the other two classes while building initial training data. The speech signals of 2000 mentally healthy people are obtained. Figure 3.2 shows the raw speech signal of a mentally healthy person. The persons were asked to record their speech for a maximum duration of three to five minutes, preferably in a closed room where external noise is at a minimum. They were told to "tell about Yourself and your future plan" and record the same. The recorded speech signal obtained by them is stored in a folder with a unique id for each file. The file is stored in wave format. the personal details, such as age, gender, occupation, and clinical history of earlier psychological treatment if any, are obtained through interaction with the subject.

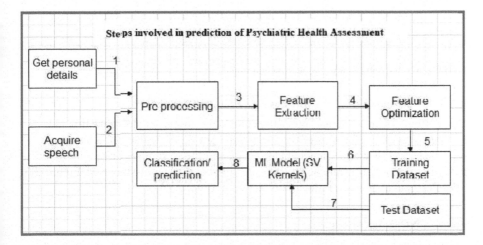

FIGURE 3.1   Steps involved in psychiatric health assessment.

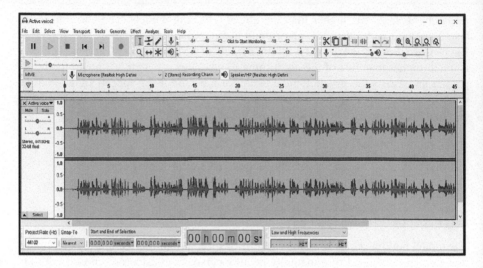

FIGURE 3.2   Sample raw speech signal of mentally healthy person.

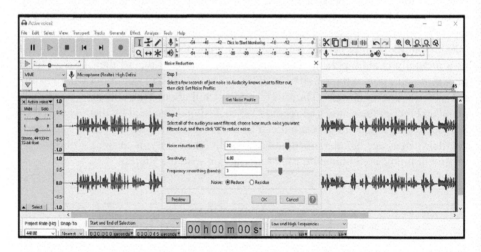

FIGURE 3.3   Applying noise reduction command.

3.3.1.1   Speech Signal Pre-processing - Noise Removal

The purpose of noise reduction is to retain only speech signals and this helps in getting the accurate features of the speech and get accurate data for a training dataset. The speech wave file may contain noise, and this is removed by applying noise reduction command available in the speech processing tool shown in Figure 3.3. Speech signal after noise reduction is shown in Figure 3.4.

3.3.2   NORMALIZATION

Apply normalization to the speech signal to retain the amplitude to the normalized level. It applies constant gain to the recorded signal and brings the amplitude to the

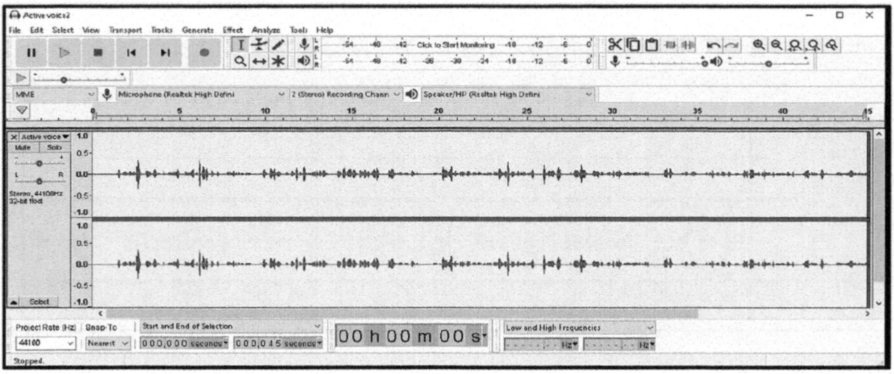

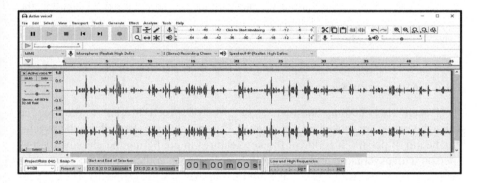

FIGURE 3.4 Speech signal after noise reduction.

FIGURE 3.5 Normalized speech signal.

fixed level. This helps to retain uniformity in the signal irrespective of how near the recording device is held to the mouth of the person. In this research loudness normalization is used to get the speech signal to the perceived level of loudness. Figure 3.5 shows the normalized speech signal.

3.3.3 FEATURE ACQUISITION AND SELECTION –ACQUIRING PAUSE COUNTS

Pause count or silence zone is the major deciding factor in the psychiatric health of a person, as a person who is suffering from a psychiatric illness such as depression gives a higher number of pauses (both small and large) due to a lack of concentration and confidence. Pause count is obtained by zero crossing the rate of the speech signal. It is the rate at which the sign change (plus to minus and vice versa) is made by the speech signal. The pause count of a psychologically healthy person, in a speech of one minute's duration, is usually seven to nine. The small silence duration of less than 0.3 seconds with no speech flow is observed and it is the time taken for normal breathing (0.2 to 0.3 seconds) while speaking. Hence, in this experiment, normal pause count is considered as nine to twelve of less than 0.3 seconds duration per

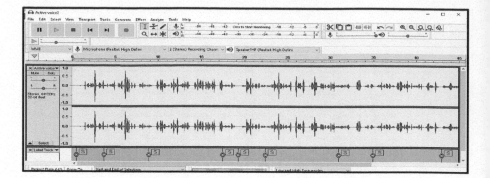

FIGURE 3.6   Pause zone count.

minute. In the present speech signal file pause count obtained is 9 for one minute's duration. The average pause count for one minute can be obtained by dividing the total pause counts by the total duration of the speech file in minutes. The pause count is shown in Figure 3.6.

3.3.4 MEASURE OF SPEECH RATE

The speech rate is nothing but the pace or speed of speech. It refers to the speed at which the words are spoken by the speaker. The speech pace also reflects the psychiatric health of person. It is one of the key features in predicting the classification as a person with psychiatric problems exhibits poor speech content both with respect to quality and content (which is nothing but the number of words spoken). The conventional speed of a psychologically healthy person is 120 to 150 words per minute. By contrast, a person with a psychiatric illness such as depression speaks at a rate of less than 80 to 100 words per minute. A still higher speed means person is experiencing anxiety, which is a psychological problem. To calculate the speech rate, python code is developed as any of the currently available signal processing softwares do not provide features for finding speech rate. The Algorithm is given below; this is developed into a Python program to obtain the speech rate.

Algorithm to find Speech Rate

Step 1.   Input noise free normalized speech signal
Step 2.   Perform speech to text translation using pydub and Speech Recognition
Step 3.   Store the output text in file
Step 4.   Perform word count
Step 5.   Divide the word count by the duration of speech file.
Step 6.   The result is the speech rate of a person

The speech rate for the sample speech signal file obtained is 133 words per minute. This speech rate is quite normal for a psychologically healthy person. Figure 3.7 shows the speech rate output.

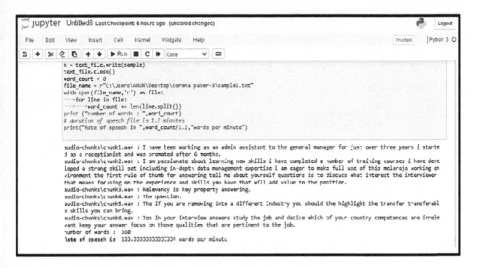

```
n = text_file.write(sample)
text_file.close()
word_count = 0
file_name = r"C:\Users\ARUN\Desktop\corona paper-3\sample1.txt"
with open(file_name,'r') as file:
    for line in file:
        word_count += len(line.split())
print("number of words : ",word_count)
# duration of speech file is 1.2 minutes
print("Rate of speech is ",word_count/1.2,"words per minute")

audio-chunks\chunk1.wav : I have been working as an admin assistant to the general manager for just over three years i starte
d as a receptionist and was promoted after 6 months.
audio-chunks\chunk2.wav : I am passionate about learning new skills i have completed a number of training courses i have deve
loped a strong skill set including in-depth data management expertise i am eager to make full use of this melaroja working en
vironment the first rule of thumb for answering tell me about yourself questions is to discuss what interest the interviewer
that means focusing on the experience and skills you have that will add value to the position.
audio-chunks\chunk3.wav : Relevancy is key property answering.
audio-chunks\chunk4.wav : The question.
audio-chunks\chunk5.wav : The if you are removing into a different industry you should the highlight the transfer transferabl
e skills you can bring.
audio-chunks\chunk6.wav : Joo in your interview answers study the job and decide which of your country competences are irrele
vant keep your answer focus on those qualities that are pertinent to the job.
number of words : 160
Rate of speech is 133.3333333333334 words per minute
```

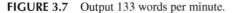

FIGURE 3.7 Output 133 words per minute.

3.3.5 LOUDNESS

A psychologically healthy person will have normal loudness in his voice. His/her voice is neither too loud nor too low. The speech will be calm. When a person is suffering from mental illness like depression, by contrast, then loudness in the voice decreases below normal and it is proven as stated in the literature survey. An algorithm is developed which is developed into python code to calculate loudness of the speech signal.

Algorithm to calculate loudness of the speech

Step 1.   Import pyloudnorm module and sound file module
Step 2.   Input the speech signal file
Step 3.   Extract sound_data and sound_rate
Step 4.   Extract speech_meter from sound_data using the built in Meter method
Step 5.   Extract speech loudness from sound_data using speech_meter method

The output of the code obtained is loudness -22.288 dB. The output is sown in Figure 3.8

3.4   BUILDING A TRAINING DATASET

The required dataset for this research is built by us due to the non-availability of suitable datasets as per our requirement. A speech sample of 2000 persons was collected by psychologically normal persons with no previous record of psychological problems. Features required are thus obtained by speech signal file and selected for model building. The required features for the present experiment were extracted and used for building training a dataset. The features extracted from these speech files are used as a benchmark dataset. Another 3000 speech samples were collected randomly by people visiting a public psychology counseling centre over a period of three months which

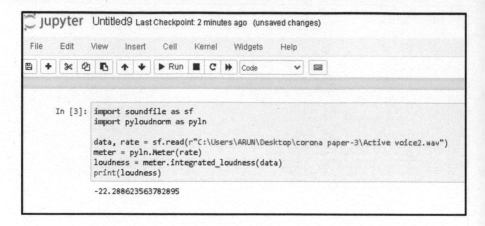

FIGURE 3.8 Output showing the loudness of speech signal.

include people with psychological problems at various stages. Required features are extracted from all the collected speech files after applying pre-processing and normalization. About 33 percent of features obtained by psychologically healthy persons and 34 percent of the features obtained by people visiting the counseling centre were used to build a rich training dataset. The remaining data is used as test data. A total of 67 percent is used as training data and the remaining 33 percent is used as test data.

The speech sound features of a psychologically healthy person acts a threshold to distinguish from other categories of psychiatric health. The features are normalized in order to obtain uniformity in the distribution of classes, to speed up the prediction and also to avoid the overfitting of the model. The training dataset is shuffled after obtaining all the required features. Classification labels are Mentally Healthy (Class value 1), Needs further _counseling (Class value 2) and Consult_ immediately (Class value 3). The problem statement of the current experiment falls under a multi-class classification and various SV Classifier kernels with its superb classification power being applied for the purposes of prediction. Features consist of personal data such as age, gender, place, occupation, and the clinical history of mental illness. Speech features are audio features: loudness, rate of speech, pause counts. However, preprocessing is not required for the personal data. If any data is missing, then it will be added manually. The speech features are the center of focus in this research which is extracted directly from the speech recording and subject to pre-processing and optimization like normalization.

3.4.1 MODEL IMPLEMENTATION ON SV CLASSIFIER USING OPTIMIZED KERNELS

In the following steps different kernels of Support Vector classifier models are applied for the prediction and assessment of the psychiatric health of a person. Kernels use a technique which speeds up the classification and optimizes the accuracy of prediction. Kernels convert inputs from low dimensional space to higher dimensional spaces by performing dot product of the input vectors. The kernels exhibited their own unique features in optimizing the prediction and classification.

The features of the dataset is complex and non-linear and hence can be tested on different kernels to obtain maximum optimality. The purpose of using different kernel optimization is to cross-evaluate the model, and compare and analyze its performance with other kernels with respect to accuracy, precision, recall and f1 score. All kernels support multi-classification and are ideal to work where multi-class classification is required. Hence, the model accuracy is taken as the average of all the accuracies predicted by different kernels. The detailed analysis of the kernel performance is examined in the following section. Figure 3.9(a, b) shows the 3D scatter plot of feature set distribution in the training dataset for loudness, rate_of_speech, pause_counts in the dataset.

3.4.2 PREDICTION MODEL USING NuSVC KERNEL CLASSIFIER

The Nu parameter of the nu-SVC classifier is used to regulate the number of support vectors. This helps in improving the classification performance by taking different

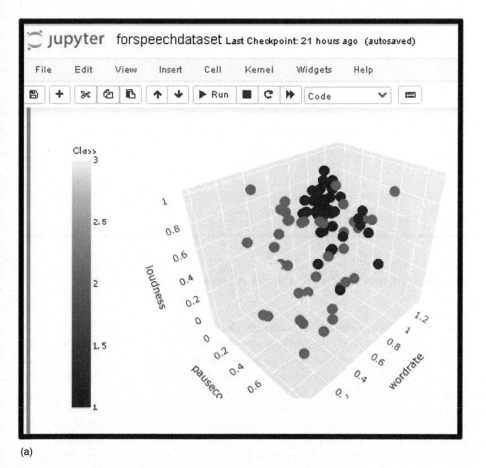

(a)

FIGURE 3.9   (a) 3D Scatter plot of features of the dataset.

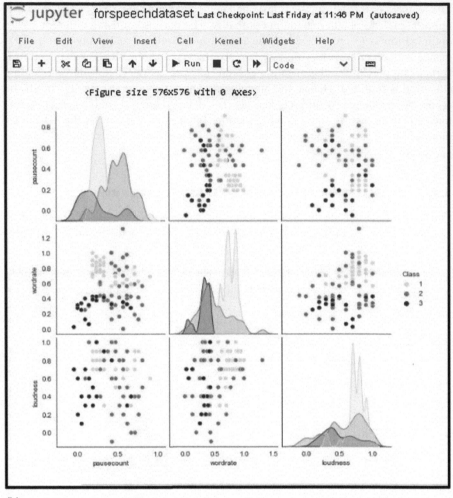

(b)

FIGURE 3.9 (CONTINUED)   (b) Pair plot distribution of features in the dataset.

values for nu. Hence, this kernel is chosen. Here the default value of nu = 0.5 is taken. If the accuracy obtained is not satisfactory then nu factor can be increased up to 0.2 units. Increasing beyond this leads to infeasible error. NuSVC supports multi-class classification facility by which dataset is classified into three different classes on the basis of person's psychiatric health using his/her extracted speech signal features. The NuSVC kernel prediction model worked with 93% accuracy. The classification report with confusion matrix and graph showing precession, recall and f1 curve for three classification is shown in Figure 3.10 (a, b).The NuSVC predicted classes with 100% precision for class 3 and for class 1 89% and for class 2 prediction obtained is 88%. The recall rate of class 1 is 90% for class 2 91% and for class 3 97%. The f1

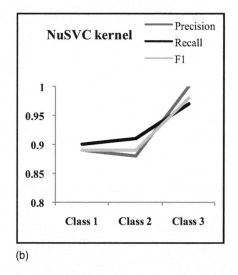

(a)

(b)

FIGURE 3.10 (a) Classification report with confusion matrix of NuSVC kernel, (b) Precision, recall, F1 curve of NuvSVC kernel classification.

score of class 1and class 2 obtained is 89% for class 3 98%. The confusion matrix shows True Positive count for class 1 is 493, for class 2 401and for class 3 640 accordingly.

3.4.3 PREDICTION EVALUATION USING ANOVA KERNEL SV CLASSIFIER

ANOVA kernel is best suited for multi-dimensional problems. As a speech dataset is complex and has many features, ANOVA kernel is chosen.

The mathematical representation of ANOVA kernel is given by Equation (3.1)

$$k(x, y) = \sum_{k=1}^{n} \exp\left(-\sigma(x^k - y^k)^2\right)^d \tag{3.1}$$

Where x, x_j represent the data for classification.

The prediction process is carried out using ANOVA kernel of SV Classifier. The model predicted with 96% accuracy. The precision rate for class 2 is 100 % whereas for class 1 and class 3 the precision rate is 95%. The recall rate for class 3 is 100%, for class 1 95% and for class 2 91%. The f1 score for class 1 and class 2 is 95% and for class 3 is 97%. The size of test data selected for ANOVA classifier is 1650. The True Positive count for class 1 is 522 for class 2 401 and for class 3 660. Figure 3.11(a, b)

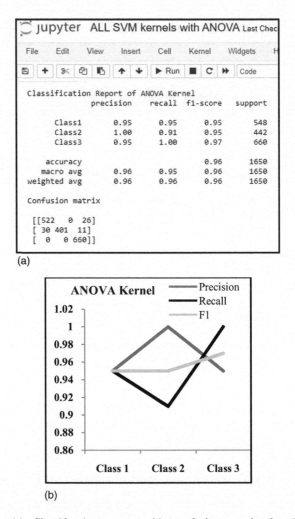

(a)

(b)

FIGURE 3.11 (a) Classification report with confusion matrix for ANOVA kernel, (b) Precision, recall, F1 curve of ANOVA kernel.

show the classification report and precision, recall f1score graph of ANOVA kernel respectively.

3.4.4 CROSS-EVALUATION OF PREDICTION USING SIGMOID KERNEL SV CLASSIFIER

Sigmoid kernel is proxy for Neural Networks and performs almost equal to double-layered perceptron of NN. Hence, this kernel is chosen. The mathematical representation of sigmoid kernel is given by Equation (3.2).

$$k(x, y) = \tan h(\alpha x^{\mathrm{T}} y + c) \qquad (3.2)$$

The prediction carried out using sigmoid kernel exhibited 88% accuracy. The precision score obtained for class 1 is 81% for class 2 80% for class 3 100%. The recall rate for class 1 is 84%, for class 2 80% and for class 3 97%. The f1 score for class 1 is 82%, class 2 80% for class 3 98%. The total True Positive count is 1534. The classification report along with the confusion matrix is shown in Figure 3.12(a). The plotting of precision, recall an f1 curve is shown in Figure 3.12(b). The sigmoid kernel, when compared with NuvSVC and ANOVA kernel, predicted with less accuracy.

3.4.5 CROSS-EVALUATION OF PREDICTION USING POLY KERNEL SV CLASSIFIER

Poly kernel (also known as polynomial kernel) gives the best results for a training dataset which is normalized. As the training data set is normalized in this current work, this kernel is chosen for prediction purposes. The model is evaluated by applying poly kernel of SV Classifier with degree 8 to evaluate the prediction accuracy. Mathematical representation poly kernel is given Equation (3.3).

$$K(X_i, X_j) = (X_I . X_J + 1)^d \qquad (3.3)$$

Where d is the degree of the polynomial.

On poly kernel SV Classifier obtained accuracy of 91% and precision score of class 1 is 82% class 2 is 100% for class 3 96%. The recall rate obtained for class 1 is 95%, class 2 74% and for class 3 100%. The f1 score for class 1 is 88%, class 2 85% and for class 3 98%. The overall accuracy of the prediction is 91%. The total True Positive count is 1623 out of 1650 test data. The prediction accuracy is less compared to previous three kernels. Figure 3.13(a, b) show classification report and graph of precision, recall and f1 score of poly kernel respectively.

3.4.6 EVALUATION WITH RBF KERNEL OF SV CLASSIFIER

Rbf (known as Radial Basis Function) kernel projects data of high level of dimension and then performs separation. It is also useful if no much information regarding the

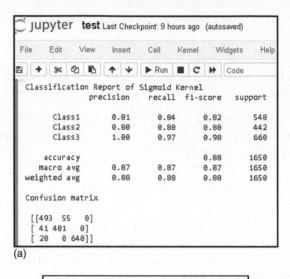

(a)

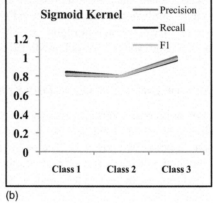

(b)

FIGURE 3.12 (a) Classification report with confusion matrix for sigmoid kernel, (b) Precision, recall, F1 curve of Sigmoid kernel.

dataset is found. As in the current work, a newly built dataset is used, and we know little about its behavior, rbf kernel is chosen. The mathematical representation of rbf kernel is given by Equation (3.4).

$$k\left(X_i, X_j\right) = \exp\left(-\gamma \left\| X_i - X_j \right\|\right)^2 \tag{3.4}$$

Where $\gamma > 0$

When SV Classifier with rbf kernel applied for prediction, the accuracy obtained is 94%. with an average precision of 87%. Rbf kernel exhibited a higher accuracy rate when compared to sigmoid and poly kernels. This is almost close to nuSVC and

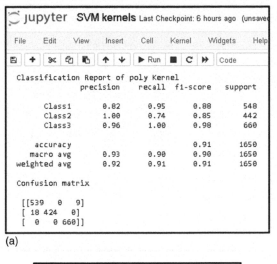

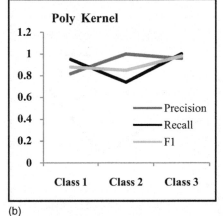

(b)

FIGURE 3.13 (a) Classification report of poly kernel, (b) precision, recall and f1 curve for poly kernel.

ANOVA kernel in prediction. Figure 3.14(a, b) show classification report and graph of precision, recall and f1 score of poly kernel respectively.

The visuals of classification performed by different kernels on speech features is shown in Figure 3.15 using scatterplot.

3.5 RESULT ANALYSIS AND DISCUSSION RESULTS ANALYSIS

The details of output for each classification and prediction along with confusion matrix obtained by all the kernels for class 1, class 2 and class 3 labels are shown in the following graphs and tables.

As per the observations of the output predicted by the various kernels, rbf kernel showed highest rate of accuracy, ANOVA kernel showed 96%, and NuSVC kernel

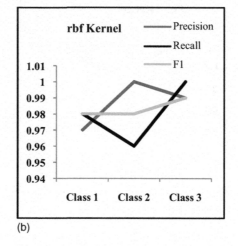

```
C Jupyter  SVM kernels  Last Checkpoint: 6 hours ago  (unsaved

File    Edit    View    Insert    Cell    Kernel    Widgets    Help

Classification Report of rbf Kernel
                 precision    recall  f1-score    support

       Class1       0.97       0.98      0.98        548
       Class2       1.00       0.96      0.98        442
       Class3       0.99       1.00      0.99        660

     accuracy                            0.98       1650
    macro avg       0.98       0.98      0.98       1650
 weighted avg       0.98       0.98      0.98       1650

Confusion matrix

[[539   0   9]
 [ 18 424   0]
 [  0   0 660]]
```
(a)

rbf Kernel

(b)

FIGURE 3.14 (a) Classification report of rbf kernel, (b) precision, recall, f1 curve of rbf kernel.

showed 93% accuracy. Others, like poly kernel, predicted with 91% and sigmoid kernel showed 88% accuracy. As per the observation, rbf kernel predicted with highest score for all classes. The precision score of rbf kernel for class 1 is 97%, for class 2 100% and for class 3 99%.

The recall score of rbf kernel for class 1 is 98%, for class 2 96% and class 3 100%. The f1 score of rbf kernel for class 1 is 98%, for class 2 98% and for class 3 99%. ANOVA and poly kernel also predicted with 100% accuracy for class 2. For class 3, NuSVC, and Sigmoid kernels predicted with 100%, which is 1% more than rbf. Overall, rbf kernel showed a very high performance. Apart from this, ANOVA kernel

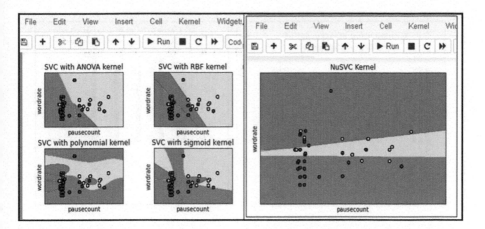

FIGURE 3.15 Visual representations of predictions by all the kernels using mesh plot.

performance stands second in prediction score, followed by NuSVC, poly and finally sigmoid kernel. The below graphs show detailed comparative analysis of performances of all the kernels considered for classification and prediction in the current model. Figure 3.16(a) shows comparison of accuracy score of each kernel. Figure 3.16(b–d) show graph- of class-wise comparative analysis of classification report made by different kernels with respect to precision, recall and f1 score.

The TP, FP, TN and FN count of both rbf and poly kernel is same for class 1, class 2 and class 3 even though, the accuracy of rbf kernel is higher when compared to poly kernel. The TP, FP, TN and FN count of NuSVC and sigmoid kernel are same for class 1, class 2, class 3 but NuSVC having more accuracy than sigmoid kernel. However, ANOVA kernel showed slightly less accuracy when compared with rbf kernel. Overall, rbf kernel stands first with highest accuracy and very good classification and prediction counts. However, we can consider the overall average accuracy of our model as 93.2%.

Table 3.1 shows the number of True Positive, False Positive, True Negative, False Negative and Accuracy score of all the kernels for classification.

The predictions made by the model matched with the psychologists' report. Hence the model is successful in assessing psychiatric health. Figure 3.17(a–c) show class-wise comparative analysis of confusion matrix and Figure 3.17(d) show overall comparison of TP (True Positive), FP (False Positive), TN (True Negative) and FN (False Negative) counts by all the kernels for three different classes.

3.5.1 COMPARISON WITH OTHER ML MODELS

The model is trained and tested with other ML algorithms such as Logistic Regression, Random Forest, Decision Tree, K-NN, XG Boost, Naive Bayes Classifier and the result obtained is shown in Table 3.2.

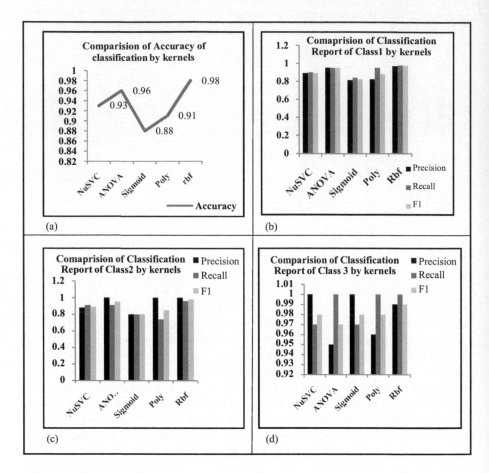

FIGURE 3.16   (a) Comparison of Accuracy of classification by kernels, (b) Comparison of Classification Report of Class1 by kernels, (c) Comparison of Classification Report of Class2 by kernels, and (d) Comparison of classification Report of Class 3 by kernels.

TABLE 3.1
Class Wise Predicted Count of TP, FP, TN, FN for Various Kernels

Kernel Type	Class1				Class2				Class3				Accuracy
	TP	FP	TN	FN	TP	FP	TN	FN	TP	FP	TN	FN	
NuSVC	493	55	1041	61	401	41	1153	55	640	20	990	0	0.93
ANOVA	522	26	1072	30	401	41	1208	0	660	0	953	37	0.96
Sigmoid	493	55	1041	61	401	41	1153	55	640	20	990	0	0.88
Poly	539	9	1084	18	424	18	1208	0	660	0	981	9	0.91
Rbf	539	9	1084	18	424	18	1208	0	660	0	981	9	0.98

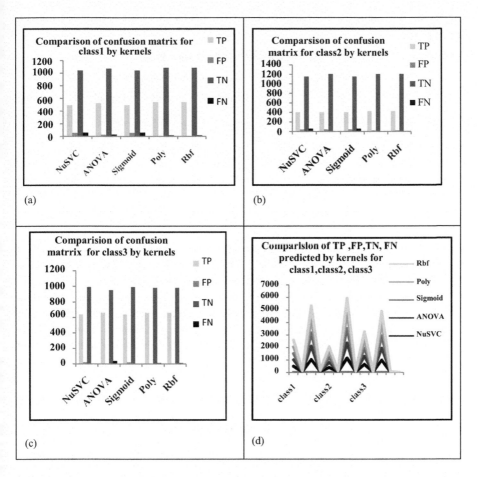

FIGURE 3.17 (a) Comparison of confusion matrix for class1 by kernels, (b)Comparison of confusion matrix for class2 by kernels, (c) Comparison of confusion matrix for class3 by kernels, and (d) Overall comparison of TP, FP, TN, FN counts by all kernels for three classes.

TABLE 3.2
Comparison of Results by other ML Models

ML Model	Accuracy (%)	Precision (%)	F1 score (%)
Logistic Regression	80.34	74.3	79.9
K-NN	82.48	77.45	80.5
Decision Tree	79.67	76.10	80.8
Random Forest	81.22	75.2	81.3
XG Boost	79.56	78.1	77.7
Naïve Baye's	81.73	76.1	81.8

TABLE 3.3

Accuracy Obtained by Kernels On Different Datasets

Dataset from Data. world	Accuracy on different Kernels of SV Classifier				
	ANOVA	NuSVC	Sigmoid	Poly	rbf
Children EmotionalDifficulty.csv	0.94	0.94	0.91	0.94	0.94
Adult Depression LGHCIndicator.csv	0.93	0.94	0.92	0.93	0.96
DOHMHCommunity Mental Health Survey.csv	0.92	0.93	0.89	0.94	0.96
Child Mental HealthProviders.csv	0.93	0.92	0.90	0.93	0.97
Teen Stress & Mental Health Poll on AfterSchool.csv	0.94	0.93	0.90	0.94	.095

The final result of classification of other ML algorithms is comparatively less than the SV Classifier with optimized kernels. The model is tested on five real-time datasets obtained and the result obtained is shown in Table 3.3.

The trained model is verified with five different datasets obtained from the data and the kernels are predicted with higher accuracy than other ML algorithms. Rbf kernel showed the highest accuracy of all the datasets. The overall average of the performance of all the kernels is considered as the model's accuracy and it is arrived at 93.2 %.

3.5.2 Discussion

The built model is capable of classifying and predicting psychological health with very high accuracy when compared to any other ML techniques and also on different datasets. The SV Classifier with various kernels is capable of optimizing the performance of SVM. The model optimized with SV kernels prediction accuracy is higher than the existing models it is demonstrated by comparing with other ML algorithms and on different datasets.

This research clearly demonstrates the role of speech in psychological assessment. It is not what the person speaks that is important, but how the person speaks matters in the preliminary investigation of psychiatric health. The reason why psychiatric health is most neglected is because it is un-noticeable and goes undetected by the person who is suffering from it and sometimes by psychologists in the initial stage. When a person visits the psychiatrist, the first thing observed is how the person speaks. A person who suffers from psychiatric problems such as depression, anxiety and trauma speaks completely differently from a person who is mentally healthy. The pattern of speech is given a higher importance than the content of the speech in the early detection of psychological problems, which is usually and keenly observed by the psychiatrist during their first visit to the patient. The psychiatrist observes pitch, loudness, pace, pauses, volume, coherence, rate and energy of the speech when the patient speaks. Collectively, these form the acoustic properties of the speech. If the person is suffering from depression, then he speaks in a lower, flatter and softer voice. His speech sounds labored, and contains more pauses. There will be frequent starts and stops. Speech sounds more strained and breathy. Speech is not well paced. Speech will have more lengthy pauses and speech will not be coherent. These characteristics of speech are captured in the speech signal. The spectral analysis of speech reveals all these traits of the person and helps in detection and prediction of psychiatric health. This model can serve as an assistant to a psychiatrist, eligible counselors in an early screening and prediction of psychiatric problems. The model built cannot be seen as a replacement for psychiatrist or counselors.

3.6 CONCLUSION, LIMITATIONS & FUTURE ENHANCEMENT CONCLUSION

The model is helpful to counselors/psychologists to determine the preliminary detection and prediction of psychiatric health status based on speech signal. It is helpful to people who hesitate to visit counseling physically as poor mental health is still regarded as a social stigma in many countries. The model can be used as preliminary screening and it also helps people living in remote or rural areas who cannot visit physically due to lack of transportation or their busy lives. It is also helpful to working people who have busy work schedules. The model is highly accurate, scientific and precise in terms of the prediction of psychiatric health status. The manual hearing of speech is inaccurate and counselors may overlook hidden speech features which play a key role in deciding the status of psychiatric health. The model can be used in further counseling sessions and the counselor can compare the speech features with the previous session. In this experiment the same person's speech was reconsidered after two or three rounds of counseling. We could see that there is a drastic improvement in loudness, rate and decrease in pauses.

3.6.1 LIMITATION

The current model works on the basis of speech features of volume, pauses and word rate. Suppose that the person has had, from birth, speech defects due to nerve or muscle defects or any other speech problem such as stuttering then, from the beginning, the model prediction will not be realistic. Hence, this model can be applied to people with no birth speech abnormalities in order to get realistic output.

3.6.2 FUTURE ENHANCEMENT

The current model is working precisely on all the kernels of SV classifiers. It can be improved further, taking into consideration the quality content of the speech by capturing and analyzing the words uttered by the person in the recorded speech. This will help in knowing whether the person speaking meaningfully and also the important words which reveal the emotions of the person. The model can be deployed using deep learning and other AI algorithms considering additional acoustic features as needed for higher precision and accuracy.

REFERENCES

[1] John, Houde, Srikantan, Nagarajan, Speech production as state feedback control. *Frontiers in Human Neuroscience*, 5, 2011, https://www.frontiersin.org/article/10.3389/fnhum.2011.00082. Doi: 10.3389/fnhum.2011.00082, Issn: 1662-5161.

[2] Li, Y., Lin, Y., Ding, H., et al. Speech databases for mental disorders: A systematic review. *General Psychiatry*, 32, e100022, 2019. Doi: 10.1136/gpsych-2018-100022.

[3] Aronson, Arnold E., *Clinical Voice Disorders: An Interdisciplinary Approach*, 3rd edn. pp. 394. Thieme, 1990. DM 78.00 hardback. ISBN 3 13 598803 1. Doi: 10.1113/expphysiol.1998.sp004249.

[4] Cohen, A.S., McGovern, J.E., Dinzeo, T.J., Covington, M.A. Speech deficits in serious mental illness: A cognitive resource issue? *Schizophrenia Research*, 160(1–3), 173–179, 2014. Doi: 10.1016/j.schres.2014.10.032.

[5] Cohen, A.S., Najolia, G.M., Kim, Y., Dinzeo, T.J. On the boundaries of blunt affect/alogia across severe mental illness: implications for Research Domain Criteria. *Schizophrenia Research*, 140(1–3), 41–45, 2012 Sep. Doi: 10.1016/j.schres.2012.07.001. Epub 2012 Jul 23. PMID: 22831770.

[6] Cohen, A.S., Hong, S.L. Understanding constricted affect in schizotypy through computerized prosodic analysis. *Journal of Personality Disorders*, 25(4), 478–491, 2011 Aug. Doi: 10.1521/pedi.2011.25.4.478. PMID: 21838563.

[7] Barch, D.M., Berenbaum, H. The relationship between information processing and language production. *Journal of Abnormal Psychology*, 1032, 241–250, 1994.

[8] Barch, D.M., Berenbaum, H. Language production and thought disorder in schizophrenia. *Journal of Abnormal Psychology*, 105(1), 81–88, 1996 Feb. Doi: 10.1037//0021-843x.105.1.81. PMID: 8666714.

[9] Jaeger, J., Berns, S., Uzelac, S., Davis-Conway, S. Neuro cognitive deficits and disability in major depressive disorder. *Psychiatry Research*, 145(1), 39–48, 2006 Nov 29. Doi: 10.1016/j.psychres.2005.11.011. Epub 2006 Oct 11. PMID: 17045658.

[10] Tate, A.E., McCabe, R.C., Larsson, H., Lundström, S., Lichtenstein, P., Kuja-Halkola, R. Predicting mental health problems in adolescence using machine learning techniques. *PLoS One*, 15(4), e0230389, 2020. Doi: 10.1371/journal.pone.0230389.

[11] Thieme, Anja, Belgrave, Danielle, Doherty, Gavin. Machine learning in mental health: A systematic review of the HCI literature to support the development of effective and implementable ML systems. *ACM Transactions on Computer-Human Interaction*, 27(5), Article 34, Publication date: August 2020.

[12] Chancellor, S., De Choudhury, M. Methods in predictive techniques for mental health status on social media: a critical review. *npj Digital Medicine*, 3, 43, 2020.

[13] Anu Priya, Shruti Garg, Neha Prerna Tigga, Predicting anxiety, depression and stress in modern life using machine learning algorithms. *Procedia Computer Science*, 1258–1267. ISSN 1877-0509(2020).

[14] Sumathi, M.R., Poorna, R.B. Prediction of mental health problems among children using machine learning techniques, (IJACSA). *International Journal of Advanced Computer Science and Applications*, 7(1), 2016.

[15] Ćosić, K., Popović, S., Šarlija, M., Kesedžić, I., Jovanovic, T. Artificial intelligence in prediction of mental health disorders induced by the COVID-19 pandemic among health care workers. *Croatian Medical Journal*, 61(3), 279–288, 2020 Jul 5.

[16] Graham, S., Depp, C., Lee, E.E., Nebeker, C., Tu, X., Kim, H.C., Jeste, D.V. Artificial intelligence for mental health and mental illnesses: An overview. *Current Psychiatry*, 21(11), 116, 2019 Nov 7.

[17] Bertoncelli, C.M., Altamura, P., Vieira, E.R., Bertoncelli, D., Solla, F. Using artificial intelligence to identify factors associated with autism spectrum disorder in adolescents with cerebral palsy. *Neuropediatrics*, 50(3), 178–187, 2019 Jun. Epub (2019 Apr 24). PMID: 31018221.

[18] Chauhan, S., Garg, A. Predictive research for mental health disease. *International Journal of Innovative Technology and Exploring Engineering (IJITEE*, ISSN: 2278-3075, 8(9S2), July 2019.

[19] Arif, M., Basri, A., Melibari, G, et al., Classification of anxiety disorders using machine learning methods: A literature review. *Insights of Biomedical Research*, 4(1), 95–110. Doi: 10.36959/584/455.

[20] Shatte, A., Hutchinson, D., Teague, S. Machine learning in mental health: A scoping review of methods and applications. *Psychological Medicine*, 49(9), 1426–1448, 2019.

[21] Mutalib, S, et. al., Mental health prediction models using machine learning in higher education institution. *Turkish Journal of Computer and Mathematics Education (TURCOMAT)*, 12(5), 2021. Doi: 10.17762/turcomat.v12i5.2181.

[22] Sandhya, P., Mahek, K. Prediction of mental disorder for employees in IT Industry. *International Journal of Innovative Technology and Exploring Engineering* (IJITEE), 8(6S), April 2019, ISSN: 2278-3075.

4 A Fuzzy-based Predictive Approach for Soil Classification of Agricultural Land for the Efficient Cultivation and Harvesting

Sandeepkumar Hegde and Rajalaxmi Hegde
NMAM Institute of Technology, Deralakatte, India

4.1 INTRODUCTION

According to their behavior, origin, or inherent characteristics, soils can be divided into various categories (soil morphology) [1]. Variations in the significance of physical characteristics to various land use and various disease theories may have an impact on the classification approach. A technical system approach to soil classification, in contrast, divides soils into categories based on their appropriateness for specific purposes and edaphic characteristics. Hundreds or thousands of years may be needed for geologic changes in soil composition, texture, and characteristics [2]. The soil data must be analyzed based on the pH for effective cultivation and harvesting. Applications of machine learning algorithms have been utilized to categorize soil by both commercial and academic institutions [3]. These methods have been applied for commercial, scientific, and industrial objectives. For instance, machine learning techniques have been applied to evaluate enormous data sets and identify insightful categorizations and patterns. Research investigations in agriculture and biology have used a variety of data analysis approaches, including decision trees, statistical machine learning, and other analysis methods [4]. This study explores the potential of machine learning techniques to enhance the analysis and pattern detection of large experimental soil profile datasets.

The goal of this effort is to comprehend potential processes underlying the aging effects in sands. This was achieved through a review of the available data from the literature and the creation of a lab testing program to categorize them according to the attributes [5]. The laboratory testing program was created so that the effects of several factors, including soil type, relative density, temperature, pH, and geographic

DOI: 10.1201/9781003363606-4

locations, could be researched [6]. Finding a collection of fuzzy rules to address a particular classification problem from training data with uncertainty is the most crucial task in the design of fuzzy classification systems [7]. In the proposed approach, the soil data were classified using the fuzzy C-Means technique through an unsupervised learning approach. The complete training dataset is transformed into fuzzy rules, and the relationships between the input variables are used to calculate the weights for each input variable that appears in the resulting fuzzy rules. The test dataset is fed into the proposed model, and the accuracy obtained with the test dataset is examined. In this chapter, C language was utilized to implement the fuzzy rules by first establishing the membership functions for the input attributes of the soil data, and then generating the initial fuzzy rules for the training data. The proposed approach's accuracy is compared to that of conventional machine learning methods like support vector machines (SVM), random forest, naive Bayes classifier, and decision tree techniques. The results of the experiments show that the proposed approach achieved better accuracy when compared to conventional machine learning techniques.

4.2 LITERATURE SURVEY

The following section summarises the various research studies that have been proposed in the field of soil classification using various machine learning approaches.

In [8] upport vector machines (SVM) were proposed for recognizing, mapping, and categorizing different types of soil. Hyperspectral data with a high spectral resolution is used in this method. When working with a tiny sample size of data, a support vector machine classifier produces accurate results. It has been found that high-dimensional datasets with few training samples benefit from the support vector machine technique. The investigated soil datasets were categorized using a technique that is proposed in [9]. By using the Naive Bayes and KNearest Neighbor algorithms, soils are divided into three categories: low, medium, and high. The Soil Testing Laboratory in Jabalpur, Madhya Pradesh, is where the data is gathered. The tuples in the dataset describe the number of nutrients and micronutrients present in the soil. By dividing these nutrients and micronutrients into two groups, it is possible to determine the soil's capacity for yield. The medium group of soils shows good yielding capabilities, according to the JNKW Jabalpur Department of Soil Science. The categories of high (H) and very high soils exhibit modern yielding capability, while the categories low (L) and very low soils do not. A categorization approach for soil texture based on hyperspectral data was presented in [10]. A random forest classifier's performance is compared to that of the Convolutional Neural Network (CNN) techniques. The soil dataset from the Land/Use and Cover Area Frame Statistical Survey (LUCAS) is used in this study. Hyperspectral and soil texture data are included. One drawback of the proposed technique is that atmospheric error, which is typically present in hyperspectral data, must be corrected. When compared to traditional statistical methods, in [11] the proposed methodology performs better which uses a limited amount of attributes from the dataset to analyze. The agricultural soil profiles were chosen to be comprehensive and to make soil classification easier. In [12] the author proposed a convolutional neural network-based empirical model to investigate the daily soil moisture retrieval for passive microwave remote sensing. The soil moisture retrieval model based on deep learning can learn detailed features from a vast amount of remote sensing data. In [13] the author developed a support vector machine-based model for the classification of soil samples with the help of numerous scientific factors. Several algorithms, characteristics, and filters are used to collect and process color photos of the soil samples. These algorithms extract numerous characteristics, including color, texture, and others. SVM only uses a small subset of the training samples that are situated at the boundaries of the class distribution in feature space to fit an ideal hyperplane between the classes. The supervised categorization's accuracy is influenced by the training data that was used. In [14] the authors proposed an improved model with more features than the current method, such as crop lists, urea levels, and soil nutrients. To categorize soils where color, energy, and HSV may be visible, image processing techniques can be employed. In [15] the authors applied J48, JRip algorithm, decision tree, and Naive Bayes classification techniques that are used on the soil datasets for the soil classification. The Naive Bayes algorithms obtained higher accuracy compared to other machine learning approaches when imposed on soil datasets.

4.3 METHODOLOGY

The architecture of the proposed approach is shown in Figure 4.1. As shown in the figure, initially soil data is given as input to the proposed model. The data are passed as input and undergo a pre-processing stage where noise and irrelevant features are filtered from the given dataset.

Once the dataset is pre-processed by removing noise and outliers, a fuzzy ruleset is defined on the extracted dataset as per functional specification from which the classification of soil will be derived. In the end, the performance of the predictive model will be evaluated.

The dataset required to experiment was gathered from the Kaggle website. The dataset is normalized using a minimax normalizer and outliers are removed using the interquartile range method. The insignificant features are removed from the dataset using the recursive feature elimination technique. Figure 4.2 depicts the flowchart of the proposed Fuzzy C means algorithm. Initially, a membership matrix is generated for the given dataset. From the generated membership matrix degree of the membership is generated using equation (4.1)

$$\mu_{jk} = 1 \Bigg/ \sum_{l=1}^{d} \left(e_{jk} \Big/ e_{kl} \right)^{\left(2/n-1 \right)} \tag{4.1}$$

Where μ_{jk} indicates the membership of the jth and k^{th} cluster centroid, 'd' represents the centers of the cluster, e_{jk} indicates the Euclidean distance between the jth and

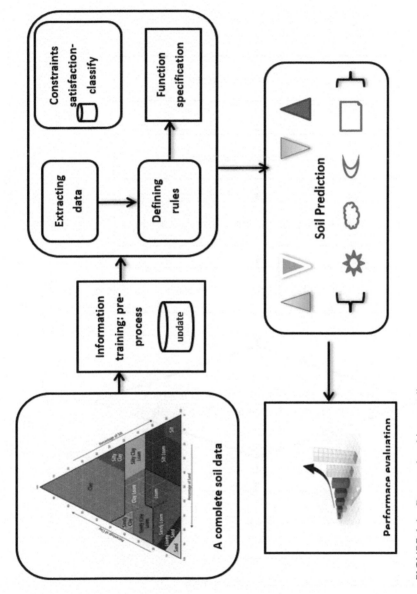

FIGURE 4.1 Proposed architecture diagram.

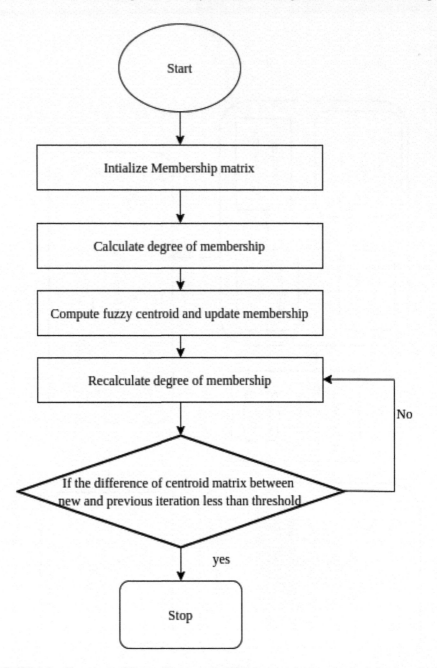

FIGURE 4.2 Flowchart of Fuzzy C means algorithm.

k^{th} cluster centroid, and 'n' is the index of fuzziness. For each of the memberships, a fuzzy centroid is derived and membership has been upgraded using equation (4.2).

$$u_k = \left. \left(\sum_{j=1}^{u} \left(\mu_{jk} \right)^n S_j \right) \middle/ \left(\sum_{j=1}^{u} \left(\mu_{jk} \right)^n \right) , \right. \quad \forall_k = 1, 2..d \tag{4.2}$$

u_k represents the kth fuzzy center, X_j represents the data points and 'k' is the objective function. The fuzzy centroid computations will be performed until the difference in the centroid matrix between the new and previous iterations will be less than the threshold.

The pseudocode of the proposed fuzzy c means algorithm is as below.

Let S = {s1, s2, s3 ..., sn} be the data points from the considered dataset and U = {u1, u2, u3 ..., uc} be the cluster centre.

1) Randomly choose the centers of the cluster 'c'
2) Compute the fuzzy membership 'μ_{jk}' as

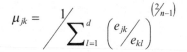

$$\mu_{jk} = \left. 1 \middle/ \sum_{l=1}^{d} \left(e_{jk} \middle/ e_{kl} \right)^{\left(2/_{n-1} \right)} \right.$$

3) Determine the fuzzy centroid 'u_k' as

$$u_k = \left. \left(\sum_{j=1}^{u} \left(\mu_{jk} \right)^n S_j \right) \middle/ \left(\sum_{j=1}^{u} \left(\mu_{jk} \right)^n \right) , \right. \quad \forall_k = 1, 2..d$$

4) Repeat stages 2 and 3 until the minimum value for 'k' is achieved.

One of the advantages of the proposed algorithm is that it obtains better results with the overlapped dataset. The fuzzy c means algorithms are applied to the considered dataset and the result obtained with the test dataset is analyzed. The section below illustrates a detailed discussion of the result obtained with the proposed approach.

4.4   RESULT AND DISCUSSION

Finding a collection of fuzzy rules to address a particular classification problem from training data with uncertainty is the most crucial task in the design of fuzzy classification systems. The values can be predictably determined by grouping soil forms. After going through the classification procedure, the database for future references has successfully been updated with soil data. The figure below indicates the result obtained with the proposed approach when it is applied to the soil dataset.

As shown in Figures 4.3 and 4.4, initially the collected soil dataset is loaded for the further visualization process. The dataset in its original form may contain noise and outliers which has to be pre-processed to obtain optimal accuracy.

As shown in Figure 4.5 a feature extraction process is carried out to extract the data from the biomass information. The dataset is classified based on different parameters such as cultivated area, forest area, and grass area. The implemented interface also has the option of displaying different information such as the number of countries, number of lands, and number of forests from which the soil dataset is taken. Figure 4.6 below illustrate the different fuzzy rules generated based on different ph parameters by applying the Fuzzy C means algorithm.

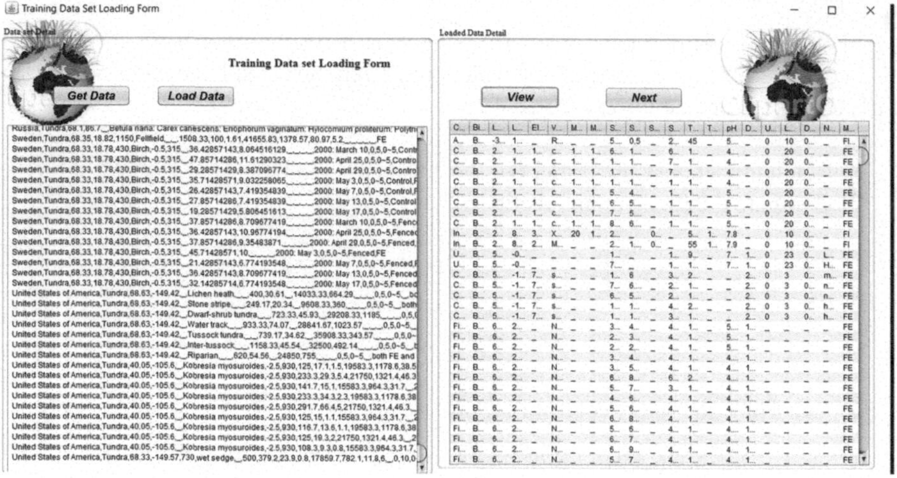

FIGURE 4.3   Snapshot of training dataset loading form.

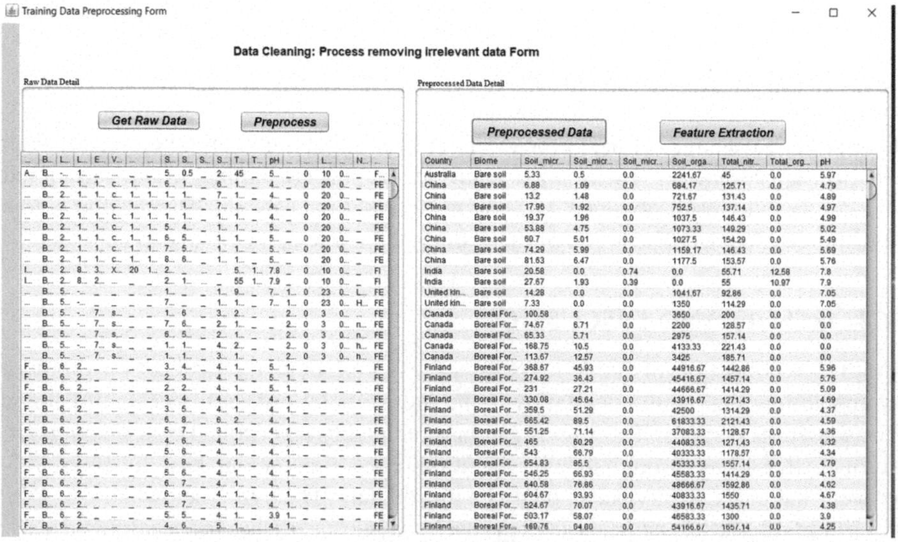

FIGURE 4.4   Snapshot of data pre-processing stage.

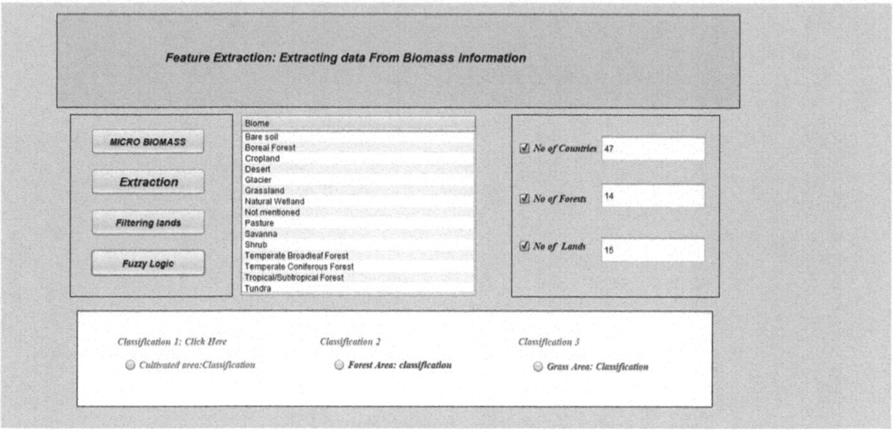

FIGURE 4.5 Snapshot of feature extraction process.

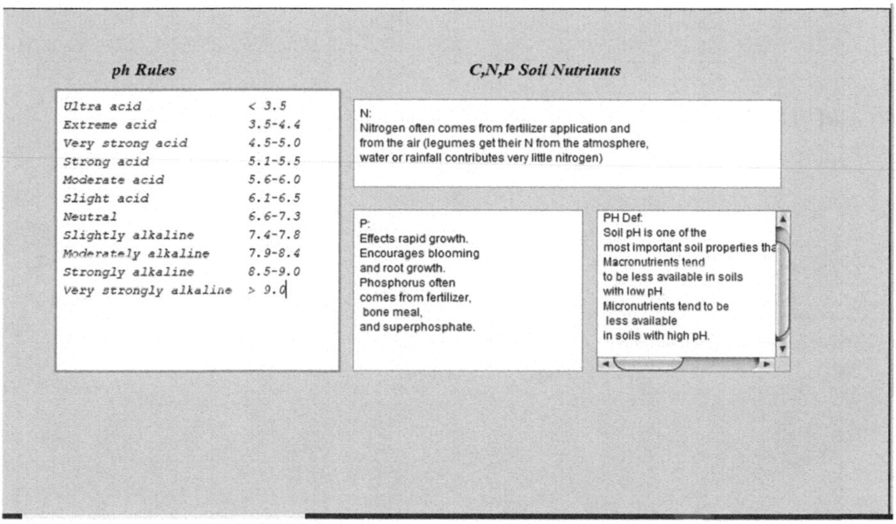

FIGURE 4.6 Snapshot of Fuzzy rules generated based on Ph parameter.

As shown in Figure 4.7, the forest area is classified using different parameters such as Temperate Coniferous Forest, Temperate Broadleaf Forest, and Tropical/Subtropical forest by applying the proposed algorithm.

As shown in Figure 4.8 cultivated lands are classified from the biome by applying Fuzzy rules. Figure 4.8 above shows the result obtained with grassland classification. The grasslands are classified from the biome using different parameters such as tundra, glacier, wetland, shrub, and pasture (Figure 4.9).

Figure 4.10 illustrates the validation rate achieved using various machine learning algorithms. From the graph, it can be evident that the proposed Fuzzy C means

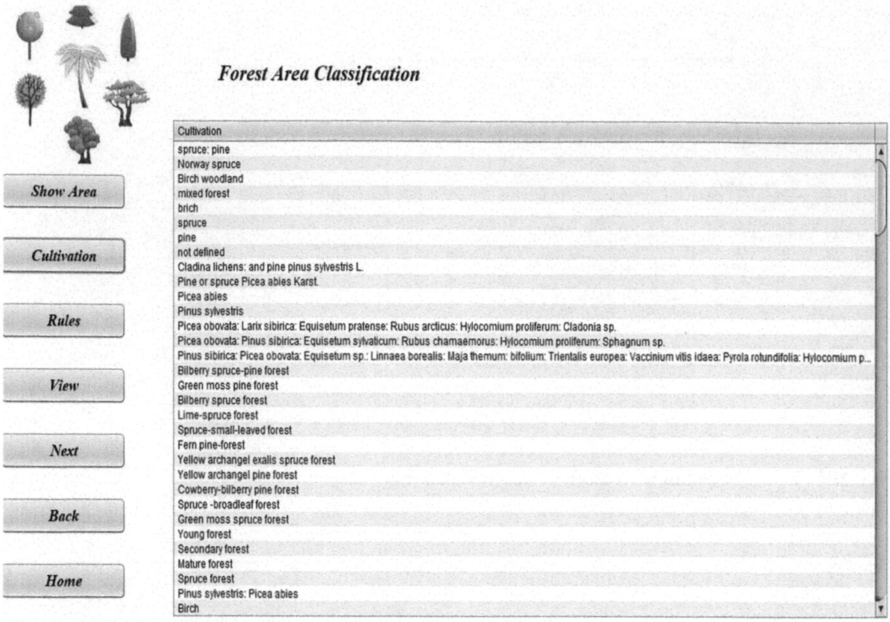

FIGURE 4.7　Snapshot of forest area classification.

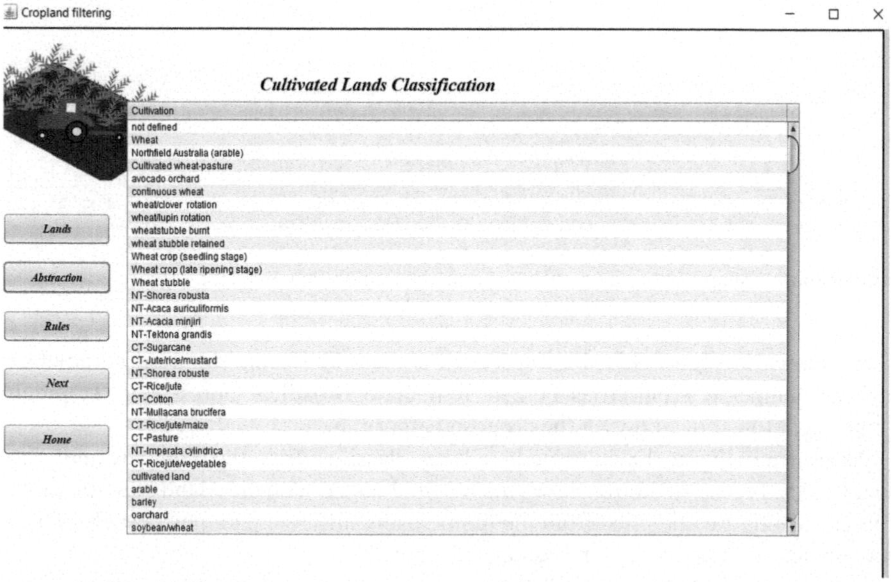

FIGURE 4.8　Snapshot of cultivated lands classification.

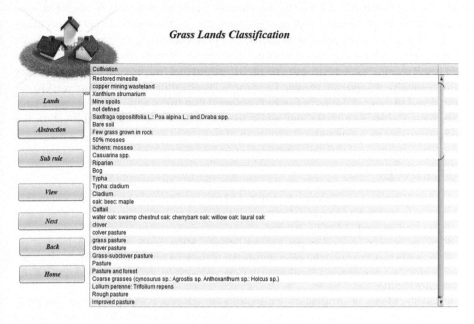

FIGURE 4.9 Snapshot of grass lands classification.

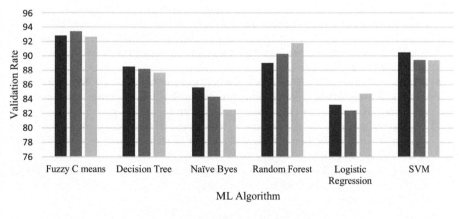

FIGURE 4.10 Accuracy analysis of machine learning algorithms.

algorithms obtained a higher accuracy and precision rate compared to the traditional machine learning approaches.

4.5 CONCLUSION

In this chapter the proposed new method to generate fuzzy rules from training data to deal with the soil classification problem was presented. The entire training dataset is converted into fuzzy rules and then the weight of each input variable appearing in the generated fuzzy rules is derived by determining the relationships between input variables. Accordingly, the test dataset is passed to the proposed model, and the accuracy obtained with the test dataset is analyzed. The performance of the proposed approach is compared with the traditional machine learning algorithms such as accuracy, precision, and recall. The experimental results illustrate that the proposed weighted fuzzy rules generation approach obtained a higher classification accuracy compared to the traditional technique. Hence it can be concluded that fuzzy approaches are more suitable for soil classification through which the efficiency of agricultural cultivation and harvesting can be improved.

REFERENCES

[1] Van Klompenburg, Thomas, Ayalew Kassahun, and Cagatay Catal. "Crop yield prediction using machine learning: A systematic literature review." *Computers and Electronics in Agriculture* 177 (2020): 105709.

[2] Rahman, S. K., A. L. Zaminur, Kaushik Chandra Mitra, and S. M. Mohidul Islam. "Soil classification using machine learning methods and crop suggestion based on soil series." *2018 21st International Conference of Computer and Information Technology (ICCIT)*. IEEE, 2018.

[3] Meier, Martin, et al. "Digital soil mapping using machine learning algorithms in a tropical mountainous area." *Revista Brasileira de Ciência do Solo* 42 (2018). https://doi.org/10.1590/18069657rbcs20170421.

[4] Wadoux, Alexandre MJ-C., Budiman Minasny, and Alex B. McBratney. "Machine learning for digital soil mapping: Applications, challenges, and suggested solutions." *Earth-Science Reviews* 210 (2020): 103359.

[5] John, Kingsley, et al. "Using machine learning algorithms to estimate soil organic carbon variability with environmental variables and soil nutrient indicators in an alluvial soil." *Land* 9.12 (2020): 487.

[6] Palanivel, Kodimalar, and Chellammal Surianarayanan. "An approach for prediction of crop yield using machine learning and big data techniques." *International Journal of Computer Engineering and Technology* 10.3 (2019): 110–118.

[7] Khosravi, Khabat, et al. "A comparative assessment of flood susceptibility modeling using multi-criteria decision-making analysis and machine learning methods." *Journal of Hydrology* 573 (2019): 311–323.

[8] Pereira, Gustavo Willam, et al. "Soil mapping for precision agriculture using support vector machines combined with inverse distance weighting." *Precision Agriculture* 23 (2022): 1189–1204.

[9] Jahwar, A. F., A. M. Abdulazeez, D. Q. Zeebaree, D. A. Zebari, and F. Y. Ahmed. (2021, July). *An integrated Gapso approach for solving problem of an examination timetabiking system.* In *2021 IEEE Symposium on Industrial Electronics & Applications (ISIEA)* (pp. 1–6). IEEE.

[10] Pandith, Vaishali, et al. "Performance evaluation of machine learning techniques for mustard crop yield prediction from soil analysis." *Journal of Scientific Research* 64.2 (2020): 394–398.

[11] Xu, Zhigang, et al. "Multisource earth observation data for land-cover classification using random forest." *IEEE Geoscience and Remote Sensing Letters* 15.5 (2018): 789–793.

[12] Xu, Xuebin, et al. "Applying convolutional neural networks (CNN) for end-to-end soil analysis based on laser-induced breakdown spectroscopy (LIBS) with less spectral pre-processing." *Computers and Electronics in Agriculture* 199 (2022): 107171.

[13] Zhu, Qian, et al. "Drought prediction using in situ and remote sensing products with SVM over the Xiang River Basin, China." *Natural Hazards* 105.2 (2021): 2161–2185.

[14] Abraham, Shiny, Chau Huynh, and Huy Vu. "Classification of soils into hydrologic groups using machine learning." *Data* 5.1 (2019): 2.

[15] Wankhede, Disha S. "Analysis and prediction of soil nutrients pH, N, P, K for crop using machine learning classifier: a review." *International Conference on Mobile Computing and Sustainable Informatics*. Springer, Cham, 2020.

5 Analysis of Smart Agriculture Systems Using IOT

S. P. Rajamohana
Pondicherry University, Karaikal, India

*S. Pavithra Shri, V. Nithyapriyaa, B. Parthiban,
A. Karthikeyan, V. B. Tharmentheran and
T. Pragatheeswaran*
PSG College of Technology, Coimbatore, India

5.1 INTRODUCTION

The Internet of Things (IoT) is a cutting-edge aspect of current technology that allows for the monitoring and managing of devices from anywhere in the world. It has the ability to converse with living creatures in a passive manner [1]. IoT technology has evolved significantly in recent years and it is now accessible to anybody.

In addition to simple and convenient sharing, IoT has developed a wide range of technologies to make human life easier, some of which can be used to provide basic necessities such as food in agricultural regions. The expansion and advancement of IoT enables us to generate renewable energy to power the setup with solar panels, creating the way for the future green world [2]. The current climatic changes are so severe that they pose a serious risk to large-scale crop production. Drones, improved tractors, and field-based sensors are examples of technologies that considerably assist farmers in increasing crop production [3]. In order to achieve greater quality and quantity in manufacturing, more safeguarding measures and regulating systems must be deployed in the field.

Agriculture employs around one-third of India's population and contributes between 15 and 16 percent of GDP. Climatic changes, soil erosion due to floods, and chemical usage near farmland have already depleted the state of agricultural land [4]. Smart farming decreases water waste and improves crop quality by using the least amount of resources. Agriculture requires a large workforce. However, today most people are not interested in agriculture because this would involve the majority of their time cultivating crops in the field and spend the entire day bringing in large harvests [5].

The use of these technologies allows for higher crop yields to be achieved quicker than with traditional agricultural methods.

DOI: 10.1201/9781003363606-5

Problems Faced:

- Inefficient soil condition
- Poor irrigation system
- Non-reliable power supply
- Incompetent scarecrow
- Lack of analysis or prediction system

This chapter makes a step towards attempting to resolve all of these issues. A passive infrared (PIR) sensor is used to predict animal movements and other unusual phenomena. When combined with an alarm or buzzer, a PIR sensor can be utilised as an electronic scarecrow. Solar panels are used to power the system, which provides endless energy and are eco-friendly [6]. We can use all of the technology available to monitor the field from any remote place to improve field productivity and automation.

5.2 LITERATURE SURVEY

Kasara Sai Pratyush Reddy [7] proposed a model that predicts the water requirement for the plants, using the decision tree algorithm. This architecture model comprises of soil moisture sensors and various weather-related sensors that dispatches the observed information to the database by using the suitable tree algorithm on the pre-processed data. The discrete value output is sent to the farmers regarding water supply through email prior.

K. N. Bhanu [8] developed a model which communicates with various parameters of the soil using Arduino and data is sent to the ThinkSpeak cloud. Threshold values are given to each sensor. Through the application of machine learning (ML) techniques to the live data, we classify the sensed data with the help of the given threshold values and based on the classification results. Using a classification algorithm, the data was intelligently classified and categorized based on the limit provided. All those values which fall above the given threshold are seen as a cause for action; all other values falling below the given threshold is kept in a cloud for further evaluation.

A.R. Al-Ali [9] presented a system that makes use of a chip controller on a single board system; to meet the necessary power, an incorporated Wi-Fi mode connection made to the solar cell. The controller detects inversive nature and generates appropriate incentive signals that aid in managing and running irrigation pump lines. A careful and routine inspection of the subsurface water level is performed to prevent the well's water from burning. In this model, there are three types of performance. First is the controlling the model in normal local mode, second is checking in mobile controlled mode and the final one is the fully logic-based controlled mode. A model reference template was drafted, then implemented and tested for the purpose of validating the proposed system.

Sourav Saha [6] concentrated on a variety of common solicitations relating to science that may work together in an agricultural plot for a healthy and good accuracy while using the least amount of labour. It also encompasses a way for checking and detecting the farming domain and the ability to record conditions from a remote location. To create the necessary renewable power supply in the field of agriculture, it makes use of a system of solar tracking which might prove to be a good and sustainable source of energy generation. It is feasible to get a precise data on soil nature by doing soil test work and measuring the humidity of the surroundings. Without any use of chemical compounds, the 'electronic scarecrow' is able to function effectively and it has the capability to link with others. A single straw man engulfs 5 metres and work for a period of 6 months only containing a 9v battery. In an attempt to reduce the workload for farmers, a Global System for Mobile communication (GSM) module has been used in this system. The employment of solar and automated lighting-controlled devices leads to significant energy conservation.

Dr. N. Suma [10] proposed a model that comprises equipment and facilities such as a distance-administered system using GPS. This also detects the level of humidity, temperature and security and it provides a good irrigation facility. Networks of wireless sensors are used by the system especially for the continuous monitoring of the properties of soil and environmental factors. At many various locations in the fields of a farm, different sensor nodes are deployed over clouds. Through any internet services, these variables controlled and interfacing sensors, Wi-Fi, camera with a good microcontroller performs the necessary activities.

P. Narayut [11] proposed intelligent farming for watering and developing roofing systems for exterior areas of cultivation and also indicating major dominating farming toward the wealth of the Thai country. In order to obtain a more accurate outcome and to smoothen the recognized values, the application of a Kalman filter can delete unwanted things or data. The recognized data, and also the weather information, is used for decision-making purposes. In order to make choices on systems certain regulations related to data and weather forecasting is created. There is a function for users to control the watering and roofing systems through digital applications manually.

T. Baranwal [12] proposed a model that addresses the challenge of combining Internet of Things (IOT) with systems that were used for safety to increase the productivity of food preservation in cereal stores. This paper establishes the procedure to resolve problems such as recognizing mouse species, warning to the cultivations and providing message based on data analysis and clarifying without human interference. In this system, the sensors and devices are connected through computer software. The success rate is 84.8 percent in the test cases.

Jash Doshi et al [13] developed a model that helps the farmers by providing the live information and visible light from censors in the field that will assist farmers in making sensible decisions. With the aid of this research, farmers will be able to increase yields and utilise their resources as efficiently as possible with little to no waste. Moreover, this system is easily operable through mobile applications and there is no prior requirement of any knowledge about it. Therefore, the scope for smart agriculture is high.

M. Safdar Munir [14] designed a model that will be useful in creating an efficient irrigation system for farmers. The decision taken is based partially on the ontology and also partially on device information. This method helps not only helps in the processing of data but also decreases the delay rate.

Adithya Vadapalli [15] advances a model which will be useful for forecasting weather data, by switching on the motor pump which will verify the moisture content of soil with the help of sensors which have been interfaced to the module Arduino-UNO. This can be operated from any kind of remote location with the advanced tech developed in networking.

Abhijit Pathak [16] put forward a model that will help agricultural workers to select the correct grain for given conditions by implementing the famous cuckoo search algorithm using IoT. The information is gathered by real-time sensors from the farming environment and is then fed to the cloud platform, i.e ThingSpeak, which is used later in the Cuckoo Search Algorithm, which will help in the selection of suitable crops for that specific soil. This will significantly increase the overall yield.

Anneketh Vij [17] proposed a model that will assist the farmers to monitor irrigation problems. This system uses non-wired sensor network to establish the connection and all fields will be recorded by modules which will send on the information to an ordinary server. Algorithms such as ML will make predictions for cultivation patterns which is based on weather and crop situations. This model will make irrigation easy.

Mrs. Vaishali Puranik [18] composed a model which illustrates a robust tool that implements real-time decisions according to the rate of irrigation, environmental parameters, weather conditions and events, such as flux flow, pressure level, and the speed of the wind are periodically sampled. The resultant data is refined based on a decision-making model in concurrence with the drools rule engine. It can be distance-controlled, and offers an open data network with shared limitation levels for information trade to farmers regarding the fertilizer supplier, and agricultural technicians which helps in improved decision-making and improved function and management.

Divyansh Thakura [19] proposes a model, which aims to improve the spraying of water on agricultural fields whenever necessary and demand that gives a useful details related recognition of obtrusion in farming field. After that, this message will be sent to farmers with the use of a cloud-based application.

Tran Anh Khoa [20] proposed a model that helps the farmers by providing real-time information such as temperature, humidity, soil moisture and visible rays from the sensors in the field that will assist the farmer to make informed decisions. With the aid of this research, farmers will be able to increase yields and utilise their resources as efficiently as possible with little to no waste. Furthermore, this system is easily operable through mobile applications and there is no prior knowledge required about it. The main benefits of using this technology are due to its capacity for long-distance communication, very low power utilization, and easy to deploy when compared to all. It can communicate to the Internet both physically and mechanically through long-range (LoRa) communication. The outcome of the trail and the computation of the smart watering method approach has an economic productivity that is a minimum of 30 percent more efficient than the current technology.

5.3 METHODS

The integration of IoT and machine learning algorithms yields excellent outcomes. We incorporated a classification technique which is a supervised learning algorithm (Figure 5.1). It examines the collected data and divides it into training and test sets. The more data fed into the model for training, the more accurate the results. The next phase is the testing phase where the sensed data is fed to the trained model to obtain the predicted output. Solar panels, which are renewable and environmentally acceptable, are used to power the proposed model. We use an Arduino UNO microcontroller for storing the data and send the data to cloud through a Wi-Fi module.

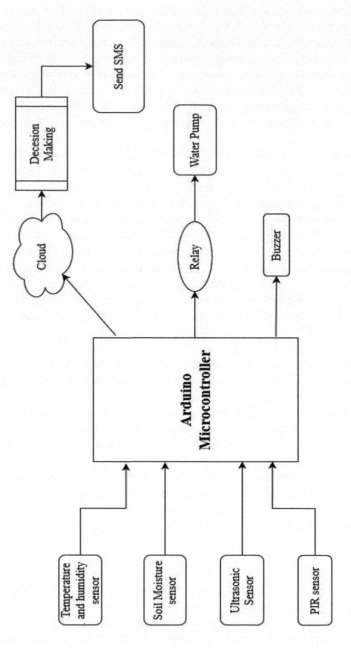

FIGURE 5.1   Block diagram of smart agriculture system.

Sensors such as the DHT11 (temperature and humidity) sensor, the PIR sensor, the soil moisture sensor, and the water level sensor are used to monitor the ambient parameters. The data collected by the sensors is then sent to the cloud for analysis. These statistics are used by the decision-making algorithm to determine how much water the soil requires. The water pump can then be turned ON with a phone call. The water pump is automatically turned OFF once the needed amount of water has been flowed.

PIR sensors are used to spot unusual bird and animal movements. When the sensor detects an unusual movement, it transmits a message to the farmer and generates a buzzer sound. To determine the amount of water required to water the field, the data acquired from the soil moisture sensor, temperature, and humidity sensor is appended to the existing dataset. The sample dataset is taken from the Kaggle repository named Agriculture and weather dataset. Temperature, humidity, soil moisture, and water flow time are the four attributes in this dataset. To forecast the amount of water necessary for the soil, this dataset was trained using the decision tree algorithm. The data from the sensor is input into this algorithm via the Cloud in order to anticipate the appropriate water content.

5.4 COMPONENTS REQUIRED

i) **Arduino UNO**

The Arduino Uno (Figure 5.2) is a microcontroller board with 14 digital pins and 6 analogue pins based on the Atmega328. The Arduino IDE is an open-source tool that executes the user's programme called sketch to get sensor readings and process it.

ii) **DTH11 Sensor**

The DHT11 (Figure 5.3) is a low-cost temperature and humidity sensor that monitors the surrounding temperature and humidity. It is a thermistor humidity sensor which measures the surrounding air. On the data pin configuration it outputs a digital signal.

iii) **Soil Moisture Sensor (YL 38)**

The image of a soil moisture sensor is shown in Figure 5.4. This sensor is used to detect and measure the soil's water humidity. This sensor works on the simple principle: it has two electrodes; soil conducts more electricity when soil moisture is high (low resistance), and soil conducts less electricity

FIGURE 5.2 Arduino UNO.

FIGURE 5.3   DTH11 sensor.

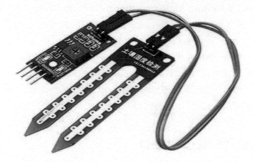

FIGURE 5.4   Soil moisture sensor.

when the soil is dry (more resistance). The electrical resistance of the soil determines the output.

iv) **Ultrasonic sensor**

The ultrasonic sensor (Figure 5.5) measures the distance between two objects using ultrasonic waves. They can reach a height of 70 feet. They are also utilised to show the water level because sound waves can bounce around in a liquid medium.

v) **GSM module**

The GSM, or Global System for Mobile Communication, module is shown in Figure 5.6. Through Short Messaging Service (SMS), GSM technology is designed to enable a data link to a remote or mobile network. This may be used to send and receive text messages as well as make and receive phone calls, just like a regular phone.

FIGURE 5.5   Ultrasonic sensor.

FIGURE 5.6   GSM module.

FIGURE 5.7   PIR sensor.

vi) **PIR sensor**

PIR Sensor, also known as a motion detection sensor, is a passive infrared sensor (Figure 5.7) that detects movement. It detects heat energy in the environment using polyelectric sensors, allowing us to detect motion.

vii) **WiFi Module**

Figure 5.8 displays a Wi-Fi module that offers low-power modes like hibernate with real-time clock (RTC) mode. An inbuilt antenna or an RF connector for an external antenna may be included in a module. The purpose of this module is to transform a serial port or TTL level into an embedded module that can comply with WiFi wireless network communication standards and has an IEEE802 wireless network protocol built in.

FIGURE 5.8   WiFi module.

5.5   FLOW DIAGRAM

We attempted to create a smart agriculture system in Proteus 8 software, which consists of an Arduino board and a microcontroller, in this work (Figure 5.9). First, the temperature and humidity are measured, and an SMS is sent to the farmer with the message "Moderate Temperature and Humidity." Then it looks for any unusual movements in the field, and, if any are found, it sends an SMS with the message "Motion Detected." The ultrasonic sensor then determines the tank's water level. The soil moisture sensor detects the amount of water in the soil. The tank pump and irrigation pump will turn on and off automatically based on the water level and the moisture content of the soil. The status of the tank pump and the watering pump will be sent to the farmer via SMS after each process (Figure 5.10).

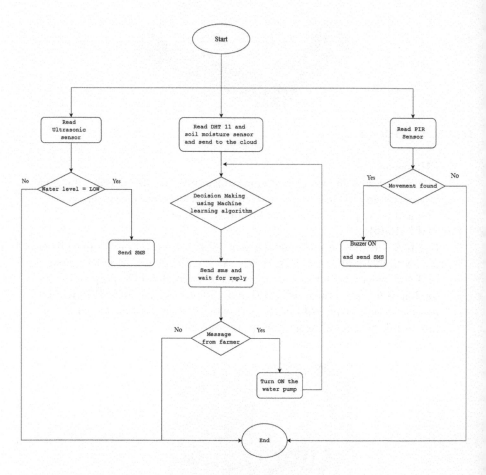

FIGURE 5.9   Flow diagram of crop monitoring system.

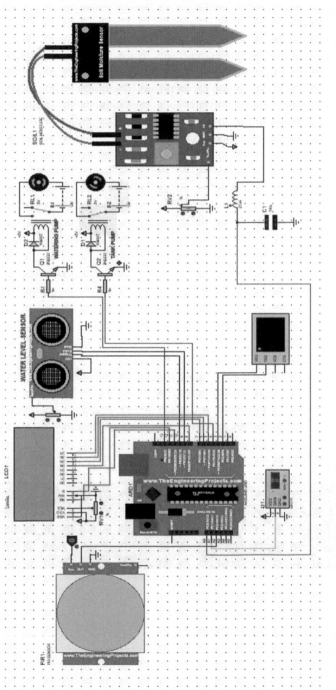

FIGURE 5.10 Implementation of crop monitoring system.

5.6   RESULTS AND DISCUSSION

The output of the above implementation is given below, which shows the SMS that is sent to the farmer.

Figure 5.11 shows the SMS message that farmer receives regarding the temperature and humidity. It displays if the temperature is low, moderate or high.

Figure 5.12 depicts the SMS messages that a farmer will get whenever a task involving the status of a water pump is completed. There are two pumps present: one is the tank pump which pumps the water to storage tank, and the other is the water tank which pumps water to the farming land. The values gathered from the data is sent to the cloud. The model is trained using real-time data as well as a dataset from the internet.

The agriculture and weather dataset from the Kaggle repository was used to train the model (see Table 5.1). The data is fed into the model, which calculates the amount of water necessary. The pump is then turned on, and the farmer will receive SMS messages indicating whether the pump is on or off.

The graph of the trained model is shown in Figure 5.13. It shows the amount of time the water needs to flow to the land. From this figure, we can conclude that the soil moisture is highly dependent on the humidity or vice versa.

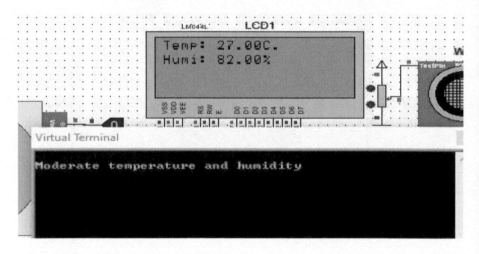

FIGURE 5.11 SMS message 1.

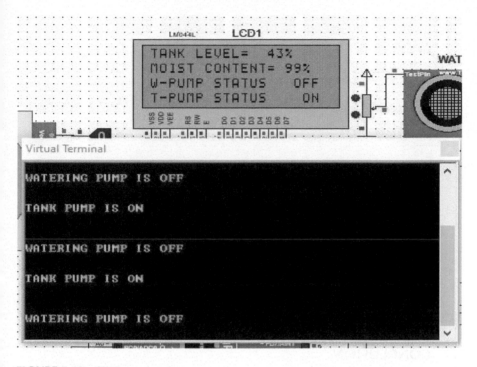

FIGURE 5.12 SMS message 2.

TABLE 5.1
Agriculture and Weather Dataset

Temperature	Humidity	Soil Moisture	Time of water flow
23.7	57.7	59.66	5
23.4	57.2	56.85	10
23.4	56.9	54.82	15
23.5	56.8	53.24	15
23.7	58	52.16	15
23.7	58.1	50.99	15
23.7	58.1	50.79	15
23.7	58.1	50.7	15
23.7	58.1	50.48	20
23.8	58.1	50.45	20
23.8	58	50.62	20
23.8	58	50.43	20
23.8	58	50.38	20
23.8	58	50.11	20
23.8	58	50.16	20
23.8	58	49.43	17
23.8	58	50.23	20
23.8	58.1	50.21	20
23.8	58.1	50.18	20

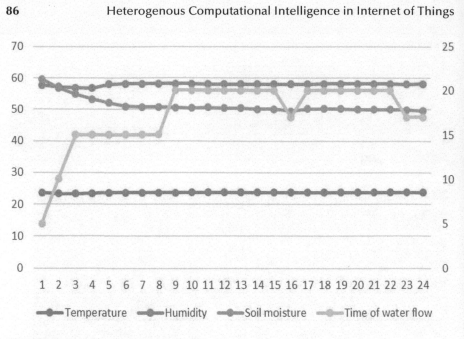

FIGURE 5.13   Graph of trained model.

5.7   CONCLUSION

This proposed model addresses all of the issues, including inadequate soil conditions, a faulty irrigation system, an unreliable power supply, and an incompetent scarecrow. The land is then irrigated with the needed amount of water using an automatic ON/OFF irrigation system. Because this model is solar-powered, it provides a renewable source of energy. To lure away birds or animals, the electric scarecrow will always emit a loud buzzer sound. This method is more effective than the traditional scarecrow strategy of placing a humanoid figure. Following that, machine learning algorithms are used. The data is classified using a decision tree classification algorithm, which yields a high accuracy rate for our model. Thus, our model tries to rectify all the problems faced by other methods and provides a smart integrated IOT system. This model can be implemented in real-time to a greater extent.

Future work could concentrate on determining soil fertility and detecting leaf disease. A smartphone application can be created to show all of the data collected, which aids in overall field monitoring. The pH sensor measures the pH value of the soil, which is used to check for soil nutrients, and alerts the farmer if the soil is too acidic or too basic can be added. Soil unfit for farming can be identified. A disease control system must be created and implemented. In field crops, diseases that occur in patches, cause significant morphological and physiological changes in crops, are economically important, and can be effectively controlled (e.g., effective fungicides, mechanical removal) are good candidates for detection using optical sensors, followed by precision agriculture disease control approaches.

REFERENCES

[1] Naser Hossein Motlagh, Mahsa Mohammadrezaei, Julian Hunt and Behnam Zakeri, "Internet of Things (IoT) and the energy sector", *Energies*, 13(2), 494, January 2020.

[2] S. Nižetić, P. Šolić, D. López-de-Ipiña González-de-Artaza and L. Patrono. "Internet of Things (IoT): Opportunities, issues and challenges towards a smart and sustainable future." *Journal of Cleaner Production*, 274, 122877.

[3] V. Saiz-Rubio and F. Rovira-Más, "From smart farming towards agriculture 5.0: A review on crop data management" *Agronomy*, 10(2), 207, February 2020.

[4] D. Satterthwaite, G. McGranahan and C. Tacoli "Urbanization and its implications for food and farming", *Philosophical transactions of the Royal Society of London. Series B, Biological Sciences*, 365(1554), 2809–2820, 2010.

[5] Janet Ranganathan, Richard Waite, Searchinger, Tim and Hanson, Craig. "How to sustainably Feed 10 billion people by 2050", in *21 Charts*, 2018.

[6] Sourav Saha, Siddhartha Paul, Sudip Halder and Kanishka Majumder "Smart Agriculture System: Better accuracy and productivity", *2017 Devices for Integrated Circuit* (DevIC-2017), 23–24 March 2017.

[7] Kasara Sai Pratyush Reddy, Y. Mohana Roopa, L. N. Kovvada Rajeev and Narra Sai Nandan, "IoT based smart agriculture using machine learning", 2020 *Second International Conference on Inventive Research in Computing Applications (ICIRCA)*, 15–17 July 2020.

[8] K. N. Bhanu, H. S. Mahadevaswamy and H. J. Jasmine, "IoT based smart system for enhanced irrigation in agriculture", *2020 International Conference on Electronics and Sustainable Communication Systems (ICESC)*, 2–4 July 2020.

[9] A. R. Al-Ali, Ahmad Al Nabulsi, Shayok Mukhopadhyay, Mohammad Shihab Awal, Sheehan Fernandes and Khalil Ailabouni, "IoT-solar energy powered smart farm irrigation system", *Journal of Electronic Science and Technology*, 17, 100017, 2017.

[10] N. Suma, Sandra Rhea Samson, S. Saranya, G. Shanmugapriya and R. Subhashri, "IOT based smart agriculture monitoring system", *International Journal on Recent and Innovation Trends in Computing and Communication*, 5(2), 177–181, 26 February 2017.

[11] P. Narayut, P. Sasimanee, C.-I. Anupong, P. Phond and A. Khajonpong, "A control system in an intelligent farming by using arduino technology", *Student Project Conference (ICT - ISPC), 2016 Fifth ICT International*, 27–28 May 2016.

[12] T. Baranwal and P. K. Pateriya, "Development of IoT based smart security and monitoring devices for agriculture", *6th International Conference-Cloud System and Big Data Engineering (Confluence)*, 14–15 Jan 2016.

[13] Jash Doshi, *Tirthkumar Patel and Santosh Kumar Bharti, "Smart Farming using IoT, a solution for optimally monitoring farming conditions", The 3rd International workshop on Recent advances on Internet of Things: Technology and Application Approaches* (IoT-T&A 2019), 4–7 November 2019.

[14] M. Safdar Munir, Imran Sarwar Bajwa, Amna Ashraf, Waheed Anwar and Rubina Rashid, "Intelligent and smart irrigation system using edge computing and IoT", *Hindawi Complexity*, 2021, 1–16, Article ID 6691571, 28 February 2021.

[15] Kurundkar, S., Patukale, S., Ekambaram, R., Kachkure, P., Sisodiva, R. and Rathod, D. *Smart urban farming system. In 2022 IEEE 9th Uttar Pradesh Section International Conference on Electrical, Electronics and Computer Engineering (UPCON)* (pp. 1–6). December, IEEE, 2022.

[16] Abhijit Pathak, Mohammad AmazUddin, Md. Jainal Abedin, Karl Andersson, Rashed Mustafa and Mohammad Shahadat Hossain, "IoT based smart system to support agricultural parameters: A case study", *The 6th International Symposium on Emerging Inter-networks, Communication and Mobility (EICM)*, August 19–21, 2019.
[17] Anneketh Vij, Singh Vijendra, Abhishek Jain and Arushi Sharma, "IoT and machine learning approaches for automation of farm irrigation system", *International Conference on Computational Intelligence and Data Science*, 2020.
[18] Vaishali Puranik, Sharmila, Ankit Ranjan and Anamika Kumari, "Automation in agriculture and IoT", *2019 4ᵗʰ International Conference on Internet of Things: Smart Innovation and Usages (IoT-SIU)*, 18–19 April 2019.
[19] Divyansh Thakura, Yugal Kumar and Singh Vijendrac, "Smart irrigation and intrusions detection in agricultural fields using IoT", *International Conference on Computational Intelligence and Data Science (ICCIDS 2019)*, 2019.
[20] Tran Anh Khoa, Mai Minh Man, Tan-Y Nguyen, VanDung Nguyen and Nguyen Hoang Nam, "Smart agriculture using IoT multi-sensors: A novel watering management system", *Journal of Sensor and Actuator Networks*, 8(3), 45, 23 August 2019.

6 AI-Enabled Internet of Medical Things in Healthcare

Rashmi Singh and Anwar Ahamed Ansari

Bansal Institute of Science & Technology, Bhopal, India

6.1 INTRODUCTION

The Internet of Things, or IOT, is the term used to define the pervasive and permanent internetworking of electronic equipment in order to facilitate data transfer and connectivity between domain-specific programs of these objects and the environment. As a result, people's lives are now much simpler than they were in the past due to IoT networking. It has been used in a variety of fields to enhance lifestyle surroundings and well-being, including agriculture, medical, pollution management, monitoring indoor air quality, and many more. The most significant use of IoT is in the medical field, where it has led to the creation of a cutting-edge tool known as the Internet of Medical Things powered by AI (AIEIOMT). One of the options offered by AIEIOMT (the AI-enabled Internet of Medical Things) is the use of wearable sensors, which people commonly use to try and achieve better health. The research areas of artificial intelligence (AI), big data, and IoT are interrelated and have an effect on the modelling and implementation of advanced personal healthcare systems. The use of wearable medical technology in conjunction with big data will make it feasible to collect massive volumes of medical data, which will, in turn, make it possible for medical professionals, such as doctors and nurses, to more accurately anticipate the future conditions of their patients. More sophisticated security measures are required since extracting information and analysis of data are complex mechanisms. AI and big data are expanding numerous opportunities for IoT-based healthcare solutions. Big data development advances fueled by AI have the ability to greatly enhance public health around the world. The use of AIEIOMT technologies lowers the total cost of preventing chronic diseases. By obtaining real-time health inputs, these technologies assist patients who are self-managing their own treatments. Through AIEIOMT, mobile applications are frequently employed in teletherapy and mHealth. The outcomes of telemedicine data analytics from these states reduce the time needed for data output processing and improve the relevancy of data interpretations.

In addition, an innovative programme known as "Personalized Preventative Health Coaches" has been developed and implemented. These experts keep experience and are relied upon to define and comprehend data pertaining to safety and health. Sensor

DOI: 10.1201/9781003363606-6

networks facilitate the monitoring of persons who are outside of a conventional healthcare surveillance system. Additionally, the examination of medical data that aids clinicians in making pertinent recommendations is made possible through wireless connectivity and machine learning (ML) integration. The research demonstrates many AIEIOMT applications in the medical areas as well as an inclusive learning strategy. It examines the various therapeutic settings in which AIEIOMT systems are used as well as the compilation methods used. Despite being a basic human right, not everyone has adequate access to high-quality healthcare. As a result of lifestyle modifications brought on by global economic, environmental, and social expansion, chronic diseases such as heart disease, cancer, and diabetes have increased significantly. These chronic diseases pose the greatest threat to human health. Additionally, hospitals are inundated with patients whenever an infectious disease spreads, which has a substantial detrimental influence on healthcare services. For instance, the continual demand on the world's healthcare resources is due to the global spread of COVID-19. In these cases, patient and data management is rendered useless.

According to professionals, the IOT environment appears to be a suitable choice for digital healthcare systems,. The transmission layer stores this data, inspects it using standard threshold levels, and reports any irregularities. It is possible that the data will be sent to the cloud for storage and sophisticated calculations. Machine learning and data mining techniques are employed in intelligent systems to detect anomalies and predict the patient's health status. The result or analysis of the data is then sent to a server in the cloud. A web-based interface allows healthcare professionals to log in, evaluate and confirm the diagnosis, and take the necessary actions.

6.2 SENSORS

Sensors can assess a person's health accurately by measuring a range of physiological parameters. The necessary medical equipment is easily accessible; nevertheless, it comes at a high price and requires a significant amount of power. Therefore, sensors are utilised in IOT-based medical systems in order to conserve electricity while also implementing low-cost and inexpensive solutions. They track a variety of vital signs and other biometric data in real time. The utilisation of sensors in IOT-based healthcare systems could ultimately result in a decline in the total number of patients requiring in-patient treatment. Specialists are utilising these biomedical sensors to develop flexible systems with machine-to-machine interfaces that enhance patient care at home and reduce waiting times for patients and medical personnel.

Table 6.1 outlines a selection of the sensors incorporated into several proposed systems. The sensors presented in this table are utilised in the process of measuring a wide variety of physiological characteristics. Temperature, electrocardiogram, and pulse rate are the three vital signs that are required in order to evaluate the overall health state of a patient. Other metrics, particularly blood pressure, are able to be measured by employing digital wristbands that are considerably easier and more compact. Blood pressure monitors are not only easily accessible, but also virtually ubiquitous in today's homes. Accelerometers are utilised to evaluate the position of the body and can be of great assistance in the event that a patient experiences a stroke

TABLE 6.1

Various Sensors Utilized in Medical Healthcare Domain

S. No.	Parameters to be Measured	Sensors used
1	Body Temperature	LM-35, DS18B20, TMP236, Thermistor
2	Room Temperature, Humidity	DS18B20,BME280, DHT11/22
3	Blood Oxygen Saturation	SPO2, MAX3010x, TCRT1000
4	Heartbeat, ECG	AD8232
5	Pulse Rate	KG011, APDS9008
6	Blood Pressure	Blood Pressure Monitor, ASDXAD015GAA5
7	Body Fat	IL300

or faints (loses consciousness). Live cameras were always also used to keep an eye on how patients are doing and to make sure that the transfer of patient information is safe. The most common types of sensors found in healthcare systems are decomposed and examined in this section.

6.2.1 TEMPERATURE SENSORS

LM-35, DS18B20, MAX30205, and TMP236 are among the temperature sensors that are utilized most frequently. The TMP236 is an analogue sensor that is both cost-effective and accurate to within 2 degrees Celsius. The temperature can be adjusted anywhere between 10 and 125 degrees Celsius. Despite this, it is not utilised to its full potential because this type of temperature sensor is an analogue one that necessitates the use of an external or internal ADC in order to generate a digital output. On the other end, the DS18B20 is a digital sensor that has an accuracy of 2 degrees Celsius and can measure temperatures between 55 and 125 degrees Celsius. The majority of its applications are found in structures and machinery for the purpose of process monitoring. A wearable patient monitoring system that utilises the DS18B20 to measure the body temperature of patient is proposed in Kaur and Jasuja [1]. The patient is supposed to wear this system.

The MAX30205 temperature sensor not only provides an accurate reading of the temperature but also acts as an alert, interrupt, and shut-down output in the event that the temperature reaches an unsafe level. Due to its high accuracy (0.1 °C) and low-voltage operation (2.7–3.3 V), the MAX30205 is ideally suited for use in wearable devices. In addition to this, its digital capabilities makes it much simpler to incorporate it into any existing system. The MAX30205 pinout is depicted in Figure 6.1 [2], which can be found here. As a result of the many applications it has in remote monitoring, the LM-35 is most commonly found in wearable sensor networks. It has a broader range than the DS18B20, which is from 55 degrees Celsius to 150 degrees Celsius, and it has a higher precision of 0.5 degrees Celsius. Temperatures can be measured with an accuracy of up to 0.25 degrees Celsius by using a thermistor instead of a temperature sensor since it is more cost-effective, trustworthy, and resistant to the effects of water.

FIGURE 6.1   MAX 30205 [2].

6.2.2   PULSE RATE SENSORS

The pulse rate is what is used to evaluate how well the heart is functioning. In the event of a crisis, it can be utilised to immediately discover the root of the problem. Various research articles make use of various methods to determine heartbeat; however, the APDS-9008 is the sensor that is used the most frequently to measure pulse rate. It is a light sensor with an analogue output that is currently being utilised in a variety of mobile electronic gadgets for the purpose of measuring the surrounding light. A low-power green infrared LED is utilised to make it function as a pulse rate sensor, and it measures the pulse by observing the light reflection that occurs with each beating. This sensor operates by reacting to changes in the amount of light that is present, and the data that gathers is processed through a low-pass filter to eliminate any high-frequency noise. After this, the signal is amplified using the operational amplifier MCP- 6001 [3].

Baker et al. [4] has examined the differences and similarities between radio frequency (RF)-based designs and photo plethysmographic (PPG) sensors for the purpose of detecting the pulse rate. The study's conclusions indicate that PPG sensors are the solution that is both affordable and efficient for usage in a healthcare application. The authors of Ruman et al. [5] describe the development of a crisis monitoring system that takes readings of the electrocardiogram (ECG), the heart rate, and the body temperature. The authors make use of a pulse sensor, which is then utilised to derive a PPG signal. A portion of this signal that was collected over a period of time equal to 1826 milliseconds is employed to calculate the person's heart rate.

6.2.3   PULSE OXIMETERS

A pulse oximeter is a device that does not require the patient to undergo any invasive procedures in order to check their blood oxygen saturation levels. This details can be used to keep an eye on a patient's health and spot any weird things that might happen. Conditions such as asthma, pneumonia, anemia, and other lung-related disorders, as well as other conditions, can be detected using a blood oximeter. The reading of arterial oxygen saturation (SpO2), which is often chosen, has been referred to as safe, convenient, noninvasive, and economical even though it is not always equivalent to the reading of peripheral oxygen saturation (SpO2) by a blood

FIGURE 6.2 MAX 30102 [7].

oximeter. This is because it measures oxygen saturation in the peripheral blood rather than in the arterial blood. In clinical applications, the pulse oximetry method has been demonstrated to be an advantageous characteristic for assessing oxygen saturation [6]. A sensor is often fastened to the patient's finger in order to obtain an accurate measurement of SpO2. Transmissive and reflecting measuring methods are both available for determining the SpO2 level. The transmissive approach is the one that is utilised more frequently. These pulse oximeters measure the blood's oxygen saturation (SpO2) by shining a light through a patient's finger veins and reading the resulting variations in light absorption caused by the presence of oxygen compared with the presence of oxygen-depleted blood. To achieve this, light is sent from finger to brain via the blood. Maxim Integrated's MAX30102 pulse oximeter sensor is widely deployed in smart healthcare systems [6]. The sensor consumes a minimal amount of power when in operation (1.8 V). As can be seen in Figure 6.2 [7], it takes up very little space and as a result can be easily included into intelligent wearable gadgets or even intelligent phones. A sophisticated pulse oximeter sensor is installed in the back of each passenger seat on Aileni et al. [8]'s jet. The fact that, during a flight, the cabin of an aeroplane may experience low pressure, low oxygen levels, and low humidity. —All of these things can put people with chronic obstructive pulmonary disease in danger. —is the easiest way to explain the goal of placing such a system in an aeroplane. As a result, it is extremely important to monitor their health and notice any abnormalities in a timely manner so that they can receive the treatment that they need.

6.2.4 ECG SENSORS

Data from an electrocardiogram (ECG) is utilised in order to monitor the normal rhythm and strength of the heart. It contributes significantly to the accuracy of the diagnosis as well as the prevention of cardiovascular disorders. As can be seen in Figure 6.3 [9], the AD8232 is a popular choice for an ECG measuring module. As a result of the fact that it may be utilised both as a an ECG graph sensor and an

FIGURE 6.3 AD8232 [9].

heartbeat sensor, it possesses a variety of applications. It is possible to utilise it as a heartbeat sensor when viewed from the front. It does this by utilising an amplifier, a buffer, and a filter to reduce the amount of power that is consumed, increase the strength of the ECG signal, and reject half of the electrode's cell capacity. The delay caused by the transition from a low cutoff frequency to a high-pass filter can be minimised thanks to the system's fast circuit restore function.

Mohammed et al. [10] demonstrates an electrocardiogram (ECG) Android app that allows people to access their data for the purpose of health monitoring. In addition, the authors of Pereira and Nagapriya [11] proposed a remote monitoring system with the intention of lowering the number of times patients needed to go to the hospital. In order to determine the patient's heart rate, this device makes use of an electrocardiogram (ECG) sensor. The authors of Uddin et al. [12] suggest a monitoring system for intensive care unit patients that makes use of a variety of physiological and environmental sensors, one of which is an electrocardiogram (ECG) sensor. Some threshold values are specified for each of the observed parameters, and in the event that any abnormality is detected, a push notice is delivered to the medical professionals.

6.2.5 PPG Sensors

Photoplethysmography, also known as PPG, is an optical measurement method that is low-cost in nature, and frequently utilised for the purpose of tracking a patient's heart rate. PPG has an advantage over other technologies because it is a non-invasive technology. In order to construct a PPG sensor, a light source and a photodetector are placed on the surface of the skin. Their purpose is to measure the fluctuations in blood circulation, which can provide a wealth of information. Recent years have seen an increase in the number of researchers interested in extracting additional useful information from the PPG signal, such as blood pressure and respiration rate [13]. The second derivative wave of a PPG signal contains essential information that is relevant to one's health. Consequently, the analysis of this waveform can assist in the diagnosis of a variety of cardiovascular diseases. Fingers, earlobes, or the patient's forehead are the areas where the PPG sensor is often positioned the most frequently. Other body regions are now being considered as potential alternatives for simpler measurement by the researchers.

6.2.6 RESPIRATION RATE SENSORS

In healthcare applications, monitoring the patient's breathing rate is essential for the identification of a wide variety of disorders, including pneumonia, asthma, and others. However, modern methods need a significant amount of technology and are not particularly efficient. In order to find a solution to this issue, non-invasive measurement techniques have been created, and these techniques are now being utilised in various intelligent healthcare applications. Because of the necessity for IoT systems to be power efficient, However, real-time monitoring of a patient's respiration rate is not feasible. Thermistors are the most common type of hardware module utilised in the process of measuring the rate of breathing. A thermistor is more affordable, consumes less power, and has reliable performance, all of which are assets for use in healthcare applications. The system described in Bhattacharya et al. [14] utilises this device along with a cloud computing-enabled architecture to communicate patient data to a web application, where authorised users can retrieve the data that has been gathered. If an irregularity is found in the patient's breathing rate or the data that has been collected, both the medical staff and the patients are notified instantly. In Azimi et al. [15], a further non-invasive method for determining a patient's respiratory health is shown and discussed. The mattress that the patient sleeps on is equipped with embedded pressure sensor arrays thanks to the inclusion of this feature in the proposed system. Monitoring a person's respiratory health with this technology is not only useful, but also extremely cutting-edge in its design.

The monitoring of a patient's respiration rate has become an essential part of the diagnostic process for a wide range of cardiopulmonary conditions; however, the standard instruments that are used to undertake this measurement are notoriously cumbersome and awkward to use on patients. Estimation of breathing rate by means of an electrocardiogram (ECG) has been the subject of a number of important research studies that have been published Sarkar et al. [16]. The use of the ECG signal to estimate the rate of respiration leads in fewer hardware components being required for observing purposes. It is well known that an electrocardiogram wave is composed of three major elements:

- The P Wave, which demonstrates that the atria have become more depolarized
- QRS Complex, which is representative of the ventricles becoming depolarized
- The T Wave, which is a component of the process of repolarization that occurs in the ventricles of the heart.

Peak amplitude variation and heart rate variability are applied for the purpose of obtaining the breathing rate from an electrocardiogram [17]. The precise amplitudes of the R-waves can be extracted using an algorithm that was developed using

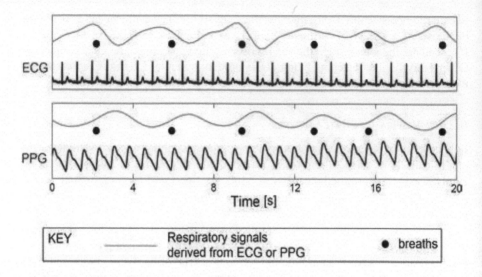

FIGURE 6.4   Estimation of respiration rate using ECG and PPG [19].

MATLAB and published in another paper [18]. Utilizing these data, pulsatile waves resulting from respiration are generated and used to calculate the patient's respiratory rate. This is done by using the data to form the waves.

The results of an algorithm that estimates the respiratory rate by using ECG and PPG data are displayed in Figure 6.4 [19]. This method of measuring the rate of breathing is proving to be effective because it does not involve any intrusive proce- dures. In addition, new respiration rate monitors that are more accurate are being made. One example of this is the invention [20] made by Strados Labs, which makes use of a device to capture lung noises and chest wall motions. The information is then sent to a web application via wireless transmission so that it can be finally processed for determining the state of the user's respiratory health.

6.2.7   BLOOD PRESSURE SENSORS

There has been a great amount of research conducted on non-invasive methods of measuring blood pressure, such as the contemporary method (the oscillometric method), which squeezes blood vessels and measures systolic and diastolic pres- sure [21]. Figure 6.5 [22] depicts a contemporary monitor that is representative of the standard model of this type of device. In the alternative method, a technique for estimating blood pressure without the use of a cuff is applied. This method relies on biomedical sensors such as ECG and PPG sensors [23]. The traditional method of measuring blood pressure needs a significant amount of equipment, which results in a significant amount of inconvenience. The development of a technique that can measure and analyse patients' blood pressures as a result of research and study developments in ECG and PPG signal processing has led to the creation of such methodology. A approach like this turns out to be useful in the long run since it less- ens the amount of money spent on the system's hardware and it makes things more

FIGURE 6.5 Typical cuff-based blood pressure monitor [22].

convenient for the patient [23, 24]. Employing artificial neural networks allows for the development of a cuffless method for continuously estimating blood pressure based on ECG and PPG inputs (ANN). For each heartbeat wave shown by the ECG and PPG data, 22 time domain features are obtained and evaluated. This makes it possible to calculate the values for both the systolic and diastolic pressures. The characteristics are inputted into the ANN module, which is then trained using the values of the arterial blood pressure collected from the PhysioNet MIMIC II database in conjunction with the data from the PPG and ECG signals. The performance of this system is evaluated by calculating the difference in the actual ABP values of the dataset and the values predicted by the ANN model. This difference is referred to as the measured performance. The findings demonstrate that the ANN model has a high degree of accuracy in its predictions. The authors have demonstrated that this method of measuring blood pressure is highly accurate and does not involve any intrusive procedures. In Simjanoska et al. [25], an estimate of the blood pressure is derived solely from the electrocardiogram data. The suggested scheme performs processing on the raw ECG data by filtering and segmenting it. Then, in order to extract characteristics from the data, a complexity analysis is carried out. In addition to this, a ML technique is implemented. This approach combines a stacking-based classification module with a regression module to provide the following predictions regarding blood pressure: systolic pressure, diastolic pressure, and mean arterial pressure. Additionally, probability distribution-based calibration can be accomplished using this method. This indicates that the model may be customised to the requirements of a specific user, which is an essential component in reaching a high level of accuracy in the outcomes.

6.2.8 Blood Glucose Monitors

Blood glucose monitors are an absolute necessity for diabetic people who wish to maintain control over their blood glucose levels. There is a substantial amount of variability in the blood glucose monitors that can be purchased. On the other hand,

FIGURE 6.6 DIAMONTECH's non-invasive blood glucose monitor [29].

non-invasive and intelligent blood glucose monitors are desirable in an IoT environment. The challenges of invasive blood glucose monitoring and the risk of needle contamination, which can cause to infections, are brought to light with reference to in Reddy and Jyostna [26]. Keeping this fact in mind, the plan that they have presented consists of the creation of blood glucose level monitors that do not require any intrusive procedures. Infrared LED, photodiode, and an AT-MEGA328 microprocessor, are all components of the sensor package that these monitors use. The majority of previously published research on systems like this one make use of IR radiations to determine the level of glucose in the blood. In addition, particular systems make use of intelligent alerting features that can send a warning to the patient in the event that an abnormality is identified. A discussion of such a system may be found in Sargunam and Anusha [27], in which the measured blood glucose level is sent wirelessly to the patient's smartphone, where it is utilised to operate the insulin infusion pump. Another system, this one referred to as iGLU, is suggested in Jain et al. [28]. An Intelligent Glucose Meter is utilised in this system. This metre utilises near infrared spectroscopy and ML models for the purpose of analysing and identifying any abnormalities in the patient data that has been collected. The information is uploaded to the cloud, where it will be stored and analysed when it is received. Endocrinologists can do remote monitoring of their patients thanks to the capabilities provided by these characteristics. Figure 6.6 [29] depicts a non-invasive blood glucose monitor that is currently being developed by DIAMONTECH, which is a company that works in this field.

FIGURE 6.7 Advancer technologies' all-in-one electromyography (EMG) sensor powered by Arduino [31].

6.2.9 EMG Sensors

The Electromyography Sensor, often known as an EMG, is utilised for the purpose of determining the electrical activity of the muscles. It is frequently utilised in the function of a control signal for a variety of prosthetic devices. With the use of this sensor, medical personnel are able to better diagnose and treat patients suffering from muscle and nerve diseases. These sensors are also used in wearable medical devices that track the patient's behaviour. EMG sensors have been shown to be indispensable in the development of systems that utilise emotion-based intelligent-information sensing. The system that is proposed in Alam et al. [30] makes use of the EMG signal in conjunction with other body vital measuring biomedical sensors in order to identify variability in face muscles and label each change with its related emotion. This technology is able to evaluate the impacted status of the patient's health and provide a diagnosis. As can be seen in Figure 6.7 [31], Advancer Technologies is also making an EMG sensor that is powered by Arduino and will be used in the medical field.

6.3 CLOUD COMPUTING

With the use of sensors in healthcare large amounts of data get collected which needs to be managed by the doctors. It becomes difficult to understand and analyse the volumes of data as it is not structured. Cloud computing helps to manage the data by not only storing it but also monitoring the security of the data with the help of various encryption algorithms. Cloud computing reduces data redundancy to maintain efficient storage space utilisation. Once the data is maintained on the cloud, AI algorithm are implemented on it. Feature extraction is done on the data, which helps in the diagnosis of diseases. The term "cloud" is a representation for networks and cloud computing refers to the manner of renting and using IT infrastructure. It denotes that the required resources are obtained over the network, depending on principles such as on-demand and easy expansion; generalised cloud computing refers to the computing mode of rent and use. IT, software, Internet-related services, and other services are among the examples of this type of service.

6.3.1 SERVICE MODELS

- Cloud Software as a Service (SaaS): A user's ability to use cloud-based applications from a service provider. The cloud provider manages the infrastructure that makes up the cloud.
- Cloud Platform as a Service (PaaS) is the ability for a customer to put applications they've bought onto the cloud infrastructure using tools provided by the service provider.
- Cloud Infrastructure as a Service (IaaS): The ability for a customer to get computing resources (like storage and a network) that they can use to deploy any software, whether it's an operating system or an application.

The healthcare systems use these services.

6.3.2 DEPLOYMENT MODELS

- Public cloud: A organization that offers services owns the cloud's infrastructure, which is accessible to the general public. Since the information collected by a healthcare monitoring system is personal to the patient, the Health Insurance Portability and Accountability Act (HIPAA) says that public clouds are not a good place to store it.
- Private cloud: In this arrangement, an organisation, a third party, or both own, run, and manage the cloud infrastructure. This gives the patient's personal health information more security, but the hospitals pay for it.
- Moreover, in the case of emergency if there is a need for more resources the servers may crash as the infrastructure is not flexible to changes in demand. In this type of situation, hybrid clouds are productive and beneficial in healthcare monitoring systems.
- Hybrid cloud: The infrastructure of the cloud is made up of multiple private clouds, as well as community and public clouds. As per need of the hour the cloud can take help of public cloud and primarily will use the services of private cloud.
- Community cloud: The cloud infrastructures in this model are shared between certain organizations, which support a certain community with shared.

6.3.3 CLOUD SECURITY

In IoT systems based on the cloud, protecting the privacy of health-related data is of the utmost importance because the medical information of any patient is extremely sensitive and private to any patient. Therefore, it is very important to safeguard the patients' data at all costs from getting in the hands of any third party not related to the patient to save the identity of the patient. This can be prevented by providing access of controlled data to limited users of the data. The user will be able to access data only after providing valid credentials such as password or face recognition that have been given to them to authenticate their identity.

Moreover, as the data is present on the cloud it has to be protected from malicious attacks so that the data cannot be manipulated. This can be accomplished by the use of various data encryption techniques. Through using Nested server security protocols, data encryption is implemented by Kaur [32]. Data that is received from the cloud is encrypted with the AES encryption technique and the decrypted at the server side to generate random keys. With the help of Shamir's Algorithm the keys are split and key server is used to store it.

6.4 MACHINE LEARNING ALGORITHMS

The information obtained from the sensors used to monitor patients in an IoT environment needs to be processed. Machine learning algorithms are applied to process the data to get meaningful information which will help in making the right diagnosis of the disease. Some of the algorithms are discussed below:

6.4.1 SUPPORT VECTOR MACHINE (SVM)

In [17], the authors have used SVM to develop a system for the diagnosis of heart disease by using the previous records of the patient and present parameters such as temperature, heartbeat and ECG sensors interfaced with raspberry pi. The accuracy with which the system will work stills needs to be mentioned and analyzed in this paper.

6.4.1.1 Ensemble Machine Learning

In Ani et al. [33], the authors have proposed a model to keep measure the current health vitals of stroke effected elderly people and would send an alert message and an email to the doctor if the parameters are not in the normal range. They compare different classifiers, namely Naïve Bayes, Random Forest, KNN, Decision Tree and Bagging, are compared and the results show that the ensemble classifiers give more accurate results than other algorithms.

6.4.1.2 Deep Learning

Deep learning techniques are a very important tool in artificial intelligence and are widely being used in healthcare systems for medical diagnostics. With the availability of large data collected through sensors in IoT-enabled healthcare systems deep learning algorithms are used to extract meaning through complex computations.

6.5 ADVANTAGES

There are numerous advantages of AIEIOMT for people, customers, businesses, community, production, and industries. IoT-based devices and software have changed the way that individuals in 1999 thought about the world. The combination of AI and IoT has resulted in significant shifts in the domain of internet connectivity. It has made a significant contribution to the growth of a wide variety of difficult fields, but particularly in the sector of medical items. Because of these factors, it has successfully bridged the communication gap between patients, medical professionals, and health-care services by virtue of its ease of use, flexibility, precision, and ability to sense data in real time. Through the use of AEIOMT, doctors and other medical professionals can carry out their jobs with greater clarity and enthusiasm while expending comparatively little mental energy.

AIEIOMT helps to improve machine and human interactions, enables real-time health monitoring systems, and encourages patient participation in decision-making. The following provides an outline of the strengths, practical uses, and constraints associated with AIEIOMT execution.

6.5.1 Benefits of Utilizing AIEIOMT

6.5.1.1 Advantages for Patients

a) Action taken in real time in response to an emergency situation.
b) Economical.
c) Reduced prevalence and economic burden as a result of fewer follow-up visits.
d) The patient's outcome and quality of life are strengthened.
e) Effective illness management and real-time disease prevention.

6.5.1.2 Service Providers in Healthcare Coverage

a) The most efficient use of the available assets and infrastructure.
b) Delay in response to a medical emergency.
c) The ability to get your prescription on time and at a reasonable price.
d) Doctors can also deliver out-of-hours medical treatments using IoT and AI.
e) Medical records are simplified for doctors to manage.

6.5.1.3 Equipment Manufacturers

a) Standardization, affinity, and consistency of the data that are already provided.
b) The ability to sense and transport health-related information to remote locations.
c) Save time and lives by automatically notifying parties of significant changes.
d) Longer and warmer lives.
e) Excellent user experience.

6.6 AIEIOMT'S LIMITATIONS

6.6.1 Technical Difficulties

a) AIEIOMT data hacking and unplanned use.
b) A lack of customary and transmission pacts.
c) Inaccurate patient data handling.
d) Data aggregation.
e) The requirement for competence in medical areas.
f) Managing collaboration and system diversity.
g) Management of system variability and collaboration.

h) Scalability, performance, and data volume.
i) Divide responsibility for managing diversity.
j) Problems with the hardware execution and layout optimization.
k) Problems with the system's memory.

6.6.2 MARKET DIFFICULTIES

a) Patient consent.
b) The excessive amount of data generated by healthcare means.
c) Suspending mobile devices.
d) Complaining about security strategies.
e) Modelling the connection between illnesses and acquired measurements.
f) Data are erratic, constantly changing, and increasing at an exponential rate.
g) Compatibility.
h) Software-based application of medical analytics.
i) Medical caution using intelligence.
j) Risks to security.

REFERENCES

[1] Kaur, A., and A. Jasuja. 2017. Health Monitoring Based on IOT Using Raspberry Pi. *2017 International Conference on Computing, Communication and Automation (ICCCA)*.

[2] https://i.ebayimg.com/images/g/t5AAAOSwIU5doa7U/s-l1600.jpgeBay. Available at: https://www.ebay.com/itm/265581254584 (Accessed: August 02, 2022).

[3] Taştan, M. 2018. IOT Based Wearable Smart Health Monitoring System. *Celal Bayar Üniversitesi Fen Bilimleri Dergisi*, 14(3): 343–350.

[4] Baker, S.B., W. Xiang, and I. Atkinson. 2017. Internet of Things for Smart Healthcare: Technologies, Challenges, and Opportunities. *IEEE Access*, 5: 26521–26544.

[5] Ruman, M.R., A. Barua, W. Rahman, K.R. Jahan, M. Jamil Roni, and M.F. Rahman. 2020. IOT Based Emergency Health Monitoring System. *2020 International Conference on Industry 4.0 Technology (I4Tech)*.

[6] Aggarwal, N.K., J. Das, and A. Aggarwal. 2010. Pulse Oximeter Accuracy and Precision at Five Different Sensor Locations in Infants and Children with Cyanotic Heart Disease. *Indian Journal of Anaesthesia*, 54(6): 531.

[7] Max30102 Pulse Oximeter & Heart-Rate Module Makerfabs. Available at: https://www. make.com/max30102-pulse-oximeter-heart-rate-module.html (Accessed: August 4, 2022).

[8] Aileni, R.M., S. Pasca, and A. Florescu. 2019. E-Health Monitoring by Smart Pulse Oximeter Systems Integrated in SDU. *2019 11th International Symposium on Advanced Topics in Electrical Engineering (ATEE)*.

[9] Monitor, S. S. L. H. R. *Sparkfun single lead heart rate monitor - AD8232, SEN-12650 - SparkFun Electronics*. Niwot, CO, USA: Sparkfun Electronics. Available at: https:// www.sparkfun.com/products/12650 (Accessed: August 16, 2022).

[10] Mohammed, J., C.-H. Lung, A. Ocneanu, A. Thakral, C. Jones, and A. Adler. 2014. Internet of Things: Remote Patient Monitoring Using Web Services and Cloud Computing. *2014 IEEE International Conference on Internet of Things(IThings), and IEEE Green Computing and Communications (GreenCom) and IEEE Cyber, Physical and Social Computing (CPSCom)*.

[11] Pereira, M., and K.K. Nagapriya. 2017. A Novel IOT Based Health Monitoring System Using LPC2129. *2017 2nd IEEE International Conference on Recent Trends in Electronics, Information & Communication Technology (RTEICT)*.

[12] Uddin, M.S., J.B. Alam, and S. Banu. 2017. Real Time Patient Monitoring System Based on Internet of Things. *2017 4th International Conference on Advances in Electrical Engineering (ICAEE)*.

[13] Castaneda, D., Esparza, A., Ghamari, M., Soltanpur, C., and Nazeran, H. 2018. A Review on Wearable Photoplethysmography Sensors and Their Potential Future Applications in Health Care. *International Journal of Biosensors & Bioelectronics*, 4(4): 195.

[14] Bhattacharya, R., N. Bandyopadhyay, and S. Kalaivani. 2017. Real Time Android App Based Respiration Rate Monitor. *2017 International Conference of Electronics, Communication and Aerospace Technology (ICECA)*.

[15] Azimi, H., S. Soleimani Gilakjani, M. Bouchard, S. Bennett, R.A. Goubran, and F. Knoefel. 2017. Breathing Signal Combining for Respiration Rate Estimation in Smart Beds. *2017 IEEE International Symposium on Medical Measurements and Applications (MeMeA)*.

[16] Sarkar, S., S. Bhattacherjee, and S. Pal. 2015. Extraction of Respiration Signal from ECG for Respiratory Rate Estimation. *Michael Faraday IET International Summit 2015*.

[17] Landis, C., M.E. O'Neil, A. Finnegan, and P.A. Shewokis. 2019. Calculating Heart Rate Variability from ECG Data from Youth with Cerebral Palsy during Active Video Game Sessions. *Journal of Visualized Experiments no*, 148.

[18] Rahman, M.T., M.A. Kadir, A.H.M.Z. Karim, and M.A. Al Mahmud. 2017. Respiration Monitoring by Using ECG. *2017 20th International Conference of Computer and Information Technology (ICCIT)*.

[19] AlekhyaSasi (n.d.) *Image search API response structure - bing search services, Image Search API response structure - Bing Search Services|Microsoft Learn*. Available at: https://learn.microsoft.com/en-us/bing/search-apis/bing-image-search/how-to/search-response (Accessed: August 17, 2022).

[20] Capp, N., V. Fauveau, Y.K. Au, P. Glasser, T. Muqeem, G. Hassen, and A. Cardenas. 2019. Strados Labs: An Efficient Process to Acquire and Characterize Clinically Validated Respiratory System Information Using a Non-Invasive Bio-Sensor. *2019 IEEE Signal Processing in Medicine and Biology Symposium (SPMB)*.

[21] Wai, K.T., N.P. Aung, and L.L. Htay. 2019. Internet of Things (IoT) Based Healthcare Monitoring System using NodeMCU and Arduino UNO. *International Journal of Trend in Scientific Research and Development (IJTSRD)*, 3(5): 755–759. https://www.ijtsrd.com/papers/ijtsrd26482.pdf

[22] Pulsedive Threat intelligence, Pulsedive. Available at: https://pulsedive.com/ioc/tse4.mm.bing.net (Accessed: August 17, 2022).

[23] Mamun, M. M. R. K., and A. Alouani, 2019. Using Photoplethysmography & ECG Towards a Non-Invasive Cuff less Blood Pressure Measurement Technique. *IEEE Canadian Conference of Electrical and Computer Engineering (CCECE)*, 2019, pp. 1–4. doi: 10.1109/CCECE.2019.8861521.

[24] Şentürk, Ü., İ. Yücedağ, K. Polat, 2018. Cuff-less continuous blood pressure estimation from Electrocardiogram(ECG) and Photoplethysmography (PPG) signals with artificial neural network. *26th Signal Processing and Communications Applications Conference (SIU)*, 2018, pp. 1–4. doi: 10.1109/SIU.2018.8404255.

[25] Simjanoska, M., M. Gjoreski, M. Gams, and A. Madevska Bogdanova, 2018. Non-Invasive Blood Pressure Estimation from ECG Using Machine Learning Techniques. *Sensors (Basel)*, 18(4): 1160. doi: 10.3390/s18041160.

[26] Reddy P. S., and K. Jyostna. 2017. Development of Smart Insulin Device for Non Invasive Blood Glucose Level Monitoring. *IEEE 7th International Advance Computing Conference (IACC)*, 2017, pp. 516–519. doi: 10.1109/IACC.2017.0112.

[27] Sargunam, B., and S. Anusha. 2019. IoT Based Mobile Medical Application for Smart Insulin Regulation. *IEEE International Conference on Electrical, Computer and Communication Technologies (ICECCT)*, 2019, pp. 1–5. doi: 10.1109/ICECCT.2019. 8869227.

[28] Jain, P., A. M. Joshi, and S. P. Mohanty. 2020. iGLU: An Intelligent Device for Accurate Noninvasive Blood Glucose-Level Monitoring in Smart Healthcare. *IEEE Consumer Electronics Magazine*, 9(1), 35–42. doi: 10.1109/MCE.2019.2940855.

[29] Assets.website-files.com. Available at: https://assets.website-files.com/5c8c0cd36dbd3c f61db07696/5d0ad71f2ab90c4febf14a76_8Hours_White_Paper.pdf (Accessed: August 18, 2022).

[30] Alam, M. G. R., S. F. Abedin, S. I. Moon, A. Talukder, and C. S. Hong. 2019. Healthcare IoT-Based Affective State Mining Using a Deep Convolutional Neural Network. *IEEE Access*, 7: 75189–75202. doi: 10.1109/ACCESS.2019,2919995.

[31] SparkFun Electronics. Available at: https://www.sparkfun.com/ (Accessed: August 17, 2022).

[32] Kaur, Chamandeep. 2020. The Cloud Computing and Internet of Things (IoT). *International Journal of Scientific Research in Science, Engineering and Technology*. doi: 10.32628/ijsrset196657.

[33] Ani, R., S. Krishna, N. Anju, M. S. Aslam, and O. S. Deepa. 2017. IoT-based patient monitoring and diagnostic prediction tool using ensemble classifier. *International Conference on Advances in Computing, Communications and Informatics (ICACCI)*, 2017, pp. 1588–1593. doi: 10.1109/ICACCI.2017.8126068.

7 Time Division Multiplexer Design for Internet of Things (IoT) Networks by Using Photonic Hetero-Structures

Anirudh Banerjee and Sheenu Rizvi

Amity School of Engineering and Technology,
Amity University, Lucknow, India

7.1 INTRODUCTION

The Internet of Things (IoT) [1–2] is an architecture in which heterogeneous computing devices are interrelated and are able to transfer data over a network without needing human–human or human–computer interaction. In IoT networks, the used devices do most of their work without needing human intervention; human interaction with the devices will only be there for giving commands or instructions and/or accessing data. The IoT networks these days are not only containing electronic devices, but also consisting of photonic or opto-electronic devices, in addition to electronic devices. Thus, an IoT network can consist of heterogeneous photonic and electronic devices. The IoT of heterogeneous photonic devices and the design of photonic devices for IoT networks are at the forefront of technology research [3–7]. Today, the photonic structures [8–15] are very popular material structures. In this chapter, a time division multiplexer is designed for IoT networks by using photonic hetero-structures. A time division multiplexer is used to delay data in IoT networks consisting of photonic devices. This photonic time division multiplexer can provide contention resolution in an IoT network consisting of intelligent photonic devices. In this scheme, each data channel transmits optical data and the multiplexed data will be available in the communication fiber. The photonic crystal structure and hetero-structures used in this design are shown in Figure 7.1. The channel 1 data reaches directly to the combiner. The channel 2 data reaches the combiner after being delayed from photonic crystal 1. The channel 3 data reaches the combiner after being delayed from the photonic hetero-structures shown. The channel 4 data also reaches the combiner after getting delayed from photonic hetero-structures shown in the figure. The layer parameters

DOI: 10.1201/9781003363606-7

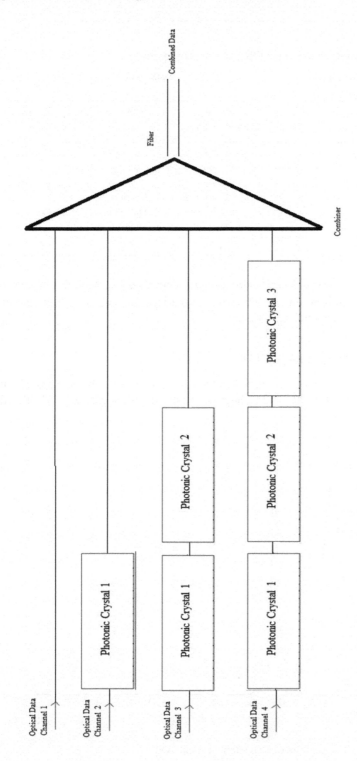

FIGURE 7.1 Time division multiplexer by using photonic hetero-structures.

TABLE 7.1

Design Parameters for Time Division Multiplexer

Channel	Structure	Delay time
1	Not used	-
2	Photonic Crystal	$n_1 = 3.3$, $n_2 = 2.05$, $n_3 = 1.46$, $n_D = 3.45$, $d_1 = 120$ nm, $d_2 = 101$ nm, $d_3 = 265$ nm and $d_D = 1.4\,\mu m$
3	Hetero-structure	$n_1 = 3.3$, $n_2 = 2.05$, $n_3 = 1.46$, $n_D = 3.45$, $d_1 = 120$ nm, $d_2 = 101$ nm, $d_3 = 265$ nm and $d_D = 1.4\,\mu m/n_1 = 3.3$, $n_2 = 2.05$, $n_3 = 1.46$, $n_D = 3.45$, $d_1 = 120$ nm, $d_2 = 101$ nm, $d_3 = 265$ nm and $d_D = 1.41\,\mu m$
4	Hetero-structure	$n_1 = 3.3$, $n_2 = 2.05$, $n_3 = 1.46$, $n_D = 3.45$, $d_1 = 120$ nm, $d_2 = 101$ nm, $d_3 = 265$ nm and $d_D = 1.4\,\mu m/n_1 = 3.3$, $n_2 = 2.05$, $n_3 = 1.46$, $n_D = 3.45$, $d_1 = 120$ nm, $d_2 = 101$ nm, $d_3 = 265$ nm and $d_D = 1.41\,\mu m/\,n_1 = 3.3$, $n_2 = 2.05$, $n_3 = 1.46$, $n_D = 3.45$, $d_1 = 120$ nm, $d_2 = 101$ nm, $d_3 = 265$ nm and $d_D = 1.42\,\mu m$

for these photonic crystal and hetero-structures are shown in Table 7.1. There are 18 material layers followed by 1 defected material layer in sequence, with 18 material layers again in each photonic crystal.

7.2 THEORY AND RESULTS

The output of these photonic crystal and hetero-structures can be computed by using the TM method [12–13]. These outputs are shown in Figures 7.2–7.4. The delay

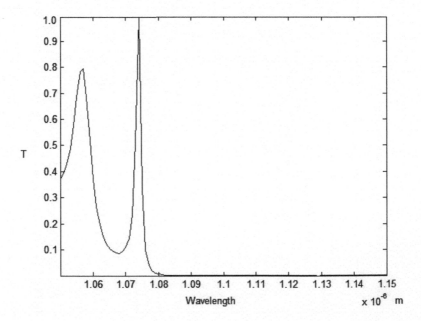

FIGURE 7.2 O/p spectrum of 1st photonic crystal used.

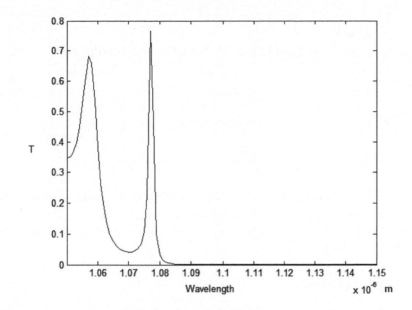

FIGURE 7.3 O/p spectrum of 2nd photonic crystal used.

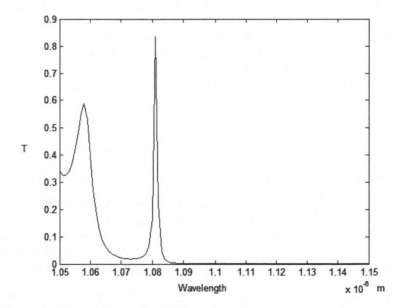

FIGURE 7.4 O/p spectrum of 3rd photonic crystal used.

times calculated for these structures are listed in Table 7.2. The channel 1 data will reach directly to the combiner, the channel 2 data will reach the combiner after 0.1480ps, the channel 3 data will reach the combiner after 0.2961ps and the channel 4 data will reach the combiner after 0.4443ps. Thereafter, these data will become

TABLE 7.2
Delay Time Calculations for Time Division Multiplexer

Channel	Structure	Delay time
1	Not used	-
2	Photonic Crystal	0.1480ps
3	Hetero-structure	0.2961ps
4	Hetero-structure	0.4443ps

combined through optical combiner and will be routed to the desired destination via optical fiber. The thicknesses of the defected layers in photonic crystal and hetero-structures are chosen in such a way that there is a time gap between the individual channels to avoid any overlap.

7.3　CONCLUSION

In this chapter, a time division multiplexer based on photonic crystal and photonic hetero-structures is proposed. The photonic crystal, photonic hetero-structures, optical combiners and optical fibers are used in this system. This system was designed for the multiplexing of 4 channels. By increasing the number of photonic crystals and photonic hetero-structures, one can design time division multiplexers for any number of channels. Further, desired time delays can be generated by these photonic crystals and photonic hetero-structures by changing their design parameters. This type of time division multiplexer finds utility in IoT networks to avoid data congestion.

REFERENCES

[1] Li, S., Xu, L. D. and Zhao, S.: The internet of things: a survey, *Information System Frontiers* 17, 243–259 (2015).
[2] Wortmann, F. and Flüchter, K.: Internet of Things, *Business and Information Systems Engineering* 57, 221–224 (2015).
[3] Aleksic, S.: A survey on optical technologies for IoT, smart industry, and smart infrastructures, *Journal of Sensor and Actuator Networks* 8, 1–18 (2019).
[4] Miladić-Tešić, S. and Marković, G.: Development of Optical Networking for 5G Smart Infrastructures, In *5th EAI International Conference on Management of Manufacturing Systems, EAI/Springer Innovations in Communication and Computing*, Springer, Cham (2022).
[5] Chen, N. and Okada, M.: Toward 6G Internet of Things and the convergence with RoF system, *IEEE Internet of Things Journal* 8, 8719–8733 (2021).
[6] Raj, R., Pandey, G. and Dixit, A.: *Tunable receiver design for spatially distributed wireless optical sensors in IoT networks*, In *IEEE International Conference on Communications (ICC)*, (pp. 1–6), IEEE, (2020).
[7] Miladić-Tešić, S., Marković, G., Peraković, D. et al.: A review of optical networking technologies supporting 5G communication infrastructure, *Wireless Networks* 28, 459–467 (2022).

[8] Abadla, M. M., Tabaza, N. A., Tabaza, W., Ramanujam, N. R., Wilson, K. S. J., Vigneswaran, D. and Taya, S. A.: Properties of ternary photonic crystal consisting of dielectric/plasma/ dielectric as a lattice period, *Optik* 185, 784–793 (2019).

[9] El-Amassi, D. M., Taya, S. A. and Vigneswaran, D.: Temperature sensor utilizing a ternary photonic crystal with a polymer layer sandwiched between Si and SiO_2 layers, *Journal of Theoretical and Applied Physics* 12, 293–298 (2018).

[10] Taya, S. A.: Ternary photonic crystal with left-handed material layer for refractometric application, *Opto-Electronics Review* 26, 236–241 (2018).

[11] Abohassan, K. M., Ashour, H. S. and Abadla, M. M.: One-dimensional ZnSe/ZnS/BK7 ternary planar photonic crystals as wide angle infrared reflectors, *Results in Physics* 22, 103882 (2021).

[12] Banerjee, A.: Enhancement in sensitivity of blood glucose sensor by using 1D defect ternary photonic band gap structures, *Journal of Optics* 48, 262–265 (2019).

[13] Banerjee, A.: Design of enhanced sensitivity gas sensors by using 1D defect ternary photonic band gap structures, *Indian Journal of Physics* 94, 535–539 (2020).

[14] Banerjee, A.: Novel applications of one-dimensional photonic crystal in optical buffer ing and optical time division multiplexing, *Optik* 122, 355–357 (2011).

[15] Banerjee, A. and Rizvi, S.: Suitability of 1D photonic band gap structures for electrical tuning of transmission spectrum in optical filters, *2018 International Conference on Computational and Characterization Techniques in Engineering & Sciences (CCTES)*, 272–275 (2018).

8 Comparative Evaluation on Various Machine Learning Strategies Based on Identification of DDoS Attacks in IoT Environment

M. Abinaya, S. Prabakeran and M. Kalpana

SRMIST, Kattankulathur, India

8.1 INTRODUCTION

In 1999, Kevin Ashton developed the concept of the Internet of Things (IoT), which resulted in a rapid revolution in the field of computing. This is a form of network of devices, either heterogenous or homogenous, in order to share information through the inter net. Various connectivity identities, such as Wi-Fi, GPRS, GSM, Ethernet, 2/3/4/5G, Zigbee, etc. are used by the IoT environment to perform tasks. The major characteristics of IoT include being dynamic in nature, scalability, security, utilization of both homogenous and heterogenous resources [1].

The sensing layer, gateways and internet layer, the support layer and the application layer are the four levels that make up the IoT architecture [2]. The sensing layer is the lowest layer, in which the smart objects are connected with the sensors. It uses low power and lower data rate connectivity to constitute the wireless sensor networks (WSN). The gateway and network layer built for data routing from sensors are applied to the third layer. The support layer, which offers on-demand storage as well as computing capabilities for data analytics, is in charge of device administration, service analytics, and data analysis. Finally, the application layer is the highest layer and is in charge of providing application-related functions to the target customers. IoT is used in many fields, including agriculture, healthcare, industry and home automation.

In the perception layer, the security challenges are eavesdropping, jamming attacks, replay attacks, node capture and cloning, and resource depletion attacks. Security problems at the network level include DDoS attacks, sybil attacks, switching attacks and so-called 'man in the middle' attacks. Security challenges in the

DOI: 10.1201/9781003363606-8

application layer include DoS attacks, session hijacking attacks, phishing attacks, and malicious code injection [3]. With regard to the IoT networks, conventional security and privacy measures do not always work. Because of the complex nature of the infrastructure, it poses a significant number of security challenges. These include heterogeneity, scale, interconnectivity, latency, cost, dynamic configuration, intelligence and proximity [4].

Computer assaults have become increasingly common in recent years. The mere possession of a computer connected to the internet dramatically increases the risk of assault. The more sensitive the data held on a computer network, the more likely it is to be attacked [5]. The behavior of internet traffic is thoroughly examined in order to discover a solution to the escalating trend of computer assaults and also to propose a viable solution to the problem. In addition, such a surveillance system is capable of generating alarms in the event that unauthorized activity is detected.

An intrusion detection system (IDS) is a device capable of identifying malicious activities present in the network or host and producing alarms when they are detected. The purpose of the IDS is to scan the informing traffic coming from the network and identify whether or not malicious activity is being detected. If any suspicious activity is found, then an alarm is generated and sent to the administrator. It is divided into two kinds based on various strategies: Network and host-based [6].

The information regarding incoming and outgoing network traffic is collected by network-based intrusion detection systems (NIDS). Sensors are placed across the network to identify suspicious activities present in the network. In host-based IDS, by contrast, the system monitors only the incoming and the outgoing traffic of the device. This generates an alert message to the administrator. IDS detects threats in two ways: anomaly-based and signature-based. When using anomaly detection, it finds both new and unknown attacks, whereas signature detection only finds known attacks [7].

Cyber assaults occur across a variety of IoT devices. In DDoS attacks, when a server receives an excessive number of service requests from several computers, it becomes overburdened and unable to respond to any of the service requests. Finally, end users are unable to access the resources and network bandwidth. The attackers identify a susceptible system in a network and install malicious malware, causing the attacking machine to perform different disruptive activities under the attacker's control. The attacker's computer causes the server to be overloaded by flooding it with bogus packets [8].

On October 21, 2016, the Dyne domain name system was the target of a series of DDoS attacks involving millions of IP addresses (DNS). The assaults were estimated to be 1.2 Tbps in size and to have involved IoT devices [9]. These assaults have sparked a crucial conversation about cybersecurity and its unpredictable nature. The scale and development of DDoS assaults were the biggest in the previous year, as per Arbor Network's 12th yearly report issued in Waterman2, and they have also risen in frequency over the past several years. Figure 8.1 shows the volume levels of various DDoS attacks over the last 15 years, with the chart indicating a massive increase in volume size in 2021. The goal is to give a comprehensive overview of DDoS assaults, preventive tactics and mitigation strategies.

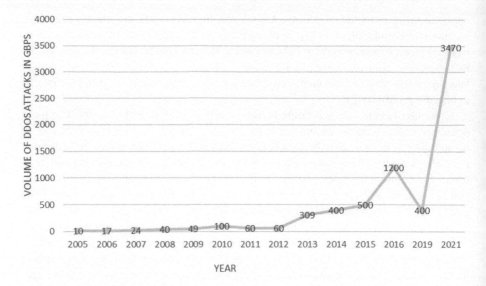

FIGURE 8.1 DDoS attacks.

The Mirai botnet managed to infect millions of IoT devices, which is used to launch distributed denial of service assaults on the businesses of Dyn. In order to identify and react to threads, machine learning techniques are utilized in various applications. This can be accomplished by analyzing the large datasets of thread intelligence and finding suspicious behavioral patterns. When similar incidents are observed, ML works automatically to deal with the trained model [10].

In general, machine learning provides several mathematical models for embedded intelligence in the IoT ecosystem. Various wireless security measures, such as traffic monitoring, intrusion detection, and botnet identification, have all been solved with machine learning algorithms. These methodologies are applied to regression and classification problems because they have the capability to extract useful information from data supplied by the sensors or individuals. ML may also be utilized to deliver intelligence services in an IoT infrastructure. The automation of threat detection problems has become increasingly popular, and ML is being applied in a variety of cybersecurity scenarios [11].

Signature-based approaches use certain traffic characteristics of known attack patterns to identify them. One of the benefits of this type of detection is that it can successfully identify all known assaults without creating a high rate of false alarms. In the existing system, signature-based methods are employed to identify the attacks and also to detect the corrupted devices via detected botnets [12]. Two primary disadvantages of signature-based techniques are that they need regular human updates of attack traffic signatures to be effective, and also that they cannot identify previously undisclosed assaults.

Under an anomaly-based approach any internet activity which can be regarded as anything out of the ordinary is viewed as an assault. This class is useful to employ because of its capacity to identify unknown attacks. The main problem with an anomaly-based approach is that it might trigger a lot of false alarms because unknown actions are labelled as abnormal [13]. A mixed algorithm can be created by combining signature and anomaly-based methods. This approach is being used to enhance known attack detection rates while lowering false positive rates for unknown attacks.

The NSL KDD dataset is one of the test datasets that is available to the public. This dataset may be used to build and test a variety of IDS models. Finding a useful dataset that meets our requirements is critical, and generating a new dataset is a costly and time-consuming procedure [14]. Similarly, by utilizing that dataset, we can only detect certain sorts of DDoS assaults that are contained in the dataset's decision class. To find the model's accuracy using several classifiers and determine which classifier offers the best results. In this chapter, we add to the field by looking at how useful it is to use machine learning algorithms to find IoT network assaults as part of a defense against IoT attack behaviors.

8.1.1 PURVIEW OF THIS STUDY AND SIGNIFICANCE

Several studies in the literature demonstrate the significance of privacy and security problems in the IoT ecosystem. Several researchers have undertaken studies on IoT network security strategies, such as machine learning, in order to provide a realistic overview of the existing methodologies [15]. The most common type of assault in the modern world is the distributed denial of service attack (DDoS). Machine learning is utilized in order to differentiate between DDoS attacks and regular traffic. As a direct result of the vast volume of data produced by connected devices, the IoT has its most significant issues in the area of data security and privacy. In the ecosystem of the internet of things, machine learning plays a vital part in the protection of data. The major significance of the chapter is summarized as follows:

- To do a literature review on Distributed Denial of Service (DDoS) attacks that use machine learning techniques.
- An assessment of various different machine learning strategies is performed in order to identify DDoS attacks in an IoT infrastructure.
- By testing a model accuracy with multiple classifiers, you can determine which classifier offers the best result.

8.1.2 ROAD MAP

This chapter is organized into several aspects in this section. The chapter outline is depicted in Figure 8.2. Section 8.1 provides an overview of IoT security. In Section 8.2, it provides an explanation of the literature study on DDoS attacks utilizing machine learning methodologies in the IoT, as well as the challenges and limitations of the research. Section 8.3 discusses IoT security in machine learning. Section 8.4 describes the many types of ML approaches in IoT security. In Section 8.5, a general overview of the types of datasets used in the area of cybersecurity is given. Section 8.6 gives the conclusion of the survey chapter.

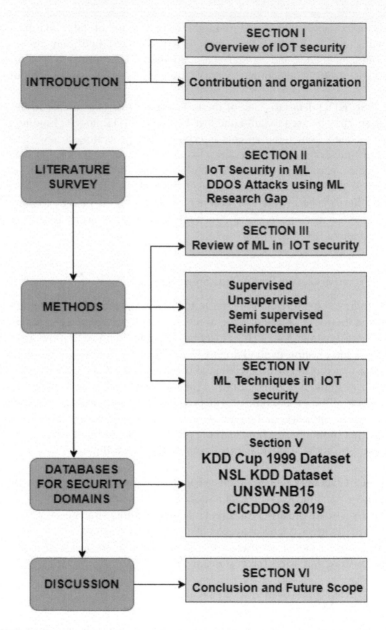

FIGURE 8.2 Paper outline.

8.2   LITERATURE SURVEY

There have been numerous surveys released that cover various areas of IoT security. Numerous detailed surveys of IoT features and possible vulnerabilities have been conducted in order to give a complete approach to IoT security as well as a plan for future work.

8.2.1 SURVEYS ON IoT SECURITY IN ML

Because the Internet of Things is a huge, complicated architectural design comprised of a range of heterogeneous systems, scalability, transparency, and dependability are the most pressing concerns to address [16]. To integrate learning-based security solutions into actual IoT systems, a number of hurdles must be overcome. Zeadally and Tsikerdekis [17] explore how machine learning techniques might help to improve IoT device security. For both host-based and network-based security solutions in the IoT context, they concentrate on the implementation of supervised, unsupervised, and reinforcement approaches. Finally, we go through some of the issues that machine learning approaches face in terms of efficiently implementing and deploying them to better safeguard IoT devices.

Various vulnerabilities and assault interfaces in IoT systems are discussed [17]. Physical devices, network services, cloud services, and web application interfaces are among the attack surfaces, each having multiple instances of security threats and possible vulnerabilities. Al-Garadi et al. [18] offers a comprehensive analysis of how machine learning and deep learning perform in the protection of IoT devices. They demonstrate how the existing solutions for the security of IoT network vulnerabilities lead to the implementation of ML and DL techniques. They also give a more detailed view of the various research problems that need to be solved in the implementation of DL/ML approaches in the IoT.

8.2.2 SURVEYS ON DDoS ATTACKS USING MACHINE LEARNING

Hussain et al. [19] presents an innovative method for the identification of intrusions that is based on ML methods. Derived from previous work on DDoS attacks, the three types of attack frames are grouped based on the features of the DDoS software. The features of attack flow are determined by analyzing normal flow data. The training process uses the random forest technique to train the features of the attack traffic received during the model detection phase. According to the findings, the proposed method has a high accuracy for current DDoS attacks.

Pei and Ji [20] investigates the scarcity of resources and the unpredictability of the edge VM to provide a solution for defending against DDoS attacks in SEC. They employ the Bayes model in order to describe the attack defense model that exists between the cooperative defender and the DDoS attacker. They find the marginal distribution for allocating resources by making sure that the cooperative defender gets more money out of it. Our Bayes approach outperforms other defense systems.

In Liu et al. [21], they presented a logical framework for classifying IoT traffic. They use this approach to classify items and extract the features from IoT traffic. In order to recover the attributes, they applied a variety of machine learning strategies. Each classifier's classification result was compared based on accuracy, algorithm training time, error rate, and other factors. Based on the results, they found a few literature gaps and made some suggestions about how to choose the right machine learning algorithm for different use cases.

In Kumar et al. [22], they analyzed the consequences of DDoS and E-DDoS attacks on smart home IoT devices and their possible implications. Wi-Fi monitors

TABLE 8.1
Comparison

Ref	Significance	Drawbacks
Ref [16]	Scholars conducted a thorough analysis of machine learning-based strategies for protecting IoT devices, data security, privacy access control, malware protec tion and ML implementation issues.	The survey is not limited to large-scale at tacks or other attacks that affect IoT systems. It is focused on machine learning-based IoT solutions. It makes no attempt to investigate DL-based solutions.
Ref [17]	Scholars created a collection of ML and DL strategies to enhance IoT security. A comprehensive study of threats is given including confidentiality, integrity and availability.	Numerous studies are analyzed, summa rized, and presented in this study. This research covers a wide range of security topics, but it does not focus on large-scale attacks on IoT systems.
Ref [18]	Researchers gave a thorough analysis of IoT network security needs, threat vectors and existing security measures related to ML and DL are discussed.	In this light, low-cost, high-efficiency IoT security measures must be addressed, as they may benefit from ML and DL as well.
Ref [25]	Researchers look at surveys that have already been done on IoT security, machine learning in IoT- and ML-based security solutions for IoT networks. They also look at how our research differs from past research in important ways.	This study looks at a variety of security issues, but it does not look at large-scale attacks on IoT devices. This research does not provide a thorough review of the literature on deep learning, but it lacks a few important components that makes an SLR unsuc cessful.
Ref [26]	Researchers gave a thorough analysis on ML in cybersecurity.	Only a few researchers have looked at the ML vulnerability problems and preventive measures that go with them.
Ref [27]	Researchers give a detailed assessment of machine learning methods for identifying the IoT devices as well as detecting corrupted or counterfeit ones.	Unsupervised device detection using behavior-independent and location diagnostic device particular attributes is currently in its early stages of development.
Ref [28]	Deep learning, big data and IoT security have all been studied in depth by researchers. The goal of the study was to find ways to secure IoT devices using deep learning techniques, assessment modules and big technologies.	This study presents an exhaustive literature assessment on deep learning. For example, at the end of their survey, the researchers did not specify the issues on research topics they intended to address.

the cut off rate and attack time for each user, allowing us to access the target's device and determine how GTK boosts DDoS attacks (Table 8.1). From either the attacker's or the victim's device's point of view, they highlighted several factors for E-DDoS, which include payload size, attack type, attack rate and victim device port states. Each device's power usage is examined.

In [23], they presented an SDN-enabled ultra-light security mechanism that may be quickly implemented without requiring a network change. This can also handle DDoS attacks in a way that does not slow down the system and reduces latency. They presented a joint defense that seamlessly blends MTD with cyberdeception, continually propagating disinformation to shift the attacker's perception and boost the architecture's efficacy and durability.

With an emerging mechanism [24], it may be possible to anticipate and prevent False Data Injection Attacks (FDIA) and DDoS attacks on 5G-enabled IoT networks. There are three levels in the architecture, an access layer, a mobile cloud computing layer, and a fog layer, each with three separate security mechanisms. To stop FDIA and DDOS attacks, they looked at the basics of how networks work and made a probabilistic Markov prediction and detection model. There was an improved rate of prediction and a significant reduction in the number of attacks was determined.

Machine learning in IoT security has been extensively studied by several researchers. They described methods to defend IoT devices against large-scale attacks. The strategies for increasing the security of IoT devices currently documented in the literature is unsuccessful.

8.2.3 RESEARCH GAP

Some of the drawbacks with respect to the categorization of traffic in the IoT networks are discussed. They created traffic on the IoT network by using a limited number of devices. When IoT devices become less complicated, classifiers need to be updated, which takes more resources. It can be overcome by increasing IoT device traffic to make it more visible [21].

Creating a machine learning model from massive data is difficult. If high-end resources are too expensive, model developers may not be able to create and fine-tune models with large datasets.

Selecting the optimal and most effective combination of attributes to distinguish DDoS attacks is a challenge based on prior research. They must not employ too many features because this would increase the controller's overhead and reaction time. DDoS attacks can be reduced by implementing an effective machine learning algorithm in an SDN environment [29].

The implementation of SDN-enabled infrastructure is required for the SDN network, which increases the cost. Expertise is required to build and manage the networks using SDN architecture.

In Alzahrani and Alzahrani [31], XG boost is an well-known and commonly used gradient boosting technique. When the number of samples or features grows, this limits both efficiency and scalability. Because of this, two new concepts are put forward: gradient-based one-sided sampling, and exclusive feature bundling. Unlike other gradient boosting methods, it is more accurate than depth or level-wise tree splitting methods.

According to Marvi and Uddin [32], the computational complexity of the existing algorithms so far implemented for DDoS attacks (RF, SVM, NB, DT, LR and KNN) is quite satisfactory. But when we consider a future enhancement, the above result is not enough with time constraints. We need to increase the computational complexity of space and time and also the accuracy. So, we need better algorithms to effectively detect DDoS attacks.

Most DDoS attack detection systems use supervised machine learning or deep learning algorithms [33]. It is extremely challenging to design supervised learning-based models for the detection of various forms of DDoS attacks using labeled datasets.

Unsupervised or semi-supervised machine learning methods have been used in several research studies to detect DDoS attacks [34–35]. These models are built using entropy-based features, which are derived from a small number of features such as source-destination IP addresses and port numbers [33]. Because these attributes can easily change depending on how the attack is set up, models made with them may not be able to find DDoS attacks that are unknown.

In current studies, a lot of data is needed for DL-based models to find relevant characteristics or spot DDoS attacks. The NSL-KDD dataset has been used to make classification models and test how well they work. Only about 150,000 samples are included in this dataset. The DL models created with such a tiny dataset are almost certainly overfit. As a result, such models perform poorly in real-world attack samples [31].

The attributes used to train ML models have a big impact on how long it takes to train them and how accurate they are. It is difficult to choose significant features for training the ML model. Using techniques for feature selection to automatically pick high-level characteristics could be a good way to solve this problem [34].

In traditional detection methods, attackers can be scattered and placed on multiple switches. The identification of such DDoS attacks can be very difficult; since switches cannot detect the attacks completely, the detection method on them may not be beneficial [35].

The current methodologies for identifying DDoS attacks in cloud computing depend on packet data. DDoS attacks often use packet data that is similar to what is used in normal scenarios, but the number of packets used in DDoS attacks can be quite large. As a result, current packet-based approaches are both unreliable and insecure [36].

8.3 REVIEW OF MACHINE LEARNING

The intention of the learning techniques is to improve performance in completing a task by training and learning from experience. The creation of new strategies and the accessibility of large datasets, as well as the rise of low-cost algorithms, have driven the modern improvement of machine learning [37].

8.3.1 SUPERVISED LEARNING

It is an algorithm that learns from the labelled data. In general, the algorithm feeds a lot of data and tells the algorithm that this data represents this label [38]. The algorithm tries to map the labels and the data so that it can recognize them. Navies Bayes (NB), Support Vector Machine (SVM), Linear Regression (LR), and K-nearest neighbors (KNN) are among the most frequently used supervised machine learning algorithms [8]. Two forms of supervised learning exist:

Classification This is about predicting a class or discrete values. From a labelled training dataset, the machine learns how to categorize the new events. The categorization output can be binary or multi-class, with either containing more than two classifications.
Regression This is about predicting a quantity or continuous values.

8.3.2 UNSUPERVISED LEARNING

It is an algorithm that learns from the unlabeled data [39]. It allows algorithms to detect patterns through self-learning and modelling. Unsupervised machine learning algorithms that are commonly used include k-means clustering, hierarchical clustering and DBSCAN approaches. There are two types of unsupervised learning:

Clustering different grouping of data points has been formed. Data points with similar characteristics will be grouped together, whereas data points with dissimilar characteristics will be grouped with another group.

Association A rule-based machine learning strategy for discovering the relationship between a large number of components.

8.3.3 SEMI-SUPERVISED LEARNING

In response to the shortcomings of both supervised and unsupervised learning, semi-supervised learning emerged as a viable alternative [40]. During the training process, it employs a mixture of labeled and unlabeled dataset. In this algorithm labelled data is limited, but unlabeled data is plentiful. Using an unsupervised learning, relevant data is first put into groups. As a result, unlabeled data becomes labeled data Table 8.2.

8.3.4 REINFORCEMENT LEARNING

This type of learning depends on the changes occurring in the environment. The smart agent interacts with its surroundings and learns how to operate in that environment [41]. In big areas, reinforcement learning (RL) may be employed in the following scenarios:

- Although there is a model of the environment, there is no analytical solution.
- Interacting with the environment is the only way to gather knowledge about it.

8.4 MACHINE LEARNING APPROACHES IN IOT

Table 8.3 summarizes the most widely used ML algorithms. These include NB, KNN, SVM, LR, RF, DT, XG boost and Adaboost. Classification algorithms include Support Vector Machine, Navies Bayes, Random Forest and Decision Trees [59].

The table compares the accuracy, precision and F1 score of several machine learning methods. Random Forest, Support Vector Machine, Navies Bayes, Decision Trees, K-nearest neighbors, Adaptive boosting and Extreme gradient boosting algorithms used

in research. Extreme gradient boosting and adaptive gradient boosting algorithms were quite accurate when compared to other methods is shown in Figure 8.3.

TABLE 8.2

Comparison

Methodology	Description	Application	Complexity
Navies bayes [19], [30]	The Bayes theorem is used to classify data, and predictors are assumed to be independent of one another.	Spam filtration, Sentimental analysis.	$O(np)$
K-nearest neighbor [30], [42], [43]	It is a classification algorithm in which some data points or data vectors are separated in to a different number of classes, and it tries to predict the classification of a new sample.	Intrusion detection, Anomalies.	$O(np)$
Support vector machine [19], [30], [43], [44]	It is a classification method that separates data using hyperplanes. It can be used to generate multiple separating hyperplanes so that the data is divided in to segments and each of these segments will contain only one kind of data.	Intrusion detection, Malware detection, Attacks in smart grids.	$O(n^2p+n^3)$
Logistic regression [30], [42], [45], [46], [47], [48]	The categorical dependent variable is predicted using logistic regression, utilizing a set of independent factors. When the dependent variable is categorical, logical regression is employed.	Descriptive statistics, Non-linear	- regression
Random for- est/ decision tree [30]–[49].	In random forest, the results of many decision trees are added together to get a single output.	Regression, Classification.	$O\,(T.D)$
XG Boost [46], [49]	It is an advanced version of the gradient boosting method that is designed to focus on computational speed and model accuracy. It supports parallelization by creating decision trees parallelly.	Regression, Classification, Ranking problems.	$O(tdx\log n)$
Ada Boost [49]	Adaptive boosting is an ensemble method in machine learning. The most frequent ADA boost algorithm is one- level decision trees, or decision trees with only one split.	Multi-classification, Regression.	$O(Tf)$

TABLE 8.3
ML Methods to Detect DDoS Attacks

Ref	Year	ML Methods	Dataset	Attack types	Acc(A)	Precision (P)	F1 Score (F1)
Ref [19]	2020	RF SVM	CICDDoS 2019	Reflection and exploitation-based attacks	99.14, 98.22	-	1, 0.98
Ref [54]	2020	ID3 RF NB LR	CICDDoS 2019	Reflection and exploitation-based attacks	-	0.78, 0.77, 0.41, 0.25	0.69, 0.62, 0.05, 0.04
Ref [55]	2020	AdaBoost J48 SVM	UNB-ISCX	DDoS	94.3, 87.9, 91.3	92.1, 79.3, 90.9	93.2, 86.3, 89.9
Ref [56]	2021	DT RF SVM NB	BoT-IoT	UDP DOS, Nor- mal, SSR, Data Theft.	99.98 100 99.82 99.86	99.55, 99.95, 99, 94.51	92.75, 95.52, 100, 99.99
Ref [57]	2020	NB DT RF	Simulated	UDP flood, SYN flood, Ping of Death, DoS	60.6 95.6 97.2	70.4, 95.7, 97.3	66.2, 95.7, 97.3
Ref [42]	2022	RF, DT, LR, KNN, ANN	UNSW-NB15	DoS, Generic, Shell code and Worms	89.29, 88.29, 82.07, 82.37, 84.80	76.9, 70.5, 50.5, 52.5, 61.0	74.12,71.4, 42.3, 49.1, 54.5
Ref [44]	2021	SVM, GBDT, RF	NSL-KDD	DoS, R2L, U2R, Probe	32.38, 78.01, 85.34	-	-
Ref [43]	2021	KNN, SVM, RF, MLP, CNN, GRU, LSTM	CICDDoS 2019	Reflection- and Exploitation- based attacks	99.97, 99.77, 96.36, 99.89, 99.13, 99.80, 99.87	99.97. 99.77, 98.51, 99.89, 99.33, 99.87, 99.88	99.97, 99.76, 97.14, 99.89, 99.19, 99.88, 99.87
Ref [45]	2021	Rf, LR, MLP, NB	CICDDoS 2019	Reflection- and Exploitation- based attacks	98.5, 79.7, 74.9, 59.6	98.5, 81.1, 79.7, 73.1	98.5, 79.5, 73.5, 52.9

(Continued)

TABLE 8.3 (CONTINUED)
ML Methods to Detect DDoS Attacks

Ref	Year	ML Methods	Dataset	Attack types	Acc(A)	Precision (P)	F1 Score (F1)
Ref [48]	2021	Ada Boost, Ex	DARPA	DoS, R2L, U2R,	75.37,	-	-
		tra trees, Gradi		Probe	76.12,		
		ent Boost, LR,			81.73,		
		MLP, RF			60.52,		
					74.58,		
					78.47		
Ref [30]	2021	KNN, SVM,	CICDDoS	Reflection and	0.98, 0.86,	0.99, 0.86,	0.99, 0.85,
		DT, NB, RF,	2019	exploitation	0.99, 0.45,	0.99, 0.66,	0.99, 0.38,
		LR		based attacks	0.99, 0.98	0.99, 0.99	0.99, 0.99
Ref [47]	2021	LR, DT, GB	BoT-IoT	UDP DOS, Nor-	99.96, 100,	99.96, 100,	99.96, 100,
				mal, SSR, Data theft	98.67	97.98	97.95
Ref [48]	2020	Bayesnet, NB,	NSL KDD	DoS, R2L, U2R,	97.18,	-	-
		DT, J48, RF		Probe	97.12,		
					99.54,		
					99.72,		
					98.83		

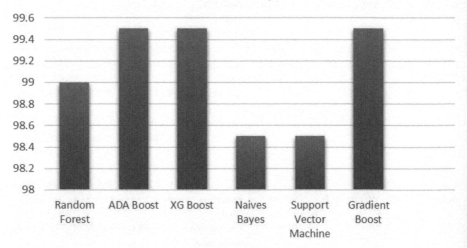

FIGURE 8.3   Comparison of ML methods.

8.5   DATASETS USED IN THE FIELD OF CYBERSECURITY

The method is evaluated using datasets to see if it would properly predict the attacks or not. The most common intrusion detection datasets are NSL-KDD, KDD-CUP 99, UNSW-NB15 and CICDDOS-2019.

8.5.1   NSL KDD DATASET

They introduced a new dataset known as NSLKDD in order to address the inadequacies of the KDDCUP dataset. Table 8.4 and Table 8.5 describes the features of NSLKDD. Compared to the KDDCUP dataset, the NSLKDD dataset provides the required benefits [50]

*   Because the test set contains no duplicated data, the classifiers will not return a biased one.
*   The test dataset has no redundant data, leading to better detection rates.
*   KDD dataset records are proportionate to hard level records.

8.5.2   KDD CUP 99 DATASET

In 1999, DARPA created the KDD '99 dataset using the network traffic from the previous dataset [51]. KDD'99 contains four types of assaults. Table 8.5 shows DoS, R2L, U2R, and Probe are depicted.

TABLE 8.4
ML Methods to Detect DDoS Attacks

Dataset	Total	Normal	DoS	Probe	R2L	U2R
KDD test+	22545	9712	7457	2422	2753	200
KDD test-	11851	2151	4342	2403	2754	201
KDD Train+	125974	67342	45926	11654	994	56

TABLE 8.5
Analysis of KDD CUP Dataset

Attack Types	Training Dataset (Percentage)	Testing Dataset (Percentage)
DoS	79.24	73.90
R2L	0.23	5.21
U2R	0.83	1.34
Probe	0.01	0.07
Normal	19.69	19.48

TABLE 8.6
Review of UNSW-NB15 Dataset

Attack Types	Training Dataset (Percentage)	Testing Dataset (Percentage)
Normal	57000	38000
Back doors	1745	580
Fuzzifiers	18180	6060
Generic	10400	3496
Worms	120	40
Exploits	33300	11132
Shell code	1138	380
DoS	12200	4080
Reconnaissance	10490	3478

8.5.3 UNSW-NB15 DATASET

It is a new dataset developed in 2015. It offers 49 characteristics and a range of regular and attacked activities, as well as 25,40,067 class labels. Of the total number of records, 2,21,876 are normal and 3,21, 283 are attacked (Table 8.6). The types of attacks in this dataset are analysis, normal, back doors, fuzzifiers, generic, worms, exploits, shell code, DoS and reconnaissance [52].

8.5.4 CICDDOS 2019 DATASET

The CICDDOS 2019 database has 50,063,112 records, including 50,006,249 for DDOS attacks and 58,863 for normal traffic. The different kinds of attacks that are included in the dataset are outlined in Table 8.7. The training dataset contains 12 DDOS at- tacks. They are NTP, LDAP, NETBIOS, SSDP, DNS, UDP, Web DDOS, TFTP, SYN, MSSQL and UDP lag [53].

TABLE 8.7
Summary of CICDDoS Attacks

Categories of Attacks	Flow Count
Network Time Protocol	1202642
Lightweight Directory Access Protocol	2179930
Network Basic Input Output System	4093279
Simple Service Discovery Protocol	2610611
Domain Name System	5071011
User Datagram Protocol	3134645
Web DDoS	439
TFTP and SYN	20082580
Microsoft SQL Server	4522492
User Datagram Protocol Lag	366461

8.6 CONCLUSION AND FUTURE SCOPE

This research provides a systematic and comprehensive review of ML algorithms for identifying intrusion detections in the IoT environment. In this chapter, a variety of techniques for identifying DDOS attacks using machine learning methodologies are examined. The model's performance is tested on several classifiers to choose the optimal classifier with high accuracy. Comparing boosted algorithms to standard machine learning algorithms, we discovered that adaptive boosting and extreme gradient boosting approaches achieved a high accuracy rate. The extreme boosting algorithms is mainly designed to enhance the computational speed and accuracy of the model. In Future work, we intend to apply optimization techniques to the proposed model in order to improve its accuracy.

REFERENCES

[1] K. K. Patel, S. M. Patel, and P. G. Scholar (2016), Internet of Things-IOT: Definition, char acteristics, architecture, enabling technologies, application & future challenges, *Int. J. Eng. Sci. Comput.*, vol. 6, no. 5, pp. 1–10.

[2] K. Singh, and D. D. Singh Toma (2019), Architecture, enabling technologies, security and pri vacy, and applications of internet of things: A survey, *Proc. Int. Conf. I-SMAC (IoT Soc. Mobile, Anal Cloud), I-SMAC 2018*, vol. 4, no. 5, pp. 642–646.

[3] P. Malhotra, Y. Singh, P. Anand, D. K. Bangotra, P. K. Singh, and W. C. Hong (2021), Internet of things: Evolution, concerns and security challenges, *Sensors*, vol. 21, no. 5, pp. 1–35.

[4] L. Babun, K. Denney, Z. B. Celik, P. McDaniel, and A. S. Uluagac (2021), A survey on IoT platforms: Communication, security, and privacy perspectives, *Comput. Networks*, vol. 192, no. April 2020, p. 108040.

[5] T. Rincy, and R. Gupta (2021), Design and development of an efficient network intrusion detection system using machine learning techniques, *Wirel. Commun. Mob. Comput.*, vol. 2021, no. 1, pp. 1–35.

[6] A. Agarwal, P. Sharma, M. Alshehri, A. A. Mohamed, and O. Alfarraj (2021), Classification model for accuracy and intrusion detection using machine learning approach, *PeerJ Comput. Sci.*, vol. 7, pp. 1–22.

[7] F. Kilincer, F. Ertam, and A. Sengur (2021), Machine learning methods for cyber security in trusion detection: Datasets and comparative study, *Comput. Networks*, vol. 188, no. October 2020, p. 107840, 2021.

[8] Aljuhani (2021), Machine learning approaches for combating distributed denial of service attacks in modern networking environments, *IEEE Access*, vol. 9, pp. 42236–42264.

[9] N. F. Syed, Z. Baig, A. Ibrahim, and C. Valli (2020), Denial of service attack detection through machine learning for the IoT, *J. Inf. Telecommun.*, vol. 4, no. 4, pp. 482–503.

[10] Constantinos Kolias, Georgios Kambourakis, Angelos Stavrou, and Jeffrey Voas (2017), DDoS in the IoT: Mirai and other botnets, *Computer (Long. Beach. Calif.).*, p. 1.

[11] V. K. Singh and M. Govindarasu (2021), A cyber-physical anomaly detection for wide area protection using machine learning, *IEEE Trans. Smart Grid*, vol. 12, no. 4, pp. 3514–3526.

[12] S. Einy, C. Oz, and Y. D. Navaei (2021), The anomaly-and signature-based IDS for network security using hybrid inference systems, *Math. Probl. Eng*, vol. 12, no. 4, pp. 3514–3526.

[13] S. Mokhtari, A. Abbaspour, K. K. Yen, and A. Sargolzaei (2021), A machine learning approach for anomaly detection in industrial control systems based on measurement data, *Electron.*, vol. 10, no. 4, pp. 1–13.

[14] A. Alshaibi, M. Al-Ani, A. Al-Azzawi, A. Konev, and A. Shelupanov (2022), The comparison of cybersecurity datasets, *Data*, vol. 7, no. 2, p. 22.

[15] N. Oliveira, I. Praça, E. Maia, and O. Sousa (2021), Intelligent cyber attack detection and classification for network-based intrusion detection systems, *Appl. Sci.*, vol. 11, no. 4, pp. 1–21.

[16] L. Xiao, X. Wan, X. Lu, Y. Zhang, and D. Wu (2018), IoT security techniques based on machine learning: How do IoT devices use AI to enhance security, *IEEE Signal Process. Mag.*, vol. 35, no. 5, pp. 41–49.

[17] S. Zeadally and M. Tsikerdekis (2020), Securing Internet of Things (IoT) with machine learning, *Int. J. Commun. Syst.*, vol. 33, no. 1, pp. 1–16.

[18] M. A. Al-Garadi, A. Mohamed, A. K. Al-Ali, X. Du, I. Ali, and M. Guizani (2020), A survey of machine and deep learning methods for Internet of Things (IoT) security, *IEEE Commun. Surv. Tutorials*, vol. 22, no. 3, pp. 1646–1685.

[19] F. Hussain, R. Hussain, S. A. Hassan, and E. Hossain (2020), Machine learning in IoT security: Current solutions and future challenges, *IEEE Commun. Surv. Tutorials*, vol. 22, no. 3, pp. 1686–1721.

[20] Y. Chen Pei, and W. Ji (2019), A DDoS attack detection method based on machine learning, *J. Phys. Conf. Ser.*, vol. 1237, no. 3, p. 032040.

[21] Liu, X. Wang, S. Shen, G. Yue, S. Yu, and M. Li (2020), A bayesian Q-learning game for dependable task offloading against DDoS attacks in sensor edge cloud, *IEEE Internet Things J.*, vol. 8, no. 9, pp. 7546–7561.

[22] R. Kumar, M. Swarnkar, G. Singal, and N. Kumar (2022), IoT network traffic classification using machine learning algorithms: An experimental analysis, *IEEE Internet Things J.*, vol. 9, no. 2, pp. 989–1008.

[23] Y. Dalal Tushir, B. Dezfouli, and Y. Liu (2020), A quantitative study of DDoS and E- DDoS attacks on WiFi smart home devices, *IEEE Internet Things J.*, vol. 8, no. 8, pp. 6282–6292.

[24] Y. Zhou, G. Cheng, and S. Yu (2021), An SDN-enabled proactive defense framework for DDoS mitigation in IoT networks, *IEEE Trans. Inf. Forensics Secur.*, vol. 16, pp. 5366–5380.

[25] H. Moudoud, L. Khoukhi, and S. Cherkaoui (2021), Prediction and detection of FDIA and DDoS attacks in 5G enabled IoT, *IEEE Netw.*, vol. 35, no. 2, pp. 194–201.

[26] E. Bout, V. Loscri, and A. Gallais (2021), How machine learning changes the nature of cyberattacks on IoT networks: A survey, *IEEE Commun. Surv. Tutorials*, vol. 24, no. 1, pp. 248–279.

[27] D. Dasgupta, Z. Akhtar, and S. Sen (2022), Machine learning in cybersecurity: A comprehensive survey, *J. Def. Model. Simul.*, vol. 19, no. 1, pp. 57–106.

[28] Y. Liu, J. Wang, J. Li, S. Niu, and H. Song (2022), Machine learning for the detection and identification of Internet of Things devices: A survey, *IEEE Internet Things J.*, vol. 9, no. 1, pp. 298–320.

[29] Ahzam et al. (2020), Deep learning and big data technologies for IoT security, *Comput. Commun.*, vol. 151, no. October 2019, pp. 495–517.

[30] A. Arfeen Marvi, and R. Uddin (2021), A generalized machine learning-based model for the detection of DDoS attacks, *Int. J. Netw. Manag.*, vol. 31, no. 6, pp. 1–22.

[31] R. J. Alzahrani and A. Alzahrani (2021), Security analysis of DDoS attacks using machine learning algorithms in networks traffic, *Electron.*, vol. 10, no. 23, p. 2919.

[32] A. Arfeen Marv, and R. Uddin (2021), An augmented K-means clustering approach for the detection of distributed denial-of-service attacks, *Int. J. Netw. Manag.*, vol. 31, no. 6, pp. 1–23.

[33] S. Hosseini and M. Azizi (2019), The hybrid technique for DDoS detection with supervised learning algorithms, *Comput. Networks*, vol. 158, pp. 35–45.

[34] Y. Gu, K. Li, Z. Guo, and Y. Wang (2019), Semi-supervised k-means ddos detection method using hybrid feature selection algorithm, *IEEE Access*, vol. 7, no. c, pp. 64351–64365.

[35] J. McHugh (2000), Testing intrusion detection systems: A critique of the 1998 and 1999 DARPA intrusion detection system evaluations as performed by Lincoln laboratory, *ACM Trans. Inf. Syst. Secur.*, vol. 3, no. 4, pp. 262–294.

[36] R. Santos, D. Souza, W. Santo, A. Ribeiro, and E. Moreno (2020), Machine learning algorithms to detect DDoS attacks in SDN, *Concurr. Comput. Pract. Exp.*, vol. 32, no. 16, pp. 1–14.

[37] G. A. Jaafar, S. M. Abdullah, and S. Ismail (2019), Review of recent detection methods for HTTP DDoS attack, *J. Comput. Networks Commun.*, vol. 2019.

[38] M. Batta (2020), Machine learning algorithms - A review, *Int. J. Sci. Res. (IJ)*, vol. 9, no. 1, pp.

[39] A. Thakkar and R. Lohiya (2021), A review on machine learning and deep learning perspectives of IDS for IoT: Recent updates, Security Issues, and Challenges, vol. 28, no. 4, pp. 3211–3243. Springer Netherlands.

[40] T. Jiang, J. L. Gradus, and A. J. Rosellini (2020), Supervised machine learning: A brief primer, *Behav. Ther.*, vol. 51, no. 5, pp. 675–687.

[41] M. Usama et al. (2019), Unsupervised machine learning for networking: Techniques, Applications and research challenges, *IEEE Access*, vol. 7, pp. 65579–65615.

[42] T. N. Alharin Doan, and M. Sartipi (2020), Reinforcement learning interpretation methods: A survey, *IEEE Access*, vol. 8, pp. 171058–171077.

[43] H. A. Ahmed, A. Hameed, and N. Z. Bawany (2022), Network intrusion detection using over sampling technique and machine learning algorithms, *PeerJ Comput. Sci.*, vol. 8, p. e820.

[44] M. Yungaicela-Naula, C. Vargas-Rosales, and J. A. Perez-Diaz (2021), SDN-based architecture for transport and application layer DDoS attack detection by using machine and deep learning, *IEEE Access*, vol. 9, pp. 108495–108512.

[45] M. Anwer, S. M. Khan, M. U. Farooq, and W. Waseemullah (2021), Attack detection in IoT using machine learning, *Eng. Technol. Appl. Sci. Res.*, vol. 11, no. 3, pp. 7273–7278.

[46] D. Zou Ortet Lopes, F. A. Ruambo, S. Akbar, and B. Yuan (2021), Towards effective detection of recent DDoS attacks: A deep learning approach, *Secur. Commun. Networks*, vol. 2021, no. September 2016, pp. 1–14.

[47] A. Abraham and V. R. Bindu (2021), Intrusion detection and prevention in networks using machine learning and deep learning approaches: A review, *International Conference on Advancements in Electrical, Electronics, Communication, Computing and Automation*, pp. 1–4.

[48] G. Karatas, and Baydoğ Mus (2021), The effects of normalization and standardization an Internet of Things attack detection, *Eur. J. Sci. Technol.*, no. 29, pp. 187–192.

[49] R. J. Alzahrani and A. Alzahrani (2021), Survey of traffic classification solution in IoT Net works, *Int. J. Comput. Appl.*, vol. 183, no. 9, pp. 37–45.

[50] S. Nandi, S. Phadikar, and K. Majumder (2020), Detection of DDoS attack and classification using a hybrid approach, *ISEA-ISAP 2020 - Proc. 3rd ISEA Int. Conf. Secur. Priv. 2020*, pp. 41–47.

[51] O. Alzahrani, and M. J. F. Alenazi (2021), Designing a network intrusion detection system based on machine learning for software defined networks, *Futur. Internet*, vol. 13, no. 5, p. 111.

[52] T. D. Diwan, S. Choubey, and H. S. Hota (2021), A detailed analysis on NSL-KDD dataset using various machine learning techniques for intrusion detection, *Turkish J. Comput. Math. Educ.*, vol. 12, no. 11, pp. 2954–2968.

[53] S. Choudhary, and N. Kesswani (2020), Analysis of KDD-Cup'99, NSL-KDD and UNSW- NB15 datasets using deep learning in IoT, *Procedia Comput. Sci.*, vol. 167, no. 2019, pp. 1561–1573.

[54] S. Moualla, K. Khorzom, and A. Jafar (2021), Improving the performance of machine learning- based network intrusion detection systems on the UNSW-NB15 dataset, *Comput. Intell. Neurosci*, vol. 2021, pp. 1–13.

[55] M. A. Ferrag, L. Shu, H. Djallel, and K. K. R. Choo (2021), Deep learning-based intrusion detection for distributed denial of service attack in agriculture 4.0, *Electron.*, vol. 10, no. 11, pp. 0–26.

[56] Y. Jia, F. Zhong, A. Alrawais, B. Gong, and X. Cheng (2020), FlowGuard: An intelligent edge defense mechanism against IoT DDoS attacks, *IEEE Internet Things J.*, vol. 7, no. 10, pp. 9552–9562.

[57] N. Ravi, and S. M. Shalinie (2020), Learning-driven detection and mitigation of DDoS attack in IoT via SDN-cloud architecture, *IEEE Internet Things J.*, vol. 7, no. 4, pp. 3559–3570.

[58] M. Shafiq, Z. Tian, A. K. Bashir, X. Du, and M. Guizani (2021), CorrAUC: A malicious Bot- IoT traffic detection method in IoT network using machine-learning techniques, *IEEE Internet Things J.*, vol. 8, no. 5, pp. 3242–3254.

[59] S. Sampalli Alsirhani, and P. Bodorik (2019), DDoS detection system: Using a set of classification algorithms controlled by fuzzy logic system in apache spark, *IEEE Trans. Netw. Serv. Manag.*, vol. 16, no. 3, pp. 936–949.

[60] M. Abinaya and S. Prabakeran (2022), Lightweight block cipher for resource constrained IoT environment—An survey, performance, cryptanalysis and research challenges, *IoT Based Control Networks and Intelligent Systems, Lecture Notes in Networks and Systems, P. No: 347-365.*

9 Simulation of Scheduling & Load Balancing Algorithms for a Distributed Data Center by Using Service Broker Policy Over the Cloud

Shivani Dubey, Vikas Singhal and Ajay Kumar Sahu
Greater Noida Institute of Technology, Greater Noida, India

9.1 INTRODUCTION

Cloud computing platforms are rapidly growing in popularity in the present day. Cloud computing, often referred to as simply "the cloud", is the delivery of on-demand computing resources over the Internet on a pay-for-use basis According to the official National Institute of Standards and Technology (NIST) definition, "cloud computing is a model for enabling ubiquitous, convenient, on-demand network access to a shared pool of configurable computing resources (e.g., networks, servers, storage, applications and services) that can be rapidly provisioned and released with minimal management effort or service provider interaction" [1]. Generally speaking, Cloud computing is a term for anything that involves the delivery of hosted services over the Internet. These services are divided into three principal categories: Infrastructure-as-a-Service (IaaS); Platform-as-a-Service (PaaS); and Software-as-a-Service (SaaS) [2]. Most IT departments are forced to spend a significant portion of their time on frustrating implementation, maintenance, and upgrade projects. At present, however, IT teams are turning to cloud computing technology to minimize the time spent on lower-value activities and allow IT to focus on strategic activities with a greater impact on business. A cloud computing service has three main distinct characteristics that differentiate it from traditional hosting: It is sold on demand, usually by the minute or the hour; it provides a property of elasticity, which means that a client can have as much or as little of a service as they need at any given time; finally, the services are

DOI: 10.1201/9781003363606-9

fully managed by the cloud service providers. Apart from all of the cloud computing advantages, there are many challenges and open issues in cloud computing research areas, such as: Security challenges [3–6]; Job scheduling [7–10]; Energy efficiency and green computing [11–14]; and Load balancing [15–18]. Load balancing is one of the vital terms in cloud computing environments and generally distributed systems which affect the system performance dependent on the amount of work allocated to the system for a specific time period. Load balancing is the process of redistributing the general system workload among system resources for improving resource utilization and system performance [19]. Load balancing has been taken into consideration so that every virtual machine in the cloud computing system does the same amount of workload and therefore by increasing the throughput and minimizing the response time, users' satisfactions will be provided. Load balancing is nothing but distributing loads among various resources in any system. In cloud architecture, the load is distributed in equal numbers at any point of time. In cloud analysis different load balancing polices and service broker policies are used for the public and private cloud in order to minimize response time and processing time. In this chapter we compare the results from the same region and different regions. Data centers from the same region are considered to be a private cloud and those from different regions are considered to be a public cloud. Cloud Analyst is a tool that is used in cloud architecture for the simulation and modeling of data. Comparing the results of public and private cloud, along with various load balancing policies and service broker policies, results in a variation in response time.

In this research, a Contractors State License Board (CSLBA) is introduced and the capabilities of crows are projected to solve the real-world multimodal scheduling optimization issue in terms of its representation, operators, control parameters, evolutionary mechanism, the performance metric, and areas of applications as presented below [16]. The suggested approach endeavors to recreate the intelligent strategy of the crows to determine the solution of scheduling optimization issues. The behaviour of flocks of crows shares many similarities with an optimization process. As illustrated by this act, crows conceal their plethora of food in concealing spots of the environment and recover the hidden food when it is required [20].

9.2   RELATED WORK

There have been some studies which have examined load-balancing performance evaluation and comprising different load-balancing algorithms in cloud computing environments, of which we will consider some in this section. In Askarzadeh [20] a comparative study of two Round Robin and Throttled virtual machine load-balancing algorithms has been proposed. In this study, Round Robin and Throttled virtual machine load-balancing policies are used along with an optimized response time service broker policy and simulation is performed by adjusting parameters to consider overall response time, data center hourly average processing times, data center request servicing times, response times according to region, user base hourly response times and total costs which have a significant effect on performance. According to the simulation results, the combination of the proposed strategy of throttled and optimized response time service broker policy has a better performance than Round Robin load-balancing algorithm in a heterogeneous cloud computing environment. Authors in have presented a review of some load-balancing algorithms in cloud computing to identify qualitative components for simulation and analyze the execution time of load-balancing algorithms. In this study, the simulation process has been executed for three load-balancing algorithms: Round Robin, Central queuing and Randomized with various combination of million instructions per second vs. VM and MIPS vs. Host. The simulation results show that the response time is inversely proportionate with MIPS vs. VM and MIPS vs. Host, but the optimum response time is achieved with the same value of MIPS vs. VM and MIPS vs. Host. A comparative study of three distributed load-balancing algorithms for cloud computing scenarios has been proposed in [21]. In this study, three representative algorithms were chosen for the comparison of performance evaluation. The first was directly based on naturally occurring phenomenon, honey bee foraging; the second sought to engineer a desired global outcome from biased random sampling; and ethe third used system rewiring which is called Active Clustering. The simulation results indicate that the honeybee-based load-balancing algorithms give better performance when a diverse population of service types is required. In addition, the simulation shows that random sampling walk performs better in confirming similar populations and degrades quickly when the population diversity increases. Active Clustering performs better as the number of processing nodes is increased similar to random walk. Authors in Ray and De Sarkar [22] discussed a performance comparison for different load-balancing algorithms of virtual machine and policies in cloud computing. In this study, four well known load balancing algorithms have been considered. The performance of Round Robin, Throttled, Execution Load and First Come First Serve Load Balancing Algorithms have been analyzed based on the average response time, the average data center request servicing time and total costs. The simulation results according to the Cloud Analyst simulator show that Round Robin has the best integration performance.

A number of studies have been conducted on the effect of service broker policy on the performance of the cloud environment. Randles et al; Mohapatra et al. [23, 24] used Cloud Analyst to represent the performance analysis of three previous broker policies in combination with different Load-balancing policies for large-scale applications using different infrastructural environments. They concluded that the service broker policy affects the overall response time of the system. Although P. M. Rekha et al. [25] analyzed various service broker policies for selecting data centers and comparing their cost, the idea of service brokering in a cloud continues to be the subject of many research works. A. Aikar et al. [26] proposed an effective data center selection algorithm for a federated cloud, in which the data center is selected based on the matrix values. The matrix is assigned to each region. This matrix contains information on the cost required for the resources of a data center and distance of the request location. A number of research works extended the service proximity-based broker policy [27, 28] and studied the case in which more than one data center is located in the selected region. D. Kapgate [29] mainly focused on implementing the predictive service broker algorithm based on the weighted moving average forecast model. This research shows how the proposed predictive service broker algorithm minimizes the response time experienced by users and the load on the data center.

9.3   CLOUD ANALYST

At the upper level of the Cloud Sim tool kit the Cloud Analyst is assembled. This kit allows for a description of the data center location with geographical representation of various users who are creating network traffic and also loads of application, number of users, resources and data centers in each data center with the help of use of functionalities of Cloud Sim. The interval in the existing simulation tools for the evaluation of applications in the cloud by the simulator Cloud Analyst where results can help the developer to finalize the estimation of larger-scale application in a geographical area where the workload is distributed on the server or data center [30]. A thorough graphical user interface (GUI) worked in Java Swing is furnished to the Cloud Analyst. This segment depicts quickly. The screen and its subsequent usage to set up and recreation execution has been represented in this segment.

1. **Characterize User Bases**: The geographical area, application's client and other properties such as the recurrence of the user and the number of clients with the number of hours are generalized with User base elements. Other side configure simulation screen has primary tab for accomplishing this task.
2. **Characterize Data Center**: The actual use of the Data Centers tab of the Configuration screen characterizes server farms which one wishes to apply in the reenactment. Characterize each and every equipment and bookkeeping parts of server farms in this case
3. **Designate Virtual Machines for the application in Data Centers**: On the configuration screen main tab, the server scenario is created to design the virtual machine for recreating and utilizing applications. A server farm characterized in the above mentioned point 2, in fact, is not incorporated into recreation until the same is allotted in the given stride. Various sorts of virtual machines in the same server farm can also be assigned by the user.
4. **Audit and change the propelled parameters**: The Configuration Screen having the advanced tab is to be changed.
5. **Audit and change system inactivity with data transfer capacity**: Networks on the Internet Qualities.
   - **Application clients**: Autonomous elements are needed to go about since movement generators and its conduct should be configurable.
   - **Internet**: The information transfer over the Internet should be reasonably demonstrated by system deferrals and data transfer capacity confine.
   - **Simulation characterized by time period**: Cloud Sim like a toolbox is intended to handle the pre-characterized arrangement of occasions (viz. accommodation of the number of cloudlets.) However, one has to change over reenactment for the time span-restricted execution when occasions are persistently produced with the help of clients unless a pre-characterized time period terminates.
   - **Service Brokers**: Cloud Sim as of now is considered to have the idea of Data Center Brokers and it plays a double part in VM administration in numerous server farms as well as steering movement towards suitable

server farms. In any case, for Cloud Analyst these two fundamental obligations were isolated and allocated to two unique substances. The Data Center Controller (depicted beneath) expands the Data Center Broker and is principally in charge of the VM administration inside of a solitary server farm and load adjusting of VM's and so on inside of that solitary server farm. The new substance CloudAppSeriveBroker was acquainted with handling the obligation of dealing with the steering of client solicitations between server farms in light of various administration business approaches.

- **GUI**: Cloud Analyst additionally presents an exhaustive GUI which can be utilized to arrange the reenactment at an abnormal state of point of interest. The GUI empowers clients to establish and perform reenactment analyzes effectively that, in addition, have advantages in demonstrating execution with precision of reenactment rationale along these lines naturally prompting general change.
- **Ability to save simulations and results**: The Cloud Analyst additionally permits clients for sparing recreation setup as an xml.file furthermore sending out of outputs to PDF position [31].

In Figure 9.1, the Cloud Analyst domain has been represented, which depicts the flow of data among various regions and data using internet technology as well as the data center controller and VM load balancing. The accompanying area portrays these segments and ideas inside and out. The three principal augmentations explained in Cloud Analyst having the Cloud Sim toolbox are mentioned as User Base, Data Center Controller & Internet. Be that as it may, before clarifying those it is proper to present the idea of "Region" [32].

1. **Region:** The entire globe is mapped in 6 areas which balances 6 significant main land areas in the whole universe in the Cloud Analyst tool. Another main substances, for instance, User Bases and Data Centers are supposed to acquire position in one of the districts. The topology collection is further applied to maintain the level of appropriate straightforwardness for enhanced scaled reproduction which are further applied in the case of Cloud Analyst. A Cloud Research Analyst in designing and then managing an organization's cloud systems, applications, policies, and strategy.
2. **Internet**: For the current scenario of the Internet the Cloud Analyst Internet has emerged as an indispensable necessity. It is a vital component that accurately reflects the existing scenario. It also indicates the movement of internet around the world by describing information-sharing delays and transmission mapping. These movements are mapped and showed among the 6 regions which are configurable.
3. **User Base**: The User Base I (UB) models a collection of clients which is considered to be a solitary unit in the reenactment (Simulation) and its principal obligation is to produce movement for the recreation. A solitary User Base might speak to a huge number of clients; however, it is designed as a solitary unit and the activity produced in synchronous blasts

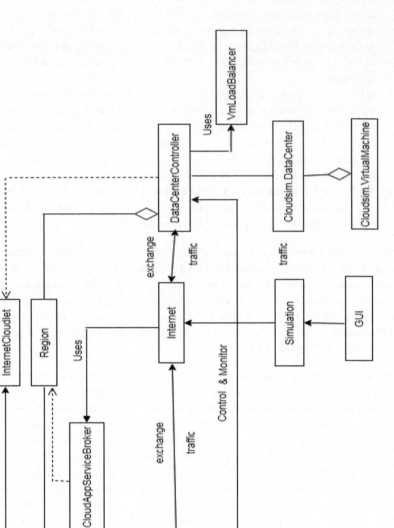

FIGURE 9.1 Cloud analyst domain.

illustrative of the span of the client base. The modeller might utilize a User Base to speak to a solitary client; however, preferably a User Base should be utilized to speak to a bigger number of clients for the effectiveness of re-enactment.

4. **Internet Cloudlet**: An Internet Cloudlet is a collection of client solicitations. The quantity of solicitations packaged into a single Internet Cloudlet is configurable in Cloud Analyst. The Internet Cloudlet conveys data; for example, the span of a solicitation execution charge, size of info and yield documents, the originator and target application id utilized for steering by the Internet and the quantity of demands.

5. **Data Center Controller**: The Data Center Controller (DCC) is considered to be the significant substance in Cloud Analyst. A solitary Server farm Controller is mapped to a solitary clouds in Data Center protest and deals with the server farm administration exercises, for example, VM creation and pulverization and does the directing of client solicitations got from User Bases through the Internet to the VMs. It can likewise be seen as the façade utilized by Cloud Analyst to get to the heart of Cloud Sim toolbox usefulness.

6. **VmLoadBalancer**: This is used to determine that VM has to assigned task to cloudlet for data processing.

9.4 CLOUD APPLICATION SERVICE BROKER

The UBs connectivity and data centers is managed by using service broker which selects the advantages for UB with facilities provided by the admin [33].

a) **Service proximity-based routing**: This is a least complex Service Broker usage, which includes some functionalities:
   - It keeps up a file about total number of data centers.
   - When Internet gets information from the client side it questions for service proximity service broker policy in the destination DCC.
   - It recovers solicitation and questions for the area vicinity list from Internet Characteristics. This rundown arranges the locales which are remained in request of least system inertness and ascertained from the district.
   - It captures main server farm situated at the most punctual/most noteworthy district in the vicinity list. On the off-chance that more than one server farm is situated in a district, one is chosen arbitrarily.

b) **Performance-optimized routing**: This approach is executed by using best response time service broker, which expands in the following steps:
   - Service broker has a list of all data centers and the best response times.
   - Internet identifies best response time service broker when it gets information by UB for DCC.

- When the Internet gets information by UB it inquires for the best response time service broker for DCC.
- Best response time service broker differentiate nearest (as far as idleness) information focus utilizing the service proximity service broker measurement.
- The server gets down and sends back the best response time to the service broker, sending its reaction to the other server.

c) **Dynamic Service Broker**:

- Proximity Service Broker or the Best Response Time Service Broker are expanded by dynamic service broker
- Dynamic service broker has server down functionality and the best reaction time recorded.
- Internet inquiries the dynamic service broker when it has any message for the destination data center controller.
- The Dynamic service broker identifies the destination point by using service proximity service broker or best response time service broker
- If exist reaction time is greater than past reaction time, the dynamic service broker recreates the best records of reaction time.

9.5 NETBEANS SOFTWARE

Netbeans (software) works as IDE (Integrated development environment) shown in Figure 9.2 to develop a Java programming environment and also supports other

FIGURE 9.2   Netbeans platform.

languages such as C, C++, PHP and HTML. NetBeans is also called as an application-based platform framework for using Java applications and other applications. IDE of NetBeans is written in Java and runs on Linux, Windows and other platforms to support a compatibility with other system configurations. It also allows applications based on IDE to develop the advance software. NetBeans application includes the other application on IDE by third-party developers [34].

9.6   CLOUD ANALYST SIMULATION

At the point when Cloud Analyst begins the principal screen is shown in Figure 9.3 in the section below. It has the recreation board for guiding the world at the privilege and the fundamental control panel board on the left-hand side. As specified, the Cloud Analyst separates the world into six districts which correspond generally with six primary major lands. Areas for components to re-enactment distinguished just from locale to straightforwardness in x and y coordinates; elements inside are area comparative to geology in the case of particular parameters. The options are countable, such as configure simulation display, internet character, run simulation and exit.

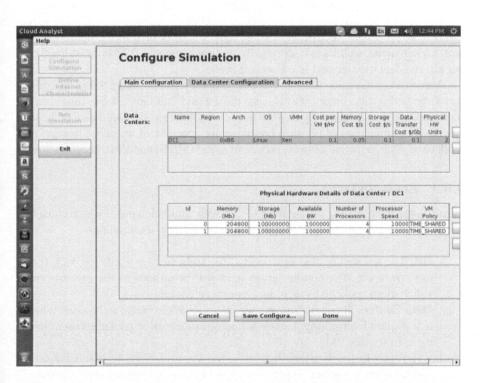

FIGURE 9.3   Configuration screen with simulation panel.

9.6.1 MAIN TAB

There is a main tab on the configuration screen which has the following components:

1. **Simulation time**: Time length of the reproduction in second, minute, hour and days.
2. **UserBase Table**: All the UB in the recreation in which each UB has taking after configuration entities; name, upload file, region, requests/user, size of data, request of data, hours at peak level, average of hour in peak level per user during the peak hours on and off-hours.
3. **Application deployment configuration**: It records how many VMs are allocated for executing application in every server farm in data centers tab; this tab has several elements such as number of virtual machines (VMs), bandwidth, memory, size of image and data center.
4. **Service broker policy**: It permits for selecting business approach between among farms which choose that server farm ought to get movement from UB. It has multiple elements: load configuration, save configuration, optimize response time, closest data center and save configuration.

9.6.2 DATA CENTER TAB

This permits you to characterize the design of a server farm. It is on top records in server farms for utilizing add or remove catches for adding or removing server farms in setup. There are different parameters in servers such as the operating system, region, name, architecture, cost/1Mb memory hour, cost/VM hour, storage cost per gb, and data transfer cost in on and off mode.

There is a configuration screen with a simulation panel in Figure 9.3 in which you can identify the data center by analyzing the 1st and 2nd table of the configuration screen appeared in the above figure with the details of the physical hardware of the data center. The components of physical hardware are; machine id, memory, storage, network bandwidth, no. of processors, processor speed (MIPS) and VM allocation policy.

9.6.3 ADVANCED TAB

Figure 9.4 represents the configuration screen with simulation panel which considers some vital components which are applied in a complete re-enactment;

1. **UB**: The test system that how many UB ought with as a solitary pack for movement era. The number given here will be utilized as the quantity of solicitations spoke to by a solitary internet cloudlet.
2. **Data Centers**: It counts how numerous solicitations ought to be dealt with as a solitary for handling. i.e. this numerous solicitations packaged and allocated to solitary VM.
3. **Executable instruction length**: It influences length of execution in solicitation.
4. **Load balancing policy**: It presents the VM based algorithms with scheduling policies; round robin, active monitoring and throttled load balancing algorithms.

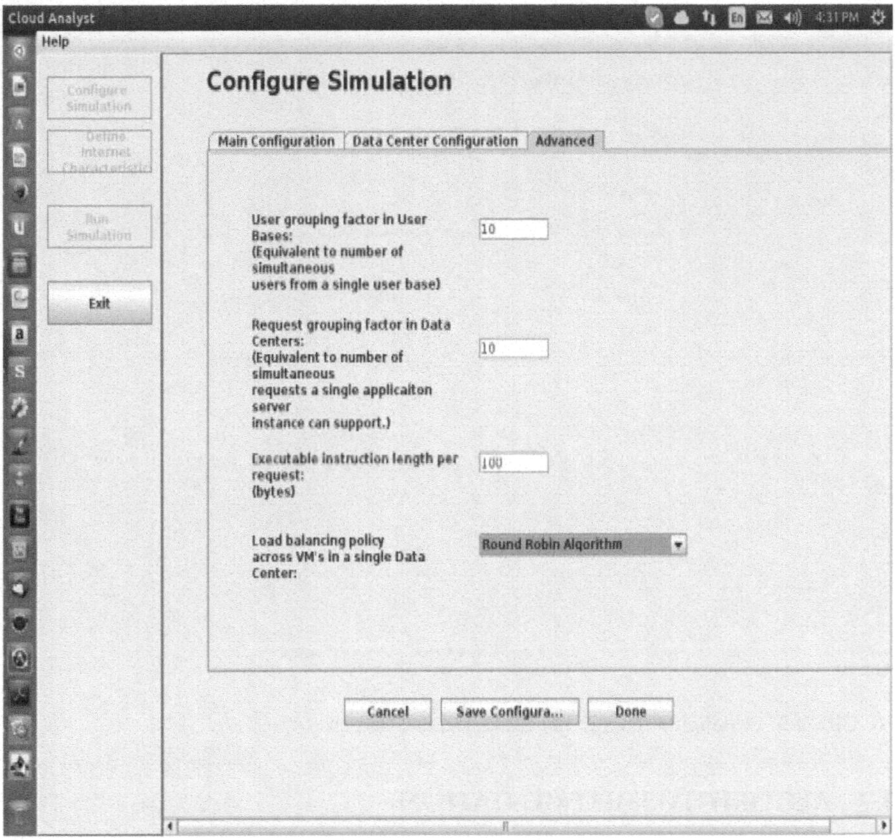

FIGURE 9.4 Configuration screen for algorithms.

9.6.4 INTERNET CHARACTERISTICS SCREEN

The internet characteristics screen is presented in Figure 9.5, which is utilized latency in Internet and bandwidth to presents delay matrix and bandwidth matrix.

9.6.5 RESULTS SCREEN

Figure 9.6 presents the display screen for resulting the simulation. There is also a go back option on the main screen. Result can be executed on the running simulated from control panel. The percentage is also shown in running screen for the completion of the simulation. This screen also displays sending requests to various data centers by UBs.

There is also a cancel button by which a simulation can be exited if any user wants to do so; otherwise the simulation will run and continue to take requests from data centers.

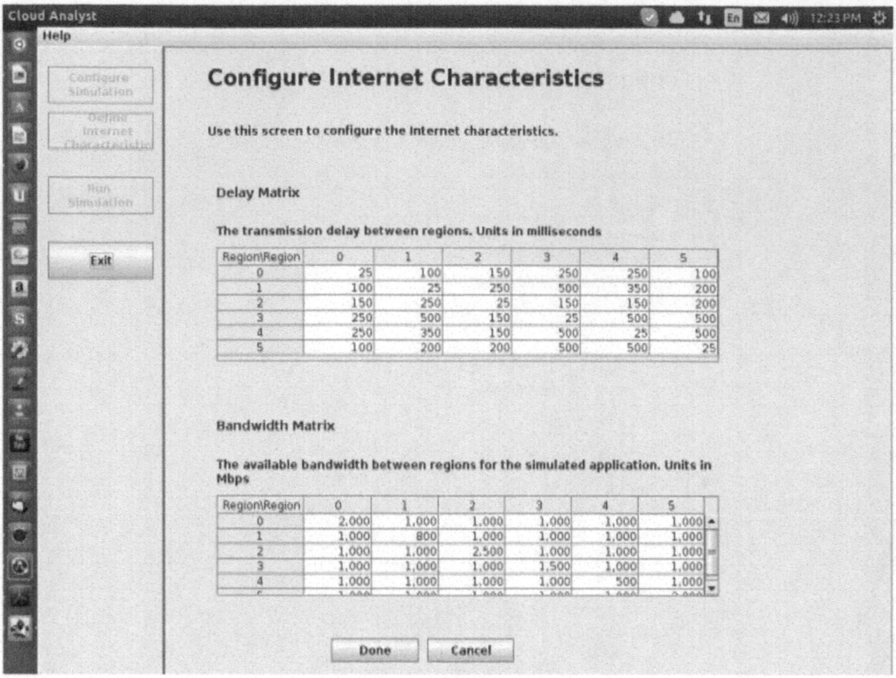

FIGURE 9.5　Configuration internet characteristics screen.

9.7　ALGORITHM IMPLEMENTATION

Cloud is a novel technique in Information Technology (IT) environments with immense infrastructure and resources. The integral aspect of cloud is load balancing. Novel load balancing in cloud computing ensures effective resource utilization. Load balancer has two categories: the static load balancer and the dynamic load balancer. We started our experiments are done through the use of the Cloud Analyst simulator. In the present-day cloud computing environment, in order to provide optimal services to customers in different geographical locations across the globe, a large number of data centers are deployed and made available all over the world and these are accessible through the internet. Every data center in the cloud environment comprises many servers of varied capacities of virtual machines. Each virtual machine can execute multiple tasks depending upon the mapping of its capacity parameters and the needs of the requested tasks.

However, the existing system does not provide the effective scheduling mechanism of the multiple tasks submitted by the customers among the VMs in data centers to achieve reasonable QoS levels. In this research paper, a CSLBA is introduced, which is capable of providing a productive allotment of user tasks on to various available resources with a focus to optimize data center load balancing, minimizing ADCPT, minimizing the AMT, minimizing energy consumption, minimizing cost of data center and minimizing AWT. The Crow Search Based Load Balancing Algorithm Crows are seen being among the world's wisest birds. As a group, crows present

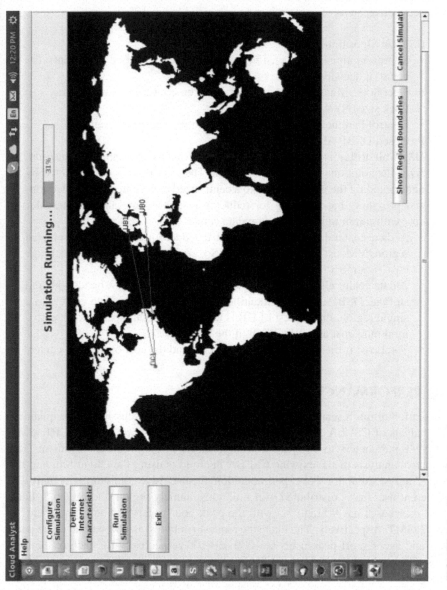

FIGURE 9.6   Simulation running screen.

outstanding illustrations of intellect and score high on knowledge assessments. Crows interact in subtle forms, and can shield and fetch food across seasons. A CSLBA is introduced in this research paper and the capabilities of crows are projected to solve the real-world multimodal scheduling optimization issue in terms of its representation, operators, control parameters, evolutionary mechanism, the performance metric, areas of applications as presented below [35].

A) CSLBA Algorithm
- Representation: D-dimensional search space where d represents the count of decision variables.
- Operators: Maximum number of iterations, awareness probability ( ), flock size (N) & flight length ( ).
- Control Parameters: Awareness probability ( ) & flight length ( ).

B) Proposed DSBP Algorithm
DSBP algorithm is simulated by the Cloud Analyst simulation kit and analyzes the solutions in geographical area. The algorithm is implemented by understanding the issues related to a centralized data center using selection- and proximity-based policy for reducing response time and data transfer cost with minimum work load on data center.
- A data center has an index, called the datacenterindex, in a selected region. VMcost is defined as a p. So, (dcTotalCost = storage*storage cost + memory*memory cost + bandwidth*bandwidthcost).
- A data center also has some parameters such as memory, bandwidth and storage. DSBP algorithm identifies if there are various data centers in a single region, the request of UB is to be executed at a data center with a minimum cost as a proportion of the total cost.
- Total cost is the combination of VM cost and the cost of the data center.

9.8 PERFORMANCE EVALUATION

This section of our research paper presents the result and discussion of the quantitative analysis of CSLBA and our proposed algorithm. Here we have ADCPT, AMT and AWT parameters to compare both algorithms in the cloud environment. The qualitative analysis of the existing CSLBA in cloud is using the Cloud Sim and the Cloud Analyst simulator. For experimentation, the user base configuration comprises 6 different user bases distributed over 6 regions, namely region 0 to region 5. Each of the user bases has 90 requests with the peak hour's start and end times being 6 and 12 GMT, respectively. The data size request (in bytes) is 100 with average peak users and average off-peak users as 1000 and 100 respectively for each of the user bases. The application deployment configuration comprises 6 different data centers, namely DC1–DC6, each having 5 virtual machines (VMs). We describe the parameters in terms of the simulator-like configurations of user, virtual machines (VMs) configuration and data center configuration with several configurations. For efficient performance of both data centers for response time and minimum cost, we test simulations of algorithms with following parameters:

TABLE 9.1
Data center Configuration for DDC

Date center id	Region id	Memory	Storage	Available bandwidth	Num ber of processors	Processor speed
DC1	1	512	1000000	1000	5	1000
DC2	2	512	1000000	1000	5	1000
DC3	3	512	1000000	1000	5	1000
DC4	4	512	1000000	1000	5	1000
DC5	5	512	1000000	1000	5	1000
DC6	6	512	1000000	1000	5	1000

TABLE 9.2
Cost Configuration in DC1-DC6

VM Cost ($)	Memory Cost ($)	Storage Cost ($)	Bandwidth Cost ($)
0.01	0.05	0.01	0.01
No. of VMs = 5	Memory = 512 MB	Images = 10000	Bandwidth = 1000

In Table 9.1, data center are presented from DC1 to DC6, there are six data center with five region ids (1–6) and the physical hardware configurations are presented. Table 9.2 is also showing the internal hardware cost for DC1 to DC6 by using cloud service provider services.

Now we have obtained the average time and average cost according to total response time of UB request and response time of each user given by selected region id. The requirement of accurate time in logistics management is required because each phase of logistics depending on each other for sharing information among the logistics partners and users. Now we tested all the existing algorithms and our proposed algorithm in the centralized and distributed data center environment.

9.9   COMPARATIVE ANALYSIS AND DISCUSSION

In the cloud environment, the experiments on the suggested CSLBA and our proposed DSBP are carried out using two distinct service broker policies, response time (RPT), Data Center Request Servicing Times and data transfer Cost (DTC). This segment of a research paper portrays the result of the experimentation performed.

Performance derived from CSLBA and our proposed DSBP algorithm simulation study presents the results in a cloud-based data center. By using Cloud Analyst, we have already simulated both load-balancing algorithms based on different components to those that are configured in geographical area. The simulated result of graphical user interface (GUI) is analyzed easily after analyzing the compared result of both algorithms' performance by using the Cloud Analyst simulation kit for the all

TABLE 9.3
CSLBA & DSBP for DTC, RT and DCPT

		Distributed Data Center			
Algorithm	DTC	Time	Avg. (ms)	Min (ms)	Max. (ms)
CSLBA	1.27	**RT**	115.15	09.50	3933.74
		DCPT	101.73	0.00	5165.11
DSBP	**0.38**	**RT**	**48.15**	0.00	53.50
		DCPT	1.42	0.00	19.11

the existing and proposed algorithms based on services polices in the cloud environment. After that, the results is evaluated the simulated response time, data center processing time and data transfer cost [36]. After getting these results we have some simulations running screen results for all existing and proposed algorithms. Table 9.3 shows the value representation of some other parameters to identify the load balancing with around 600 users from a multiple UB which are accessed the services simultaneously. The CSLBA and proposed algorithms support these requests simultaneously and give the result.

9.10   CONCLUSION & FUTURE SCOPE

Cloud computing services offers a logistics information system which provides information distribution and storage. In order to provide a solution for the issues in information distribution among the systems, logistics management uses service management of cloud computing. Information management system of logistics in cloud computing which is accountable for collection of information, its execution, distribution, deployment and at the end it concludes to logistics information collaboration.

Hence CSLBA and DSBP give better results in a cloud-based data center environment over the cloud. As a matter of fact, DSBP basically minimizes network congestion, higher latency and cost so that the various problems of multiple Demand of Service in LIS can be efficiently solved. Thus, the DSBP plays a very significant role in filling the gap among different geographical area, enhancing the resource-sharing process maintaining transparency, improving data protection measures, providing security features and subsequently protecting various business applications. Thus, the DSBP algorithm has been implemented by using the Cloud Analyst simulator kit which, in turn, finally analyzes the result graphically. The CSLBA and DSBP are simulated using the CloudSim simulator and then the comparative analysis around the existing load-balancing algorithm is carried out, based on different parameters such as ADCPT, AMT and AWT. The experimental results illustrated that the proposed CSLBA outperformed the ACOLBA for all of the parameters considered for comparison, and thus it can be identified as the optimal load-balancing scheduling algorithm. In future, the proposed CSLBA could be hybridized with other load-balancing meta-heuristic scheduling algorithms to solve the multi-objective scheduling optimization problem. It can be very much implied that cloud computing, which has now been increasingly identified as a technology which will have a remarkable impact on information technology and its related areas in the years to come. However, the Cloud is still in its initial, critical phase and is required to be resolved for the apprehension of the real-world scenario, which is logically depicted and explained by cloud techniques. Load balancing has a critical role to play the apprehension of an open cloud computing federation. In view of the above, this current research study has laid down a solid foundation for the future research work in cloud computing for LIS.

REFERENCES

[1] Mell, P. and T. Grance, The NIST definition of cloud computing. *National Institute of Standards and Technology*, 2009. 53(6): p. 50.
[2] Jadeja, Y. and K. Modi. Cloud computing-concepts, architecture and challenges. in Computing, Electronics and Electrical Technologies (ICCEET), *2012 International Conference on. 2012*. IEEE.
[3] Behl, A. Emerging security challenges in cloud computing: An insight to cloud security challenges and their mitigation. *Information and Communication Technologies (WICT), 2011 World Congress on*. 2011. IEEE.
[4] Hong-Hui, C., Cloud Computing Security Challenges. *Computer Knowledge and Technology*, 2011. 24: p. 014.
[5] Li, J., et al., L-EncDB: A Lightweight Framework for Privacy-Preserving Data Queries in Cloud Computing. *Knowledge-Based Systems*, 2014, 79: pp. 18–26.
[6] Pauliesther, C.M., et al., Towards Secure Cloud Computing Using Digital Signature. *Journal of Theoretical and Applied Information Technology*, 2015. 79(2): pp. 185–190.
[7] Oussalah, M., et al., Job Scheduling in the Expert Cloud based on Genetic Algorithms. *Kybernetes*, 2014. 43(8): pp. 1262–1275.
[8] Pop, F., et al., Deadline Scheduling for Aperiodic Tasks in Inter-Cloud Environments: A New Approach to Resource Management. *The Journal of Supercomputing*, 2014. 71: pp. 1–12.
[9] Dashti, S.E. and A. Masoud Rahmani, A New Scheduling Method for Workflows on Cloud Computing. *International Journal of Advanced Research in Computer Science*, 2015. 6(6).
[10] Calheiros, R.N. and R. Buyya. Energy-Efficient Scheduling of Urgent bag-of-tasks Applications in Clouds Through DVFS. *6th International Conference on Cloud Computing Technology and Science (CloudCom)*. 2014. IEEE.
[11] Gong, L., et al. Study on Energy Saving Strategy and Evaluation Method of Green Cloud Computing System. *Industrial Electronics and Applications (ICIEA), 2013 8th IEEE Conference on. 2013*. IEEE.
[12] Jain, A., et al. Energy Efficient Computing-Green Cloud Computing. *Energy Efficient Technologies for Sustainability (ICEETS), 2013 International Conference on*. 2013. IEEE.
[13] Hsu, C.-H., et al. Energy-aware Task Consolidation Technique for Cloud Computing. *Cloud Computing Technology and Science (CloudCom), 2011 IEEE Third International Conference on*. 2011. IEEE.
[14] Dashti, S.E. and A.M. Rahmani, Dynamic VMs Placement for Energy Efficiency by PSO in Cloud Computing. *Journal of Experimental & Theoretical Artificial Intelligence*, 2015. 28(1–2): pp. 97–112.

[15] Xu, F., et al., Managing Performance Overhead of Virtual Machines in Cloud Computing: A Survey, State of the Art, and Future Directions. *Proceedings of the IEEE*, 2014. 102(1): pp. 11–31.

[16] Nuaimi, K.A., et al. A Survey of Load Balancing in Cloud Computing: Challenges and Algorithms. *Network Cloud Computing and Applications (NCCA), 2012 Second Symposium on*. 2012. IEEE.

[17] Mesbahi, M., A.M. Rahmani, and A.T. Chronopoulos. Cloud Light Weight: A New Solution for Load Balancing in Cloud Computing. in *Data Science & Engineering (ICDSE), 2014 International Conference on*. 2014. IEEE.

[18] Kargar, M.J. and M. Vakili, Load Balancing in MapReduce on Homogeneous and Heterogeneous Clusters: An In-depth Review. *International Journal of Communication Networks and Distributed Systems*, 2015. 15(2–3): pp. 149–168.

[19] Alakeel, A.M., A Guide to Dynamic Load Balancing in Distributed Computer Systems. *International Journal of Computer Science and Information Security*, 2010. 10(6): pp. 153–160.

[20] Askarzadeh, A. A Novel Metaheuristic Method for Solving Constrained Engineering Optimization Problems: Crow Search Algorithm. *Computers and Structures*, vol. 169, no. May, pp. 1–12, 2016.

[21] Behal, V. and A. Kumar. Cloud Computing: Performance Analysis of Load Balancing Algorithms in Cloud Heterogeneous Environment. *Confluence The Next Generation Information Technology Summit (Confluence), 2014 5th International Conference-*. 2014. IEEE.

[22] Ray, S. and A. De Sarkar, Execution Analysis of Load Balancing Algorithms in Cloud Computing Environment. *International Journal on Cloud Computing: Services and Architecture (IJCCSA)*, 2012. 2(5): pp. 1–13.

[23] Randles, M., D. Lamb, and A. Taleb-Bendiab. A Comparative Study Into Distributed Load Balancing Algorithms for Cloud Computing. *Advanced Information Networking and Applications Workshops (WAINA), 2010 IEEE 24th International Conference on*. 2010. IEEE.

[24] Mohapatra, S., K. Smruti Rekha, and S. Mohanty, A Comparison of Four Popular Heuristics for Load Balancing of Virtual Machines in Cloud Computing. *International Journal of Computer Applications*, 2013. 68(6): pp. 33–38.

[25] Wickremasinghe, B. and R. Buyya, Cloud Analyst: A CloudSim-based Tool for Modelling and Analysis of Large Scale Cloud Computing *Distributed. Computing Project CSSE Department University of Melbourne*. 2009. 22(6): pp. 433–659.

[26] Bala, M., Performance Evaluation of Large Scaled Applications using Different Load Balancing Tactics in Cloud Computing. *International Journal of Computer Applications*, 2013. 76(14): pp. 17–22.

[27] Dakshayini, R.P.M.A.M., Service Broker Routing Polices in Cloud Environment: An International Survey. *Journal of Advances in Engineering & Technology (IJAET)* 2014. 6 (6): pp. 2717–2723.

[28] Jaikar, A., G.-R. Kim, and S.-Y. Noh, Effective Data Center Selection Algorithm for a Federated Cloud. *Advanced Science and Technology Letters*, 2013. 35: pp. 66–69.

[29] Limbani, D. and B. Oza, A Proposed Service Broker Strategy in Cloud Analyst for Cost-Effective Data Center Selection. *International Journal of Engineering Research and Applications (IJERA)*, 2012. 2(1): pp. 793–797.

[30] Sharma, V., R. Rathi, and S.K. Bola, Round-Robin Data Center Selection in Single Region for Service Proximity Service Broker in Cloud Analyst. *International Journal of Computers & Technology*, 2013. 4(2a1): pp. 254–260.

[31] Kapgate, D., Weighted Moving Average Forecast Model based Prediction Service Broker Algorithm for Cloud Computing. *IJCSMC*, 2014. 3(2): pp. 71–79.

[32] Wickremasinghe, B. Cloud Analyst: A CloudSim-based Tool for Modelling and Analysis of Large Scale Cloud Computing Environments, 2009.

[33] Howell, F. and R. Macnab, SimJava: A Discrete Event Simulation Library for Java, *Proc. of the 1st International Conference on Web-based Modeling and Simulation*, SCS, Jan. 2008.

[34] Wickremasinghe, Bhathiya, *Cloud Analyst: A CloudSim-based Tool for Modelling and Analysis of Large Scale Cloud Computing Environments, Distributed Computing Project, CSSE Dept*, University of Melbourne, 433–659, July, 2009.

[35] Mishra, Rakesh Kumar, and Bhukya, Sreenu Naik, Service Broker Algorithm for Cloud-Analyst. *International Journal of Computer Science and Information Technologies*, 2014. 5(3): 3957–3962.

[36] Caron Eddy, and Rodero-Merino Luis, Auto-Scaling, Load Balancing and Monitoring in Commercial and Open Source Clouds, Research Report, January 2012.

10 Facts Analysis to Handle the COVID-19 Pandemic Situation in an Efficient Way

Soma Datta

Sister Nivedita University, Newtown, India

Nabendu Chaki

University of Calcutta, Kolkata, India

10.1 INTRODUCTION

Severe acute respiratory syndrome (SARS) was first reported officially for a particular demographic area on December 2019. This syndrome was then reported throughout the world within a very short span of time [1]. It was caused by a RNA virus, called SARS-CoV2 or COVID-19. According to [2] the mutation rate of this virus is quite high, at around 30.53%. 95 full length genomic sequence of SARS-CoV2 were identified at the beginning of the year 2020. Later, more than 2785 different genomic sequences of this virus had been identified up to the beginning of 2021 Nakamichi, Shen, Lee, Lee, Roberts, Simonson, Roychoudhury, Andriesen, Randhawa, Mathias, [3]. This increases the difficulty level of SARS-CoV2 vaccine-related researches. This virus has spread all over the world. The World Health Organization (WHO) declared it as global pandemic on 11 March 2020 [4].

The spreading rate of this virus is much higher than its ancestor SARS-CoV. Some of the strain (genomic variations) of this virus is more infectious than its earlier strain. At the time of writing (1 September 2021), approximately 218.8 million around the globe are reported as COVID-19 positive, of whom 4.6 million people had died (Worldometer Accessed April 21, 2021). As per WHO, to date there is no specific common antivirus agent available for the treatment of all SARS-CoV2 virus strains. Depending on the condition of the patient, the treatment procedure varies. The entire COVID-19 patient pool could be roughly categorized into three groups: the asymptomatic group, the mild condition group and the acute respiratory distress syndrome group. Sometimes, an asymptomatic patient can be treated at home whereas other two groups need special care.

DOI: 10.1201/9781003363606-10

10.1.1 Past Scenario

This section describes the facts those are associated with this COVID-19 pandemic.

10.1.1.1 Transmission Medium

Some evidence has been found, which indicates that COVID-19 may be an airborne disease [5]. However, globally acceptable health organizations such as the WHO, the Centers for Disease Control (CDC), etc. had, at the time of writing (1 May 2021), not yet declared that COVID-19 is an airborne disease.

10.1.1.2 Limitations of Vaccine Technology

The different genomic sequences of this SARS-CoV2 virus have been found in different demographic areas and the mutation rate of this virus is very high [6, 7]. Thus, it is very difficult to prepare a vaccine that will act upon most of the different genomic sequences of this virus [8]. At present, almost all publicly available vaccine acts as an immunity buster but this does not ensure that the virus will not attack WHO (Accessed May 14, 2021a). This indicates that we may have to face multiple waves (surge) of this SARS-CoV2 virus attack Abdool Karim and de Oliveira (2021); Pilz, Chakeri, Ioannidis, Richter, Theiler-Schwetz, Trummer, Krause, and Allerberger (2021) in the near future. Wearing masks along with being fully vaccinated are the protective measures; those we have to adopt.

10.1.1.3 Adverse Effects of Protective Measures

Wearing a face mask outdoors or even indoors is the most effective armor to protect from COVID-19 virus attack. However, wearing a N95 respirator or surgical face mask for a long duration can, in itself, result in many adverse effects. For example, The frequency of mouth breathing increases. This may alter the pattern of breathing and may also change the respiratory milieu. Sometimes, airway symptoms have also been observed due to wearing a N95 respirator for a long duration (that is, more than three hours a day) [9, 10]; Radhakrishnan, Sudarsan, Raj, and Krishnamoorthy 2021).

In parallel with the COVID-19 pandemic, depression becomes another silent epidemic that is not happening in the limelight (Ravens-Sieberer, Kaman, Erhart, Devine, Schlack, and Otto 2021). Children to adults, all age groups are victimized more or less. Increasing aggression in the child age groups is the reflection of their feelings of insecurity. They are addicted to computer or mobile games to reduce their levels of anxiety. The condition of underprivileged children group is even more miserable since they do not have the infrastructure to attend online classes, or to talk with friends and teachers (Egan, Pope, Moloney, Hoyne, and Beatty 2021). Adults are also anxious about their future and family (Usher, Durkin, and Bhullar 2020).

It is a matter of hope that a considerable number of European countries are able to reduce daily COVID-19 positive cases (Worldometer Accessed April 21, 2021). They have revoked some restrictions upon their citizens such as night curfew etc.

10.1.1.4 Revoking of Restrictions Causes Surges in Pandemic

In India, the second wave of this pandemic proved devastating. In the first week of May 2021, the situation was almost out of control in the capital of India and other most important cities. The situation was very chaotic. The physician community of India has warned of the situation regarding the second wave but the government has not taken sufficient precautionary steps to tackle the second wave. Within this pandemic situation, the government conducts a lot of state-level elections. During the election, different political parties made an uncountable number of public gatherings and rallies to establish their influence. Some of the public gatherings and rallies were crowded with more than 0.4 million people (INDIA TODAY accessed May 14, 2021a). As a consequence, the pandemic situation becomes uncontrollable in some areas in India. International support is required to tackle this chaotic situation. The Madras high court (in India) has accused the election commission (a government body that conducts elections in India), in this regard THE WIRE (Accessed May 14, 2021); INDIA TODAY (Accessed May 14, 2021b).

Hence, it is a matter of a long time span when COVID-19 becomes an endemic disease from a pandemic disease. Hence, we have to deal with future surges of this pandemic. Research articles show different influencing factors of this pandemic situation [11–13] it is a multidimensional challenge. It is tough enough to locate the most influential factors that need to be addressed in order to reduce the vulnerability of the pandemic situation.

10.2 METHODS

The entire methodology section is divided into three consecutive parts. In the first part, a Cybernetic Influence Diagram (CID) is used to determine the major influencing factors of this pandemic situation. In the second part, a specific influence factor (obtained from the first part) is analyzed in more detail with empirical data. The third part describes an outline of the household system which may reduce the probability of COVID-19 infection transmission from outdoor to indoor.

10.2.1 Determining the Major Influencing Factors

At the time of analyzing a problem, our cognitive analytical skill becomes confused when the number of interlinked influencing parameters of the problem increases. In such a situation, system thinking tools are used to analyze the problem. The use of system thinking tools began 1956. A number of revolutions have been observed in existing system thinking tools and in addition to this very many new tools have been developed to strengthen the power of system thinking. The Cybernetic Influence diagram (CID) [14–16] is one of such tools. The crude form of this tool was developed by Tata Consultancy Service Ltd. in 2011. CID is a directed graph with nodes and edges. Each directed edge denotes the influences between two factors (node). Consider a CID with an edge and two nodes (influencing factors). If there is a proportional influence upon the destination node (factor) by the source node then the connected edge should show the positive symbol; this can be considered to be the weight of the directed edge. If there is an inversely proportional influence by the source node on the destination node then there should be a negative symbol upon the directed edge. In the case of a circuit in the CID, all symbols of the directed edges in a circuit must not be the same. This would indicate infinity gain; which indicates instability. CID assists to find all influencing factors (including missing factors) along with influence; this ultimately helps to model the problem.

Figure 10.1 shows the major influencing factors associated with "New COVID-19 cases" using CID. For the sake of simplicity, not all influencing factors are considered; otherwise, it will be very complex to understand. It is clear from the CID that "New COVID-19 cases" indirectly reduce both economic growth and mental health.

"New COVID-19 cases" are indirectly influenced by "Tightening social gathering rules", "Healthcare expenses for prevention", and "Awareness and personal protection equipment".

As per the CID, "Tightening social gathering rules" cannot be used for a long-term solution; it indicates instability as per CID rules. Consider the circuit "New COVID-19 cases", "Probability of lockdown", "Tightening social gathering rules", and back to "New COVID-19 cases"; apparently, it looks stable because the gain is not infinite. However, if we consider the adjoin circuit "New COVID-19 cases", "Probability of lockdown", "Tightening social gathering rules", "Depression", "Tendency to disobey social gathering rules" and finally "New COVID-19 cases", the gain of this circuit is infinite as per CID rules. So, it indicates instability. All influences of the circuits are also positive; so this indicates instability. Hence, we have to focus on other influences that reduce "New COVID-19 cases" from other directions. Those are "Healthcare expenses for prevention" and "Awareness and personal protection equipment".

10.2.2 ANALYZED THE SELECTED INFLUENCING FACTOR

The "Healthcare expenses for prevention" includes the discovery, manufacturing, and distribution of effective vaccine for COVID-19. At present, almost all publicly available vaccine acts as an immunity buster but does not ensure that the virus will not attack [17]. This indicates that, we have to face multiple waves (surge) of this SARS-CoV2 virus attack [18, 19] in near future.

A considerable number of European countries are able to reduce daily COVID-19 positive cases [20]. It could be assumed that the people of those countries are following the health guidelines provided by the respective government health agencies, these are part of "Awareness and personal protection equipment". The most common guidelines are as follows-

- Wearing of mask and maintain the mask related instructions properly.
- Clean the exposed body part with soap and alcohol based sanitizer for at least 20 second.
- Maintain social distancing.
- Ensure the safety of food items before eating.

In addition to these, some other hidden factors are there to assist in reducing the daily positive cases for those European countries. Table 10.1 shows a sample study for

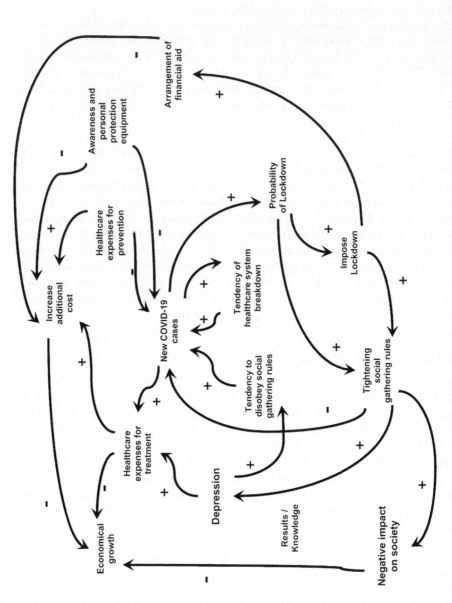

FIGURE 10.1 CID for finding major influencing factors associated with "New COVID-19 cases".

TABLE 10.1

A Sample Study for Those European Countries with Daily COVID-19 Positive Cases and Temperature

Date	France		Italy		Germany	
	New	Temperature	New	Temperature	New	Temperature
	COVID-19 case/day (3 days moving average) Worldometer (Accessed April 21, 2021)	at capital city (Paris) Ac-cuWeather (Accessed July 12, 2020) In degree Celsius	COVID-19 case/day (3 days moving average) Worldometer (Accessed April 21, 2021)	at capital city (Rome) Ac-cuWeather (Accessed July 12, 2020) In Degree Celsius	COVID-19 case/day (3 days moving average) Worldometer (Accessed April 21, 2021)	at capital city (Berlin) Ac-cuWeather (Accessed July 12, 2020) In degree Celsius
10-3-20	278	15	1423	16	255	11
15-3-20	849	17	3213	18	1023	12
20-3-20	1628	17	5172	18	3494	9
25-3-20	3071	13	5073	13	4150	10
30-3-20	3862	11	5078	18	5338	4
5-4-20	3791	23	4569	21	5109	16
10-4-20	4170	26	3996	22	4836	16
15-4-20	3601	21	2931	18	2300	16
20-4-20	1802	23	2930	20	1889	15
25-4-20	1654	22	2674	22	1955	15
30-4-20	414	15	2017	22	1417	19
5-5-20	663	21	1229	24	682	12
10-5-20	428	23	1071	27	817	24
20-5-20	478	29	643	26	626	21
30-5-20	1916	26	510	20	467	18
10-6-20	386	21	255	22	213	22
20-6-20	639	25	282	29	570	20
30-6-20	448	22	147	30	381	24
10-7-20	647	25	228	33	411	25
30-7-20	1092	33	284	38	758	23
21-8-20	4108	23	810	36	1639	22
10-9-20	7810	21	1469	33	1494	18
30-9-20	7810	20	1670	23	2191	15
20-10-20	19879	15	10694	18	6388	12
10-11-20	27141	12	31203	16	15720	8
30-11-20	8244	11	21209	13	14146	2
20-12-20	14401	10	16508	15	25449	1
20-1-21	17497	5	18809	10	20009	3
31-1-21	20797	7	12512	15	10364	-1

two European countries. This table shows daily new COVID-19 positive cases with respect to the temperature of the capital of those countries. The data are collected from World-O-Meters [21] and AccuWeather website AccuWeather [22].

This data pattern gives a hazy idea that when the "moving average" of environmental temperature is gradually increasing then the daily new COVID-19 positive cases are decreasing. It may, of course, be a combined effect of health guidelines and the increase in environmental temperature. It could be argued that if this is the case then why do tropical regions (comparatively warm weather) have a considerably large number of COVID-19 positive cases. The lack of consciousness about health guidelines and high population density are the major reasons behind the new positive cases in tropical regions.

10.2.2.1   Evidence 1

As per the WHO document, SARS-CoV2 could not survive beyond 56^0C WHO (Accessed July 14, 2020). That means increasing environmental temperatures creates an adverse condition to SARS-CoV2 [23].

10.2.2.2   Evidence 2

Table 10.2 shows a comparative study of the COVID-19 daily infection rate per million between India and Nepal. India and Nepal are two neighboring countries which share a lot of cultural and behavioral similarities. However, the main difference between these two countries is the climate, since India is much warmer than Nepal. Table 10.2 shows the hike in daily infection rate per million population (at the time of the second wave of COVID-19 in Indian subcontinent) [24], [25]. There are a lots of political gatherings that have been organized in India from March 21 to May 21 for state-level elections which have influenced the daily infection rate [26, 27]. In Nepal, the general election is due to be held next year. Thus, the political gathering is not an issue for a hike in the daily infection rate for Nepal. At present, the daily infection rate per million population of Nepal exceeds the daily infection rate in India. There is a high chance that the change in the daily infection rate is influenced by low temperature.

TABLE 10.2
Comparative Study of the COVID-19 Daily Infection Rate Per Million Between India and Nepal

Date	Daily Infection Rate per million in Nepal	Daily InfectionRate per million in India
11-5-21	309	288
2-5-21	241	265
21-4-21	75	226
10-4-21	10	110
30-3-21	5	52

10.2.2.3 Evidence 3

According to earlier WHO guidelines COVID-19 was not an airborne disease; it spreads only through droplets [28]. However, this statement has been challenged by several groups of scientists. Thereafter, the WHO partially changed its guideline [29]. It can be thought that the floating particles in the air may transport the virus over long distances. If the virus survives in the floating particles of the air, then it is clear that the environmental temperature has an impact upon the spreading of this virus.

Hence, there is a chance of COVID-19 surge after the end of the summer season.

10.2.3 Managing Mechanism to Reduce Spreading Rate of COVID-19

The availability of a successful vaccine or the discovery of proper drugs that are dedicated to this disease could provide a permanent solution to the pandemic. However, the availability of these permanent solutions are uncertain. Hence, for this time being we have to depend on the time being temporary safety solutions to reduce the potential danger of future surges of the pandemic.

One article shows that SARS-CoV2 virus spreads through droplets and also from aerosol emissions from the nose or mouth of the infected person [30, 31]. It shows that in some situations, an outdoor environment is safer than an indoor environment with poor ventilation [32].

In the next subsequent section, we will discuss the necessity of different household systems and provide a guideline for future household systems that need to be developed to reduce the spreading of the new strains of SARS-CoV2 virus at the end of the summer season.

In the subsequent sections, we will discuss the functionality and provide a guideline for the future household systems which are needed to be developed to reduce the spreading of the new strains of SARS-CoV2 virus at the end of the summer season. Future household systems need to be developed to address the following matters:

- Disinfect the personal belongings, necessary for outdoor use, like winter clothing.
- Modify the room air conditioning system to reduce the density of infectious aerosol particles.
- Design the next-generation outdoor mask or respirator to reduce stresses on the lungs.
- Wearable smart devices for health condition tracking for COVID-19 patients and estimate the risk factors.
- Blending the real-time "Augmented Reality" features with modern home fitness equipment to reduce mental and physical tresses.

In this document, we provide some hypothetical models for the selected systems mentioned above. Some technical details are also given. These details are important for the physical implementation of these devices.

10.2.4   THE HOUSEHOLD HEALTH SAFETY SYSTEMS TO DISINFECT OUTDOOR CLOTHES

The wearing of masks may protect us in outdoor settings but clothes may carry this virus around in our homes, where we are generally not using masks. It is difficult to disinfect outdoor clothes (particularly winter clothes) on a daily basis.

10.2.4.1   Present Household Disinfection Systems for Clothes and Personal Belongings

Household disinfecting systems have a great impact in this regard. At present, a lot of standard and nonstandard household systems are available in the market to disinfect belongings. Most of them are UV-based with poor safety measures. Only UV-C (100–280 nm) with a proper intensity level can kill this type of virus [32]. But this C-type UV is dangerous for human eyes. UV also acts as a stimulant for mutation [31], that may lead to skin carcinoma. WHO does not recommend UV for sanitization [30].

Furthermore, the UV-C-based system cannot disinfect the wrinkle and floppy fur portion of clothes. So, thermal-based systems are suitable to disinfect outdoor clothes (especially winter clothes). Samsung AirDresser is an expensive device that can disinfect clothes through the use of steam. It works like a "German steam iron" in a closed chamber. The main drawback of this system is that it uses steam; if steam is used on unclean clothes then it fixes the dust particles permanently on the outer surface of the clothes.

10.2.4.2   The Outline of Household Health Safety Systems to Disinfect Outdoor Clothes

When designing household systems to disinfect clothes using thermal energy the following factors should be borne in mind:

(1) The mode of transmission of heat should be convection; otherwise un-uniform heating may damage the clothes.
(2) The quantity of heat generation should be controlled in such a way that the surface temperature of the target object should be greater than $70^0 C$ and less than the tolerance temperature of the targeted material.
(3) The disinfection process should be confined in a closed area with minimum air circulation. Thermal blower (like hair dryer) cannot be used for this purpose. It may blow the virus into room air.

As an example, an outline of the winter clothes disinfection system is discussed in this subsection. This system should be deployed within a small separated wardrobe, placed near the main door. The block diagram of the system is shown in Figure 10.2.

In this figure, the dark lined box denotes the periphery of the closed wardrobe. Inside this, a an article of winter clothing is hanging upon a specially designed hollow hanger. The three red circles denote three low-speed air blowers which are connected with the specialized hollow hanger. These three blowers receive hot air from

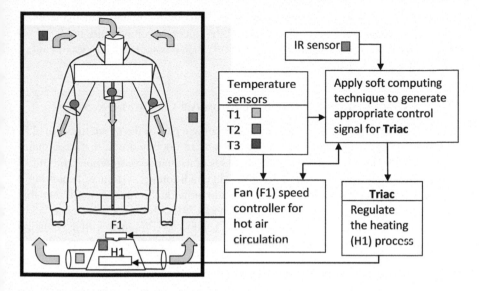

FIGURE 10.2   Block diagram of the proposed conceptual system.

the inlet (near the top of the hanger) portion and project the hot air in the inner side of the cloth. There are three temperature sensors marked with three different green shades. These are denoted by T1, T2 and T3. The blue solid arrows denote the direction of hot air flow. H1 is a heater to heat the air. The heating process is precisely controlled by the control unit via Triac. F1 denotes a fan. Its speed can be controlled by a separate speed controller. This F1 is used to control the volume of hot air within the closed wardrobe. The orange square near the H1 is an IR sensor. It is used to measure the heat radiation level of the heating coil. It acts as a sensor to take feedback at the time of generating control signal for H1. In this method, the convection mode of heat transmission is used. The heating arrangement is placed at the bottom of the wardrobe for this mode of heat transmission. The operational workflow of the system would be as follows:

(1) Place the winter clothes upon the specialized hanger and close the wardrobe.
(2) When the system starts up, it sends a precise control signal to the Triac to start the heater (H1).
(3) The T1 sensor, the IR sensor and speed of the F1 are organized in such a way that the emitting hot air temperature (t) from the heating module should lie in between $70^0 < t < threshold$.
(4) By following the principle of convection, the hot air will be deposited in the top portion of the closed wardrobe.
(5) When T3 senses the preferred ambient temperature then it starts the blowers. It is marked with a red circle in Figure 10.2.
(6) When T2 senses the threshold temperature, the heater (H1) and fan (F1) are controlled in such a way that the temperature which is sensed by all the sensors should not exceed the threshold.

The selection of the *threshold* temperature depends on the material of the clothes. Cotton can tolerate 220°C whereas for wool the tolerance temperature is 150°C [4] Hence, if the tolerance temperature is set to 80°C then it is safe for all types of clothes and it is also able to disinfect the clothes.

10.2.5 UP-GRADATION OF INDIVIDUAL ROOM AIR CONDITIONING SYSTEM

Today, room air conditioning systems have become a part of the urban lifestyle [29]. In winter, room air heating and in summer room air cooling are desirable in maintaining comfort levels. Both of these processes consume a considerable amount of energy. Energy optimization in individual air conditioning system is becoming a major concern. These lead to poor ventilation in individual rooms. A study says that poor ventilation increases the spreading of the COVID-19 virus [12]. Hence, additional AI-controlled room ventilation systems need to be combined with the existing individual room air conditioning systems.

10.2.5.1 The Outline of AI-based Room Ventilator System

The design of an AI-based indoor room ventilation system to increase the quality of room air should include the following properties:

- Inlet and outlet ventilators point should be placed far away from each other. The inlet point should fetch fresh air from the outdoors.
- Both outlet and inlet air should be treated by C-type UV.
- The AI-based system would accelerate the air exchange process when the temperature difference between the outdoor and the preferred indoor air temperature is at a minimum. This would optimize energy usage.
- The air filter of the air conditioning system should be disinfected automatically at periodic intervals. Proper use of static electricity increases the performance of the air filter.
- When the room is not in use, the air ventilator would work at full capacity.

10.2.6 DESIGN OF NEXT GENERATION MASK

Masks with a higher filtration capacity (N95-N100) are essential for use in the healthcare domain. This type of mask uses different fiber layers as a barrier against the tiny particles. This process creates resistance at the time of inhalation and exhalation. Wearing this type of mask for a long time increases stresses upon lungs and creates feelings of discomfort.

The next-generation mask should be designed in such a way that it reduces the resistance at the time of inhalation and exhalation, without compromising safety. Mechanical arrangement with chemicals may be effective in this circumstance. Preliminary work has begun to do this. However, the acceleration of the progress to carry out these works on urgent basis is required.

10.3 RESULTS

On the basis of discovered facts (Section 10.2.2), a hypothetical conclusion could be established. This suggests that there is a high chance that this COVID-19 pandemic situation will stay for a long time with multiple surges. These surges have a relation with the environmental temperature. Hence, the threats of pandemic will be around for a long time. This increases the difficulty levels of physical and mental struggles. Within this chapter, the discussion is not restricted within the boundary of establishing this hypothetical conclusion. We also focus on the outline of the future research and development trends (Section 10.2.4–10.2.6) for household healthcare systems.

10.4 CONCLUSION

It is a matter of time when COVID-19 morphs from a pandemic disease to an endemic disease. Until this comes about, we have to face multiple surges of this disease. If the situation grows out of control, then a 'lockdown'-like painful solution will have to be adopted, which has an adverse effect on the economy. Hence, a large number of studies are required for different household systems to control the spread of this disease in parallel with research in medical science. In this document, the outline of some conceptual models has been discussed to combat the COVID-19 pandemic situation. The physical implementation will requires a large amount of research. As an example, in this outdoor winter clothing disinfecting system, the synchronization among different computing and control unit Petri Net model is useful [26]. This document gives a direction for product-based research to reduce the effect of a COVID-19 surge in upcoming days.

ACKNOWLEDGEMENT(S)

The authors would like to thank Dr. Biswajit Modak for giving us relevant domain knowledge.

DISCLOSURE STATEMENT

Not Applicable

CONFLICT OF INTEREST

Authors state that there is no conflict of interest.

FUNDING

No funding has been received.

REFERENCES

[1] Tanu Singhal. A review of coronavirus disease-2019 (covid-19). *The Indian Journal of Pediatrics*, 1–6, 2020.

[2] Changtai Wang, Zhongping Liu, Zixiang Chen, Xin Huang, Mengyuan Xu, Tengfei He, and Zhenhua Zhang. The establishment of reference sequence for sars-cov-2 and variation analysis. *Journal of medical virology*, 92(6):667–674, 2020.

[3] WHO. *First data on stability and resistance of SARS coronavirus compiled by members of WHO laboratory network*, Accessed July 14, 2020. URL https://www.who.int/csr/sars/ survival 2003 05 04/en/.

[4] Worldometer. *COVID-19 Coronavirus Pandemic*, Accessed April 21, 2021. URL https://www.worldometers.info/coronavirus/.

[5] R Karthik, R Menaka, M Hariharan, and GS Kathiresan. AI for COVID-19 detection from radiographs: Incisive analysis of state of the art techniques, key challenges and future directions. *IRBM*, 43(5):486–510, 2022.

[6] Tommaso Celeste Bulfone, Mohsen Malekinejad, George W Rutherford, and Nooshin Razani. Outdoor transmission of sars-cov-2 and other respiratory viruses: a systematic review. *The Journal of Infectious Diseases*, 223(4):550–561, 2021.

[7] Wenzhao Chen, Nan Zhang, Jianjian Wei, Hui-Ling Yen, and Yuguo Li. Short-range airborne route dominates exposure of respiratory infection during close contact. *Building and Environment*, 176:106859, 2020.

[8] Suzanne M Egan, Jennifer Pope, Mary Moloney, Clara Hoyne, and Chlóe Beatty. Missing early education and care during the pandemic: The socio-emotional impact of the covid-19 crisis on young children. *Early Childhood Education Journal*, 1–10, 2021.

[9] SS Abdool Karim, and T de Oliveira. New SARS-CoV-2 variants-clinical, public health, and vaccine implications. *The New England Journal of Medicine*, 384(19):1866–1868, 2021.

[10] P Ghosh, D Bhattacharjee, and M Nasipuri. Intelligent toilet system for non-invasive estimation of blood-sugar level from urine. *IRBM*, 41(2):94–105, 2020.

[11] P Ghosh, D Bhattacharjee, and M Nasipuri. Dynamic diet planner: A personal diet recommender system based on daily activity and physical condition. *IRBM*, 42(6):442–456, 2021.

[12] Trisha Greenhalgh, Jose L Jimenez, Kimberly A Prather, Zeynep Tufekci, David Fisman, and Robert Schooley. Ten scientific reasons in support of airborne transmission of sars-cov-2. *The Lancet*, 397(10285):1603–1605, 2021.

[13] INDIA TODAY. *Madras HC holds Election Commission responsible for 2nd Covid wave, says officials should be booked for murder*, Accessed May 14, 2021. URL https://www.indiatoday.in/india/story /madras-hc-election-commission-covid-wave-officials-booked-murder-1795082-2021-04-26.

[14] Ironing Lab. *The Best Steam Iron Advice and Reviews*, Accessed May 14, 2021. URL https://ironinglab.com/.

[15] Supriya Kummamuru and Narayana Mandaleeka. Modeling the business system by applying cybernetic concepts. In *2016 IEEE Conference on Norbert Wiener in the 21st Century (21CW)*, 1–6. IEEE, 2016.

[16] Kwok-Hung Chan, JS Malik Peiris, SY Lam, LLM Poon, KY Yuen, and Wing Hong Seto. The effects of temperature and relative humidity on the viability of the SARS coronavirus. *Advances in Virology*, 2011:734690, 2011.

[17] K Mackenzie and Hermann Joseph Muller. Mutation effects of ultra-violet light in drosophila. *Proceedings of the Royal Society of London. Series B-Biological Sciences*, 129(857):491–517, 1940.

[18] Kenji Nakamichi, Jolie Z Shen, Cecilia S Lee, Aaron Lee, Emma A Roberts, Paul D Simonson, Pavitra Roychoudhury, Jessica Andriesen, April K Randhawa, Patrick C Mathias, et al. Hospitalization and mortality associated with sars-cov-2 viral clades in covid-19. *Scientific Reports*, 11(1):1–11, 2021.

[19] Stefan Pilz, Ali Chakeri, John PA Ioannidis, Lukas Richter, Verena Theiler-Schwetz, Christian Trummer, Robert Krause, and Franz Allerberger. Sars-cov-2 re-infection risk in Austria. *European Journal of Clinical Investigation*, 51(4):e13520, 2021.

[20] Nandhini Radhakrishnan, Shyam Sudhakar Sudarsan, K Deepak Raj, and Srinivasan Krishnamoorthy. Clinical audit on symptomatology of covid-19 healthcare workers and impact on quality-of-life (QoL) due to continuous facemask usage: A prospective study. *Indian Journal of Otolaryngology and Head & Neck Surgery*, 1–8, 2021.

[21] Veerendra K Rai and Sanjit Mehta. Systems approach to as-is state formation of an engagement: A case study illustration. In *2012 IEEE International Systems Conference SysCon 2012*, 1–6. IEEE, 2012.

[22] Ulrike Ravens-Sieberer, Anne Kaman, Michael Erhart, Janine Devine, Robert Schlack, and Christiane Otto. Impact of the covid-19 pandemic on quality of life and mental health in children and adolescents in Germany. *European Child & Adolescent Psychiatry*, 1–11, 2021.

[23] Kim Usher, Joanne Durkin, and Navjot Bhullar. The covid-19 pandemic and mental health impacts. *International Journal of Mental Health Nursing*, 29(3):315, 2020.

[24] WHO. *Getting the COVID-19 Vaccine*, Accessed May 14, 2021a. URL https://www. who.int/news-room /feature-stories/detail/getting-the-covid-19-vaccine.

[25] WHO. *Modes of transmission of virus causing COVID-19: implications for IPC precaution recommendations*, Accessed May 14, 2021b. URL https://www.who.int/news-room/ commentaries/detail/modes-of-transmission-of-virus-causingcovid-19-implications-for-ipc-precaution-recommendations.

[26] WHO. *Raising awareness on ultraviolet radiation*, Accessed May 14, 2021c. URL https://www.who.int/activities /raising-awareness-on-ultraviolet-radiation.

[27] WHO. *Transmission of SARS-CoV-2: implications for infection prevention precautions*, Accessed July 9, 2022. URL https://www.who.int/publications/i/item/modes-of-transmission-of-virus-causing-covid-19-/implications-for-ipc-precaution-recommendations.

[28] World Health Organization et al. Virtual press conference on covid-19-11 March 2020. *Last accessed*, 25, 2020.

[29] World Health Organization et al. Evaluation of covid-19 vaccine effectiveness: interim guidance, 17 March 2021. Technical report, World Health Organization, 2021.

[30] Zhixiang Xie, Yaochen Qin, Yang Li, Wei Shen, Zhicheng Zheng, and Shirui Liu. Spatial and temporal differentiation of covid-19 epidemic spread in mainland china and its influencing factors. *Science of The Total Environment*, 744:140929, 2020.

[31] Zaria Gorvett, BBC. *Theres only one type of UV that can reliably inactivate covid-19 and it's extremely dangerous*. Accessed July 14, 2020. URL https://www.bbc.com/future/article/20200327-can-you-kill-coronavirus-with-uv-light.

[32] Jian Hua Zhu, Shu Jin Lee, DY Wang, and HP Lee. Effects of long-duration wearing of n95 respirator and surgical facemask: a pilot study. *Journal of Lung, Pulmonary & Respiratory Research*, 4:97–100, 2014.

11 Experimental and Computational Investigation of Acoustic Erosion in C$_2$H$_5$OH

Vipulkumar Rokad

KSV University, Gandhinagar, India

Divyang Pandya

LDRP Institute of Technology & Research, Gandhinagar, India

Pavan Bhatt

VPMP Polytechnic, Gandhinagar, India

11.1 INTRODUCTION

Vibro Cleaner is developed using the pressure acoustic transient technique. In this, the walls of the tank react as a transient between the piezoelectric transducer and the solvent [1, 2]. As a source of ultrasound, a piezoelectric transducer PZT4 with 40 kHz frequency [3] has been stuck at the outer bottom surface of a tank which transmits electronic signals toward mechanical vibrations and then pressure acoustic waves into liquid media through tank wall transience [4]. The positive and negative pressure phase difference generates cavitation bubbles called blisters [5, 6]. These bubbles strike over the surface of an object which needs to be cleaned. In the presence of acoustophoretic and drag forces, it reacts fatigue-like damage with contaminations on the surface of the part [7, 8]. The erosion phenomenon is the motion study of particles with particle trajectories of turbulence fluid flow [8]. Repetitive interaction of fluid particles to the contaminations of the object surface, Erosive wear acts and removes sticky contaminations from the surface of parts [9]. The properties of the solvent are another affecting factor that improves the efficiency of the cleaning process by adding chemical like reactions. This acoustic cleaning is most suitable for the removal of dust, rust, oil and other sticky adhesives from the object surface. This investigation is especially developed for the cleaning of small critical components such as jewelry, ornaments, coins, electronic components, disk drives and watch parts etc. using low quantities of solvents [1, 2].

DOI: 10.1201/9781003363606-11

11.2 TECHNICAL BACKBONE

11.2.1 PIEZOELECTRICITY

Piezoelectricity is a phenomenon that converts mechanical stress into electrical charges by means of crystal. In the presence of an electrical field, the crystal stretches in its length. When mechanical stress is excreted, the crystal geometry shows dipole moments to generate net polarization. Thus, the electric field reacts as proportional to the stress applied. This is known as the generator effect called the direct piezoelectric effect [6].

$$S_i = S_{ij}^E T_j + d_{mi} E_{in} \tag{11.1}$$

$$D_n = d_{nj} T_j + \varepsilon_{nm}^T E_{in} \tag{11.2}$$

11.2.2 SOLID–LIQUID INTERFACE

In an ultrasonic cleaning tank, sound waves produced from the piezoelectric transducer are reflected into the liquid by means of tank wall transient. The standing wave is produced as a result. When the piezoelectric transducer is stuck at the outer bottom surface of the tank, a positive direction – x – is taken toward the surface of planar liquid from the tank bottom [4–6]. As a result, reflected waves from a liquid surface are expressed as follows:

$$p_i = p_{a,i} \sin\left(-kx + \omega t\right) \tag{11.3}$$

$$p_r = -p_{a,i} \sin\left(kx + \omega t\right) \tag{11.4}$$

11.2.3 BUBBLE FORMATION

When ultrasound intensity exceeds the tensile strength of the medium, this leads to the formation of large number of small voids or cavities having empty spaces called cavitation bubbles [10]. The critical pressure (PB) required to form a cavity with radius Re is as follows:

$$P_B \sim P_H + \frac{0.77\sigma}{Re} \tag{11.5}$$

11.2.4 BUBBLE GROWTH

When the cavitation bubble is much bigger than the original nucleus, the effect of viscosity, non- condensable gas, and surface tension becomes negligible. Thus, the simplified Rayleigh equation has been applied as when $P_{inf} < P_v$. [10].

$$\dot{R} \cong \sqrt{\frac{2}{3} \frac{p_v - p_\infty}{\rho}} \tag{11.6}$$

11.2.5 BUBBLE COLLAPSE

A bubble violently collapses after expanding during the ultrasound rarefaction effect, when the bubble radius reaches a critical stage [11]. When the bubble collapses, the Rayleigh-Plesset equation is expressed with bubble wall acceleration as below.

$$\ddot{R} = -\frac{3R^2}{2R} + \frac{1}{\rho_0 R}\left[p_g + p_v - \frac{2\sigma}{R} - \frac{4\mu R}{R} - p_0 - p_s(t) \right] \tag{11.7}$$

When a bubble collapses violently and $\dot{R}^2$ increases, the first term on the right-hand side becomes dominant and the second term becomes negligible. So, the equation becomes [10]:

$$\ddot{R} \approx -\frac{3\dot{R}^2}{2R} \tag{11.8}$$

11.2.6 EROSION PHENOMENON

Erosion is the operation of material loss and surface scour due to the cavitation effect. Cavitation erosion is time-dependent and fatigue-like damage. Material degradation terminology is blanketed by means of the ASTM G-40 standard related to erosion done by the cavitation effect. In step with the ASTM G-32 standard, a mean depth of the erosion is the average thickness of material eroded from a specified facet space, typically, calculated by the average material loss and dividing that by means of density and specified surface area of the material [12, 13].

$$MDE = \frac{\Delta m}{(\rho * A)} \tag{11.9}$$

The Mean Depth of Penetration Rate (MDPR) is the rate of average eroded material volume loss per unit surface area with respect to time. MDPR is inversely proportional to the ultimate resilience of the material. It is related to imply intensity of abrasion penetration [14]:

$$MDPR = \frac{MDE}{t} \tag{11.10}$$

11.3 COMPUTATIONAL MODEL AND SIMULATION

For computations investigation, a computational model is prepared using 2D axisymmetric in COMSOL Multiphysics software. The cylindrical-shaped tank of size 170 mm diameter x 95 mm height with 1 mm wall thickness has been used to study the conceptual principle of Vibro Cleaning and the effect of different solvents on the erosion rate. The 40 kHz frequency PZT4 piezoelectric transducer has been used with 230 V.

Multiple modules of COMSOL Multiphysics have been coupled to accumulate the paramount results. Here, the acoustic module has been coupled with the CFD module to achieve significant solutions for the research. The acoustic module operates considering various phases, including pressure acoustic-transient, solid mechanics–linear elastic, and electrostatics whereas the CFD module operates considering terms like turbulence fluid drift in the environment of the bubbly waft k-ε model and fluid glide particle-tracing having various erosion modules. Fluid flow particle-tracing indicates the kinetics of fluid particles and also particle interaction with objects for achieving the erosive cleaning rate [15, 16]. Here, solvents like C_2H_5OH also known as ethanol and water have been chosen as cleaning media in the computational model to study the efficiency of the cleaning process. PZT-4 transducer is annexed on the outer bottom surface of the tank wall that transmits electronic signals into the sound waves. Because of this sound stain impact, the tank wall surface vibrates perpetually which creates a pressure phase distinction of poor and superb to get acoustic stress waves by means of cavitating bubbles. These cavitating bubbles hit and explode on the part surface, which requires it to be unsullied. The facet of the component is cleaned because of the perpetuated bombing of diminutive cavities (Table 11.1).

Meshing is also crucial and paramount in achieving stringent results for wave generation. Here, COMSOL default meshing method extra-fine has been culled. It includes the biggest and smallest element sizes of 2 and 0.1 respectively. In summary, the magnification rate is 1.3 considering the curvature effect of 0.6. The resolution of the slender vicinity is taken as 0.2. Refer to Figure 11.1 (a) for the geometric model and Figure 11.1(b), for the mesh model [15].

For the simulation, COMSOL Multiphysics-5.3a is utilized [15]. The investigation of sound waves and acoustic waves are accumulated by applying frequency domain to investigate the replications of a legitimate stress level in a stress transient-acoustic module. The materials, stainless steel as a tank and mild steel as an object, have been set as solid domains with solvent as a fluid domain. The piezoelectric transducer is set into the electrostatic term to transform piezoelectric signals into acoustic properties. Here, bubbly fluid flow is utilized to get turbulence acoustic streaming with a solver-stationary that responds to the kinetics of fluid in congruous ways. The module-particle tracing is used for the motion of particle trajectories in fluid motion flow utilizing solver-time depended. The erosion rate has been found

TABLE 11.1
Properties of Materials

Parameters	Stainless Steel	Mild Steel
Density (kg/m)	8000	7850
Young's modulus (Pa)	20.3×10^{10}	21×10^{10}
Poisson's Ratio	0.27	0.30
Bulk modulus (Pa)	15.1×10^{10}	14×10^{10}
Shear modulus (Pa)	8.1×10^{10}	7.0×10^{10}

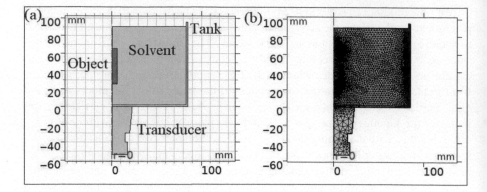

FIGURE 11.1   (a) Geometric model (2D Axisymmetric), (b) Mesh model.

based on particle interaction with the object surface in the circumstances of drag pressure and acoustophoretic-radiation pressure [15, 16].

11.4   EXPERIMENTAL INVESTIGATION

For the experimental investigation, a small cylindrical-shaped tank has been used which is made of stainless steel because of its properties, such as high elasticity, anti-wear and anti-corrosive etc (Table 11.2). To boost the cleaning process more effectively, two different solvents have been advanced: water and ethanol. For research purposes, a two-liter capacity tank has been used. Water is a commonly used solvent, is not harmful to either humans or nature. Ethanol is frequently used for sticky contaminants such as adhesives, oil etc. with disinfection. Refer to Table 11.3 for the properties of solvents.

When power is applied, the transducer attached to the bottom of the tank converts sound waves into mechanical vibration which transfers over the tank wall (Figure 11.2). By means of the tank wall transient, the pressure acoustic waves have been generated into solvents and, due to the cavitation effect, generated bubbles strike over the surface of the object to remove the contaminations.

TABLE 11.2
Specifications of Transducer

Parameters	PZT 4 Transducer
Frequency (kHz)	40
Power (W)	60
Radiating Surface (mm)	45
Length (mm)	55
Density (kg/m^3)	7500
Permittivity Constant	8.854×10^{-12}
Relative Permittivity	$\varepsilon_{T11} = 1475$; $\varepsilon_{T12} = 1475$; $\varepsilon_{T13} = 1300$

TABLE 11.3
Properties of Solvents

Parameters	Water	C_2H_5OH
Density (kg/m³)	8000	785
Speed of Sound (m/s)	1482	1100
Temperature (°C)	20	20
Dynamic Viscosity (Pa*s)	1.0×10^{-3}	1.1×10^{-3}
Kinematic Viscosity (m/s)	1.0×10^{-6}	1.4×10^{-6}
Surface Tension (N/m)	0.079	0.022
Vapour Pressure (Pa)	2.2×10^3	5.3×10^3
Thermo-Conductivity (W/m*K)	0.58	0.014
Specific heat (J/kg*K)	4183	2400
Volume Expansivity (1/K)	207×10^{-6}	1090×10^{-6}

FIGURE 11.2   Experimental set-up.

11.5   RESULTS AND DISCUSSION

In this research, COMSOL Multiphysics software has played a vital role in making CAD models and achieving appropriate simulation results. The erosion rate has been found using two different modules like acoustic and CFD in the presence of two different solvents: water and ethanol. The acoustic module is used to study the acoustic pressure and sound pressure level by cavitation effect while the CFD module has been applied for the investigation of particle trajectories in turbulence fluid flow with spherical wave radiation. The finnie erosion module is coupled to find the erosion rate Figures 11.3 to 11.6).

Simulation results show that, with a frequency of 40 kHz, the acoustic pressure 3.19×10^3 Pa, 2.47×10^3 and sound pressure level 187 dB, 192 dB have been achieved for liquid media water and ethanol respectively. 2D and 3D axisymmetric views are shown for more clarity about the results.

In addition, 7.27×10^4 Pa and 3.1×10^5 Von Mises stresses have been found for water and ethanol respectively (Figure 11.7). For a sonic streaming flow of cavitation bubbles into fluid, the bubbly fluid k-ε model and RANS turbulence are merged to know the motion of particle trajectories and interaction with part surfaces (Figure 11.8).

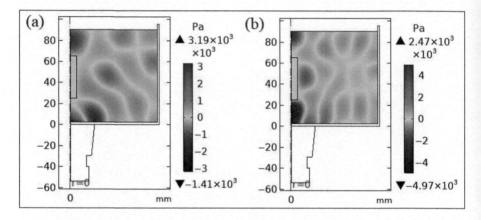

FIGURE 11.3   Acoustic pressure, Pa; (a) Water, (b) C_2H_5OH.

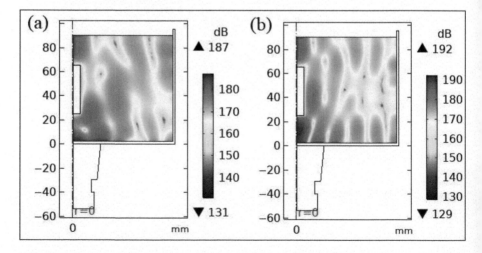

FIGURE 11.4   Sound pressure level, dB; (a) Water, (b) C_2H_5OH.

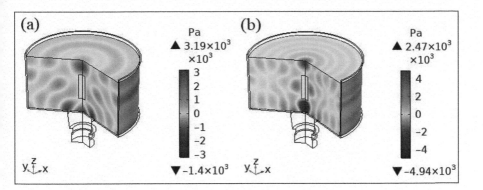

FIGURE 11.5 Acoustic pressure (3D), Pa; (a) Water, (b) C₂H₅OH.

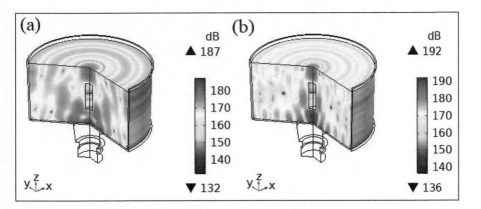

FIGURE 11.6 Sound pressure level (3D), dB; (a) Water, (b) C₂H₅OH.

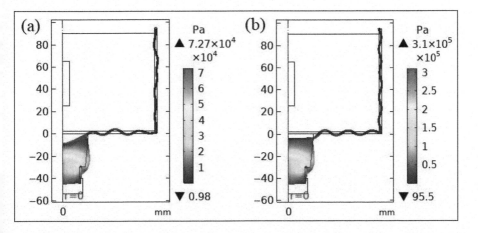

FIGURE 11.7 Von Mises stresses, Pa; (a) Water, (b) C₂H₅OH.

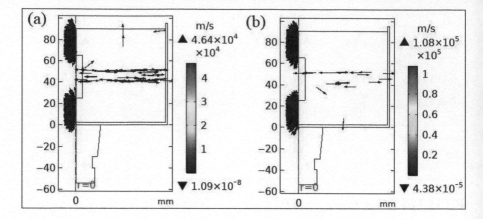

FIGURE 11.8   Particle trajectory; (a) Water, (b) C_2H_5OH.

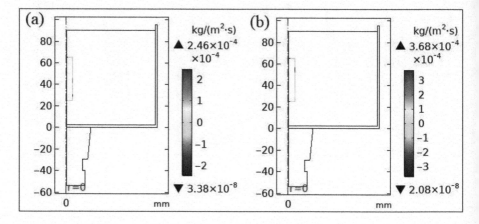

FIGURE 11.9   Erosion rate, kg/m²s; (a) Water, (b) C_2H_5OH.

In the presence of Stokes drag law in the company of the Basset rare fraction effect and an acoustophoretic radiation force, the erosion phenomenon has been studied and the erosion rate has been calculated as 2.46×10^{-4} kg/m²s, 3.68×10^{-4} kg/m²s for water and ethanol respectively (Figure 11.9).

From experimental investigation, water and ethanol have been used as solvents for the same process time of 5 minutes for each process. The specimen size of 12 diameter x 40 length has been used for the investigation.

The result shows that the solvent gave a significant effect on improving the cleaning rate (Table 11.4). Water gives lower erosion rates such as 1.110×10^{-4} kg/m²s and 1.061×10^{-4} kg/m²s while ethanol gives higher erosion rates such as 2.211×10^{-4} kg/m²s and 4.423×10^{-4} kg/m²s. Water is a commonly used and easily available solvent, whereas ethanol (C_2H_5OH) is costly and has nature-affecting properties (Table 11.5).

TABLE 11.4
Experimental Results

Sr No	Solvents	Weight before cleaning (grams)	Weight after cleaning (grams)	Material Loss (grams)	Erosion rate (kg/m²s)
1	Water	34.500	34.450	0.050	1.110×10^{-4}
2	Water	34.040	33.992	0.048	1.061×10^{-4}
3	C_2H_5OH	35.050	34.950	0.100	2.211×10^{-4}
4	C_2H_5OH	35.090	34.995	0.095	2.101×10^{-4}

TABLE 11.5
Comparison of Simulation Results Vs Experimental Results

Sr No.	Solvents	Simulation Result Erosion Rate (kg/m²s)	Experimental Results Erosion Rate (kg/m²s)
1	Water	2.46×10^{-4}	1.110×10^{-4}
2	Water		1.061×10^{-4}
3	C_2H_5OH		2.211×10^{-4}
4	C_2H_5OH	3.68×10^{-4}	2.101×10^{-4}

11.6 CONCLUSION

According to the acquired outcomes, it has been concluded that COMSOL Multiphysics gives more adequate results. The computational model is well-defined to predict congruous cleaning rates. The simulation results show a 2.46×10^{-4} kg/m²s and 3.68×10^{-4} kg/m²s erosion rate for water and C_2H_5OH respectively. The simulation results have been verified with an experimental investigation by considering the same parameters. The experimental results show average erosion rates of 1.110×10^{-4} kg/m²s, 1.061×10^{-4} kg/m²s and 2.211×10^{-4} kg/m²s and 4.423×10^{-4} kg/m²s for water and C_2H_5OH respectively. Hence, it also leads to the conclusion that C_2H_5OH gives a better cleaning rate as validated experimentally.

ACKNOWLEDGMENTS

Authors would love to be renowned for the guide acquired from the Green Ksv Skill Development center, Gandhinagar for providing machine tools, tooling, and instruments.

CREDIT AUTHORSHIP CONTRIBUTION STATEMENT

Vipulkumar Rokad: Conceptualization, Methodology, Software, Investigation, Data curation, Formal analysis, Writing – original draft. **Divyang H. Pandya**: Validation, Supervision.

REFERENCES

[1] Rokad, V., "Development of 2D axisymmetric acoustic transient and CFD based Erosion model for Vibro cleaner using COMSOL multiphysics", *Mathematical Modeling, Computational Intelligence Techniques and Renewable Energy*, Vol. 2, 2021, pp. 203–213. https://doi.org/10.1007/978-16-5952-2_18

[2] Rokad, V., "Development of 3D improved acoustic transient model for vibro cleaner using COMSOL Multiphysics", *Materials Today Proceedings*, Vol. 44, No. 1, 2021, pp. 732–736. https://doi.org/10.1016/j.matpr.2020.10.635

[3] DeAngelis, D. A., "Performance of PZT8 versus PZT4 piezoelectric materials in ultrasonic transducers" *Science Direct Physics Procedia*, Vol. 87, 2016, pp. 85–92. https://doi.org/10.1016/j.phpro.2016.12.014

[4] Duran, F., "Design and implementation of an intelligent ultrasonic cleaning device," *Intelligent Automation and Soft Computing*, Vol. 25, No. 3, 2019, pp 441–449. https://doi.org/10.31209/2018.11006161

[5] Tangsopa, W., "A novel ultrasonic cleaning tank development by harmonic response analysis and computational fluid dynamics", *Metals*, Vol. 10, No. 335), 2020, pp 1–18. https://doi.org/10.3390/met10030335

[6] Tangsopa, W., "Development of an industrial ultrasonic cleaning tank based on harmonic response analysis", *Ultrasonics*, Vol. 91, 2019, pp. 68–76. https://doi.org/10.1016/j.ultras.2018.07.013

[7] Lewis, J. P., "A 2D finite element analysis of an ultrasonic cleaning vessel: Results and comparisons", *International Journal of Modeling and Simulation*, Vol. 27, No. 2, 2015, pp. 181–185. https://doi.org/10.1080/02286203.2007.11442415

[8] Mirek, P., "Field testing of acoustic cleaning system working in 670MWTHCFB boiler", *Chemical and Processes Engineering*, Vol. 34, No. 2, 2013, pp. 283–291. https://doi.org/10.2478/cpe-2013-0023

[9] Vetrimurugan, "Ultrasonic and megasonic cleaning to remove nano-dimensional contaminations from various disk drive components", *International Journal of Innovation Research in Science, Engineering and Technology*, Vol. 2, No. 11, 2013, pp. 5971–5977.

[10] Lais, H., "Numerical modelling of acoustic pressure field to optimize the ultrasonic cleaning technique for cylinders", *Sonochemistry*, Vol. 45, 2018, pp. 7–16. https://doi.org/10.1016/j.ultsonch.2018.02.045

[11] Bretz, N., "Numerical simulation of ultrasonic waves in cavitating fluids with special consideration of ultrasonic cleaning", *IEEE-Ultrasonics Symposium*, 2005, pp. 703–706. https://doi.org/10.1109/ULTSYM.2005.1602948

[12] Dursun, H., "Experimental investigation of the cavitation erosion of a flat aluminum part using a sonotrode test device", *Materials and Technology*, Vol. 53, No. 5, 2019, pp. 637–642. https://doi.org/10.17222/mit.2018.255

[13] Rokad, V., "Erosive investigation of various erosion models for vibro cleaner developed based on ultrasonic technique using COMSOL Multiphysics", *Journal of Engineering, Science and Technology*, Vol. 13, No. 2, 2021, pp. 33–41. http://dx.doi.org/10.4314/ijest.v13i2.4

[14] Krella, A. K., "Cavitation Erosion – Phenomenon and test rigs", *Advances in Materials Science*, Vol. 18, No. 2(56), 2018, pp. 15–26. https://doi.org/10.1515/adms-2017-0028

[15] Introduction to COMSOL multiphysics – user's guide, Version 5.3a, 2017.

[16] Zhong, L., "COMSOL Multiphysics Simulation of Ultrasonic Energy in Cleaning tanks",*COMSOL Conference*, 2015.

12 A Novel Facial Emotion Recognition Technique using Convolution Neural Network

Shuva Biswas, Tonny Saha, Prayas Banerjee and Soma Datta

Sister Nivedita University, Kolkata, India

12.1 INTRODUCTION

Human beings do not want to express their emotions verbally. They just expect that the person next to them will understand these emotions without being told how we actually feel. Facial expressions are the vital identifiers of human feelings, because it corresponds to the emotions [1, 2]. For the majority of time, the facial expression is a nonverbal way of emotional expression, and it can be considered as concrete evidence to uncover whether an individual is speaking the truth or not. The current approaches primarily focus on facial investigation, keeping the background intact [3, 4]. Hence, they retain a lot of un-necessary and misleading features that confuse the CNN training process [5]. This chapter focuses on seven essential facial expression classes reported: angry, disgust, fear, happy, sad, surprise and neutral. The Facial Emotion Recognition using CNN algorithm presented here aims for expressional examination and to characterize the given image into these seven essential emotion classes [6, 7].

Reported techniques on facial expression detection can be described as two major approaches. The first one is distinguishing expressions that are identified with an explicit classifier. The second one is making characterization dependent on the extracted facial highlights. The automatic facial expression recognition system has many applications such as understanding human behaviour, the detection of mental disorders, and synthetic human expressions [8, 9]. The two popular methods used mostly in the literature for the automatic facial expression recognition systems are geometry-based and appearance-based. This book chapter presents a quick survey of facial expression recognition. Currently, an FER system plays an important role in artificial intelligence and serves as a potential real-world application in different areas for psychological studies, driver fatigue monitoring, interactive game design, portable mobile application to automatically insert emotions in chat and assistance systems for autistic people, facial nerve grading in medical field, an emotion detection system used by disabled to assist a caretaker, a socially intelligent robot with emotional intelligence and so on [10].

DOI: 10.1201/9781003363606-12

This approach has been widely used in the field of diversion, training, online business, wellbeing and security. In our work, we propose a technique to recognize the feeling by utilizing facial information. This will anticipate whether or not the individual is happy, disgusted, afraid, sad, angry, neutral or surprised. We have utilized Keras having Tensor Flow back-ended and OpenCV to prepare the model and the dataset utilized is from the Kaggle website [11–13]. The main contributions of this research work are as listed below:

- Five layers of Convolutional Neural Network with two fully-connected layers have been proposed.
- The FER2013 dataset is an imbalance dataset. A good balancing protocol has been used to balance the dataset using oversampler.
- Some pre-processing to the images such as normalization is used to avoid basic noises.
- The authors have added dropout layers, image augmentation and 'early stopping' to the CNN model to avoid overfitting.

12.2 LITERATURE REVIEW

Facial expression is the common signal for all humans to convey mood. These tools have application in many fields, such as robotics, medicine, driving assist system and lie detector. Thus, there are many attempts to make an automatic facial expression analysis tool. Recent advancement in facial expression recognition (FER) have made improvements in neuroscience and cognitive science. Further development in computer vision. Machine learning techniques have made emotion identification more accurate and accessible. In recent years, researchers have made significant progress detecting automatic facial expression [14–16]. Among those, few expression recognition techniques categorise the face into a set of classical emotions, such as happiness, sadness and anger etc. Other researchers try to recognize the individual muscle position and movements that the face can produce. Facial Action Coding System (FACS) [17, 18] is the well-known psychological framework to describe the entirety of facial movements. FACS is a system that also classify human facial movements by their appearance on the face using Action Units (AU) which contains 46 individual elements of visible facial movement Tian et al. (2001); Bartlett et al. (2006). Bayesian Networks, Neural Networks and the multi-level Hidden Markov Model (HMM) Cohen, Sebe, Sun, Lew, and Huang (2003); Padgett and Cottrell (1996) have all been used for facial expression recognition. Few of these techniques have the drawbacks of recognition rate and timing.

Ekman et al. Cohen et al. (2003) proposed seven basic emotions, irrespective of culture in which a human grows like anger, fear, happiness, sadness, contempt Matsumoto (1992), disgust, and surprise. Sajid et al. Sajid, Iqbal Ratyal, Ali, Zafar, Dar, Mahmood, and Joo (2019) found out the influence of facial asymmetry as a marker of age estimation. They have worked on the facial recognition technology (FERET) dataset [19]. In this research work, the authors have identified that right face asymmetry is better than left face asymmetry. Face pose from different angles also remains a challenge with face detection. Ratyal et al. Ratyal, Taj, Sajid, Ali,

Mahmood, and Razzaq (2019a); Ratyal, Taj, Sajid, Mahmood, Razzaq, Dar, Ali, Usman, Baig, and Mussadiq (2019b) proposed the solution for variability in facial pose appearance in their research work. They have used three-dimensional pose-invariant approach using subject-specific descriptors Ratyal, Taj, Bajwa, and Sajid (2018). There are many issues, such as excessive makeup pose and expression which are solved using convolutional networks [20, 21].

Recently, researchers have made extraordinary advances in facial expression detection Xie and Hu (2018); Danisman, Bilasco, Ihaddadene, and Djeraba (2010); Mal and Swarnalatha (2017) which have led to improvements in neuroscience Parr and Waller (2006) and cognitive science. In addition, the development in computer vision Kong, Heo, Abidi, Paik, and Abidi (2005) and machine learning Xue, Mao, and Zhang (2006) makes emotion identification much more accurate. As a consequence, facial expression recognition is growing rapidly as a sub-field of image processing. Among the possible applications are psychiatric observations Kim, An, Ryu, and Chung (2007), drunk driver recognition Ernst (1934), human–computer interaction Kim et al. (2007), and the most important of these is the lie detector. In research work Anil and Suresh (2016) states a hybrid approach that incorporate multi-modal information for facial emotion recognition. In this research work, the authors have chosen two different speakers using two different languages. The evaluation is carried out with three different media clips: (1) audio information of the emotions only; (2) video information of the emotions only; and (3) both audio and video information. The results of audio and facial recognition are provided as input to the weighing matrix.

The authors of ref. [22] study emotional recognition using facial expressions. For this purpose they have used Microsoft Kinect to conduct a 3D modelling of the face. This involves two 2 cameras of Microsoft Kinect: one works with visible light and the other works with infrared light. According to their results, accuracy reaches 90%. Facial expression is the common signal for all humans to convey the mood. Facial expression analysis tools have application in many fields, such as robotics, medicine, driving assist system and lie detector Lucey, Cohn, Kanade, Saragih, Ambadar, and Matthews (2010). Thus, there are many attempts to make an automatic facial expression analysis tool. Recent advances in FER have made improvements in neuroscience and cognitive science. Further developments in computer vision and ML have made emotion identification more accurate and accessible. Table 12.1 shows a comparative study of a number of recent research studies [23–25].

12.3 PROPOSED METHODOLOGY

This section describes different phases of this research work in different sub-sections.

12.3.1 CONVOLUTIONAL OPERATION

Convolutional Neural Network (CNN) is the most popular way of analysing images. CNN differs from a multi-layer perceptron (MLP) as it contains hidden layers, called convolutional layers. In the context of a convolutional neural network, a convolution is a linear operation that involves the multiplication of a set of weights with the

TABLE 12.1
List of Previous Work

Year	Dataset	Accuracy (%)	Architecture
2021	JAFFE	95.24	CNN architecture
2021	FERC-2013	70.14	CNN architecture
2021	FER2013	72.14	7 Convolutional layers
2021	FER2013	79.5	6 C layers, pre-processing steps
2019	JAFEE, CK+	55	The existing VGG model is used by fine-tuning
2018	CK+	83	feature extraction from face region and Emotion classification using Fuzzy Classifier
2017	CFEE	95.71	CNN architecture based on AlexNet
2017	RaFD	74.79	CNN architecture based on AlexNet
2017	CK+	93.21	CNN combined with facial landmarks
2017	MMI	77.50	CNN combined with facial landmarks
2017	FERA	77.42	CNN combined with facial landmarks
2017	DISFA	58.00	CNN combined with facial landmarks

input, much like a traditional neural network. Given that the technique was designed for two-dimensional input, the multiplication is performed between an array of input data and a two-dimensional array of weights, called a filter or a kernel. The proposed method is based on a five-level CNN framework. Here, the conventional CNN network module is used to extract primary feature maps (FM) [19]. The feature maps (FM) are generated by tracking down relevant facial points of importance. Figure 12.1 shows the presentation of feature map and line detector. FM is directly related to changes in expression. The FM is obtained using a basic perceptron unit applied on a background-removed face image. In the proposed FER model, we also have two non-convolutional perceptron layers that is the dense layer as the last stage. Each of the convolutional layers receives image as input that is pixels in the image, transforms it, and then outputs it to the next level [26]. A filter is used to create the feature maps that are a result of the filters convolving around the input image pixels. This convolving operation of filters with a fixed number of strides is called the convolutional operation. In each layer, there are a certain number of filters that generates exactly the same number of feature maps as the number of filters. Different types of filters, including line detector, edge detector, circle detector, and corner detector filters are used at the start of the convolutional layer 1. The consecutive layers then detect the features such as eyes, ears, lips, nose, cheeks, etc. [15]. Here is a demonstration of how filter produces output.

12.3.2 POOLING OPERATION

The pooling layer reduces the spatial size of a convolved feature. This is done to decrease the computations required to process the data and extract dominant features which are rotation- and position-invariant [27, 28]. There are two types of pooling, namely max pooling and average pooling. Max pooling returns the maximum value

0	0	0	1	1	0	0	0
0	0	0	1	1	0	0	0
0	0	0	1	1	0	0	0
0	0	0	1	1	0	0	0
0	0	0	1	1	0	0	0
0	0	0	1	1	0	0	0
0	0	0	1	1	0	0	0
0	0	0	1	1	0	0	0

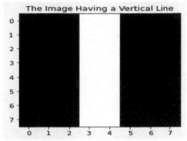

(a) Representation of a vertical line

0	1	0
0	1	0
0	1	0

(b) Vertical line detector filter

0.0	0.0	3.0	3.0	0.0	0.0
0.0	0.0	3.0	3.0	0.0	0.0
0.0	0.0	3.0	3.0	0.0	0.0
0.0	0.0	3.0	3.0	0.0	0.0
0.0	0.0	3.0	3.0	0.0	0.0
0.0	0.0	3.0	3.0	0.0	0.0

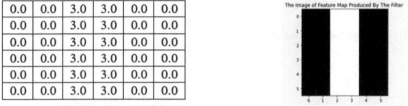

(c) The feature map after convolving the filter across the image

FIGURE 12.1   Representation of feature map and line detector.

from the portion of the image covered by the kernel, while average pooling returns the average of the corresponding values. Figure 12.2 shows the outputs obtained by performing max and average pooling on an image.

12.3.3 FULLY CONNECTED LAYER

Neurons in a fully connected layer have connections to all neurons in the previous layer. This layer is found towards the end of a CNN. In this layer, the input from the previous layer is flattened into a one-dimensional vector and an activation function is applied to obtain the output [29, 30].

12.3.4 DROPOUT LAYER

Dropout is used to avoid overfitting. Overfitting in an ML model happens when the training accuracy is much greater than the testing accuracy. Dropout refers to ignoring neurons during training so they are not considered during a particular forward or backward pass, thereby leaving a reduced network. These neurons are chosen randomly and an example is shown in Figure 12.3. The dropout rate is the probability of training a given node in a layer, where 1.0 means no dropout and 0.0 means all outputs from the layer are ignored.

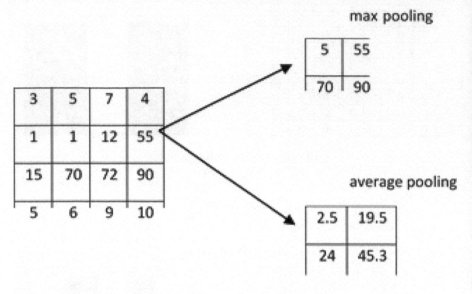

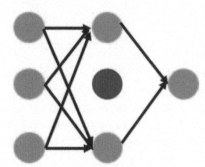

FIGURE 12.2   Max and average pooling.

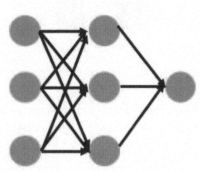

Neural Network without Dropout   **Neural Network with Dropout**

FIGURE 12.3   Dropout in neural network.

12.3.5   BATCH NORMALIZATION

Training a network is more efficient when the distributions of the layer inputs are the same. Variations in these distributions can make a model biased. Batch normalization is used to normalize the inputs to the layers [31, 32].

12.3.6   ACTIVATION FUNCTION

Softmax and Rectified Linear Unit (ReLU) are activation functions commonly used in CNNs and are described below. The softmax function is given by equation (1). ReLU stands for rectified linear unit, and is a type of activation function. Mathematically, it is defined as $y = \max(0, x)$.

$$\text{Softmax}(Z)_i = \frac{e^{zi}}{\sum_{j=1}^{N} e^{zj}} \tag{12.1}$$

12.3.7 COLLECTION OF DATASET

We have used the FER2013 dataset which is available in Kaggle. The dataset is available in two formats. One is of a folder containing images and another is of CSV format. We have used the second one Kaggle (Accessed November 30, 2022) Sambhare (Accessed March 30, 2022).

The total FER-2013 dataset is 35,887 consisting of 7 (seven) different types of micro expression, and marked with labels based on 7 (seven) different classifications starting from the index label 0 to 6 Sambhare (Accessed March 30, 2022).

12.3.8 SAMPLES OF DATASET

12.3.8.1 Train Dataset

The train dataset has images of seven basic emotions in separate folders. We have plotted three images from each seven emotions.

12.3.8.2 Test Dataset

The test dataset has images of seven basic emotions in separate folders. We have plotted three images from each seven emotions. The test dataset images are totally distinct from those of the train dataset. Figure 12.4–12.6 shows different test data sample.

12.3.9 DATASET ANOMALIES

The FER 2013 dataset is well known and was used in the Kaggle competition. The data must be prepared for input to the CNN because there are some issues with this dataset, as discussed below. The input to the model should be an array of numbers, so images must be converted into arrays Kaggle (Accessed November 30, 2022). Some dataset challenges are given in the following subsections.

12.3.9.1 Imbalance

A dataset is said to be imbalanced if there is a significant disproportion among the number of samples in each class. The problem with an imbalanced dataset is that the model tends to bias towards the class having a higher number of samples. In our case the happy class has 7215 sample images and the disgust class has 436 sample images. Thus, most of the prediction will be biased towards the happy expression. We have performed the augmentation to remove the biasness of the model. Data augmentation increases the amount of data using techniques such as cropping, padding, rotating, shifting, horizontal flipping etc. We have used the resampler to balance the dataset Çeliktutan, Ulukaya, and Sankur (2013); Ebrahimi Kahou, Michalski, Konda, Memisevic, and Pal (2015).

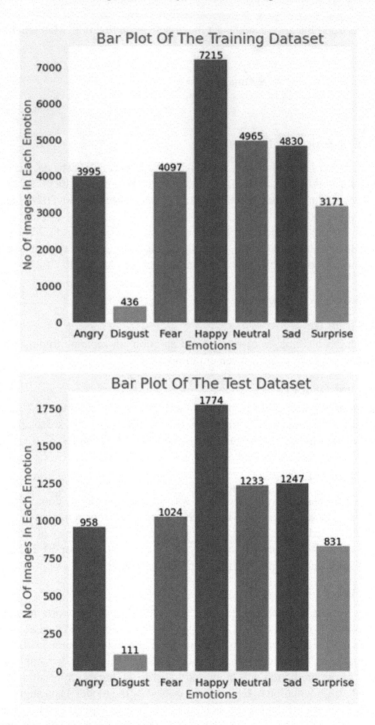

FIGURE 12.4   Bar plot of the training and test dataset.

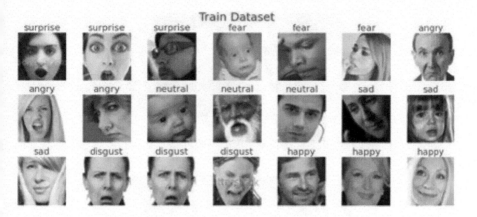

FIGURE 12.5 Train dataset samples.

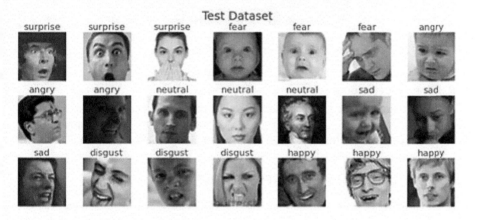

FIGURE 12.6 Test dataset samples.

12.3.9.2 Contrast Variation

In visual perception of the real world, contrast is determined by the difference in the colour and brightness of the object and other objects within the same field of view. In the dataset some images are too dark while some are too light. As images contain visual information, higher-contrast images have more information than lower-contrast images. Our CNN model takes images as input Ebrahimi Kahou et al. (2015).

12.3.9.3 Intra-class Variation

Intra-class variation defines how image variations occur between different images of one class. The similarity between samples within the same class is typically measured by the Intra-class Correlation coefficient. In our dataset there are some irrelevant images in each class. To make the model performance better irrelevant images should be removed Ebrahimi Kahou et al. (2015). Figure 12.7 shows sample Intra-class variation images.

FIGURE 12.7 Examples of intra-class variation images.

FIGURE 12.8 Examples of occluded image.

12.3.9.4 Occlusion

Occlusion happens when part of the image is covered. This can occur when a hand covers a part of the face such as the right eye or nose. A person wearing sunglasses or a mask also creates occlusion. Figure 12.8 shows sample occluded images.

12.4 MACHINE-LEVEL REPRESENTATION OF AN IMAGE

An image is represented by numbers that correspond to the pixel intensities. The array module in NumPy is used to convert an image into an array and obtain the image attributes. Figure 12.9 shows an image in the happy class from the FER 2013 dataset converted into a NumPy array.

```
array([[[144, 144, 144],
        [144, 144, 144],
        [143, 143, 143],
        ...,
        [121, 121, 121],
        [121, 121, 121],
        [121, 121, 121]],
       ...,
       [[100, 100, 100],
        [100, 100, 100],
        [100, 100, 100],
        ...,
        [117, 117, 117],
        [120, 120, 120],
        [120, 120, 120]]], dtype=uint8)
```

FIGURE 12.9 Happy image from the FER 2013 dataset converted into an array.

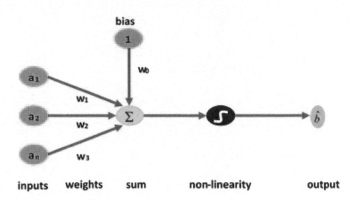

FIGURE 12.10   The basic structure of neuron.

12.5   MATHEMATICAL BACKGROUND

12.5.1   CONVOLUTIONAL NEURAL NETWORKS

The fundamental building block of a Neural Network is a neuron. Figure 12.14 shows the structure of a neuron. Forward propagation of information through a neuron happens when inputs a_1 to a_n are multiplied by their corresponding weights and then added together. This result is passed through a nonlinear activation function along with a bias term which shifts the output. The bias is shown as w_0 in Figure 12.10. For an input vector $a = a_1, a_2, ..., a_n$ and weight vector $w = w_1, w_2, ..., w_n$ the neuron output is

$$b^1 = g\left(w_0 + \sum_{i=1}^{n} a_i w_i\right) \qquad (12.2)$$

The output is between 0 and 1, which makes it suitable for problems with probabilities. The purpose of the activation function is to introduce nonlinearities in the network since most real-world data is nonlinear. The use of a nonlinear function also allows Neural Networks to approximate complex functions.

Neurons can be combined to create a multi-output Neural Network. If every input has a connection to every neuron it is called dense or fully connected. A deep Neural Network has multiple hidden layers stacked on top of each other and every neuron in each hidden layer is connected to a neuron in the previous layer Zafar, Ashraf, Ali, Iqbal, Sajid, Dar, and Ratyal (2018); Ali, Zafar, Riaz, Hanif Dar, Iqbal Ratyal, Bashir Bajwa, Kashif Iqbal, and Sajid (2018).

12.5.2   THE PROPOSED CNN ARCHITECTURE

The architecture of proposed CNN (Convolutional Neural Network) is represented in Figure 12.11. The network has five blocks of CNN and the final layer as the fully connected layer. In the CNN architecture the input image is fed to the first convolutional layer, having the input shape of 48x48 and having one channel. After each convolutional layer there is a batch normalization to normalize the data. And after

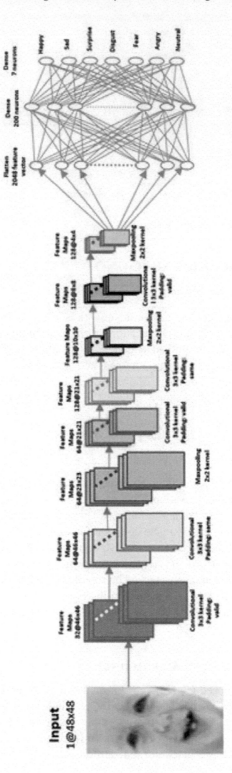

FIGURE 12.11 The proposed CNN architecture.

each block of convolutional layer there is a Max Pooling layer which reduces the size given to it to half of its size using 3 x 3 kernel Ebrahimi Kahou et al. (2015). At the final layer, there is a dense layer that is connected to the flattened layer. We have used ReLU as the activation function in the hidden layer and the softmax as the activation function at the output layer.

12.5.3 DIFFERENT TYPES OF FILTERS

The convolution operation is used to extract high-level features such as edges from an input image. In our model, we have several convolutional layers. In each layer, there are a certain number of filters that are convolved around the input image from top-left to bottom-right with a fixed number of strides Danisman et al. (2010). After each convolution operation one feature map is generated. In the final layer, all the feature maps are combined and flattened to feed to the dense layer. The convolutional filter is shown in Figure 12.12. The sample filtered output is shown in Figure 12.13. The filters of different convolutional layers are shown in Figure 12.14 to Figure 12.17.

After applying the filters to the image:

12.6 EXPERIMENT DETAILS

This section will describes the details of the experimental results.

12.6.1 TRAINING DETAILS

As we have downloaded the FER2013 CSV file thus we are given with three types of data: Training Data, PrivateTest and PublicTest. We have used the *train test split*()

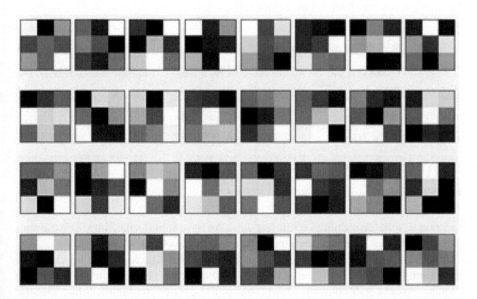

FIGURE 12.12   The convolutional filters.

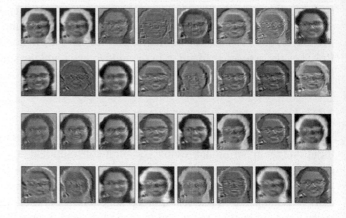

Input Image

FIGURE 12.13 Filtered output.

FIGURE 12.14 The filters of 2nd convolutional layer.

FIGURE 12.15 The filters of 3rd convolutional layer.

function to split the training and the test data. We have split the data into 90% training data and 10% test data. We have set the learning rate as 0.0001.

The learning rate is a configurable parameter. If we set a high learning rate then the training process will converge very fast and if we set a low learning rate then the training process will converge slowly, but in the case of the high learning rate the weights are not particularly accurate when compared with a low learning rate

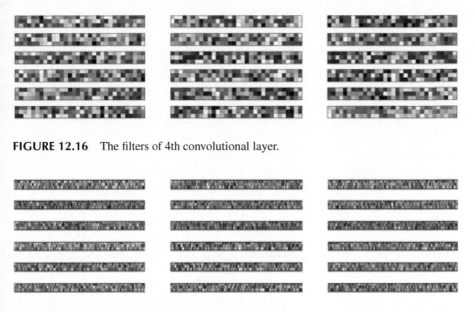

FIGURE 12.16 The filters of 4th convolutional layer.

FIGURE 12.17 The filters of 5th convolutional layer.

Danisman et al. (2010). The number of epochs is the number of times a dataset is passed forward and backward through the Neural Network. The dataset is divided into batches to lower the processing time and the number of training images in a batch is called the batch size.

12.7 RESULTS

The implementation of pre-processing steps was done using tensorflow, keras and Python. All the experiments were carried out using a GPU-based CNN Library [8].

12.7.1 CONFUSION MATRIX

A Confusion matrix is an N x N matrix used to evaluate the performance of a classification model, where N is the number of target classes. The matrix compares the actual target values with those predicted by the machine learning model (Figure 12.18).

TABLE 12.2
CNN Model Result

Iteration number	Number of Epochs	Accuracy	Loss	Val Accuracy	Val Loss
1	40	0.9832	0.0511	0.8420	0.9840
2	26	0.9474	0.1557	0.8281	0.7995
3	36	0.9887	0.0363	0.8420	0.9608
4	33	0.9622	0.1122	0.8252	0.9196

TABLE 12.3
Accuracy Comparison of Data Augmentation

Preprocessing	Accuracy	Validation Accuracy
Without Data Augmentation	54	44
With Data Augmentation	97	83

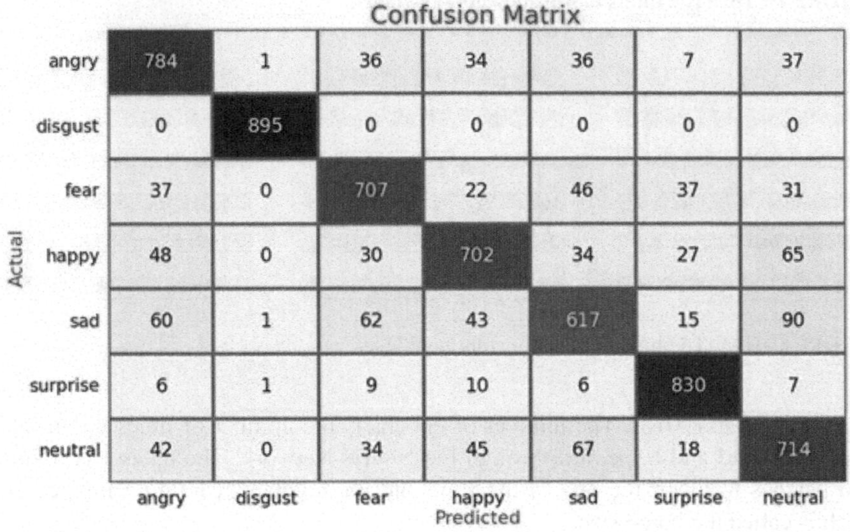

FIGURE 12.18   Confusion matrix.

12.7.2   Performance Metrics

TABLE 12.4
Classification Report-1

Classes	Precision	Recall	F1-Score	Support
0	0.80	0.84	0.82	935
1	1.00	1.00	1.00	895
2	0.81	0.80	0.80	880
3	0.82	0.77	0.80	906
4	0.77	0.69	0.73	888
5	0.89	0.96	0.92	869
6	0.76	0.78	0.77	920

12.7.3   Accuracy and Loss Curve

Figure 12.19 shows the representation of accuracy and lost curve.

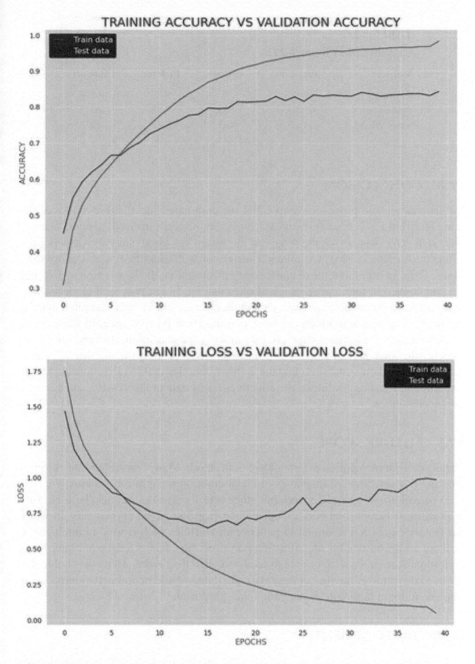

FIGURE 12.19   Accuracy and loss curve.

TABLE 12.5

Classification Report-21

Metrices	Precision	Recall	F1-Score	Support
accuracy			0.83	6293
macro avg	0.83	0.83	0.83	6293
weighted avg	0.83	0.83	0.83	6293

12.8 CONCLUSION

In this chapter, we propose a deep CNN for automated facial expression recognition algorithm for seven expressions: happy, sad, angry, surprised, neutral, fear and disgusted. The structure of the proposed algorithm has good generality and classification performance. First, we collect a variety of well-classified, high-quality databases. Then, in order to remove unnecessary information, the face region is detected, cut and converted into a gray image of one channel. In the proposed algorithm, the data augmentation which increases the number of training images is applied to solve the overfitting problem which degrades classification performance. In the existing CNN structure, the optimal structure for reducing the execution time and improving the classification performance was determined by adjusting the number of feature maps in the convolutional layer and the number of nodes in the fully-connected layer. Experimental results confirmed the effectiveness of data preprocessing and augmentation techniques.

12.9 FUTURE SCOPE

Facial emotion recognition is now a topic of research. Many researchers are currently working to overcome the loopholes of facial emotion recognition systems. We have used convolutional neural network but other neural networks can also be used, such as Recurrent Neural Network or other deep learning-based approaches. In CNN, the feature extraction is similar to pattern recognition which is used in intelligence, military and forensics for identification purposes. As CNN is a deep learning-based algorithm, it requires a lot of data to feed and train the model. Thus, we should find a way to use a lower number of resources and data to build neural network models to implement them to mobile phones and other platforms.

ACKNOWLEDGEMENT(S)

The authors would like to thank Dr. Biswajit Modak for giving us relevant domain knowledge.

DISCLOSURE STATEMENT

Not Applicable

CONFLICT OF INTEREST

Authors state that there is no conflict of interest.

FUNDING

No funding has been received.

REFERENCES

[1] Lisa A. Parr and Bridget M. Waller. Understanding chimpanzee facial expression: insights into the evolution of communication. *Social cognitive and affective neuroscience*, 1(3):221–228, 2006.

[2] Md Zia Uddin, Mohammed Mehedi Hassan, Ahmad Almogren, Mansour Zuair, Giancarlo Fortino, and Jim Torresen. A facial expression recognition system using robust face features from depth videos and deep learning. *Computers & Electrical Engineering*, 63:114–125, 2017.

[3] Peter Burkert, Felix Trier, Muhammad Zeshan Afzal, Andreas Dengel, and Marcus Liwicki. *Dexpression: Deep convolutional neural network for expression recognition. arXiv preprint arXiv:1509.05371*, 2015.

[4] Mahdi Ilbeygi and Hamed Shah-Hosseini. A novel fuzzy facial expression recognition system based on facial feature extraction from color face images. *Engineering Applications of Artificial Intelligence*, 25(1):130–146, 2012.

[5] Mangayarkarasi Nehru and S. Padmavathi. Illumination invariant face detection using viola jones algorithm. In *2017 4th International Conference on Advanced Computing and Communication Systems (ICACCS)*, pages 1–4. IEEE, 2017.

[6] Y-I. Tian, Takeo Kanade, and Jeffrey F. Cohn. Recognizing action units for facial expression analysis. *IEEE Transactions on Pattern Analysis and Machine Intelligence*, 23(2):97–115, 2001.

[7] Marian Stewart Bartlett, Gwen Littlewort, Mark Frank, Claudia Lainscsek, Ian Fasel, and Javier Movellan. Fully automatic facial action recognition in spontaneous behavior. In *7th International Conference on Automatic Face and Gesture Recognition (FGR06)*, pages 223–230. IEEE, 2006.

[8] Gwen Littlewort, Marian Stewart Bartlett, Ian Fasel, Joshua Susskind, and Javier Movellan. Dynamics of facial expression extracted automatically from video. In *2004 Conference on Computer Vision and Pattern Recognition Workshop*, page 80. IEEE, 2004.

[9] Manas Sambhare. *FER-2013 database, version 1*, 2013. Accessed March 30, 2022. URL https://www.kaggle.com/msambare/fer2013/metadata.

[10] Ira Cohen, Nicu Sebe, Yafei Sun, Michael S Lew, and Thomas S Huang. Evaluation of expression recognition techniques. In *International Conference on Image and Video Retrieval*, pages 184–195. Springer, 2003.

[11] Curtis Padgett and Garrison Cottrell. Representing face images for emotion classification. *Advances in Neural Information Processing Systems*, 9, 1996.

[12] David Matsumoto. More evidence for the universality of a contempt expression. *Motivation and Emotion*, 16(4):363–368, 1992.

[13] Muhammad Sajid, Naeem Iqbal Ratyal, Nouman Ali, Bushra Zafar, Saadat Hanif Dar, Muham-Mad Tariq Mahmood, and Young Bok Joo. The impact of asymmetric left and asymmetric right face images on accurate age estimation. *Mathematical Problems in Engineering*, 2019.

[14] Naeem Iqbal Ratyal, Imtiaz Ahmad Taj, Muhammad Sajid, Nouman Ali, Anzar Mahmood, and Sohail Razzaq. Three-dimensional face recognition using variance-based registration and subject-specific descriptors. *International Journal of Advanced Robotic Systems*, 16(3):1729881419851716, 2019a.

[15] Naeem Ratyal, Imtiaz Ahmad Taj, Muhammad Sajid, Anzar Mahmood, Sohail Razzaq, Saa-Dat Hanif Dar, Nouman Ali, Muhammad Usman, Mirza Jabbar Aziz Baig, and Usman Mussadiq. Deeply learned pose invariant image analysis with applications in 3d face recognition. *Mathematical Problems in Engineering*, 2019, 2019b.

[16] Naeem Ratyal, Imtiaz Taj, Usama Bajwa, and Muhammad Sajid. Pose and expression invariant alignment based multi-view 3d face recognition. *KSII Transactions on Internet and Information Systems (TIIS)*, 12(10):4903–4929, 2018.

[17] Siyue Xie and Haifeng Hu. Facial expression recognition using hierarchical features with deep comprehensive multipatches aggregation convolutional neural networks. *IEEE Transactions on Multimedia*, 21(1):211–220, 2018.

[18] Taner Danisman, Ioan Marius Bilasco, Nacim Ihaddadene, and Chaabane Djeraba. Automatic facial feature detection for facial expression recognition. In *Fifth International Conference on Computer Vision Theory and Applications (VISAPP) 2010*, volume 2, pages 407–412, 2010.

[19] Hari Prasad Mal and P Swarnalatha. Facial expression detection using facial expression model. In *2017 International Conference on Energy, Communication, Data Analytics and Soft Computing (ICECDS)*, pages 1259–1262. IEEE, 2017.

[20] Seong G Kong, Jingu Heo, Besma R Abidi, Joonki Paik, and Mongi A Abidi. Recent advances in visual and infrared face recognition review. *Computer Vision and Image Understanding*, 97(1):103–135, 2005.

[21] Yu-li Xue, Xia Mao, and Fan Zhang. Beihang University facial expression database and multiple facial expression recognition. In *2006 International Conference on Machine Learning and Cybernetics*, pages 3282–3287. IEEE, 2006.

[22] Do Hyoung Kim, Kwang Ho An, Yeon Geol Ryu, and Myung Jin Chung. A facial expression imitation system for the primitive of intuitive human–robot interaction. In *Human robot interaction*. IntechOpen, 2007.

[23] Huber Ernst. Evolution of facial musculature and facial expression. *The Journal of Nervous and Mental Disease*, 79(1):109, 1934.

[24] J. Anil, and L. Padma Suresh. Literature survey on face and face expression recognition. In *2016 International Conference on Circuit, Power and Computing Technologies (ICCPCT)*, pages 1–6. IEEE, 2016.

[25] Pawel Tarnowski, Marcin Kolodziej, Andrzej Majkowski, and Remigiusz J Rak. Emotion recognition using facial expressions. *Procedia Computer Science*, 108:1175–1184, 2017.

[26] Patrick Lucey, Jeffrey F Cohn, Takeo Kanade, Jason Saragih, Zara Ambadar, and Iain Matthews. The extended Cohn-Kanade dataset (CK+): A complete dataset for action unit and emotion-specified expression. In *2010 IEEE Computer Society Conference on computer vision and pattern recognition-workshops*, pages 94–101. IEEE, 2010.

[27] Zibo Meng, Ping Liu, Jie Cai, Shizhong Han, and Yan Tong. Identity-aware convolutional neural network for facial expression recognition. In *2017 12th IEEE International Conference on Automatic Face & Gesture Recognition (FG 2017)*, pages 558–565. IEEE, 2017.

[28] Kaggle. *Kaggle Facial Images*, Accessed November 30, 2022. URL https://www.kaggle.com/c/challenges-inrepresentation-learning-facial-expressionrecognition-cha

[29] Oya Çeliktutan, Sezer Ulukaya, and Bülent Sankur. A comparative study of face landmarking techniques. *EURASIP Journal on Image and Video Processing*, 2013(1):1–27, 2013.

[30] Samira Ebrahimi Kahou, Vincent Michalski, Kishore Konda, Roland Memisevic, and Christo-Pher Pal. Recurrent neural networks for emotion recognition in video. In *Proceedings of the 2015 ACM International Conference on multimodal interaction*, pages 467–474, 2015.

[31] Bushra Zafar, Rehan Ashraf, Nouman Ali, Muhammad Kashif Iqbal, Muhammad Sajid, Saa-Dat Hanif Dar, and Naeem Iqbal Ratyal. A novel discriminating and relative global spatial image representation with applications in CBIR. *Applied Sciences*, 8(11):2242, 2018.

[32] Nouman Ali, Bushra Zafar, Faisal Riaz, Saadat Hanif Dar, Naeem Iqbal Ratyal, Khalid Bashir Bajwa, Muhammad Kashif Iqbal, and Muhammad Sajid. A hybrid geometric spatial image representation for scene classification. *PloS one*, 13(9):e0203339, 2018.

13 Using Machine Learning to Detect Abnormalities on Modbus/TCP Networks

Yatish Sekaran, Tanmoy Debnath, Taeesh Azal Assadi, Sai Dileep Suvvari and Shubh Oswal

B.M.S. College of Engineering, Bengaluru, India

13.1 INTRODUCTION

Recently, in the advent of the Fourth Industrial Revolution, smart factories with strong connection-oriented characteristics have emerged, escaping from the closed network concept. Unlike a closed network base factory environment, the Industrial Control System (ICS) of a smart factory tends to be connected to the external internet, which means that the system is exposed to several security threats that have not been considered hitherto. Therefore, there is a need to come up with countermeasures against attacks coming from external networks.

In this chapter, we studied which detection model and which feature extraction method would be most efficient for detecting network anomalies, such as distributed denial of service (DDoS), during network attacks. We limit the target to Modbus/TCP for network protocol and only consider machine learning-based detection models because the rule-based model needs manual rule generation and management, taking more cost than a learning-based model in the long term.

Regarding learning-based anomaly detection models, we focused on the following two factors:

feature extraction: which feature best represents abnormal behavior?
Detection model: which model is most accurate and efficient (i.e. fast)?

We conducted intensive research on the two topics, the outcome of which is as detailed below.

13.2 APPROACHES

13.2.1 DATASET

In training anomaly detection models, the quality of the dataset being used is very important. Unfortunately, we could not get hardware to simulate the City Public

DOI: 10.1201/9781003363606-13

Service (CPS) environment, so we should continue our research by using the existing dataset. The dataset used in the study, CYBER-SECURITY MODBUS ICS DATASET [1], is a dataset that exists in IEEE data port. It simulated the following small industrial networks and then generated several anomalies, such as DDoS/MITM. We created a dataset by extracting features from each packet of the original dataset and labeling each of them by attack type [2]. The composition of the dataset that we created is as follows.

Datasets class type	
Type	**number(packet)**
Normal	1208554(during attack) + 521686
MITM	47083
Modbus Query Flooding	893233
Ping Flooding	754232
TCP SYN Flooding	698758
Total	4123546

Portion of Train and Test set	
Usage	**number(packet)**
Train	2474127 (60%)
Test	1649419 (40%)

We limited the number of feature data from attack packets to balance normal, and attack packets feature data [3] in the datasets. We used 60% of them for training, and used the remaining 40% for testing. We did feature engineering by using this dataset, by limiting some features in training and testing anomaly detection models [4].

13.2.2 Overview

To simultaneously evaluate the extracted feature set and the performance of the detection model, we construct the framework as follows.

The framework is largely divided into pre-processing and evaluation steps. In the pre-processing step, feature information is extracted from packets in the pcap file, and features are fused to form multiple feature sets [5]. In the subsequent evaluation phase, models are trained and tested for each feature set to evaluate their performance (Figure 13.1).

13.2.3 Preprocessing Step

We determine that basic information which is extractable from individual packets can be utilized to detect anomalies in Modbus/TCP environments [6]. Therefore, protocol

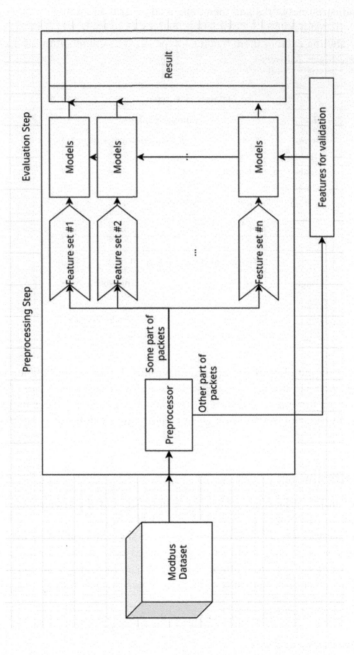

FIGURE 13.1   Framework overview.

type, data length, TCP flag, ARP opcode, ICMP type, ICMP code information was extracted from each packet, and the above information was set to feature set candidates [7]. Information extracted from these individual packets will be collectively referred to as "Packet Information" from now on and its detailed explanation is shown below.

Packet Information	
Features	feature location in full vector
Protocol type	[0]
Data length	[1]
TCP flag	[2~7]
ARP op	[8~11]
ICMP type	[12~19]
ICMP code	[20~27]

In addition, since abnormalities occur across multiple packets rather than one packet, we cut the packet's sequence into a two-second window and extract features below. We will collectively call this "Flow Information" from now on (Figure 13.2).

Flow information(N Sec)	
Features	feature location in full vector
number of packets from same src ip	[28]
number of packets from same dst ip	[29]
number of packets from same src ip, src port	[30]
number of packets from same dst ip, dst port	[31]
number of IP address to same dst ip	[32]
number of source port from same src ip to same dst ip	[33]
number of destination port from same src ip to same dst ip	[34]
Total bytes size from same src ip	[35]
Total bytes size from same dst ip	[36]
number of ICMP packets from same src ip	[37]
number of TCP SYN packets from same src ip	[38]
number of ICMP packets to same dst ip	[39]
number of TCP SYN packets from same dst ip	[40]

13.2.4 EVALUATION STEP

This step is the part where the model is trained and tested using the feature set extracted earlier. The result of this step is performance indicators for each model and

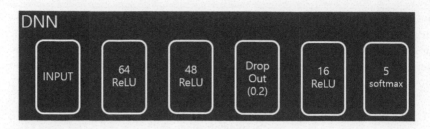

FIGURE 13.2   Shape of DNN model.

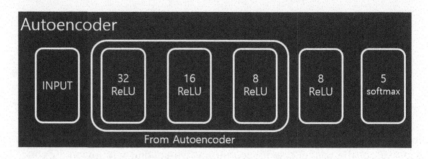

FIGURE 13.3   Shape of autoencoder model.

used feature set such as learning time, processing time, and accuracy. The learning-based model used in this study is as follows:

SVM: SVM is a machine learning algorithm that calculating maximum-margin hyperplane that can classify the input data. In this study, we used rbf (Radial Basis Function) as kernel, give C = 8, gamma = 0.1, and limited maximum iteration to 500 times.

DT: DT makes decision trees that can classify new input by evaluating the input value with tree of conditions. In this study, we give default parameter to DT model (no limitation of max. depth and max. leaf of tree).

Random Forest: Random Forest make Forest containing multiple DT from input data and make final decision by combining each decision from DT. We set the number of DT to 50 in Random Forest model (Figure 13.3).

K Means: K Means make n clusters that minimize the total within-cluster variance. We set the number of clusters to 5.

DNN: DNN is a supervised neural network model, and its model shape is shown as below.

Autoencoder model: We first trained the Autoencoder in an unsupervised manner. Then we make new neural net using Autoencoder and did supervised training. The shape of the final Autoencoder model is shown below.

13.3   EVALUATION

This section discusses the evaluation result of the framework.

13.3.1 ENVIRONMENT

We set up the evaluation environment as follows.

Evaluation Environment	
OS	**Windows 10**
CPU	AMD Ryzen 3600XT (6C12T)
GPU	NDIVIA GeForce GTX 1660 SUPER
RAM	24GB
Runtime	Python 3.8 & Jupyter notebook

13.3.2 FEATURE SET

The number of all possible feature sets is 2^{41}, and testing all possible feature sets is almost impossible [8]. So we arbitrarily selected five feature sets that are considered as meaningful in this project. Below are the feature sets we selected (Figures 13.4 to 13.8):

1. Full feature: Using all extracted features as feature set.
2. Extended flow information: All flow information with basic packet information (protocol type, data length).
3. Flow information only: Feature set contains only flow information.
4. Limited flow information: Some flow information ([35, 37, 38]) were dropped from the above feature set.
5. Packet information only: Feature set with all packet information and without flow information.

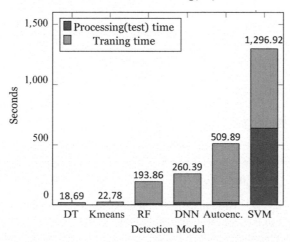

FIGURE 13.4 Feature set #1.

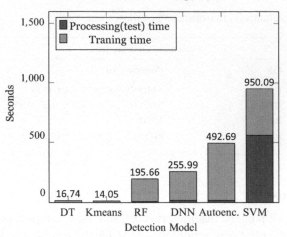

FIGURE 13.5   Feature set #2.

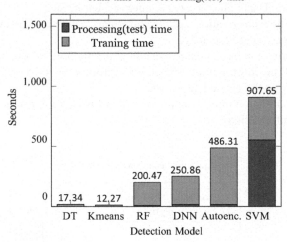

FIGURE 13.6   Feature set #3.

13.3.3 PERFORMANCE

We evaluated the performance of each model with selected feature sets.

Each detection model showed relatively similar performance across the feature sets. To sum up, it is as follows:

- In most cases, DT, Kmeans showed the highest performance among detection models in terms of training and test(process) time.
- DNN, Autoencoder, Random Forest models showed the second-fastest performance. They spent more training times, but they showed fast detection speed in comparison with DT and Kmeans model.

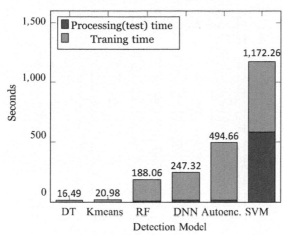

FIGURE 13.7   Feature set #4.

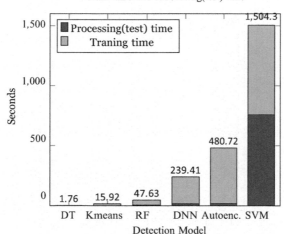

FIGURE 13.8   Feature set #5.

- SVM showed low performance in most cases, including both training time and test time.
- Reducing the number of features in feature set reduced training time and test time of some model, such as SVM.

13.3.4 ACCURACY

We evaluated the accuracy of each model with selected feature sets (Figures 13.9 to 13.13).

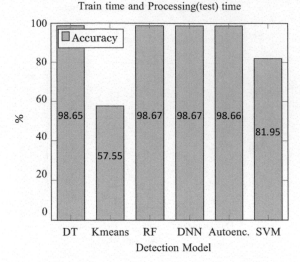

FIGURE 13.9 Feature set #1.

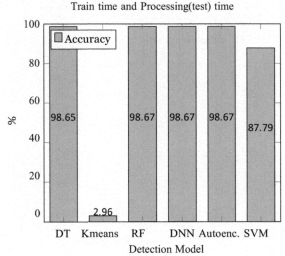

FIGURE 13.10 Feature set #2.

Each detection model showed relatively similar performance across the feature sets. To sum up, it is as follows:

- In most cases, feature sets containing flow information showed high accuracy across detection models. It is, even if the accuracy of a specific detection model is low on average, the model with a feature set including flow information showed higher accuracy than one without flow information relatively.

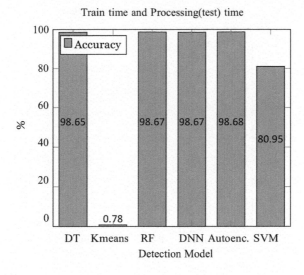

FIGURE 13.11 Feature set #3.

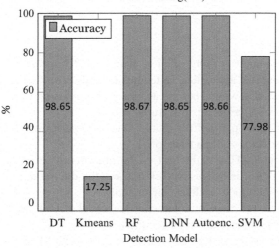

FIGURE 13.12 Feature set #4.

- DT, DNN, Autoencoder, Random Forest showed the highest accuracy among detection models in terms of detection accuracy.
- SVM showed the second accurate result. But there is a large difference in the accuracy between the above models.
- Kmeans model was more inaccurate than the others, being lower than 50% in most cases. It showed a weak correlation between feature selection and accuracy.

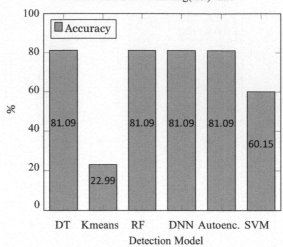

Train time and Processing(test) time

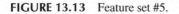

FIGURE 13.13   Feature set #5.

13.3.5 EVALUATION SUMMARY

From the evaluation of the feature set and detection model, we could reach some conclusions:

- Flow information is more efficient than packet information when detecting Modbus/TCP anomalies. Detecting anomaly with packet information of each packet also works, but the accuracy of only using flow information is almost the same as using all features.
- Removing some parts of the feature increases performance slightly, but it reduces the accuracy in a trade-off.
- In this project, DT was the best model in terms of performance accuracy. We guess that it is because attack types in the dataset are simple or DT is indeed a good model to detect an anomaly.
- DNN, Random Forest, and autoencoder model also showed an acceptable level of performance and high accuracy.
- Other two models are not recommended to be used. SVM shows less accuracy and worse performance than other models, and the Kmeans model failed to detect anomalies properly.

13.4   FUTURE WORK

Section 13.4 discusses the limitation of the project and future research topics.

13.4.1   COLLECTING DATASET AND DETECTION MODEL

In this project, we used a packet third-party dataset available since we do not have access to the real-world or simulated industrial network [9]. The dataset used in this project is well generated, but attack types are not varied enough. Collecting more datasets is required for these reasons.

Coverage: models have to detect various attack types/scenarios.
Validation: accuracy of the trained model have to be robust against multiple
    datasets in detecting an anomaly.

Therefore, collecting available datasets with more attack types/scenarios and generating a dataset by ourselves can be one of the future studies. In addition, recently devised learning-based models need to be applied to the framework. Including the latest learning-based models into our framework should also be considered as future work.

13.4.2 FEATURE ANALYSIS

Because of the lack of time, we did not analyze exactly which feature is helpful in detecting each particular type of attack [10]. It should be done because we can reduce features of a feature set that are not useful in detecting any anomaly attack. Analyzing the relation between each feature and accuracy of detecting specific attack type/scenario.

13.5 CONCLUSION

We proposed the framework for evaluating feature set and learning-based models to efficiently and accurately detect Modbus/TCP anomalies. We evaluated five different feature sets with various learning-based models. Among feature sets and models, feature sets containing the information about packet flow showed high accuracy, and DT, DNN, Random Forest, and Autoencoder models showed high performance and accuracy enough to be applied in the real world. We expect the project result will assist in designing the ICS anomaly detection model in the future.

REFERENCES

[1] Ivo Frazão, Pedro Abreu, Tiago Cruz, Helder Araújo, and Paulo Simões. *Cyber-security modbus ics dataset*, 2019.
[2] Lucas Macena Lima da Silva. *Controle industrial com Modbus/TCP e microcontrolador esp8266*. 2022.
[3] Zhengjun Hao, Asadullah Asadullah, Surindar Wawale, and Subrata Das. Application of Modbus double-layer communication network technology in intelligent management of urban traffic equipment. *International Journal of System Assurance Engineering and Management*, 13(1):197–202, 2022.
[4] Stefano Giglio, Bryan Kelly, and Dacheng Xiu. Factor models, machine learning, and assct pricing. *Machine Learning, and Asset Pricing*, 14, 2022.
[5] Guo-Ming Sung, Chun-Ting Lee, Zhang-Yi Yan, and Chih-Ping Yu. Ethernet packet to USB data transfer bridge ASIC with Modbus transmission control protocol based on FPGA development kit. *Electronics*, 11(20):3269, 2022.
[6] Tiago Martins and Sergio Vidal Garcia Oliveira. Enhanced Modbus/TCP security protocol: Authentication and authorization functions supported. *Sensors*, 22(20):8024, 2022.

[7] Eduardo Mosqueira-Rey, Elena Hernández-Pereira, David Alonso-Ríos, José Bobes-Bascarán, and Ángel Fernández-Leal. Human-in-the-loop machine learning: A state of the art. *Artificial Intelligence Review* 56(4):1–50, 2022.

[8] David Rolnick, Priya L. Donti, Lynn H. Kaack, Kelly Kochanski, Alexandre Lacoste, Kris Sankaran, Andrew Slavin Ross, Nikola Milojevic-Dupont, Natasha Jaques, Anna Waldman-Brown, et al. Tackling climate change with machine learning. *ACM Computing Surveys (CSUR)*, 55(2):1–96, 2022.

[9] F Katulić, D Sumina, I Erceg, and S Groš. Enhancing Modbus/TCP-based industrial automation and control systems cybersecurity using a misuse-based intrusion detection system. In *2022 International Symposium on Power Electronics, Electrical Drives, Automation and Motion (SPEEDAM)*, pages 964–969. IEEE, 2022.

[10] Emily Sullivan. Understanding from machine learning models. *The British Journal for the Philosophy of Science*, 2022.

14 Face Recognition System Using CNN Architecture & Its Model with Its Detection Technique Using Machine Learning

Sonali R. Chavan and Swati Sherekar

Sant Gadge Baba Amravati University, Amravati, India

14.1 INTRODUCTION

Facial recognition systems have been used in a wide range of applications, including video surveillance, e-passports, and so on. The most prevalent biometric employed is the face. Face recognition systems, on the other hand, are vulnerable to attacks through the use of fake faces. Face spoofing is a sort of attack in which a fake face is displayed in front of the camera. Such attacks come in a variety of forms, including print attacks, video attacks, and 3D mask attacks. To detect face spoofing, a secure system is necessary [1]. Facial spoofing detection attempts to determine whether or not a face image is genuine. Facial recognition systems employ facial traits to validate the user's identification. One of the key problems in this respect is the security of facial recognition technologies. Spoofing attacks on face recognition systems, such as pictures, masks, and video attacks, are possible. The most basic security requirement is the protection of information. Traditional authentication mechanisms, such as usernames and passwords, are easily compromised. Biometric applications are becoming increasingly popular, and they are more secure than other legitimate applications. In a biometric authentication system, two processes are carried out: enrolment and verification. Enrolment is the process of producing a biometric reference template for a single individual and storing it for future comparison. Verification is the process of comparing the query biometric template to the reference one in order to make a decision. Biometric features used include the face, fingerprint, and palm. The most frequent face is the typical biometric application because it is simple to use, direct, and non-intrusive.

DOI: 10.1201/9781003363606-14

14.2　FACE SPOOFING ATTACK

Facial spoofing is a vulnerability that occurs when an attacker attempts to trick the facial recognition system by using printed images, films, or 3D masks of a legitimate person in order to gain access to the system's resources. There are two types of face spoofing: Two-dimensional face spoofing and three-dimensional face spoofing. Photographs and movies are used to produce 2D face spoofing, Whereas 3D face spoofing is done with a 3D mask, which is more expensive. Spoofing occurs when an attacker presents a bogus face in order to get authentication [2].

Facial spoofing is a vulnerability in the system that arises when an attacker attempts to fool a facial recognition system with printed photographs, videos, or a 3D mask of a genuine human in order to access to the system's resources. A spoofing attack occurs when an attacker employs a fake face to get authentication [3].

The biggest vulnerability with biometric systems is face spoofing. In spoofing attacks, biometrics is employed for high security applications. Because actual or real images are commonly used on social networking sites such as Facebook, Instagram, Orkut, and WhatsApp, facial recognition spoofing is a very common threat [4]. For the purposes of authentication, the attacker provides false evidence to the biometric system, leading in a spoofing attack [5]. There are two methods of face spoofing, i.e. 2D and 3D spoof, which are shown below in Figure 14.1. 2D attacks can be categorized into photo attacks and video attacks. A 3D spoof attack is also known as a Mask attack [6]. Photo attacks are readily carried out by uploading photographs taken with a digital camera to social networking sites. The enhanced

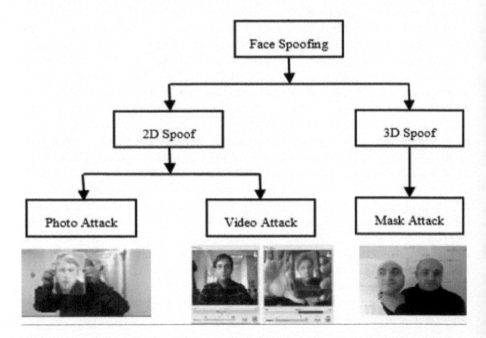

FIGURE 14.1　Classification of the face spoofing attack.

variant of the photo attack is a video attack. To carry out this attack, the attacker attempts to collect video shots by a digital camera, a mobile device, or any tablet. The 3D Mask attack is a more sophisticated variation of the photo and video attack [7, 8].

14.2.1 TYPES OF ATTACKS IN FACE SPOOFING

a. **Photo Attack**

The photo attack is a sort of 2D spoof in which an attacker exposes a photo to a biometric device, such as the screen of a mobile phone or tablet, in order to gain access to a system. This image may possibly have been captured with a digital camera or downloaded from a social media site such as Facebook, Twitter, or Instagram. Photographic masks are a more advanced type of photo attack in which high-resolution prints of the eyes and mouth are morphed. At the moment of the attack, the impersonator is positioned behind the attacker so that certain facial movements, such as eye blinking, can be duplicated [9].

These fraudulent access attempts are carried out by giving the identifying system with an image of the genuine user. It's likely either that the intruder took the shot with a digital camera, or that the user downloaded it from the internet and submitted it to one of the most popular online social networking sites.

The photograph can then be printed on paper (print printing) or displayed on the screen of a digital device, such as a smartphone or tablet (digital photo attacks). A slightly more advanced type of photo attack that has also been studied is the use of photographic masks. These masks are made of high-resolution printed images that have had the eyes and mouth removed. The impersonator is placed behind the attacker at the time of the attack, allowing certain facial movements, such as eye blinking, to be mimicked [10].

b. **Video Attack**

This is a more advanced type of photo attack. In this approach, the attacker uses a mobile phone, tablet, or digital camera to record a video of a genuine person, and then plays the footage during facial recognition to get access to the biometric modality due to proper movement of the face part. As a reason, these attacks are becoming more difficult to identify and detect [9].

These are known as replay attacks in some cases. They are a more polished take on the old photo spoofs. The attacker in this case does not use a static image, but rather a digital device (e.g., a mobile phone, tablet, or laptop) to replay a video of the genuine client. Such attacks came as the next stage in the evolution of face spoofing and are more difficult to detect since they mimic not only the 2D texture of the face but also its movement [10].

c. **3D Mask Attack**

The 3-D mask attack is a more complex variant of video and photo attacks due to the depth components in the facial characteristics. In a 3D mask attack, the attackers generate a 3D mask of the actual person (who is being impersonated), making anti-spoofing systems more difficult to implement. These attacks are less common when compared with the other types. 3D masks are commonly made from a range of materials and sizes, including paper, plastics, and silicon [9].

In other cases, the spooning artefact is a 3D mask of the underlying client's face, making effective defences more difficult to create. Because the complete 3D structure of the face is duplicated, using depth cues to avoid the two types of attacks outlined above becomes worthless in the face of this specific threat.

Although the concept of avoiding a biometric system by wearing a mask that imitates the face of another user has been discussed for some time, these attacks are far less common than the other two methods. Face-mask spoofing has just lately begun to be properly investigated, with the collection of the first mask-specific datasets, which include masks of various materials and sizes [10].

14.3 BASIC PROCESS OF FACE RECOGNITION

Facial recognition is accomplished in four discrete steps: gathering and identifying face photographs; pre-processing them; extracting features from them; and matching and recognising them. Face detection and image collecting are techniques for determining whether or not there are faces in pictures or video streams. If a face is detected in an image, the relevant regions of the image should be eliminated and the face found. When a face is found in a video stream, it must be tracked using facial features, including the nose, eyes, mouth, and contours. Image pre-processing, which has the primary purpose of minimising interruptions, includes the elimination of aberrations and the greying of images. Image pre-processing in facial recognition using image sets is much simpler or can even be skipped because an image set contains more information, and, regardless of how effective the information is, the features of an individual can be described effectively as long as the information is considered in an overall view.

One strategy for lowering computational costs is feature extraction, which involves extracting a small amount of meaningful information from a huge amount of raw data to represent a face. An individual is linked to numerous images in the image set facial recognition technique; thus, his features are formed up of the features of each image. While retaining recognition accuracy, feature extraction can drastically reduce computation expenses (Figure 14.2). The process of comparing the extracted features of an unlabelled face to the features of labelled faces in the database, and identifying which face in the database the unlabelled face matches based on the degree of similarity, is known as image identification and recognition.

It is challenging for state-of-the-art face recognition algorithms to create models with good recognition accuracy when using a small number of training samples for a single class without pretraining. The amount of face samples for each person in the current public face sample collections is relatively small. Deep learning struggles to construct a good network model in the absence of sufficient data. The accuracy of facial recognition is principally controlled by feature extraction and matching algorithms. Finally, data is critical in the creation of a good network model [11].

In this figure, the complete process of face recognition is given in some detail.

- Face Detection: a method of picking an area of interest (such as a face) from a video or image sequence.
- Face Image Pre-processing: The captured face image cannot be used as the ultimate source for facial recognition because it could also include unwelcome details such as ear, neck, clothing accessories, and jewellery. The possibility of receiving inaccurate characteristics for further processing increases due to the variability of this additional information. The quality of the acquired image can be improved through pre-processing by using various image processing techniques, such as alignment, normalisation, standardisation, and noise removal (Figures 14.2).
- Feature Extraction: Feature extraction is the step in which some crucial attributes or characteristics of the objects are extracted. This is transformed into a 1D vector in multiple applications. Features may include colour, texture & shape.
- Pattern Matching/Feature Classification: This compares the video sequence or image sequence from the stored databases and it will generate its similarity scores. In a similar manner, threshold value is calculated and it is used to classify a claim identity as it is accepted or not [12].

14.4 BIOMETRIC SYSTEM

Biometric systems are now widely understood to be subject to manipulation. Direct and indirect attacks are the two main types of attacks. Direct attacks, often known as spoofing, are a type of cyber-attack. Presentation assaults are conducted outside the sensor. The digital bounds of the biometric system Intruders, on the other hand, carry out indirect attacks inside the bounds of the digital world. Take malicious hackers on the internet. You may disregard the feature extractor and the comparator since these attackers might be trying to modify the data (Figure 14.3).

Biometrics is formed from the Greek words bio (life) and metric (measurement) (to measure). A biometric recognition system's purpose is to determine or verify an individual's identity. Based on his/her behavioural and/or biological traits. The category of characteristics includes a number of applications. These programmes are used for a variety of things, including computer security, airport security checks, and criminal identification. They are used for things like mobile device log-ins, securing private data within buildings, and controlling access to infrastructure. Applications for characteristics are also used to manage the rights to digital material. Voice mail, transaction authentication, and secure teleworking are a few examples of particular applications within the traits domain. Various biometrics have been researched, ranging from the most basic to the most advanced, fingerprint, iris, face, and voice, among others. Gait, hand-grip, ear, and electroencephalograms are among some of the newer modalities. Each modality has its own set of advantages and disadvantages. Facial

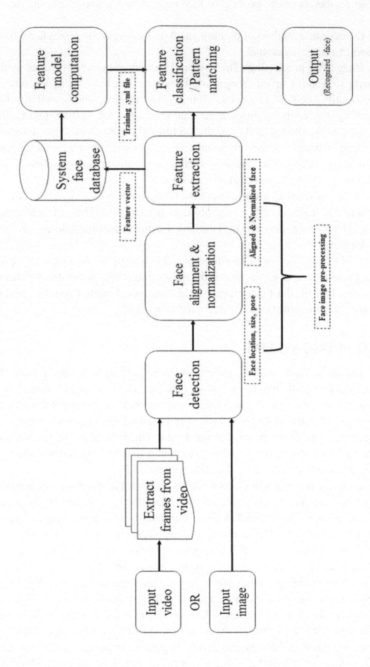

FIGURE 14.2 Basic process of face recognition.

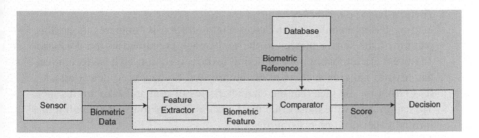

FIGURE 14.3   A generic biometric system.

recognition, for example, is one of the most widely used technologies. This is a natural method; it is a socially acceptable biometric. Humans employ various methods of identification on a daily basis. Typically, biometric systems operate in one of two modes: 1) verification (or authentication); or 2) identification. The goal of an authentication system is to validate or deny a claimed identity (one-to-one matching), but the goal of an identification system is to identify a specific person (one-to-many matching). Although the two modes have certain differences, their most basic operation, namely feature-to-reference comparison, is the same.

A biometric sample (for example, a face image) is first obtained from a sensor (e.g., a digital camera). The sample's biometric features (such as facial intensity, colour, or texture) are then retrieved. These are a set of parameters (or coefficients) that give a compact representation of the biometric sample that is more discriminative and pattern-recognition-friendly. Variations in biometric features should be minimised due to the acquisition or environmental factors when distinguishing between biometrics obtained from several people.

The properties of a given biometric sample are compared to a single (verification) or a set of (identification) biometric references collected previously during an enrolment phase to establish or verify the identity corresponding to that sample. These comparisons are conducted by a comparator, which generates a score based on how comparable features and references are. In the case of verification, the decision is acceptance or rejection, while, in the case of identification, the decision is the identity of the closest match [13].

14.5   FACE SPOOFING DETECTION CLASSIFICATION APPROACHES

Several approaches for face spoofing detection are introduced by researchers. Existing face spoofing detection techniques are classified into

    a) Texture-based approaches
    b) Motion-based approaches
    c) Image quality-based approaches
    d) Frequency approaches.
    e) Other approaches.

a. *Texture-based approaches*

Texture-based techniques can detect photo attacks. It compares the texture pattern of the sensor images to the real image contained in the database. Texture descriptors are used to define texture variations. These techniques use texture patterns such as print failures and blurriness to detect attacks. It is based on the idea that the characteristics of real and fake are distinct. This approach is the most often used since it is easy to use, although it has limited generalisation possibilities.

b. *Motion-based Approaches*

These strategies compare the motion pattern of a real user to the image collected by the sensor. It is based on the premise that two-dimensional faces move differently than three-dimensional faces. This technique uses lip moment, head rotation, and eye blinking to distinguish between the actual and faked faces. Optical flow analysis of video sequences is used in motion-based analysis. For motion-based analysis, high-quality photos are necessary.

c. *Image quality-based approaches*

The technique's goal is to identify the quality difference. This technique is predicated on the premise that fake faces are of lower quality than actual faces. Image quality is measured using features such as chromatic moment, blurriness, chromatic moments, and specular reflection.

d. *Frequency-based Approaches*

Frequency-based techniques in this approach use noise signals in recovered footage to distinguish between live and fake faces. For the detection of face spoofing attacks, these techniques rely on frequency analysis. It works on the idea that the frequency of captured videos will vary.

e. *Other Approaches*

Deep learning algorithms and person-specific approaches have recently gained prominence in the identification of face spoofing. Convolution neural network (CNN) was used for face spoofing detection in the deep learning approach. Enrolment samples are used in person-specific techniques to identify face faking. Other approaches used in the detection of face spoofing include 3D depth, infrared, and vein flow detection [14].

14.6   STEPS OF FACE RECOGNITION EXPRESSION

The facial detection system consists of number of steps which includes pre-processing, face identification, feature extraction, facial component & at last classifier for the result in terms of fake face & real face, i.e. binary classification result (Figure 14.4).

1. Pre-processing: This is the very first step in the image processing system. In this step, raw data is collected and performs some operation on it. The raw data consists of images which are not held in a standard format i.e these images contain noise, illumination variation, different sizes etc. In the pre-processing step noise is removed, and the image is enhanced and resized.

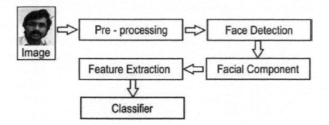

FIGURE 14.4   Steps in face detection.

2. Face Detection: After the pre-processing of the image the next goal is to remove all the unwanted noise and features are extracted, i.e here the face is extracted for further processing. This stage is called is face detection.
3. Facial Component: This is the stage where some regions of the face is selected, such as nose, eyebrows, eyes, mouth, lips etc.
4. Features Extraction: This is stage where the necessary features are selected for further classification. This stage also filters the raw data form where we take only that data which are going to be classified.
5. Classifier: The main work of classifier is to classify the image whether it is fake or real. At this stage, it going to use different classifiers such as CNN, SVM, Random Forest etc. This is the final stage in every system that identifies the fake or the real face [15].

14.7   ARCHITECTURE OF FACE TRACKING APPROACHES

In computer vision, tracking is the important area. Figure 14.5 indicates the overview of the face tracking approaches. Face tracking can be divided into three main groups: the first is head-based, the second is facial features-based and the third is real-time tracking. The head features approach is further classified as model-based, shape-based and colour-based.

Real-time approaches are again divided into Condensation, Meanshift, Kalman Filter and Croma based. Finally, model-based approaches are divided into two categories: the Active Appearance Model and the Exemplar Model.

1. Head-Based Approaches
   a. **Model-Based Approach**
      For tracking, the author employs an active appearance model, which is a parametric model, to generate an effective method that solves the disadvantage of posture. The variations and lighting fluctuate with the camera's view field.
   b. **Shape- and colour-based approach**
      The author integrates the condensation method with both the skin film's colour and facial structure to effectively follow the facial expression under diverse lighting variations.

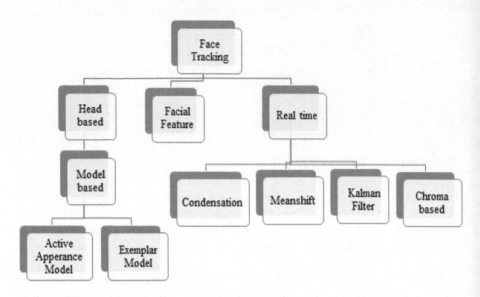

FIGURE 14.5 Architecture of face tracking approaches.

2. Facial Features-based approach

The author integrates the continuous brightness facial detection algorithm with a facial monitoring Kalman filter that enhances the speed and precision of the entire object tracking model.

3. Real-time Tracking Approach

Because of the real-time face tracking in each frame, these approaches have recently piqued the interest of viewers. These following are some of the real-time face tracking approaches that have been employed [16].

- Condensation
- Meanshift
- Kalman filter
- Chroma-based

14.8 FACE SPOOFING DETECTION TECHNIQUE

Shilpa Garg et al.'s DeBNet is a tool for classifying real and artificial faces and extracting deep information from facial features. The developed technique for liveness detection is reliable and effective and produces the best results when compared to the existing one. During an experiment, a number of parameters are employed, such as the NUAA Dataset, which provides a 99% detection rate and a 0.31 half total failure rate. Additional parameters include detection accuracy, positive predictive value, true negative rate, and others. As a result of employing deep learning to extract the features, this DeBNet technique achieves the highest detection rate but is quite time-consuming [17].

By utilising a Deep Learning Algorithm, the authors Gustavo B. Souza and colleagues suggest a brand-new, effective technique called deep Boltzmann machine (DBM). DBM has the ability to handle intricate patterns and difficult-to-create features by collecting and works show features from raw data. While existing algorithms detect malicious behaviour in the database with an accuracy rate of up to 68%, the proposed technique achieves a higher level of accuracy, close to 86%, and has a flatter ROC curve. The results show that by using the LivDet data on the CUDA platform, the proposed method exceeds earlier techniques in terms of threat accuracy rate as well as the capacity for using less labelled data [18].

An approach for identifying face spoofing attacks that is non-intrusive and relies on a single frame sequence is presented by authors Aziz Alotaibi et al. A specific deep CNN was built to extract complex attributes from input blurred frames. The synthetic face image has fewer edges as well as a flat area surrounding the eye, nose, mouth, and cheek areas after the input films are twice rebuilt, obliterating all sharp edges and shifting the pixel positions. By the application of several factors, including the false negative rate and false admission rate, as well as working with the Active Attacks data to use a machine learning technique, the half absolute error rate will be reduced [19].

To determine if an iris image is authentic or fake, author Waleed S.-A. Fathy and colleagues created the Feature Selection Algorithm. Multi-level two-dimensional wavelet decomposition is used to acquire the approximate value & characteristics of the wavelet channel. Features are classified by Euclidean distance and appropriate mixing techniques. The system's performance is improved by using an effective feature selection strategy, which lowers the computational burden. The classification accuracy of CASIA IRIS SYN is 100% and it uses 4,444 of roughly 10,000 composite pictures. The proposed attribute selection classifier integration decreases dimensionality while still carefully examining the connection between statistical variables and not ignoring features that offer additional information. These outcomes also indicate that using the original [20].

14.9 TAXONOMY OF DEEP CNN ARCHITECTURE

Machine learning and deep learning are recent areas which are used to solve the problem of face recognition. In taxonomy, taken the different classification of CNN and their deep learning architecture. Thus, all architecture is used for face detection or face recognition. Machine learning and deep learning plays a very important role in advanced face spoofing and detection. The traditional model of the face recognition system does not provide accurate predictions when compared to this deep learning algorithm. This chapter discusses some of the architecture of the deep CNN-based algorithm (Figure 14.6).

14.9.1 LeNet Architecture

LeCuN proposed LeNet in 1998 (LeCun et al. 1995). It is well known because it was the first CNN to demonstrate cutting-edge efficiency on hand-digit text

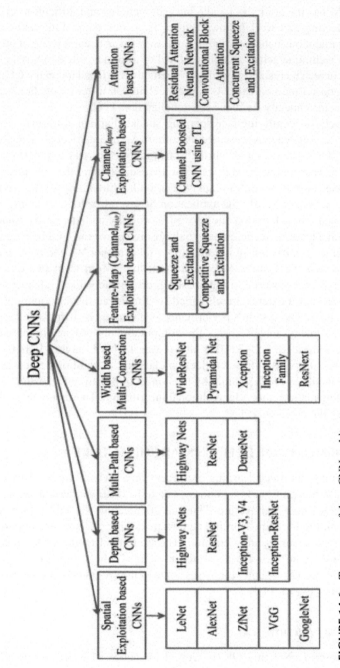

FIGURE 14.6 Taxonomy of deep CNN architecture.

categorization. It can identify digits without being impacted by minor distortions, rotation, or changes in position and scale. LeNet is a feed-forward neural network (NN) composed of five alternating convolutional and pooling layers, followed by two fully connected layers. In the mid-2000s, GPUs were rarely used to accelerate training, and even CPUs were slow. The major limitation of traditional multi-layered fully connected NN was that it treated every pixel as a distinct input and applied a transformation to it, which imposed a high computation burden at the moment.

LeNet took advantage of the image's underlying foundation, which is that neighbouring pixels are correlated to one another and feature patterns are dispersed across the input frame. Convolution with trainable parameters is thus a productive method for the extraction of common traits at numerous places with a very few parameters. The conceptions of training, where each pixel was viewed as a completely separate input parameter from its neighbourhood and neglected the correlation between them, was altered by gaining knowledge with freely distributable parameters. LeNet was the initial CNN architecture that could not only reduce the amount of parameters but also immediately learn features from raw pixels.

14.9.2 ALEXNET ARCHITECTURE

LeNet, on the other hand, began the past of the deep CNN., During this period, however, CNN was restricted to hand-digit classification methods and did not do well across all image classes. AlexNet is widely regarded as the initial deep CNN architecture, achieving ground-breaking results in classification tasks and classification techniques. Krizhevsky proposed AlexNet, which improved the learning capability of the CNN by trying to make it deeper and employing many parameterization strategies. Figure 14.7 depicts the basic architectural design of AlexNet. In the mid-2000s, device constraints limited the learning ability of deep CNN architectures by limiting their dimensions. In order to take advantage from deep CNNs' representational ability. To overcome hardware constraints, AlexNet was trained in parallel on two NVIDIA GTX 580 GPUs.

In Alex Net, extension of the layers was up to 8 layers to classify the diverse category of the images. Due to depth generalization, various resolutions could be taken, but when depth is increase an overfitting problem occurred. To solve this problem, overlapping subsampling and local response is used to enhance the generalization by decreasing the overfitting. Due to the learning approach, it has proven to be more popular than all the other CNN architecture [21].

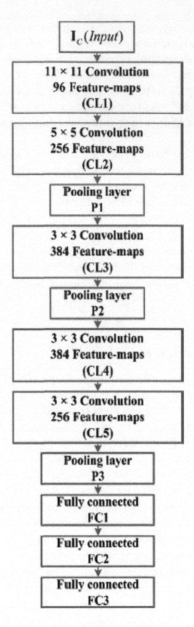

FIGURE 14.7　Basic layout of AlexNet with its layers.

14.10　CONCLUSION

The human face is a very important biometric factor used in everyday security processes due to its unique characteristics. For authentication purposes, it is widely used in large-scale applications, as the demand for biometric technology is increasing. It leads to research work in the field of face spoofing attack, which is a challenging task for the researcher. In recent years, more researchers have given increased focus to detecting the differences between real and genuine faces. In this chapter, the types of face spoofing attacks, biometric systems that are vulnerable to the face spoofing attack, the CNN architecture model used in detecting real or fake faces are discussed here. This gives a detailed study of different models which will be used in the detection of faces, either real or fake. Researchers can take this advantage to outline their further research in the field of the face spoofing attack.

REFERENCES

[1] S. R. Chavan, S. S. Sherekar, V. M. Thakare. "A Survey on Social Networking Attacks: Issues and Challenges", *National Conference on Recent Advances in Science and Technology*, ISSN: 2277 (Ajanta) 5730, 5–6. March 2019.

[2] "Factors Related to the Improvement of Face Anti-Spoofing Detection Techniques with CNN Classifier," Presented *International Conference on Computational Intelligence and Computing Applications (ICCICA)* organized by G. H. Raisoni college Nagpur at 26–27. November 2021.

[3] N. Daniel, A. Anitha, "A Study on Recent Trends in Face Spoofing Detection Techniques," *3rd International Conference on Inventive Computation Technologies (ICICT)*, pp. 583–586, doi: 10.1109/ICICT43934.2018.9034361, 2018.

[4] S. R. Chavan, S. S. Sherekar, V. M. Thakare, "Traceability Analysis of Face Spoofing Detection Techniques Using Machine Learning," *International Conference on Innovative Trends and Advances In Engineering and Technology (ICITAET)*, Shegaon, India, pp. 84–88, doi: 10.1109/Icitaet47105.2019.9170212, 2019.

[5] W. Sun, Y. Song, H. Zhao, Z. Jin, "A Face Spoofing Detection Method Based on Domain Adaptation and Lossless Size Adaptation," *IEEE Access*, vol. 8, pp. 66553–66563, doi: 10.1109/ACCESS.2020.2985453, 2020.

[6] A. Alotaibi, A. Mahmood "Deep Face Liveness Detection Based on Nonlinear Diffusion Using Convolution Neural Network," *Signal, Image and Video Processing*, vol. 11, pp. 713–720, doi:10.1007/s11760-016-1014-2, 2017.

[7] Oeslle Lucena, Amadeu Junior, Vitor Hugo G Moia, Roberto Souza, Eduardo Valle, Roberto Lotufo. "Transfer Learning Using Convolutional Neural Networks for Face Anti-Spoofing," doi:10.1007/978-3-319-59876-5, 2017.

[8] M. Singh, A.S. Arora "A Novel Face Liveness Detection Algorithm with Multiple Liveness Indicators," *Wireless Personal Communications*, vol. 100, pp. 1677–1687, doi:10.1007/s11277-018-5661-1, 2018.

[9] S. Kumar, S. Singh, J. Kumar "A Comparative Study on Face Spoofing Attacks," *International Conference on Computing, Communication and Automation (ICCCA)*, pp. 1104–1108, doi: 10.1109/CCAA.2017.8229961, 2017.

[10] J. Galbally, S. Marcel, J. Fierrez, "Biometric Antispoofing Methods: A Survey in Face Recognition," *IEEE Access*, vol. 2, pp. 1530–1552, doi: 10.1109/ACCESS.2014.2381273, 2014.

[11] L. Wu, S. Liu. "Comparative Analysis and Application of LBP Face Image Recognition Algorithms," *International Journal of Communication Systems*, vol. 34, pp. e3977, doi: 10.1002/dac.3977, 2021.

[12] M.K. Rusia, D.K. Singh, "A Comprehensive Survey on Techniques to Handle Face Identity Threats: Challenges and Opportunities," *Multimedia Tools and Applications*, doi: 10.1007/s11042-022-13248-6, 2022.

[13] A. Hadid, N. Evans, S. Marcel, J. Fierrez, "Biometrics Systems Under Spoofing Attack: An Evaluation Methodology and Lessons Learned," *IEEE Signal Processing Magazine*, vol. 32, no. 5, pp. 20–30, doi: 10.1109/MSP.2015.2437652, 2015.

[14] N. Daniel, A. Anitha, "A Study on Recent Trends in Face Spoofing Detection Techniques," *International Conference on Inventive Computation Technologies (ICICT)* pp. 583–586, doi: 10.1109/ICICT43934.2018.9034361, 2018.

[15] J. Anil, L. P. Suresh, "Literature Survey on Face and Face Expression Recognition," *International Conference on Circuit, Power and Computing Technologies (ICCPCT)*, pp. 1–6, doi: 10.1109/ICCPCT.2016.7530173, 2016.

[16] R. Vij, B. Kaushik, "A Survey on Various Face detecting and Tracking Techniques in Video Sequences," *International Conference on Intelligent Computing and Control Systems (ICCS)*, pp. 69–73, doi: 10.1109/ICCS45141.2019.9065483, 2019.

[17] S. Garg, S. Mittal, P. Kumar, V. Anant Athavale, "DeBNet: Multilayer Deep Network for Liveness Detection in Face Recognition System," *7th International Conference on Signal Processing and Integrated Networks (SPIN)*, pp. 1136–1141, doi: 10.1109/SPIN48934.2020.9070853, 2020.

[18] G. B. Souza, D. F. S. Santos, R. G. Pires, A. N. Marana, J. P. Papa, "Deep Boltzmann Machines for Robust Fingerprint Spoofing Attack Detection," *International Joint Conference on Neural Networks (IJCNN)*, pp. 1863–1870, doi: 10.1109/IJCNN.2017.7966077, 2017.

[19] A. Alotaibi, A. Mahmood, "Enhancing Computer Vision to Detect Face Spoofing Attack Utilizing a Single Frame from a Replay Video Attack Using Deep Learning," *International Conference on Optoelectronics and Image Processing (ICOIP)* pp. 1–5, doi: 10.1109/OPTIP.2016.7528488, 2016.

[20] W. S. -A. Fathy, H. S. Ali, I. I. Mahmoud, "Statistical Representation for Iris Anti-spoofing Using Wavelet-based Feature Extraction and Selection Algorithms," *34th National Radio Science Conference (NRSC)*, pp. 221–229, doi: 10.1109/NRSC.2017.7893480, 2017.

[21] A. Khan, A. Sohail, U. Zahoora et al. "A Survey of the Recent Architectures of Deep Convolutional Neural Networks," *Artificial Intelligence Review*, vol. 53, pp. 5455–5516, doi: 10.1007/s10462-020-09825-6, 2020.

15 Network Security Configuration for Campus LAN Using CPT

P. Saleem Akram, Lavanya Veeranki,
Anjali Kakarla and Tejaswini Pamidimukkala
Koneru Lakshmaiah Education Foundation, Guntur, India

15.1 INTRODUCTION

Given the rapid growth of networks today, we have paid considerable attention to the confidentiality of the network connection. And even though our network protection means are now advanced, there are many difficulties in managing the information system, which is a special network provider, because of the large number of clients and the near-universal availability of the network. As desktops and networking technologies continue to expand in the current world, increased and solid system and network security has become increasingly crucial and essential. The expansion of the networked computer has exposed several systems to multiple types of internet attacks. Recognition, verification, permission, and surveillance equipment may be used to preserve the security, accessibility, responsibility, and provenance of computer equipment or network infrastructure [1]. There is no set of rules and guidelines for creating a secure network. Network security must be tailored to an organization's policies and procedures.

The campus network is crucial and performs an important role in the workplace. Atmosphere, moisture, nourishment, and housing are all as important as network technology and stability. Threats to desktop structure security and system infrastructure are invariably significant concerns [2]. An arrangement design is a sovereignty network dominated by a community college located in a specific geographic region and may also be a metropolitan area network (MAN). A desktop system administrator faces numerous difficulties in ensuring highly scalable, strong performance and stability. Multiple people belong in a subnet, each with its resource availability. Network administrators may desire the restriction of access to particular portions of the network and prevent confidential material from "spilling" between various portions of the network or from the company's network to the global Internet. It is hard for network administrators to translate these high-level strategies and project goals at the level of specific devices when they are not based on a network-wide point of view.

DOI: 10.1201/9781003363606-15

15.2   BLOCK DIAGRAM

Figure 15.1 represents the block diagram of the university campus network architecture; we will access the university services data. The Access layer, Distribution layer, Core layer, Server Farm, and data center are present in the university campus network. E-learning, Internet connectivity, VPN remote access, and site-to-site VPN are present in university sensors which play a major role in data transfer. All these are going to be accessed through remote sensors. By this, the data has been sent from one to another without any data loss. We are configuring a username and password to secure your data using university services [3]. ISP A, ISP B, PSTN, and FRAME RELAY are working at a service provider end. With the help of this service provider end, the remote sensors will access the data of the end users.

15.3   REQUIRED RESOURCES

In our work, we utilized various types of gadgets to demonstrate various interconnect scenarios. Most gadgets, such as PCs, are attached via connectors. However, a few of them, such as PCs, were wirelessly connected. We used wireless devices as a wireless connection provider. The appliance abridgment is as follows:

1. Routers
2. Layer 3 Switch
3. Layer 2 Switch
4. Access Point

15.4   CONFIGURATION STEPS

1. Create topology on the Cisco Packet tracer platform and perform basic settings, including SSH on routers and 12 switches [4].
2. Configure VLANs and perform trunk and access operations.
3. Secure the 12 switches by the switch port.
4. Perform IP addressing to all interfaces and subnetting according to the VLANs.
5. Configure OSPF on network devices like routers and switches.
6. Perform static IP Addresses to server room devices.
7. Configure the DHCP server.
8. Inter VLAN Routing and DHCP Helper address on 12 switches.
9. Configure the Wireless network.
10. Verify the output and test the results.

15.5   WORKING METHODOLOGY

After the basic setup of the topology and basic settings in the Cisco Packet tracer, we have to proceed with further steps, and we should configure step-wise.

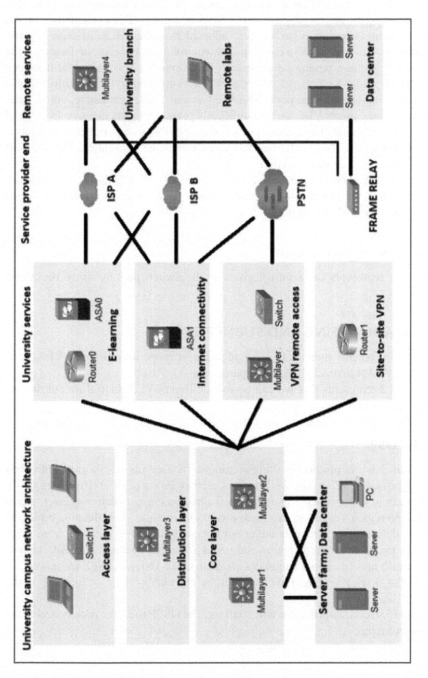

FIGURE 15.1 Network architecture.

15.5.1 VLANs

VLANs are an accumulation of locally linked local area networks (LANs) that strengthen security and regulate LANs' radio addresses. Consequentially, in the secured network segment, VLANs were adopted in some places to segregate the smart objects into various VLANs [5]. The environment consists of factors. First of all, it will arrange separate departments in diverse VLANs, which will reduce the levels of traffic. Second, VLAN is used for extra security. It will block malicious users from utilizing the ports. The five types of VLAN are native, voice, data, management, and preset VLANs; default VLAN presently exists in every switch and is assigned to all ports. Thus, those ports are simple for outside rather than interior criminals to exploit. Thus, switching to VLAN versus the conventional VLAN will give all connections more protection.

Figure 15.2 represents the schematic diagram of the VLANs configuring all switches to differentiate the blocks and perform Trunk mode to access different VLANs and access Modes in the VLAN.

15.5.2 SWITCH PORT SECURITY

Figure 15.3 represents the security given to the switch port by using the above commands.

15.6 IP ADDRESSING AND SUBNETTING

Table 15.1 represents that we have divided the network into different VLANs to allow each VLAN to reach different departments.

Table 15.2 represents that we can perform different VLANs to different departments as performed above.

15.6.1 OSPF

OSPF is an Internet protocol routing technique focused on the Shortest Path First (SPF) algorithm. OSPF exists for Interior Gateway Protocol (IGP) [6]. In an OSPF area, devices or systems in the same region retain the same connection dataset, which explains the region's architecture. Each modem or framework in the area builds its link-state dataset from link-state advertising messages (LSAs) received from other devices or mechanisms in the region and LSAs generated by itself. An LSA is a unit of data which has data about neighbors and path costs. Using the SPF technique, we can find the shortest path and avoid a loop by calculating the root focused on the link-state dataset.

Figure 15.4 represents that we will configure the OSPF to all the routers according to the above figure.

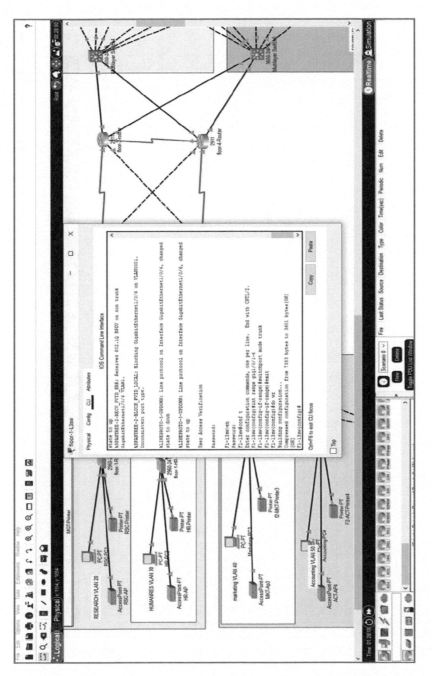

FIGURE 15.2 VLAN configuration with devices.

FIGURE 15.3　Switch port security for all switches.

TABLE 15.1

Performing Subnetting

Department	Network Address	Subnet Mask	Host address range	Broadcast address
Management	192.168.10.0	255.255.255.192/26	192.168.10.1-192.168.10.62	192.168.10.63
Research	192.168.10.64	255.255.255.192/26	192.168.10.65-192.168.10.126	192.168.10.127
Human Resources	192168.10.128	255.255.255.192/26	192.168.10.129-192.168.10.190	192.168.10.191

TABLE 15.2

Different Networks of VLAN

Department	Network Address	Subnet Mask	Host address range	Broadcast address
Marketing	192.168.10.192	255.255.255.192/26	192.168.10.193-192.168.10.254	192.168.10.255
Accounts	192.168.11.0	255.255.255.192/26	192.168.11.1-192.168.11.62	192.168.11.63
Finance	192168.11.64	255.255.255.192/26	192.168.11.65-192.168.11.126	192.168.11.127

Figure 15.5 represents the OSPF configuring d on all routers to find the shortest path to transfer the data from the source to the destination.

15.6.2 DHCP

DHCP stands for Dynamic Host Configuration Protocol, a user-/server-based procedure that automatically assigns a Network address and other network configurations to an Internet Protocol (IP) host, such as the IP protocol and broadcast address. To enter the system and its assets, each gadget on a TCP/IP-based system must be assigned a specific unicast IP address [7]. Network devices for computer systems or computers relocated from one VLAN to another have to be directly programmable without DHCP; IP for computer systems deleted from the system must be individually recaptured.

Figure 15.6 represents the DHCP assigned to all the networks, i.e., VLANs of different departments so that we can get the IP address to PCs connected to the particular department from the DHCP server.

15.7 WIRELESS CONNECTIVITY

Figure 15.7 represents that we have taken the laptop to connect the laptop to access the pointer wirelessly by giving usernames and passwords to the access pointers so that we can access Wi-Fi from the laptop by entering the correct password.

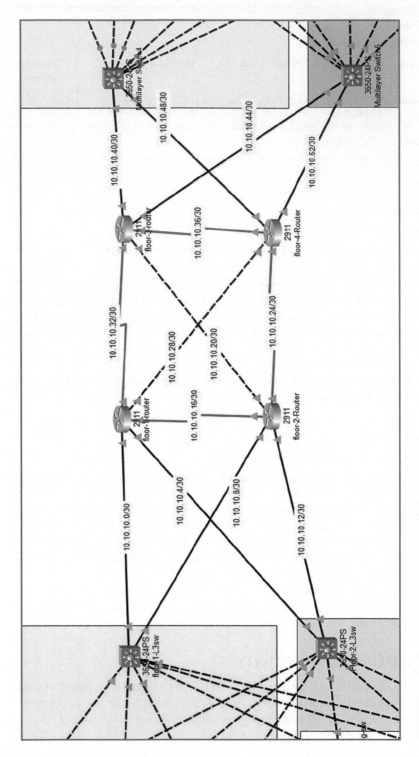

FIGURE 15.4 Topology of routers that can perform OSPF.

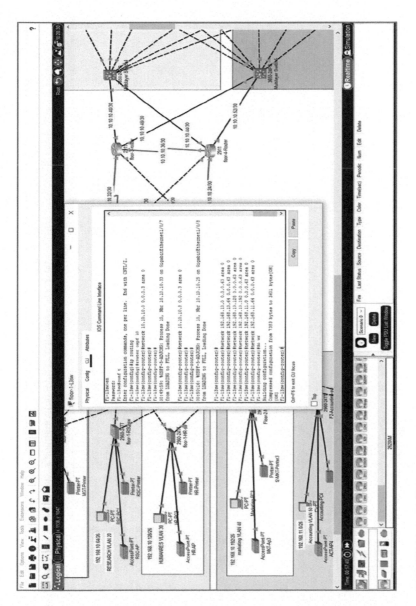

FIGURE 15.5 OSPF configuration.

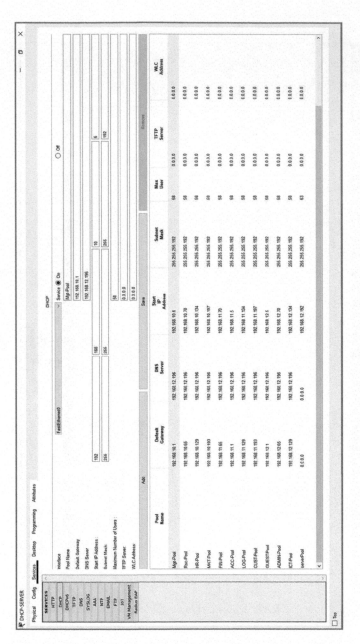

FIGURE 15.6 DHCP server configuration with IP addresses in server.

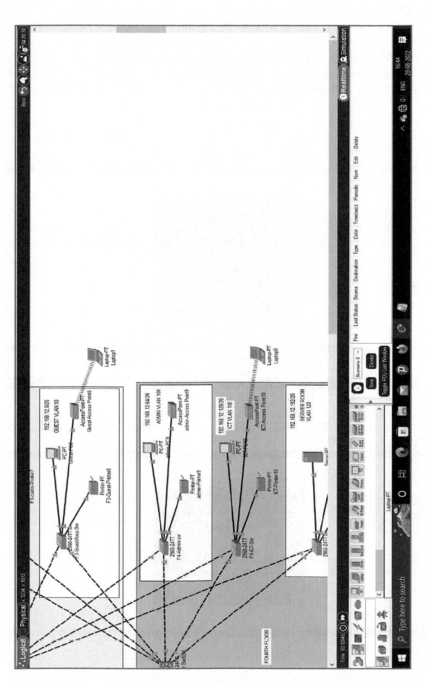

FIGURE 15.7 Wireless connectivity from access points.

15.8　SIMULATION

Figure 15.8 shows that packets that are passed/transmitted from the PC to the laptop connected wirelessly are successful. We should take a laptop so that we have to connect wireless to the Access pointer and connect to Wi-Fi using Username and Password. After connecting, therefore, we have to check the connection by pinging the IP address of the laptop in any PC from the network. So Figures 15.8(a, b) represent the successful transmission of packets.

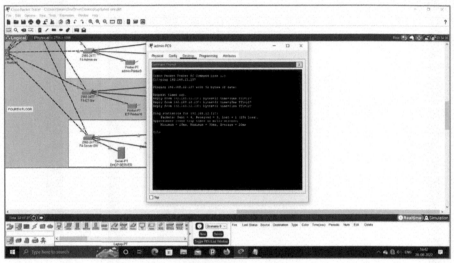

(a)

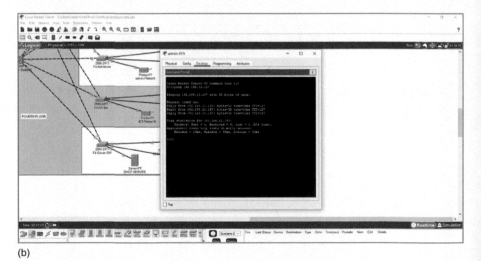

(b)

FIGURE 15.8　(a) Pinging from PC to laptop, (b): Pinging from PC of one department to laptop.

15.9   RESULTS AND CONCLUSION

After the successful configuration of VLAN, OSPF, DHCP, and all protocols mentioned on all devices, such as layer two switches, layer three switches, and routers, we have to check the successful connection. Hence, we used DHCP to get the address for all PCs in the network by the DHCP server so that we have used access pointers in network to get Wi-Fi to connect our gadgets. Access pointers provide security so that each Wi-Fi-enabled device will need to enter a security code like Username and Password to reach the network and ensure that packets of data are successfully sent from the sender to the receiver.

It has already been discovered that the campus area network's Wi-Fi is insecure and vulnerable to hacking due to poor security setups in a few WAPs. Even so, most people will connect to WAPs using the strictest WPA2-PSK security rules via the most recent Samsung Android users. This opens up new possibilities for IT Services to capitalize on this pattern. Most security technology is software-based, as also are some hardware components. Likewise, the security system comprises provisions built into the underlying computer network infrastructure, rules set by the system administrator to guard against unapproved network resources and their resources, and the efficiency (or lack thereof) of all these components. Network security is an important research area that is receiving increasing attention as the network size increases.

Security risks and access technologies should be analyzed to determine the appropriate security system. Data encryption is mostly application, but it also includes various hardware components. Furthermore, data security includes a provision made in an underlying computer network infrastructure, policies implemented by the system administrator to safeguard the connectivity and infrastructure assets from unauthorized access, and the efficiency (or lack thereof) of these indicators when combined.

An optimal network protection strategy should be devised with a profound comprehension of security risks, preferred attackers, the amount of protection required, and the elements that make a system susceptible to attack. Encoding, authorization processes, intrusion prevention, information security, and security software are all among the tools for reducing a user's security vulnerabilities.

Moreover, implementing security network guidelines can help mitigate external threats and prevent staff members from introducing the risk of misconfiguration, thereby safeguarding the system.

REFERENCES

[1] Sulaimon Adeniji Adebayo, Bachelor's Thesis (UAS) Network Security, Degree Program in Information Technology Specialization: Internet Technology.

[2] Network Architecture and Security Issues in Campus Networks, Mohammed Nadir Bin Ali, Fourth International Conference on Computing, Communications and Networking Technologies (ICCCNT) 2013.

[3] S.A. Khan, "A STRIDE Model Based Threat Modelling Using Unified and-or Fuzzy Operator for Computer Network Security," *International Journal of Computing and Network Technology*, vol. 5, no. 01, pp. 13–20, 2017.

[4] A.H. Ahmed, M.N. Al-Hamadani. "Designing a Secure Campus Network and Simulating It Using Cisco Packet Tracer," *Indonesian Journal of Electrical Engineering and Computer Science*, vol. 23, no. 1, pp. 479–489, 2021.

[5] M. Naagas, E. Mique, and T. D. Palaoag, "Defense-through-deception Network Security Model: Securing University Campus Network from DOS/DDOS Attack," *Bulletin of Electrical Engineering and Informatics*, vol. 7, no. 4, p. 593600, 2018, DOI: 10.11591/eei.v7i4.1349.

[6] M. Jahanirad, A.L.N. Yahya, and R.M. Noor, Comprehensive Network Security Approach: Security Breaches.

[7] https://www.youtube.com/watch?v=NLMqmaBvD8Q

16 Advancements in IoT-Based Smart Environmental Systems

*Shashwat Gupta, Pradeep Kumar, Shikha Singh,
Garima Srivastava and Bramah Hazela*

Amity University (U.P) Lucknow Campus, Lucknow, India

16.1 INTRODUCTION

There is now a lot of talk about the Internet of Things (or IoT) and how it will affect everything from how we travel and shop to how manufacturers manage their inventories. But what is it? How does it function? And how significant is it really? The IoT is the idea of connecting any gadget to the Internet and other connected devices (Figure 16.1). The IoT is a vast network of interconnected devices and people, all of which gather and exchange information about their environments and how they are used [1]. That encompasses an extraordinary variety of items of all sizes and shapes, such as self-driving cars with sophisticated sensors that can detect objects in their path and smart microwaves that cook food for us automatically. It also includes wearable fitness devices that monitor our heart rate and the number of steps we take each day in order to provide us with personalized exercise recommendations. Even connected footballs are available that can monitor how far and quickly they are thrown and record those facts using an app for future practice. Nowadays, sometimes, computers like the Raspberry Pi are used in creating cost-effective IoT systems [2].

This chapter tries to further explain the role of IoT in numerous facets of daily life with a focus on intelligent environmental systems. Along with providing light on security concerns related to IoT devices, this chapter will also highlight different existing IoT standards and frameworks.

Sensor-equipped devices and items are linked to an IoT platform, which combines data from many devices and employs analytics to communicate the most important information with programs designed to answer certain requirements. These robust IoT solutions can precisely identify which information is helpful and which may be safely disregarded. This data can be used to identify trends, generate recommendations, and identify potential issues before they arise. For instance, the owner of a

DOI: 10.1201/9781003363606-16

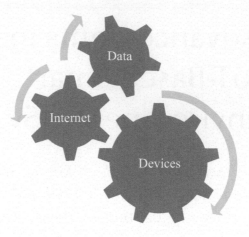

FIGURE 16.1   Internet of Things [3].

company that manufactures cars could be interested in learning which add-ons, such as leather seats or alloy wheels, are the most popular. They can do it by the means of IoT technologies:

- Use sensors to identify which showroom spaces are the busiest and where patrons remain the longest.
- Analyze the available sales data in-depth to determine which components are selling the quickest.
- Automatically match supply and sales data to prevent the run-out of popular goods.

One can make informed judgments about which items to start stockpiling based on current information thanks to linked devices, which helps them save both money and time. The ability to improve procedures comes with the insight provide by sophisticated analytics. We can automate some chores thanks to smart systems and objects, especially if they are monotonous, time-consuming, repetitive, or even hazardous. To show how this appears in practice let's look at some samples of IoT devices [4]:

- Home Security
  IoT is the main force behind safe and secure houses. IoT connections are used to link a range of sensors, lights, alarms, and cameras—all of which can be managed from a smartphone—to offer security around the clock.
- Activity Trackers
  Alerts and security are provided via smart home security cameras. Activity trackers are sensor-based gadgets that may continuously monitor and communicate important health markers. We may monitor and control our oxygen levels, hunger, physical activity, and blood pressure.

- Industrial Security and Safety
  To identify trespassers, IoT-enabled detection systems, cameras, and sensors can be installed in restricted areas. Additionally, they may spot little chemical leaks and pressure buildups before they turn into larger issues and rectify them.
- Augmented Reality Glasses
  Wearable computer-enabled glasses known as augmented reality (AR) glasses enable users to add additional information, such as 3D animations and films, to real-world surroundings.
  Users can access Internet apps with the assistance of the information, which is shown within the glasses' lenses.
- Motion Detection
  Vibrations in huge structures such as buildings, bridges, dams, and others can be picked up by motion sensors. These tools can spot structural irregularities and disturbances that might trigger disastrous breakdowns. They can also be employed in places that are prone to earthquakes, landslides, and floods [5].

An overview of the IoT is given at the beginning of the chapter, followed by a brief overview of its history. The motivation behind picking the subject for investigation is covered in the following section. IoT-based smart environmental systems, such as those for smart homes, smart factories, smart cities, and smart transportation, as well as how IoT is used to disaster management, are described in Section 16.4. In Section 16.5, it is discussed how IoT is assisting in the monitoring of various environmental health conditions based on the quality of the water we drink, the air we breathe, and the knowledge of the presence of toxic gases in our environment so that appropriate action could be taken to either control them or be ready to fight against them. Section 16.6 discusses various IoT standards and frameworks, security concerns with IoT devices, how to secure IoT devices, and the ratio of effort required to defend against an attack to that required to secure it. Towards the end after discussing the advantages and disadvantages of the IoT-based smart environment system, the conclusion and potential future applications are discussed.

16.2   BRIEF HISTORY OF THE INTERNET OF THINGS

The idea of embedding sensors and intelligence into physical items was initially considered in the 1980s, when some university students intended to alter a Coca-Cola vending machine so that its contents could be tracked remotely. However, the technology was cumbersome, and development was slow. Kevin Ashton, a computer scientist, created the phrase "Internet of Things" in 1999. While working for Procter & Gamble, Ashton recommended putting radio-frequency identification (RFID) chips on items to follow them along the supply chain. To catch the executives' attention, he allegedly slipped the then-buzzword 'internet' into his presentation. And the term remained with him. The public's interest in the IoT began to increase during the following ten years as more and more linked gadgets entered the market.

LG debuted the very first smart refrigerator in 2000, the first iPhone was released in 2007, and by 2008, the number of linked gadgets had surpassed the human population of the Earth. Google began developing self-driving cars in 2009, while Google's Nest smart thermostat, which enabled the remote management of central heating, joined the market in 2011 [6, 7].

The IoT application that has been implemented will have a big impact on the networking, connection, and communicative protocols. IoT applications may be divided into many distinct categories depending on how they are used, just as there are several different IoT devices. Here are a few of the most typical:

- Consumer IoT: Mostly for daily use. For instance, household appliances, speech recognition software, and light fixtures.
- Commercial IoT: Mostly utilized in the transportation and healthcare sectors. Smart monitors and pacemakers, for instance.
- Military Things (IoMT): IoT technologies are mostly applied in the military through the usage of military things. Robotic surveillance and combat biometrics, for instance.
- Industrial IoT (IIoT): This technology is mostly utilized for industrial applications, such as those in the manufacturing and energy industries. Examples include industrial big data, smart agriculture, and digital control systems.
- Infrastructure IoT: IoT infrastructure is mostly utilized in smart cities for connection. For instance, management and sensor systems for infrastructure.

16.3 MOTIVATION BEHIND IOT

People who use the Internet of Things can live and work more intelligently and have total control over their lives. IoT is crucial to business in addition to providing smart home automation devices. With the help of IoT, organizations can see in real time how their systems actually function, gaining insights into anything from equipment performance to supply chain and logistics activities.

People that use the IoT may lead more intelligent lives, do jobs more effectively, and have complete control over their daily lives. In addition to offering smart home automation devices, IoT is essential for business. It enables businesses to monitor the real-time performance of their systems, providing insights into equipment performance, supply chain and logistics operations, and much more. As more businesses see the potential of linked devices to keep them competitive, IoT will continue to gain momentum as one of the most crucial technologies of everyday life [8]. Every smart device connected to an Internet of Things (IoT) network has one of the most fundamental characteristics: the ability to gather a larger collection of newly created data and send it over the internet to the recipient server [9]. By utilising complex algorithms to analyse vast amounts of data, machine learning may assist in demystifying the hidden patterns in IoT data. In crucial operations, automated systems applying statistically determined actions can augment or completely replace manual procedures [10]. We shall be connected in ways that are incredibly futuristic in the coming years. Integration of IoT and AI will open new avenues for cutting-edge applications in numerous industries.

16.4 INTERNET OF THINGS-BASED SMART ENVIRONMENTAL SYSTEM

16.4.1 SMART HOME

Over the past decade or so, there has been a significant surge in the production of new "smart" devices that can connect to the Internet and be controlled remotely by apps. A network of devices and other items known as the "Internet of Things" includes electronics, sensors, software, and communication capabilities (IoT). It has led to the development of a cloud-based IoT-based system for the construction of smart homes as well as the most recent cloud computing technology [11, 12]. The idea of a "Smart Home," coupled with ubiquitous network coverage and integrated computer technology, is taking on increasing importance for residents of highly urbanized places [13] as referred in Figure 16.2.

16.4.2 SMART HEALTH

The use of real-time health and tracking systems in the healthcare industry has improved patient care, diagnosis, maintenance of medical and diagnostic equipment, and remote procedures. Patient happiness depends on connected healthcare making the right judgments, taking the appropriate actions, and providing smart treatments. The importance of IoT in healthcare is depicted in Figure 16.3. The following is a list of benefits that IoT devices may offer healthcare organizations [14, 15]:

- Patient costs are decreased, and health is remotely monitored.
- Shorten the duration of the patient's hospital stay.
- Patients receive individualized care via gadgets like blood pressure cuffs, heart rate monitors, and glucose meters. These gadgets may also remind users of their calorie intake, doctor visits, and activity monitoring.

FIGURE 16.2 Smart home [13].

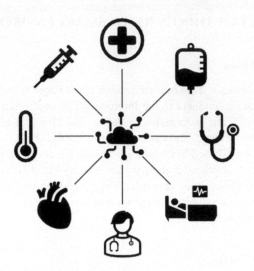

FIGURE 16.3   Importance of IoT in healthcare [16].

- Medical equipment locations may be tracked in real-time using IoT devices with sensors.
- Asset supervision.

16.4.3 SMART CITY

Smart city technologies aim to ease daily burdens and increase productivity while addressing problems with public safety, traffic, and the environment. Smart Utility Meters, Smart Transportation, Smart Waste Management Systems, Smart Air Quality Monitors, Smart Road Traffic, Smart Parking, Smart Grids, and other technologies are among the most widely used smart city technologies. Cities may link and control various infrastructures and public services with the aid of IoT. The variety of use cases is quite wide, ranging from linked public transportation and waste management to smart lighting and traffic. The results are what they share in common. When IoT solutions are used, energy costs are decreased, natural resource utilization is maximized, cities are safer, and the environment is healthier.

Municipalities should adopt a consistent strategy when designing a practical and scalable architecture for smart cities, nevertheless, to reap these benefits. When implemented quickly and with good design, smart city solutions may be implemented with less investment in IoT development while yet having room for growth [17, 18].

16.4.4 SMART FACTORIES AND INDUSTRIES

The Industrial Internet of Things, or IIoT, is the primary impetus behind the 4th industrial revolution. Danish IIoT projects have been developed by the Center for the 4th Industrial Revolution of the World Economic Forum. Amazing social efficiencies are being produced by these projects. The manufacturing sector is now the one investing the most in the IoT. The top IoT uses in manufacturing include:

- Production flow monitoring, which results in flow optimization, waste reduction, and a decrease in extra work in process inventories.
- Remote equipment management, which enables monitoring and upkeep of equipment performance and cost savings.
- Notifications of condition-based maintenance, which improve machine availability.
- Supply chains increase the effectiveness of production and supply chain operations by enabling the tracking of assets and vehicles using IoT technologies.

16.4.5 SMART TRANSPORTATION

Two of the top difficulties facing transportation and logistics are speed and scheduling. Through automation and the optimization of business processes, IoT devices are poised to improve the intelligence and efficiency of the transportation industry. IoT gives useful insights into acquired data, assisting the sector in the following ways:

1. Lower costs and more profitability
2. Improving travel efficiency
3. Enhanced operational effectiveness
4. Less energy consumption and traffic
5. Enhanced security
6. Makes real-time visibility possible
7. Promotes better fleet management
8. Aids in maintaining the health of the vehicle
9. Warehouse administration [14]

16.4.6 IoT USAGE IN DISASTER MANAGEMENT

IoT offers more effective options for disaster management that might transform preparedness strategies. Governments may benefit from better evacuation and relief procedures. IoT can gather and monitor data when it comes to natural catastrophes and emergency preparation since it is best suited for automation. Experts can keep an eye on magma movement, seismic activity, water levels, and much more by using the right tools and software. As a result, they can issue warnings about impending disasters.

The different ways that IoT can aid in disaster management are as follows (depicted in Figure 16.4):

1. **Filling the infrastructural gap**
   90% of deaths brought on by natural catastrophes, according to the UN, take place in developing or low-income nations. Typically, there is inadequate infrastructure for safety and escape. Infrared sensors can monitor floods, infrared sensors can detect earthquakes, and placing sensors on trees may

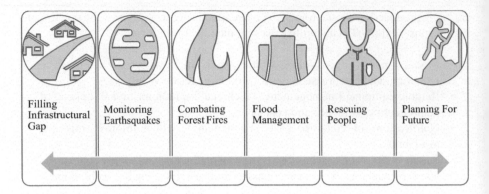

| Filling Infrastructural Gap | Monitoring Earthsquakes | Combating Forest Fires | Flood Management | Rescuing People | Planning For Future |

FIGURE 16.4   IoT usage in disaster management [19].

assist predict when forest fires will start. All of these examples show how IoT can fill in the infrastructure gap affordably. IoT will thereby transform the disaster management system from one that is reactive to one that is proactive.

2. **Earthquake management**

Since it was impossible to predict where or how hard an earthquake will strike, experts have been baffled by them for many years. Monitoring seismic activity is now possible thanks to IoT. The following fixes would considerably enhance earthquake management:

- Applications for mobile devices that have acceleration sensors built in can forecast earthquakes.
- Smart sensors on structures can monitor earthquake activity.
- Governments can save many lives and valuable resources by evacuating the area in advance of the earthquake.

3. **Forest fire management**

This natural disaster significantly harms wildlife and vegetation, from the Amazon Forest fires to catastrophic wildfires in Australia. The following approaches can make fighting wildfires more effective when using IoT's proactive approach:

- When the perfect circumstances for a forest fire appear to be coming together, sensors that monitor the carbon dioxide and humidity levels in the sky can send out alerts.
- To enable early detection, these sensors can be fastened to trees.
- For improved rescue strategies, they can also provide notifications to firefighters and comprehensive information about the extent of the fire.

4. **Flood management**

Farmers and livestock owners are very concerned about floods as a result of natural disasters. They may be ordinary floods or floods brought on by other catastrophes like cyclones or tsunamis.

- Using sensors, increasing water levels may be monitored and signaled, which can aid with flood prediction.

- To calculate flood levels and issue appropriate notifications, experts employ big data and cloud technologies.
- The government works to evacuate the region and safeguard all property in the event of tsunamis or storms.

5. **Rescue and relief operations**

   As soon as a natural disaster occurs, rescue teams and relief efforts are underway in full force. Plans are created in great detail to locate survivors, give them food, medicine, and shelter, and repair the property. IoT can increase the effectiveness of these efforts:

   - The aviation sector has seen enormous advances because of IoT. As a result, airlift operations and supply drops may be made more effective.
   - Mobile or radio signals can be located using certain devices. As a result, it is simpler to locate and save survivors.
   - Rescue personnel may more easily locate casualties by using GPS devices, which can provide them with precise information.

     AI-based technology and intelligent traffic systems can assist move people and goods more quickly.

6. **Future planning**

   Governments can be more prepared for natural catastrophes with the aid of IoT. Even if most of them cannot be prevented, the harm they inflict may be somewhat managed. Artificial intelligence, deep learning, and sensor technology can be used to forecast the potential severity of disasters. IoT may be used by governments all around the world in disaster management systems to improve preparation and reduce losses. IoT has the potential to revolutionize emergency preparation by:

   - Assisting professionals in catastrophe prediction
   - Utilizing it in conjunction with augmented reality to teach rescue personnel
   - IoT has the potential to revolutionize emergency preparation by [20]

16.5 ENVIRONMENTAL MONITORING USING IOT

The regular gathering of measurements and data from our physical surroundings using sensors and linked devices is known as IoT-based environmental monitoring. Sensors can monitor temperature, moisture, water levels, leaks, and other physical characteristics in irrigation systems, pipelines, tanks, weather stations, maritime applications, and industrial machinery located everywhere on the Earth. The information may then be processed utilizing edge computing technology by intelligent, connected devices with embedded communications modules, which can then transfer urgent data to the cloud or a data center for additional processing or analysis. Another motivating aspect is the drive toward green technology, which is supported by these environmental monitoring and cleanup technologies. Applications like energy systems, agricultural use cases, wastewater and water management, operations on oil and gases, and pollution control projects may all acquire more understanding of their distant operations and enhance procedures to lessen their effect and avert calamities.

Real-time analysis of water treatment readings, air quality measures, water and fuel flows, and other data is conceivable using information acquired throughout a whole industrial deployment. The majority of the time, users use an analytical dashboard that aggregates this data and displays trends, spikes, and anomalies, obviating the need to plan expensive truck rolls to each remote installation, which also consumes gasoline. The data-driven methodology offers the crucial insights required for resource management and predictive and preventive maintenance.

1. **Water Quality Monitoring**

   Today, technology is required to help the management and conservation of clean water, as water is a crucial resource for the health of the world and its inhabitants. Utilizing IoT-based solutions for water quality monitoring aids in the management of this priceless resource and the prevention of pollution. Water in structures, water treatment facilities, irrigation systems, and industrial operations may all be evaluated using IoT systems.

   These cutting-edge IoT-based smart water monitoring devices provide precise assessments of pollutants, oxygen levels, other variables, and pH levels. IoT technology makes it possible to identify dangerous materials before they enter buildings and residences. Cutting-edge technology supports our continued health and well-being. Several instances include:
   - Monitoring of municipal water treatment
   - Monitoring of groundwater and stormwater
   - Agriculture irrigation management and surveillance
   - Monitoring the quality of drinking water and city water

2. **Air Quality Monitoring**

   Greenhouse gases (organic substances including carbon monoxide, hydrocarbons, and chemicals) are released into the atmosphere by industrial activities. Additionally, as is common knowledge, the quality of our air and the environment are impacted by car emissions and livestock methane.

   Science and industry can bring about change via air quality monitoring. These crucial measurements provide the information needed for cities to manage their metropolitan areas, for businesses to lessen their environmental effect, and for automakers as a whole to continuously develop emission-reducing designs. Even using IoT to control city traffic flow can significantly lower automobile emissions and promote cleaner air. Examples of air quality monitoring in the real world include:
   - Monitoring for carbon monoxide in residences and structures
   - Methane monitoring in waste management and agriculture
   - Monitoring of the ambient air for toxins, lead, and pollutants

3. **Energy Monitoring**

   Energy monitoring is crucial to conservation due to the limited global energy supplies. IoT-based solutions can give us the management tools and insights we need to optimize our usage of energy. Today's top energy suppliers are quickly incorporating a variety of IoT monitoring and mitigation approaches to curb usage, as well as clean energy solutions to cut energy use and encourage sustainability. These methods can reduce costs for everyone who uses the electric grid in the process. Numerous energy management objectives are supported by energy monitoring:

- Use of fossil fuels in households and companies is being reduced
- Establishing grid stability
- Avoiding energy use spikes and the resulting equipment malfunctions and service interruptions

4. **Toxic Gas Detection**

Poisonous gas detection systems examine the air quality in a variety of industrial processes to find dangerous, toxic, and flammable gases that are present in the atmosphere, allowing us to spot pollutants before they endanger human health or the environment. These devices gauge the amount of a particular gas in the air. These systems can immediately send out important signals and start processes such as turning down valves, turning off systems, and starting fire alarms and chemical mitigation systems thanks to IoT connection. Here are a few instances of actual harmful gas monitoring:

- Toxic or pyrophoric (instantaneously combustible) gases must be monitored for safety.
- Monitoring of H_2S or CO in petrochemical and refinery applications, parking lots, and enclosed places like warehouses
- Workplace hazardous gas detection to safeguard employees from exposure to corrosive and toxic gases wherever they may be present
- In mining operations, hazardous gas monitoring [21]

16.6   IOT STANDARDS AND FRAMEWORKS

There are a number of new IoT standards, including the ones listed below:

- The Internet Engineering Task Force (IETF) has developed an open standard called IPv6 over Low-Power Personal WANs (6LoWPAN) (IETF). Any low-power radio may interact with the internet thanks to the 6LoWPAN standard, including 804.15.4, Bluetooth Low Energy (BLE), and Z-Wave (for home automation).
- ZigBee is a wireless network with a low data rate and minimal power that is mostly utilized in industrial environments. The IEEE (Institute of Electrical and Electronics Engineers) 802.15.4 standard is the foundation of ZigBee. Dotdot, the global IoT language developed by the ZigBee Alliance, enables smart items to communicate and cooperate safely across any network.
- LiteOS is a Unix-like operating system (OS) for wireless sensor networks. LiteOS supports smart homes, wearables, intelligent industrial apps, smartphones, and the Internet of Vehicles (IoV).
- OneM2M is a machine-to-machine service layer that can link devices by being incorporated into hardware and software. OneM2M, a worldwide standardization organization, was established to generate reusable standards that would allow IoT applications from many industry verticals to interact.

- The Object Management Group (OMG) created Data Distribution Service (DDS), which is an IoT standard for real-time, scalable, and high-performance M2M connectivity.
- Asynchronous messaging via wire is supported by the open-source Advanced Message Queuing Protocol (AMQP). AMQP allows for interoperable and secure transmission between businesses and apps. The protocol is utilized in IoT device management and client-server communications.
- The IETF created the Constrained Application Protocol (CoAP), which describes how low- power, compute-constrained devices can function in the Internet of Things.
- A WAN protocol, called Long Range Wide Area Network (LoRaWAN), was created to accommodate massive networks, such as smart cities with millions of low-power devices.

There are several IoT frameworks, including (shown in Figure 16.5):

- A cloud computing platform for IoT called **Amazon Web Services (AWS)** IoT was introduced by Amazon. With the help of this framework, smart devices will be able to securely connect to and communicate with other connected devices as well as the AWS cloud.
- The **Arm Mbed IoT** platform allows for the creation of IoT applications using Arm microcontrollers. By incorporating Mbed tools and services, the Arm Mbed IoT platform aims to give IoT devices a scalable, connected, and secure environment.
- The **Azure IoT Suite from Microsoft** is a platform made up of a number of services that let users connect with and receive data from their IoT devices as well as carrying out different operations on that data, such as multidimensional analysis, transformation, and aggregation.
- A platform for the quick implementation of IoT applications is **Google's Brillo/Weave**. Brillo, an Android-based operating system enabling the

FIGURE 16.5 IoT frameworks.

creation of embedded low-power devices, and Weave, an IoT-focused communication protocol that acts as the device and cloud's common language, make up the platform's two key pillars.

- **Calvin** is an open-source Internet of Things platform created by Ericsson for creating and administering distributed applications that allow devices to communicate with one another. Calvin comes with a runtime environment for managing applications that are already running as well as a development framework for programmers creating new applications [8].

16.7   SECURITY IN IOT DEVICES

IoT devices face a number of security issues that put the businesses and organizations adopting them at risk. If these devices are not adequately safeguarded, the network of the organisation may become vulnerable. A wide range of possible cybersecurity risks are better defended against by IoT devices with embedded security [22]. These devices need to be safeguarded from sophisticated attacks, especially if the devices' design or manufacturing processes established the framework for the attacks, as is the case with Hardware Trojans [23]. Here are a few significant IoT security issues:

- Improper management of security concerns associated with gadgets, which mostly arise because these devices don't receive regular upgrades.
- Devices are susceptible to password hacking or brute force attacks due to weak credentials and default passwords.
- Devices are susceptible to various assaults due to the ongoing hybridization of malware and ransomware strains.
- When IoT botnets are used to mine cryptocurrencies, the confidentiality, integrity, and accessibility of data stored on IoT devices are put at risk.
  1. **IoT security issues at various IoT architectural levels**
     The perception layer, network layer, and application layer are the three levels of the IoT architecture that provide security problems (Figure 16.6).
     1.1 **Perception layer**
        The perception (or senses) layer's goal is to gather environmental data with the use of actuators and sensors. The perception layer security issues are as follows:
        - Sensor nodes connected by wireless technology exchange signals. Disturbing waves can be used to reduce their effectiveness.

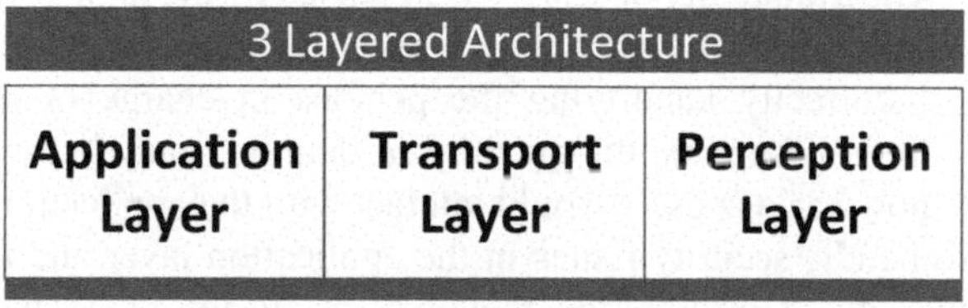

3 Layered Architecture		
Application Layer	**Transport Layer**	**Perception Layer**

FIGURE 16.6   Three layers of IoT architecture [24].

- The sensor nodes of IoT devices can be intercepted by attackers when they are operating outdoors. Attackers have access to the device's hardware.
- The topology of the network can change since nodes might be relocated.
- Radio-frequency identification (RFID) devices and sensors make up the majority of the IoT perception layer. Due to their constrained processing and storage capabilities, they are vulnerable to IoT security risks.
- By replaying or faking an IoT device's identification information, replay attacks can take advantage of the secrecy of the perception layer.

     By implementing encryption, authentication, and access controls, these IoT security issues may be solved.

1.2 **Network layer**

Data routing and transmission to multiple IoT hubs and devices linked to the Internet are made possible by the network layer of the IoT architecture. The following are the security issues that the network layers face:

- Data privacy and confidentiality are at risk as a result of remote access techniques and data transfers. Attackers can use traffic analysis, passive monitoring, or eavesdropping to their advantage.
- Heterogeneous network components make it difficult to use current network protocols.
- The secure communication channel can be compromised if the keying material of the devices is made public.

By implementing protocols and IoT security software, these network layer security issues may be solved, allowing an IoT item to react to unusual actions and circumstances.

1.3 **Application layer**

The application layer fulfills the IoT's goal by developing an intelligent environment. The data's veracity, consistency, and secrecy are ensured by this layer. The following are the IoT security problems at the application layer:

- Since each application has a distinct authentication system in place to protect data privacy and identity authentication, integrating them might be difficult.
- The availability of service is impacted by the high overhead costs that many connected devices place on apps that analyze data.
- Incorrectly identifying the persons in charge of maintaining these programs, the quantity of data that may be revealed, and how various users would interact with the application.

To handle security issues in the application layer and manage the quantity of information that may be disclosed, as well as how, when, and by whom, we need the appropriate tools [25].

2. **Methods of Securing IoT Devices**

To ensure IoT security, there are a few broad defensive measures that we may use. Using permitted software in IoT devices is one of them. Additionally, before collecting or sending data, an IoT device should authenticate itself on the network when it is turned on. Firewalls must be installed in order to filter packets transmitted to IoT endpoints because of their constrained memory and processing capacity. Furthermore, we must make sure that fixes and upgrades are applied without using additional bandwidth. When preparing for the security of IoT devices, we need to take into account a few special security procedures in addition to normal security measures. We must guarantee network security, device security, and system security for the whole Internet of Things infrastructure and system. To protect IoT devices, we may apply the following security procedures:

- Maintain IoT device isolation and physical access protection to ensure physical security.
- Use tamper-resistant IoT devices: Use tamper-resistant IoT devices that deactivate themselves when tampered with.
- Patching software and updating firmware: As soon as the manufacturer provides a new firmware update or patch, be diligent about updating it.
- Perform dynamic testing: It reveals both code flaws and hardware-based security issues.
- Data protection during device disposal: Establish protocols for disposing of IoT equipment as it becomes outdated. Devices that have been improperly dumped can be used for a variety of nefarious activities and to threaten privacy.
- Use strong authentication to prevent password stealing. Steer clear of utilizing default passwords. For authentication, use complex passwords and avoid educated guessing.
- The usage of adaptive authentication should be promoted: Contextual data and machine learning techniques are used in adaptive authentication, also known as context-aware authentication (CAA), to determine the likelihood of malice. The user will be prompted for a multi-factor token if the risk is high.
- Use robust protocols and encryption: Ensure safe data transfer via a variety of IoT protocols by utilizing robust encryption (Bluetooth, Zigbee, Z-Wave, Thread, Wi-Fi, cellular, 6LoWPAN, NFC, etc.)
- Reduce the device's bandwidth: Limit network capacity and bandwidth to the bare minimum needed for the device to operate in order to protect it against distributed denial of service (DDoS) assault brought on by the Internet of Things.
- Segment the network: By combining IP address ranges, virtual local area networks (VLANs), and other techniques, networks can be divided into smaller local networks. This enables the creation of various security zones and the representation of various firewall-controlled segments.

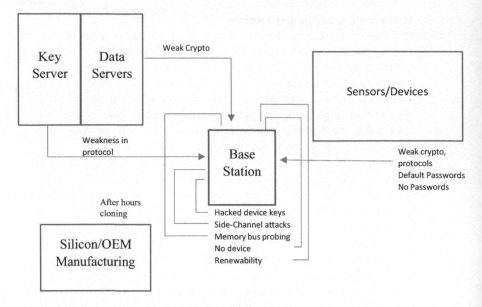

FIGURE 16.7   Embedded security in IoT devices.

- Prevent the leaking of sensitive personally identifiable information (PII) by preventing the ability to find these devices. So that the IoT device can be found by authorized clients, suitable service methods and authentication protocols are required.

3. **Embedded Security in IoT Devices**

   The attack surface's breadth, and some of the vulnerabilities that can be used against linked systems, are depicted in the diagram above (Figure 16.7). These can be grouped into:

   - **The network attack surface**
     - The network attack surface includes every point of network contacts, from end device nodes to the server.
   - **The software attack surface**
     - From the end device, via the network, and all the way to the server, every running piece of code has the potential to have exploitable flaws.
   - **The physical attack surfaces**
     - Physical assaults provide an attacker the most access to a device if it is not secured. This may take the form of intrusive hardware assaults or debugging probes.

   Attackers have the freedom to choose where to launch their attacks; thus, we must carefully consider countermeasures for the entire system.

Security is a trade-off between financial advantage and expense. Any system can be hacked given enough time, money, and knowledge, thus it's crucial to build a system that makes an attacker's attempt unprofitable (i.e. An attack's effort or expense

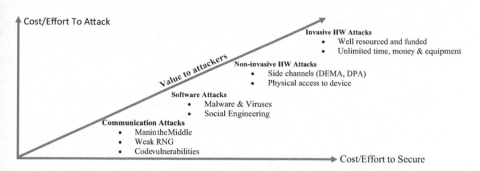

FIGURE 16.8 Effort to attack vs effort to secure ratio.

considerably surpasses any potential reward for the perpetrator.). Attack types may be categorized based on the amount of money spent, the sort of attacker, and the tools employed. These include:

- intrusive assaults that cost a lot (such as sophisticated micro probing a chip or reverse engineering)
- To reduce costs:
  - assaults from passive software (using a code's accidental security flaws for gain)
  - Communication-related attacks (such as those that take advantage of internet protocol, cryptography, or key management flaws)

Depending on the value of assets and the price of security features, security is always a trade-off between economic cost and benefit. The graph in Figure 16.8 shows the effort to attack versus effort to secure ratio. Data and services must be safeguarded for the Internet of Things to succeed, and when that balance is struck, new markets and possibilities may be created.

The best method for establishing security often involves combining several strategies, but this relies on the amount of protection that is suitable for each unique device.

- **Device Identity**: For accountability to be enforced, device identity is required. Digital certificates are used by organizations to secure their digital communication utilizing public key infrastructure (PKI). Digital certificates are employed to carry out a number of security measures, including device authentication, host-to-host communication security, and TLS/SSL communication security. PKI is an excellent infrastructure for device identity and authentication because of its scalability. The device maker must take this into account and combine PKI with an appropriate certificate management solution due to the short lifespan of digital certificates.
- **Hardware Security Module (HSM)**: Because widely accessible IoT devices are vulnerable to physical assaults, it is necessary to deploy tamper-resistant hardware security modules to safeguard data such as cryptographic keys and functions like data encryption, PIN verification, etc. A physical

device called an HSM is used to add an extra layer of protection to critical applications, data, and cryptographic keys. The HSM device can be utilized as a standalone unit, integrated into other hardware, or linked to a server. By implanting a semiconductor chip with a unique identification in each device, it is possible to improve the legitimacy of each device by giving each one a distinct electronic identity. Key injection is the term for this action. Utilizing HSMs, which create a Root of Trust for the key injection process and are crucial to maintaining its integrity, is one way to accomplish this goal. These keys can be generated, secured, and managed by HSMs.

- **Trusted Platform Module (TPM)**: TPM was developed by the Trusted Computing Platform Alliance (TCPA) as a hardware implementation of the TCPA standard with an emphasis on protecting the privacy and boosting security. TPM is a discrete, embedded hardware, or firmware solution that combines safe micro processing with additional cryptographic capabilities. TPM hardware provides the platform's root of trust and can create a chain of trust to extend its trust to other platform components. The TPM uses an integrated RSA engine, which is capable of 2048-bit RSA encryption and decryption while performing digital signature and key wrapping. The built-in hash function in TPM may be used to calculate the hash values of modest amounts of data. TPM employs a collection of specialized Platform Configuration Registers (PCR), which may be accessed by external applications and hold a single cryptographic hash. Each boot chain binary generates a hash of the next binary, extends it into the PCRs, and logs it in the measurement log. To verify the accuracy of the measurement log, the sequence of these measured values may be compared to recent PCR values. TPM further offers attestation by using its attestation key to sign the PCR values. Platform authentication is accomplished through the use of Attestation Identity Keys (AIK). AIKs are created using certificates that are accessible within TPM [26].

16.8   PROS AND CONS OF AN IOT-BASED SMART ENVIRONMENT

16.8.1   Advantages of IoT

1. **Communication**
   IoT promotes device connectivity, commonly referred to as Machine-to-Machine (M2M) communication. Since the physical equipment may remain linked as a result, absolute transparency is possible with fewer inefficiencies and higher quality.

2. **Automation and Control**
   There is a significant level of automation and control in operation as a result of physical items becoming connected and controlled digitally and centralized via wireless infrastructure. Without human involvement, machines can interact with one another, producing output more quickly and on schedule.

3. **Information**

   Increased knowledge facilitates wiser decision-making. Knowledge is power, and more knowledge is better, whether it be for important decisions like knowing what to buy at the grocery store or if our firm has enough supplies and widgets.

4. **Monitor**

   Monitoring is the second most evident benefit of IoT. More information that previously could not have been easily gathered can be provided if we are aware of the precise amount of goods we have on hand or the air quality in our home. For instance, being aware of our need for more milk or printer ink might prevent us from making a subsequent trip to the shop. Monitoring product expiry dates may and will increase safety.

5. **Time**

   The time that may be saved as a result of IoT could be substantial, as suggested by the preceding instances. We could all use more time in the hectic world we live in today.

6. **Money**

   Saving money is the IoT's main benefit. The Internet of Things will be widely used if the cost of the tagging and monitoring hardware is less than the money saved. IoT essentially demonstrates to be highly beneficial to individuals in their everyday routines by enabling the appliances to effectively connect with one another, saving energy and money. Our systems are more effective when data can be exchanged and transmitted amongst devices before being translated as needed.

7. **Automation of daily tasks leads to better monitoring of devices**

   The Internet of Things (IoT) enables us to automate and regulate daily processes while preventing human interference. Communication between machines aids in keeping processes transparent. It also results in task homogeneity. Additionally, it can keep up the level of service. In an emergency, we can also behave as is required.

16.8.2 Disadvantages of IoT

1. **Compatibility**

   As equipment from many manufacturers is linked, the problem of tag and monitoring compatibility arises. Even if all the manufacturers agree on a single standard, this drawback will still exist because of technical problems. We have Bluetooth-capable gadgets now, yet compatibility issues still remain with this technology! Customers may only purchase appliances from one manufacturer as a consequence of compatibility difficulties, creating a monopoly for that company.

2. **Complexity**

   A broad and intricate network, the IoT. Serious repercussions will result from any hardware or software malfunctions or flaws. Even a power outage can be quite inconvenient.

3. **Lesser Employment of Menial Staff**
The automation of daily tasks may result in the loss of employment for unskilled employees and assistants. This may cause problems with unemployment in the community. Any new technology will have problems such as these, but they can be solved through knowledge. Naturally, as daily tasks become more automated, there will be less need for human resources, particularly for laborers and less educated staff. This might lead to problems with unemployment in the society.
4. **Technology Takes Control of Life**
Technology will have an ever-increasing influence on and dependence on our life. The younger generation is already dependent on technology in many spheres of life. We must determine how much of our everyday life we are ready to automate and subjugate to technological control [27].

16.9   CONCLUSION AND THE FUTURE SCOPE OF IOT DEVICES

Nearly every aspect of our lives and society are now being impacted by IoT devices. Whether it's improving healthcare, making our cities smarter, making factories smarter, or controlling calamities, its good impacts are obvious to everyone. When it comes to the environment, its effects are also very noticeable. All of these factors are quantifiable and subject to immediate control, including air quality index, water quality, poisonous gas concentrations, etc. With its limitless advantages, society and the environment are moving toward a better and more intelligent version of themselves. In the future, a lot can be done to increase its popularity. The predictions for the IoT's future growth are upbeat since the technology is still in its early stages. In the upcoming years, we will be connected in ways that are regarded to be unimaginably futuristic. Integration of IoT and AI will create new possibilities for innovative applications across several industries. The following technologies are included in the future range of IoT devices:

- **The voice controller of Google Home**
  The Google Home voice controller is one of the most frequently utilized Internet of Things devices today. For many different things, like lights, thermostats, volume control, and more, it provides voice-activated services.
- **Voice controller for the Amazon Echo Plus**
  The voice controller for the Amazon Echo Plus is a popular and reliable IoT device on the market. It offers a wide range of voice-activated features, including as call answering, setting timers and alarms, checking the weather, and much more.
- **Doorbell Cam for August**
  We can answer the door remotely using the August Doorbell Cam, an Internet of Things (IoT) device. It continuously captures changes in motion and shadowy activities at our entryway.
- **August Smart Lock**
  Customers may manage their doors with the August Smart Lock, an established IoT security device, from any location. It strengthens the security of our homes and helps to repel thieves.

- **Foobot**
  Foobot, an Internet of Things (IoT) device, can accurately measure indoor pollution. It helps to raise the standard of the air within buildings including residences, coffee shops, offices, and public spaces.

REFERENCES

[1] Gomez, C., Chessa, S., Fleury, A., Roussos, G., & Preuveneers, D. (2019). Internet of Things for enabling smart environments: A technology-centric perspective. *Journal of Ambient Intelligence and Smart Environments, 11*(1), 23–43.

[2] Ibrahim, M., Elgamri, A., Babiker, S., & Mohamed, A. (2015, October). Internet of things based smart environmental monitoring using the Raspberry-Pi computer. In *2015 Fifth International Conference on Digital Information Processing and Communications (ICDIPC)* (pp. 159–164). IEEE.

[3] *All about the internet of Things (IoT).* (2019, November 1). *Tridens; Tridens Technology.* https://tridenstechnology.com/all-about-the-internet-of-things-iot/

[4] Clark, J. (2016, November 17). *What is the Internet of Things, and how does it work?* IBM Business Operations Blog. https://www.ibm.com/blogs/internet-of-things/what-is-the-iot/

[5] Duggal, N. (2021, April 5). *What are IoT devices: Definition, types, and 5 most popular ones for 2023.* Simplilearn.com; Simplilearn. https://www.simplilearn.com/iot-devices-article/

[6] Castle, A. (2021, April 7). *IoT Technologies explained: History, examples, risks & future.* Vision of Humanity. https://www.visionofhumanity.org/what-is-the-internet-of-things/

[7] Chin, J., Callaghan, V., & Allouch, S. B. (2019). The Internet-of-Things: Reflections on the past, present and future from a user-centered and smart environment perspective. *Journal of Ambient Intelligence and Smart Environments, 11*(1), 45–69.

[8] Gillis, A. S. (2020). What is Internet of Things (IoT). *IoT Agenda.*

[9] Kalnoor, G., & Gowrishankar, S. (2021). IoT-based smart environment using intelligent intrusion detection system. *Soft Computing, 25*(17), 11573–11588.

[10] *Machine learning (ML) for IoT.* (n.d.). Software AG. Retrieved November 2, 2022, from https://www.softwareag.com/en_corporate/resources/what-is/machine-learning.html

[11] Mocrii, D., Chen, Y., & Musilek, P. (2018). IoT-based smart homes: A review of system architecture, software, communications, privacy and security. *Internet of Things, 1,* 81–98.

[12] Oh, J., Yu, S., Lee, J., Son, S., Kim, M., & Park, Y. (2021). A secure and lightweight authentication protocol for IoT-based smart homes. *Sensors, 21*(4), 1488.

[13] Tao, M., Zuo, J., Liu, Z., Castiglione, A., & Palmieri, F. (2018). Multi-layer cloud architectural model and ontology-based security service framework for IoT-based smart homes. *Future Generation Computer Systems, 78,* 1040–1051.

[14] Peranzo, P. (2022, May 5). *Imaginovation. Imaginovation | Top Web & Mobile App Development Company Raleigh.* https://imaginovation.net/blog/8-sectors-benefit-from-iot-development-in-2021/

[15] Mohamed, S. A. S. (2019, October 3). *How IoT in healthcare benefits the medical industry.* DeveloperOnRent - Blog. https://www.developeronrent.com/blogs/iot-healthcare

[16] (n.d.). Data-Flair,Training. Retrieved November 2, 2022, from https://data-flair.training/blogs/how-iot-works/

[17] Grizhnevich, A. (2018). IoT for smart cities: Use cases and implementation strategies. *Science Soft.*

[18] Insider Intelligence. (2022, April 15). *How IoT and smart city technology works: Devices, applications and examples*. Insider Intelligence. https://www.insiderintelligence.com/insights/iot-smart-city-technology/

[19] *IoT can help in disaster management*. (2020, October 29). *Allerin.com*. https://www.allerin.com/blog/iot-can-help-in-disaster-management-heres-how

[20] (n.d.). Mytechmag.com. Retrieved November 2, 2022, from https://www.mytechmag.com/iot-in-disaster-management/

[21] *IoT-based environmental monitoring: Types and use cases*. (n.d.). *Digi.com*. Retrieved November 2, 2022, from https://www.digi.com/blog/post/iot-based-environmental-monitoring

[22] *What is embedded security?* (2021, January 13). *Check Point Software*. https://www.checkpoint.com/cyber-hub/network-security/what-is-embedded-security/

[23] Sidhu, S., Mohd, B. J., & Hayajneh, T. (2019). Hardware security in IoT devices with emphasis on hardware Trojans. *Journal of Sensor and Actuator Networks, 8*(3), 42.

[24] Thomaz, J. (2021, August 24). *Learn IoT from scratch #4 - IoT protocols & architecture*. DEV Community https://dev.to/josethz00/learn-iot-from-scratch-4-iot-protocols-architecture-46g8

[25] Joshi, S. (2021, May 5). *What is IoT security? How to keep IoT devices safe*. Learn. g2.com; G2. https://learn.g2.com/iot-security

[26] *Securing the embedded IoT world*. (n.d.). *Iotsecurityfoundation.org*. Retrieved November 2, 2022, from https://www.iotsecurityfoundation.org/securing-the-embedded-iot-world/

[27] Quek, T. (2017, February 14). *The advantages and disadvantages of Internet Of Things (IoT)*. Linkedin.com. https://www.linkedin.com/pulse/advantages-disadvantages-internet-things-iot-tommy-quek

17 An Application of Convolutional Neural Networks in Recognition of Handwritten Digits

Preeti Choudhury, Kashish Thakur and Soma Datta

Sister Nivedita University, Kolkata, India

17.1 INTRODUCTION

The handwritten digit recognition will become an ability of computers to recognize the human handwritten digits because it becomes a hard task for the machines as the handwritten digits are not perfect and can be made in different forms. Thus, handwritten digit recognition will be the solution to this problem by using the images of the digit to recognize the digit present in the image. In this project, we have chosen to focus on recognizing handwritten digits available in different languages [1]. We have decided to use the MNIST dataset for English digits, the CMATERDB dataset for Bengali digits, the CMATERDB/Devanagari dataset for Devanagari digits, and the CMATERdb/Telugu dataset for Telegu digits. The challenge in this project is to use more than one type of language digit for recognition which makes the whole project complex. The use of the Adam optimization technique helps to maximize the overall accuracy of the handwritten digits recognizer. The aim of the project is to develop a hybrid model of a powerful Convolutional Neural Network (CNN) for the recognition of handwritten digits of different languages from the MNIST dataset, the CMATERdb dataset, and the CMATERdb/Devanagari dataset. The contributions of the proposed method are as follows:

- Develop a new deep architecture using multiple stages of convolutional Neural Network layers.
- Achieving state-of-the-art performance on noisy handwritten digits.
- All the parameters of CNN architecture to deliver the best recognition accuracy among peer researchers for MNIST digit recognition [2].

DOI: 10.1201/9781003363606-17

The rest of the chapter is organized as follows: Section 17.2 describes the literature survey in the field of handwriting recognition. Section 17.3 describes the CNN architecture-based proposed method along with description of each subphase respectively. Section 17.4 discusses the findings and presents a comparative analysis; and Section 17.5 presents the conclusion and suggestions for future directions.

17.2 LITERATURE SURVEY

There are various existing methods that are being used to solve the problem of handwritten digit recognition. Ali and Zeeshan proposed a model for the MNIST dataset where they used the method of CNN Architecture with DeepLearning4j framework; they have experienced a huge variation in the error rates and accuracy of the model [3]. The model is also limited to identifying digits of similar size and only in the English language. The other models proposed by Hanmandlu that have used RNN [4] Architecture with the Hidden Markov model have applied a dataset of 4750 samples of English and Hindi digits which resulted in slow and complex training procedures that have made the entire process sequences more difficult and longer [16]. They proposed another model that was implemented using the CNN model and the Stochastic Gradient Descent (SGD) optimizer using the DHCD dataset. They used Stochastic Gradient Descent (SGD) in their model, which is updated very frequently and which may lead to several oscillations that make the minima steps noisier in nature [27–29]. The existing model for handwritten digit recognition proposed by Anshul Gupta and Manisha Srivastava is based on the Neural Network Toolbox (NNL) and Support Vector Machine (SVM) methods, where they have implemented the MNIST dataset to record their final results. The SVM algorithm that they have used is not suitable for a large number of datasets as it tends to perform poorly or unwell on noisy data [10]. We have analyzed all the limitations of the existing models and incorporated them in our proposed model [5].

Badrinarayanan et al. [30–32] proposed a deep convolution network architecture for semantic segmentation which is known as SegNet and consists of an encoder network. The proposed method used max-pooling indices of a feature map [6]. The method is also analyzed and compared with existing techniques for road scene and indoor understanding. Gupta et al. reported in [33] a novel multi-objective optimization framework to identify the most informative local regions from a set of character images. The work was validated on isolated handwritten English numerals, especially MNIST images, handwritten Bangala numerals and also handwritten Devanagari characters. The authors used features extracted from a CNN in their model and achieved 95.96% recognition accuracy. Nguyen et al. [34] used a multi-scale CNN in their proposed method to extract spatial classification features for handwritten mathematical expression (HME). The local features and spatial information of HME images were used for clustering HME images [23–25]. The work validated with high performance for the CROHME dataset. The authors also concluded that classification can be improved by training the CNN with a combination of global max pooling and global attentive pooling. Ziran et al. [35] proposed a faster R-CNN-based framework for text, word location and recognition in historical books.

17.3   PROPOSED METHOD

In the first step, the data bases, including MNIST dataset, CMATERdb dataset, CMATERdb/devanagari dataset, CMATERdb/telugu dataset, have been intensively studied to understand their properties. After the establishment of the environment by importing the essential python libraries to create the proposed CNN model, the specific datasets are loaded. The dataset are also printed to analyze the data of all three said datasets. The datasets are already divided into train data and test Data [7]. In the case of the MNIST dataset, the images are 28 x 28 x 1 NumPy arrays whereas in CMATERdb, CMATERdb/devanagari, and CMATERdb/telugu datasets the images are 32 x 32 x 3 NumPy arrays. Figure 17.1 shows the block diagram of the proposed method. The initial steps of our research work is to organize inputs and define user inputs before creating the model.

A basic CNN comprises three components, namely, the convolutional layer, the pooling layer, and the output layer. The pooling layer is optional sometimes. The typical CNN architecture with three convolutional layers is well adapted for the classification of handwritten images [8]. It consists of the input layer, multiple hidden layers (repetitions of convolutional, normalization, pooling), and a fully connected and an output layer. For training, the model we use sparse_categorical cross-entropy loss with Adam optimizer. The detailed description of every layer is defined in the next subsections.

17.3.1   THE INPUT LAYER

The input data is loaded and stored in the input layer. This layer describes the height, width, and several channels of the input image [9].

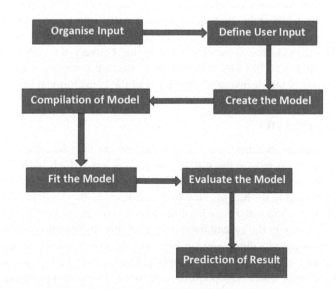

FIGURE 17.1   Block diagram of proposed method.

17.3.2 Hidden Layers

The hidden layers are the backbone of the CNN architecture. They perform a feature extraction process where a series of convolution, pooling, and activation functions are used. The distinguishable features of handwritten digits are detected at this stage. Figure 17.2 shows the architecture of our proposed CNN Model for the project where every step of the architecture is displayed [10].

17.3.3 Convolutional Layer

The convolutional layer is the first layer placed above the input image. It is used for extracting the features of an image. The n x n input neurons of the input layer are convoluted with an m x m filter and in return deliver $(n - m + 1) \times (n - m + 1)$ as output. It introduces non-linearity through a neural activation function. The main contributors of the convolutional layer are receptive field, stride, dilation, and padding, as described in the following paragraph. CNN computation is inspired by the visual cortex in animals. The visual cortex is a part of the brain that processes the information forwarded from the retina. It processes visual information and is subtle to small subregions of the input. Similarly, a receptive field is calculated in a CNN, which is a small region of an input image that can affect a specific region of the network [11]. It is also one of the important design parameters of the CNN architecture and helps in setting other CNN parameters. It has the same size as the kernel and works similarly to the foveal vision of the human eye works for producing sharp central vision. The receptive field is influenced by striding, pooling, kernel size, and depth of the CNN. Receptive field (r), effective receptive field (ERF) and projective field (PF) are all examples of terminology used in calculating effective subregions in a network. The area of the original image influencing the activation of a neuron is described using the ERF, whereas the PF is a count of neurons to which neurons project their outputs. Stride is another parameter used in CNN architecture. It is defined as the step size by which the filter moves every time [12]. Astride value of 1 indicates the filter sliding movement pixel by pixel. A larger stride size shows less overlapping between the cells. The concept of padding is introduced in CNN architecture to make it more accurate. Padding is introduced to control the shrinking of the output of the convolutional layer.

17.3.4 Pooling Layer

After the convolution operation, we perform the pooling to reduce the dimensionality. This enables us to reduce the number of parameters, which both shortens the training time and combats overfitting. Pooling layers down sample each feature map independently, reducing the height and width, and keeping the depth intact. The most common type of pooling is the max pooling, which takes the max value in the pooling window. Contrary to the convolution operation, pooling has no parameters [13]. It slides a window over its input, and simply takes the max value in the window.

Pooling is a form of non-linear down-sampling. There are several non-linear functions to implement pooling, where max pooling is the most common. It partitions the input image into a set of rectangles and, for each such sub-region, outputs the maximum.

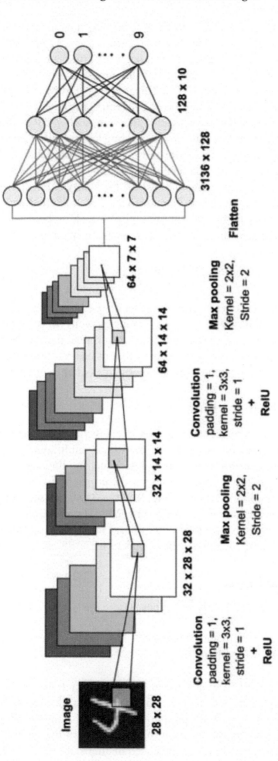

FIGURE 17.2 Architecture of our CNN model.

Intuitively, the exact location of a feature is less important than its rough location relative to other features. This is the idea behind the use of pooling in CNNs. The pooling layer serves to progressively reduce the spatial size of the representation, reduce the number of parameters, memory footprint, and amount of computation in the network, and hence to also control overfitting [14]. This is known as down-sampling. It is common to periodically insert a pooling layer between successive convolutional layers (each one typically followed by an activation function, such as a Rectified Linear Unit [ReLU] layer) in a CNN architecture. While pooling layers contribute to local translation invariance, they do not provide global translation invariance in a CNN, unless a form of global pooling is used. The pooling layer commonly operates independently on every depth, or slice, of the input and resizes it spatially [21, 22]. A very common form of max pooling is a layer with filters of size 2 × 2, applied with a stride of 2, which subsamples every depth slice in the input by 2 along both width and height, discarding 75% of the activations, as we can observe from equation 17.1

$$f_{X,Y}\left(S\right) = \max_{a,b=0}^{1} S_{2X+a,2Y+b}. \tag{17.1}$$

In this case, every max operation is over 4 numbers. The depth dimension remains unchanged (this is true for other forms of pooling as well). In addition to max pooling, pooling units can use other functions, such as average pooling or ℓ2-norm pooling. Average pooling was often used historically but has recently fallen out of favor compared to max pooling, which generally performs better in practice.

17.3.5 FULLY CONNECTED LAYER

Fully connected layers connect every neuron in one layer to every neuron in another layer. It is, in principle, the same as the traditional multilayer perceptron neural network (MLP). After several convolutional and max-pooling layers, the final classification is done via fully connected layers. Neurons in a fully connected layer have connections to all activations in the previous layer, as seen in regular (non-convolutional) artificial neural networks [18–20]. Their activations can thus be computed as an affine transformation, with matrix multiplication followed by a bias offset (vector addition of a learned or fixed bias term).

17.3.6 ACTIVATION LAYER

Activation functions are generally two types, These are

- Linear or Identity Activation Function
- Non-Linear Activation Function.

Generally, neural networks use non-linear activation functions, which can help the network learn complex data, compute and learn almost any function representing a question, and provide accurate predictions. They also allow back-propagation because they have a derivative function that is related to the inputs . ReLU is the most widely used activation function. It is used in almost all the convolutional neural networks and deep learning tasks. For the output layer, we used the Softmax activation function in our model.

17.3.6.1 ReLU (Rectified Linear Unit)

This is one of the most popular activation functions which we have used in the hidden layer of our CNN model. The formula is deceptively simple: $(0,)$ max$(0,z)$. Despite its name and appearance, it's not linear and provides the same benefits as Sigmoid but with better performance so we have used this activation function in our model (Figure 17.3).

Its main advantage is that it avoids and rectifies vanishing gradient problems and is less computationally expensive than tanh and sigmoid [17]. For activations in the region $(x < 0)$ of ReLU, the gradient will be 0 because of which the weights will not get adjusted during descent (Figure 17.4). That means those neurons which go into that state will stop responding to variations in error/input (simply because the gradient is 0, nothing changes). When we compare it with the sigmoid activation function, it looks like Figure 17.5.

17.3.7 OUTPUT LAYER

The output from the hidden layer is then fed into a logistic function like sigmoid or softmax which converts the output of each class into the probability score of each class. The output nodes provided the final precision of every digit in the dataset with respect to the input given [15]. It uses the non-linear function, Softmax Activation

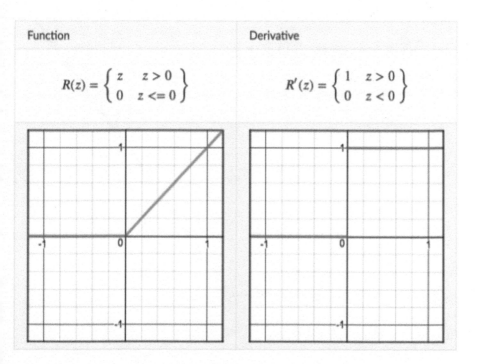

Function	Derivative
$R(z) = \begin{cases} z & z > 0 \\ 0 & z <= 0 \end{cases}$	$R'(z) = \begin{cases} 1 & z > 0 \\ 0 & z < 0 \end{cases}$

FIGURE 17.3 ReLU activation and its derivative.

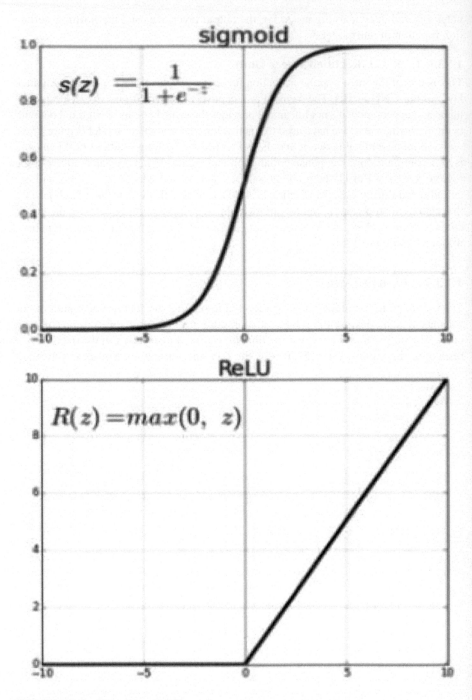

FIGURE 17.4   Sigmoid vs ReLU graph.

```
# ReLU activation function
def relu(z):
    return max(0, z)


# Derivative of ReLU Activation Function
def relu_prime(z):
    return 1 if z > 0 else 0
```

FIGURE 17.5 ReLU activation function and its derivative.

Function, to predict the final output of the system. The output layer of fully connected neural networks is connected to the CNN output layer with a non-linear function. It helps to record the final output of the given input of all digits of different datasets respectively.

17.3.7.1 Softmax Activation Function

The Softmax function, also known as Softargmax or the normalized exponential function, is a function that takes as input a vector of n real numbers and normalizes it into a probability distribution consisting of n probabilities proportional to the exponentials of the input vector [16]. A probability distribution implies that the result vector sums up to 1. Needless to say, if some components of the input vector are negative or more significant than one, they will be in the range (0, 1) after applying Softmax. The Softmax function is often used in neural networks, to map the results of the output layer, which is non-normalized, to a probability distribution over predicted output classes.

The Softmax function σ is defined by the following formula equation 17.2.

$$\sigma(o_i) = \frac{e^{o_i}}{\sum_{j=1}^{n} e^{o_j}} \tag{17.2}$$

where the index i is in $(0, ..., n\text{-}1)$ and o is the output vector of the network

$$o = (o_0, o_1, ..., o_{n-1})$$

17.4 RESULTS

Many researchers contributed to the huge field of digit recognition. Murthy and Hanmandlu proposed a character recognition system that featured the various individual features based on the different priorities and relied on the final accuracies of distinct features that were implemented in the proposed system [17]. They used the recurrent neural network through the Hidden Markov model to determine the exact order of characters in the handwritten script, where they have received an accuracy of about 95%. The Hidden Markov model is also implemented by Schmidhuber and Graves for the handwritten recognition system of Arabic words, in which they achieved an overall accuracy of about 92% [9] whereas our proposed model has an accuracy of 96% for the CMATERdb dataset. Ali and Shaukat used the Convolutional Neural Network (CNN) model and MNIST Dataset to recognize the English handwritten digits with an overall accuracy of 99% [3] (Figure 17.6). In our proposed model, we have achieved an accuracy of 99% with an application of the CNN model with the Softmax Activation function (Figure 17.7). Several researchers have implemented the system of Bangla Handwritten Digit recognition using the CMATERDB dataset and achieved an accuracy of 99% by using deep convolutional neural networks and encoding models (Figures 17.8 and 17.9) [23, 26]. We have incorporated four different languages in our model that gives an overall accuracy of 96% (Figures 17.10–17.13). Table 17.1 shows Configuration details and accuracy achieved for CNN with four layers.

```
Confusion Matrix :
[[ 976    1    0    0    0    0    1    1    1    0]
 [   0 1131    0    3    0    0    0    0    0    1]
 [   0    0 1025    5    0    0    0    2    0    0]
 [   0    0    1 1008    0    1    0    0    0    0]
 [   0    0    1    0  970    0    1    0    0   10]
 [   0    0    0   11    0  880    1    0    0    0]
 [   2    4    0    0    2    4  946    0    0    0]
 [   0    1    6    1    0    1    0 1013    1    5]
 [   6    0    1    9    0    1    1    0  954    2]
 [   1    1    0    4    2    3    0    0    1  997]]
Accuracy Score is 0.99
```

FIGURE 17.6 Confusion matrix of MNIST dataset.

```
Classification Report :
              precision    recall  f1-score   support

           0       0.99      1.00      0.99       980
           1       0.99      1.00      1.00      1135
           2       0.99      0.99      0.99      1032
           3       0.97      1.00      0.98      1010
           4       1.00      0.99      0.99       982
           5       0.99      0.99      0.99       892
           6       1.00      0.99      0.99       958
           7       1.00      0.99      0.99      1028
           8       1.00      0.98      0.99       974
           9       0.98      0.99      0.99      1009

    accuracy                           0.99     10000
   macro avg       0.99      0.99      0.99     10000
weighted avg       0.99      0.99      0.99     10000

AUC-ROC: 0.9999150956379128
LOGLOSS Value is 0.04160486554402858
```

FIGURE 17.7 Classification report, AUC-ROC, and LOGLOSS value of MNIST dataset.

```
Confusion Matrix :
[[ 98   0   0   0   0   2   0   0   0   0]
 [  0  96   0   0   1   0   0   0   1   2]
 [  0   0  98   0   1   0   0   1   0   0]
 [  1   1   0  96   0   1   1   0   0   0]
 [  0   1   0   0  98   0   0   1   0   0]
 [  0   0   0   2   0  98   0   0   0   0]
 [  0   0   0   3   0   2  95   0   0   0]
 [  0   1   1   0   0   1   0  97   0   0]
 [  0   0   0   0   0   0   0   0 100   0]
 [  0   9   0   0   2   0   1   0   0  88]]
Accuracy Score is 0.964
```

FIGURE 17.8 Confusion matrix of CMATERdb dataset.

```
Classification Report :
              precision    recall  f1-score   support

           0       0.99      0.98      0.98       100
           1       0.89      0.96      0.92       100
           2       0.99      0.98      0.98       100
           3       0.95      0.96      0.96       100
           4       0.96      0.98      0.97       100
           5       0.94      0.98      0.96       100
           6       0.98      0.95      0.96       100
           7       0.98      0.97      0.97       100
           8       0.99      1.00      1.00       100
           9       0.98      0.88      0.93       100

    accuracy                           0.96      1000
   macro avg       0.96      0.96      0.96      1000
weighted avg       0.96      0.96      0.96      1000

AUC-ROC: 0.9990899999999999
LOGLOSS Value is 0.12413596006213329
```

FIGURE 17.9 Classification report, AUC-ROC, and LOGLOSS value of CMATERdb datase.

```
Confusion Matrix :
[[48   0   0   0   0   0   0   2   0   0]
 [ 0  48   1   0   0   1   0   0   0   0]
 [ 0   0  47   2   0   0   0   0   0   1]
 [ 0   0   1  44   1   0   2   1   0   1]
 [ 0   0   0   2  46   1   0   1   0   0]
 [ 0   0   0   0   3  46   0   1   0   0]
 [ 0   0   0   0   1   2  46   0   0   1]
 [ 2   1   0   0   0   0   0  44   3   0]
 [ 3   0   0   0   1   0   0   1  45   0]
 [ 0   0   0   1   1   0   0   0   0  48]]
Accuracy Score is 0.924
```

FIGURE 17.10 Confusion matrix of CMATERdb/devanagari dataset.

```
Classification Report :
              precision    recall  f1-score   support

           0       0.91      0.96      0.93        50
           1       0.98      0.96      0.97        50
           2       0.96      0.94      0.95        50
           3       0.90      0.88      0.89        50
           4       0.87      0.92      0.89        50
           5       0.92      0.92      0.92        50
           6       0.96      0.92      0.94        50
           7       0.88      0.88      0.88        50
           8       0.94      0.90      0.92        50
           9       0.94      0.96      0.95        50

    accuracy                           0.92       500
   macro avg       0.92      0.92      0.92       500
weighted avg       0.92      0.92      0.92       500

AUC-ROC: 0.9952799999999999
LOGLOSS Value is 0.34845251558929474
```

FIGURE 17.11 Classification report, AUC-ROC, and LOGLOSS value of CMATERdb/devanagari dataset.

```
Confusion Matrix :
[[48  2  0  0  0  0  0  0  0  0]
 [ 1 49  0  0  0  0  0  0  0  0]
 [ 0  0 49  0  0  1  0  0  0  0]
 [ 0  0  0 50  0  0  0  0  0  0]
 [ 0  0  0  0 48  2  0  0  0  0]
 [ 0  0  0  1  2 46  0  1  0  0]
 [ 1  0  0  0  0  0 48  0  0  1]
 [ 1  0  1  0  0  0  0 48  0  0]
 [ 0  0  0  0  0  0  0  0 50  0]
 [ 0  0  0  0  0  0  1  0  0 49]]
Accuracy Score is 0.97
```

FIGURE 17.12 Confusion matrix of CMATERdb/telugu dataset.

```
Classification Report :
              precision    recall   f1-score    support

           0     0.94       0.96      0.95         50
           1     0.96       0.98      0.97         50
           2     0.98       0.98      0.98         50
           3     0.98       1.00      0.99         50
           4     0.96       0.96      0.96         50
           5     0.94       0.92      0.93         50
           6     0.98       0.96      0.97         50
           7     0.98       0.96      0.97         50
           8     1.00       1.00      1.00         50
           9     0.98       0.98      0.98         50

    accuracy                          0.97        500
   macro avg     0.97       0.97      0.97        500
weighted avg     0.97       0.97      0.97        500

AUC-ROC: 0.9993244444444445
LOGLOSS Value is 0.09618368887582517
```

FIGURE 17.13   Classification report, AUC-ROC, and LOGLOSS value of CMATERdb/ telugu dataset.

TABLE 17.1

Configuration Details Along with Accuracy and Time

Model	Layer	k	s	d	p	i/p	o/p	r	Accuracy & Time
Case 1	Layer1	3	2	1	1	28	14	3	95.36% (38s)
	Layer2	3	2	1	1	14	7	7	
	Layer3	3	2	1	1	7	4	15	
	Layer4	3	2	1	1	4	2	31	
Case 2	Layer1	3	2	2	2	28	14	3	96.10% (35s)
	Layer2	3	2	2	2	14	7	13	
	Layer3	3	2	1	1	7	4	21	
	Layer4	3	2	1	1	4	2	33	
Case 3	Layer1	5	2	2	2	28	14	9	96.81% (32s)
	Layer2	3	2	2	2	14	7	13	
	Layer3	3	2	1	1	7	4	25	
	Layer4	3	2	1	1	4	2	37	

17.5   CONCLUSION & FUTURE WORK

We would like to conclude that with the aim of improving the performance of the handwritten digit recognition, we have evaluated the variants of the convolutional neural networks to avoid complex pre-processing, costly feature extraction, and a complex approach to a traditional recognition system. Through extensive evaluation using an MNIST dataset, CMATERdb dataset, CMATERdb/devanagari dataset, and CMATERdb/telugu dataset we achieved an overall accuracy rate of 96.309% with the Adam optimizer for the databases. The effect of increasing the number of convolutional layers in CNN architecture on the performance of handwritten digit recognition is clearly presented through the experiments. In the future, we are aiming to enhance our proposed model's overall accuracy by testing our different datasets on various predicting methods. We will predict our handwritten digits using different existing algorithms such as Random Forests, Decision Trees, KNN, SVM, and Gaussian Naive Bayes so that we can identify the efficient algorithm for our handwritten digits which can help us to achieve better accuracy than our existing model.

17.5.1 DECLARATION OF COMPETING INTEREST

The authors declare that they have no known competing financial interests or personal relationships that could have appeared to influence the work reported in this chapter.

REFERENCES

[1] Ahlawat, Savita, Amit Choudhary, Anand Nayyar, Saurabh Singh, and Byungun Yoon. "Improved handwritten digit recognition using convolutional neural networks (CNN)." *Sensors* 20, no. 12 (2020): 3344.
[2] Ahlawat, Savita, and Amit Choudhary. "Hybrid CNN-SVM classifier for handwritten digit recognition." *Procedia Computer Science* 167 (2020): 2554–2560.
[3] Ali, Saqib, Zeeshan Shaukat, Muhammad Azeem, Zareen Sakhawat, and Tariq Mahmood. "An efficient and improved scheme for handwritten digit recognition based on convolutional neural network." *SN Applied Sciences* 1, no. 9 (2019): 1–9.
[4] Alwzwazy, Haider A., Hayder M. Albehadili, Younes S. Alwan, and Naz E. Islam. "Handwritten digit recognition using convolutional neural networks." *International Journal of Innovative Research in Computer and Communication Engineering* 4, no. 2 (2016): 1101–1106.
[5] Bisht, Mamta, and Richa Gupta. "Multiclass recognition of offline handwritten Devanagari characters using CNN." *International Journal of Mathematical, Engineering and Management Sciences* 5 (2020): 1429–1439.
[6] Qiao, Junfei, Gongming Wang, Wenjing Li, and Min Chen. "An adaptive deep Q-learning strategy for handwritten digit recognition." *Neural Networks* 107 (2018): 61–71.
[7] Das, Nibaran, Ram Sarkar, Subhadip Basu, Mahantapas Kundu, Mita Nasipuri, and Dipak Kumar Basu. "A genetic algorithm based region sampling for selection of local features in handwritten digit recognition application." *Applied Soft Computing* 12, no. 5 (2012): 1592–1606.
[8] Dutt, Anuj, and Aashi Dutt. "Handwritten digit recognition using deep learning." *International Journal of Advanced Research in Computer Engineering & Technology (IJARCET)* 6, no. 7 (2017): 990–997.
[9] AlKhateeb, Jawad H., Jinchang Ren, Jianmin Jiang, and Husni Al-Muhtaseb. "Offline handwritten Arabic cursive text recognition using Hidden Markov Models and re-ranking." *Pattern Recognition Letters* 32, no. 8 (2011): 1081–1088.
[10] Gupta, Anshul, Manisha Srivastava, and Chitralekha Mahanta. "Offline handwritten character recognition using neural network." In *2011 IEEE International Conference on Computer Applications and Industrial Electronics (ICCAIE)*, pp. 102–107. IEEE, 2011.
[11] Hou, Yawei, and Huailin Zhao. "Handwritten digit recognition based on depth neural network." In *2017 International Conference on Intelligent Informatics and Biomedical Sciences (ICIIBMS)*, pp. 35–38. IEEE, 2017.

[12] Hussain, Mahbub, Jordan J. Bird, and Diego R. Faria. "A study on cnn transfer learning for image classification." In *UK Workshop on computational Intelligence*, pp. 191–202. Springer, Cham, 2018.

[13] Shrivastava, Shailedra Kumar, and Sanjay S. Gharde. "Support vector machine for handwritten Devanagari numeral recognition." *International Journal of Computer Applications* 7, no. 11 (2010): 9–14.

[14] LeCun, Yann, Lawrence D. Jackel, Léon Bottou, Corinna Cortes, John S. Denker, Harris Drucker, Isabelle Guyon et al. "Learning algorithms for classification: A comparison on handwritten digit recognition." *Neural Networks: The Statistical Mechanics Perspective* 261, no. 276 (1995): 2.

[15] LeCun, Yann. "The MNIST database of handwritten digits." http://yann.lecun.com/exdb/mnist/ (1998).

[16] Muppalaneni, Naresh Babu. "Handwritten Telugu compound character prediction using convolutional neural network." In *2020 International Conference on Emerging Trends in Information Technology and Engineering (ic- ETITE)*, pp. 1–4. IEEE, 2020.

[17] Murthy, OV Ramana, and M. Hanmandlu. "A study on the effect of outliers in devanagari character recognition." *International Journal of Computer Applications* 975 (2011): 8887.

[18] Neves, Renata FP, Alberto NG Lopes Filho, Carlos AB Mello, and Cleber Zanchettin. "A SVM based off-line handwritten digit recognizer." In *2011 IEEE international conference on systems, man, and cybernetics*, pp. 510–515. IEEE, 2011.

[19] Pal, Anita, and Dayashankar Singh. "Handwritten English character recognition using neural network." *International Journal of Computer Science & Communication* 1, no. 2 (2010): 141–144.

[20] Pedregosa, Fabian, Gaël Varoquaux, Alexandre Gramfort, Vincent Michel, Bertrand Thirion, Olivier Grisel, Mathieu Blondel et al. "Scikit-learn: Machine learning in Python." *Journal of Machine Learning Research* 12 (2011): 2825–2830.

[21] Shamim, S. M., Mohammad Badrul Alam Miah, Masud Rana Angona Sarker, and Abdullah Al Jobair. "Handwritten digit recognition using machine learning algorithms." *Global Journal of Computer Science and Technology* (2018).

[22] Shawon, Ashadullah, Md Jamil-Ur Rahman, Firoz Mahmud, and MM Arefin Zaman. "Bangla handwritten digit recognition using deep cnn for large and unbiased dataset." In *2018 International Conference on Bangla Speech and Language Processing (ICBSLP)*, pp. 1–6. IEEE, 2018.

[23] Shopon, Md, Nabeel Mohammed, and Md Anowarul Abedin. "Bangla handwritten digit recognition using autoencoder and deep convolutional neural network." In *2016 International Workshop on Computational Intelligence (IWCI)*, pp. 64–68. IEEE, 2016.

[24] Siddique, Fathma, Shadman Sakib, and Md Abu Bakr Siddique. "Handwritten digit recognition using convolutional neural network in Python with tensorflow and observe the variation of accuracies for various hidden layers." (2019).

[25] Soman, Soumya T., Ashakranthi Nandigam, and V. Srinivasa Chakravarthy. "An efficient multiclassifier system based on convolutional neural network for offline handwritten Telugu character recognition." In *2013 National conference on communications (NCC)*, pp. 1–5. IEEE, 2013.

[26] Swethalakshmi, Hariharan, Anitha Jayaraman, V. Srinivasa Chakravarthy, and C. Chandra Sekhar. "Online handwritten character recognition of devanagari and telugu characters using support vector machines." In *Tenth international workshop on Frontiers in handwriting recognition*. Suvisoft, 2006.

[27] Team, T. "TensorFlow Datasets: a collection of ready-to-use datasets."

[28] Paper, David, and David Paper. "TensorFlow Datasets." *State-of-the-Art Deep Learning Models in TensorFlow: Modern Machine Learning in the Google Colab Ecosystem* (2021): 65–91.

[29] Younis, Khaled S., and Abdullah A. Alkhateeb. "A new implementation of deep neural networks for optical character recognition and face recognition." *Proceedings of the New Trends in Information Technology* (2017): 157–162.

[30] Long, J., Shelhamer, E., and Darrell, T. Fully convolutional networks for semantic segmentation. In *Proceedings of the IEEE Conference on Computer Vision and Pattern Recognition*, Boston, MA, USA, 7–12 June 2015.

[31] Chen, L.-C., Papandreou, G., Kokkinos, I., Murphy, K., and Yuille, A.L. DeepLab: Semantic image segmentation with deep convolutional nets, atrous convolution, and fully connected CRFs. *IEEE Transactions on Pattern Analysis and Machine Intelligence* 2018, 40, 834–848.

[32] Noh, H., Hong, S., and Han, B. Learning deconvolution network for semantic segmentation. In *Proceedings of the IEEE International Conference on Computer Vision*, Araucano Park, Las Condes, Chille, 11–18 December 2015.

[33] Gupta, A., Sarkhel, R., Das, N., and Kundu, M. Multiobjective optimization for recognition of isolated handwritten Indic scripts. *Pattern Recognition Letters* 2019, 128, 318–325.

[34] Nguyen, C.T., Khuong, V.T.M., Nguyen, H.T., and Nakagawa, M. CNN based spatial classification features for clustering offline handwritten mathematical expressions. *Pattern Recognition Letters*. 2019.

[35] Ziran, Z., Pic, X., Innocenti, S.U., Mugnai, D., and Marinai, S. Text alignment in early printed books combining deep learning and dynamic programming. *Pattern Recognition Letters* 2020, 133, 109–115.

18 Uses of Artificial Intelligence and GIS Technologies in Healthcare Services

Sushobhan Majumdar

Jadavpur University, Kolkata, India

18.1 INTRODUCTION

Healthcare (or healthcare-related services) involves the assimilation and improvement of various processes such as prevention, diagnosis, treatment, illness, injury etc. Healthcare services are a very crucial issue for all countries around the world. After COVID-19, the necessity and demand for good healthcare services are growing on a daily basis. At this time healthcare systems around the world face various kinds of challenges in achieving sustainable health conditions for the improvement of population health, improving the patient care system, raising the cost for the healthcare-related services etc. In the case of developing countries the problem of overpopulation, the increasing tendency of growing chronic diseases, and the insufficient availability of hospital beds are among the major problems.

Artificial intelligence (AI) is the integration and combination of various algorithms such as computing technologies, the creation of a variety of software packages and applications and the secure transmission of data among a variety of activities. Core technologies that are deeply engaged with the AI technologies are machine learning, deep learning, speech recognition, generation of natural language, robotics, biometric identification etc. Now AI is being used in various public sectors such as manufacturing industries, business hubs, and automobile engineering industries [1]. Machine learning is one of the major sub-branches of AI, which has been used for healthcare-related services. In the present day, various computational techniques have been used for healthcare research. Deep learning is a also major aspect of machine learning which is mainly used for the advance in healthcare technologies [2, 3].

The uses of GIS in healthcare services have also been increasing daily. It also helps the user with the integration of the data, and the visualization and analysis of the data. At present, GIS can also be used for the improvement of public health. Using the GIS platform the patients and its relatives can identify the nearest hospitals with precise location i.e. distance, latitude, longitude etc. Now various hospital authorities use GIS for the improvement of patient-related services. It also helps the hospitals to managing and best utilize their resources in a sustainable manner.

18.1.1 PREVIOUS RESEARCH

Intelligence about health refers to the applications of AI technologies and data science technologies to provide new and rapid technologies for advances in health and healthcare-related services [4]. Health intelligence can also be used for the social media analytics for syndromic surveillance [5]. It can also be used for the predictive modeling of healthcare for chronic diseases [6], for the delivery of healthcare products and medical imaging technologies [7].

AI and GIS technologies are interrelated with the modern healthcare technologies, with its various sub-branches. For this reason health intelligence can be described as AI applications to increase the quality of human health from the personal level to the community level [8]. For the improvement of community health, proper health planning and management is required. Communities of population-level health planning are the major issues of the public health system. In the case of individual-level planning, treatment and diagnosis can be carried out through medication, treatment or by changing genetics, its environment and changing lifestyle [9, 10]. For these types of advantages of using AI technologies the performance of healthcare and healthcare-related services have been increasing very rapidly, which is mainly due to its high performance and cloud computing technologies [11, 12]. Tran et al. [13], defines that AI plays a vital role in global health research because of its evolutionary nature. In a few cases bibliometric analysis or bibliometric research has been used for the study of healthcare and health-related services. Connelly et al. [14] suggests that robotic intelligence is one of the powerful tools to be used under AI. Robotic assisted surgery is one of the essential tools for health research in the present day. Now it has been used in different fields such as urological, orthopedic applications etc. Guo et al. [15] were trying to find out the recent applications of AI through the month of December, 2019. In that study, the researchers focus on the applications of AI on health and also provide an idea of how the newest applications of AI can help health professionals. Choudhury and Asan's [16] research was based on the systematic review of the AI-based literature to identify the degree of health risk of the patients. In that research the researchers were carried out their study over 53 cases.

Geographical Information System (GIS) is the sub-branch of spatial science research. Now various types of spatial science tools and technologies have been used for the advancement of healthcare services as it is easy to understand and analyze and can easily visualize real-world phenomena. Now GIS technologies and AI algorithms are interlinked with one another with the help of Geospatial Artificial Intelligence (GeoAI technologies). These GeoAI technologies are a combination of various methods such as GIS, data mining, data integration, computing technologies, the management of big data etc. (Jing et al. 2018). GeoAI is one of the important technologies that is now being for the better tracking of location to take action for the enhancement of human health. GeoAI technology represents a new domain of intelligence in public health to take quick action and precise location techniques that can be used for the improvement of human health. GeoAI technologies can also be used for both the community and the individual level. It can also help with the integration of data, facilities of remote sensing technologies, data mining, data cloud and computing etc. It is one of the major drivers behind the smart city development by reducing the levels of death of patients from chronic diseases, the innovation of new medication techniques and new technologies for the treatment purposes.

18.1.2 OBJECTIVE

Both AI and GIS are new technologies. In the case of healthcare technologies both these technologies have been integrated. In this research, an effort has been done to find out the uses of AI and GIS in the case of healthcare and healthcare-related services. Side-by-side emphasis has also been given on the recent challenges and its possible solutions for the application of these technologies.

18.2 DATABASE AND METHODOLOGY

18.2.1 DATA

This research is based on the empirical research, in which empirical data has been used. Most of the data in this research has been taken from users when they are performing the application of processing AI and GIS technology.

18.2.2 METHODOLOGY

In recent years, various disciplines started their research using AI technologies. Thus, in this research an effort has been carried out to find out uses of AI technology with the geography discipline. In most cases AI technologies have been used for disease-mapping purposes. It helps the users to extract the information from the different resources. Now various technologies have been used with GIS for the management of public health and services. The first step of the GIS is to find out the uses of AI and GIS in the case of public health.

18.3 RESULTS AND ANALYSIS

18.3.1 GLOBAL ARTIFICIAL INTELLIGENCE [1]

AI is now one of the fastest growing industries not only in India but also across the world. It is also among the highest-growing industries in India. According to Healthcare Market Size Reports, the market size of AI was USD3.25 per capita (approx.) in 2018. It has been predicted to grow by up to 41.5 percentage points by 2025.

18.3.2　Uses of AI and GIS in India for Healthcare Services

According to the report of health informatics, the uses of AI will rapidly change the entire healthcare systems of India. AI and its various modern technologies, such as data science machine learning, creates huge opportunities for improvements in healthcare services. It also creates huge employment in India which indirectly strengthens the economy of India. Healthcare industries are also regarded as knowledge-intensive industries as it depends on the storage and coding of the data or industries. Today the collection of medical information has been increased hugely because it gathers various types of information such as behavioural, clinical, sociocultural, environment data etc. The use of this technology is so intensive today that everyday huge amounts of data are stored by using this technology. AI technology is responsible for the revolutionary changes of healthcare services in India because of its extensive application in healthcare services. It provides a huge role in the diagnosis of diseases, protocol development, treatment monitoring, and health system care and management.

18.4　INDIAN CONTEXT

The demand for the uses of AI technology has increased hugely in recent periods after the outbreak of COVID-19. This outbreak is also responsible for the paradigm shift of digital healthcare services in India. (Karim et al. 2019) suggests that it is time for India to introduce modern technology from the traditional technological system which minimizes the gap between the old healthcare system and new healthcare techniques. The healthcare sector in India is now a rapidly growing industry in India because of its increasing revenues and also for increasing market share. This also helps in completing various healthcare procedures such as booking appointments, the sales of medicine etc.

18.5　DISCUSSION

18.5.1　The role of AI in Healthcare

Now AI technologies play a vital role for the growth and development of healthcare-related services. At present, not only artificial intelligence but also its various sub-branches such as robotics, big data etc. have been playing a vital role in the improvement of healthcare services. It also opens a new era of opportunities by providing new technology in a faster way. Now healthcare services are related with various other processes such as the integration of the data, data mining etc. In recent years, the sphere of public health services have been hugely increased because it is now related to other activities such as storing of data, and the coding of data which includes mainly four principal types of data: clinical, genetic, behavioral and environmental. Different healthcare practitioners, medical researchers as well as patients produce vast amounts of data daily which are cumulatively stored in the server.

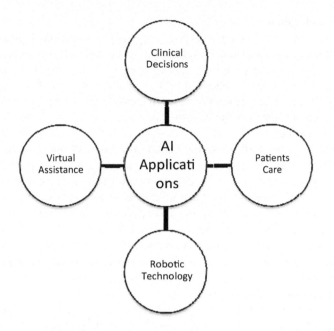

FIGURE 18.1   The application of AI in healthcare.

Both AI and GeoAI technology are bringing huge changes in the history of healthcare research that are unprecedented. Although not all the work is completely based only on the AI technologies, it is now associated with other processes such as data mining, robotics, image asset recognition etc. Not only this, but medical AI technology also plays an important role by maintaining and managing electronic health records (EHRs), the diagnosis of the patient's problem, maintaining the protocol for treatment, monitoring health conditions of the patient, proper medication and the management of the public information system. Figure 18.1. shows the applications of AI in healthcare.

AI and Clinical Decisions
With the help of AI technologies, users can easily store, manage and process larger sets of data. Through the AI technologies, users can easily maintain the database which is one of the major steps of Data Base Management System (DBMS). Using this technology the health professionals and practitioners can easily diagnose patient's diseases with the help of the decision support system. Through the AI technologies users, and also researchers, can easily keep all kinds of medical records for future uses.

Enhancing Patients' Care
Using AI technology, health practitioners can easily improve patients' care by reducing the level of stress of the patients. It also helps the patients in saving the patients' expenditure including their health queries through the instant solution of their problems.

Robotic Technology

AI, with its robotic technology system, can easily speed up medical practices with making delicate incisions as robot do not tire during lengthy surgery. For this reason, doctors can perform surgeries over many hours with the help of a few professionals. Using a robotic system, new surgical methods can be developed. With the help of this kind of modern technology, the chances of tremors and accidental movements can be reduced.

Virtual Assistance

AI systems are also performing the virtual assistance of nurses and can perform a huge range of tasks in a shorter span of time. Through the virtual assistance system, patients can get best and effective guidance and treatment according to their desired time. Patients can take those virtual assistance 24/7 time whenever they need. Using the virtual assistance systems, patients can easily share their queries and get instant solutions or treatment. Now in the case of various countries regular interactions have been made with the help of virtual management systems and it reduces the frequency of unnecessary hospital visits.

Proper Diagnosis of Problems

AI also helps the doctors to detect, and diagnose the diseases more accurately in a faster way. With the help of this technology health professionals can easily increase their efficiency and the accuracy of the diagnosis of the problem. It is also a cost-effective method which helps the patients to get their treatment at a cheaper rate.

18.5.2　Role of GIS in Healthcare

GIS is another modern technology which was introduced a few decades ago.

18.5.3　The Overview of Geo-intelligence

GIS is another modern technology which was introduced a few decades ago. Now AI algorithms have been added with GIS technologies. For this reason users can perform various GIS functions, including spatial data processing and the analysis of algorithms. Now with the help of GIS technology and AI algorithms it has gradually become the main focus of geoscience research and geo-information research.

Geo- Intelligence:

This is a comparatively new term and issues which is associated with the techniques of visualization, discussion and analysis, decision-making strategy with the help of GIS, remote sensing and satellite systems. GIS technology is the most unique of all the technological advances, which establishes it as a separate discipline. GIS technologies consist of four other technologies: data coding, geo-visualization, geographic design and decision-making. User's complexity of using GIS decreases from the beginning to the end. Another major advantage of using this technology is the output of GIS technology, i.e. map, data etc., can also be used in the case of other analysis. It is also very user-friendly.

Neo-thinking of AI-GIS Algorithms:
AI and GIS combination will be any one of the followings:

1. Geo-AI: It is the processing of the data or it is one of the data processing techniques in which GIS technology and AI algorithms can be integrated and merged under the same domain.
2. Use of AI for GIS: AI in GIS can be used to increase the functional ability of GIS techniques and it is less time-consuming.
3. GIS and AI Integration: It enhances the power of visualization and analytical techniques. After the completion of the data integration process, the acceptability of the data will be hugely increased.

Recent uses of AI and GIS:
Core themes of each GIS application are related with the geographic location i.e. latitude and longitude. The sphere of using GIS and AI technologies that have been hugely increased daily. For this reason, it has been hugely used in the disease mapping such as pest control and management and various computation intelligence researches. Satellite images are one of the essential tools for performing GIS as it provides real-time images to the user with a precise location and with minimum chances of errors. Now satellite images have been largely used in case of making health reports, measurement of air and water pollution etc. The uses of GIS are relatively high in the case of urban areas than in the other areas.

User challenges:
GIS technologies are associated with data science developments such as machine learning and data mining with geography. Industrial geography provides valuable insights and benefits to both industrial geographers and industrialists. While industrial geographers gain useful knowledge and understanding of the spatial patterns, location factors, and economic dynamics of industries, industrialists can utilize this information to make informed decisions about their businesses. Therefore, industrial geography serves as a beneficial discipline for both users, contributing to the growth and success of industrial sectors.

Recognition of image:
Recognition of the image can only be done in the recognition software. The main aim of this image recognition software is to search the assets and scrutinize how those assets are interlinked. Type features and meters of road on photos are also another feature of this software. This image recognition software maintains its accuracy when each of the images is connected with the precise location and each precise location contains a geotag. To perform this algorithm properly, integration and management of the data are very much needed through the database management system.

Utility mapping
Each map contains a specific purpose. The purpose and objective of making maps changed very rapidly according to the user's requirements and objectives. For the purposes of utility mapping, machine learning and data mining techniques can be applied.

Data reduction

Reduction of the data can be termed as data cleansing. Through the data reduction techniques users can easily reduce the percentage of errors or incorrect data. GIS data often called the historical data mostly by the engineers as it records and saves previous years of data. Users can easily perform research with these kinds of data.

4. **Limitations**:

Like any other, this research work also has some limitations that could be addressed by more in- depth future studies. The main problem of AI and GIS integration is that the cost of using this technology is very high. All of the software has to be bought by the researchers. For this reason the uses of this technology is very much lower in the case of developing countries than it is in the case of the developed countries. Efficient users are required for the use of this technology.

This is a new research area. For this reason, a much lower number of professionals is use this technology. For security reasons and in the interests of privacy, the work of ethical frameworks is needed as large amounts of data are stored in this server. For the sharing and storing of the data, standard norms are required at the international level. There is a lack of proper training data for AI algorithms.

18.6   CONCLUSIONS

There is an emerging role of GeoAI for health and healthcare services. It integrated both geography and AI. This integration is particularly helpful for the population which extends up to the national health level. GeoAI has been principally used for environmental and health modeling as it links the precise location with its data. It has also been used to explore their role for health outcomes. This research therefore adopts a qualitative approach for the analysis of uses and applications of AI and GIS techniques. There are also some limitations that will affect future research regarding AI and GIS studies.

In India, AI faces a lots of challenges regarding its uses because of the lack of professional users. One of the major aims of AI is human interference, but it is unable to collect and information for various reasons. In many cases, AI mainly used for the health measures, diagnosis of the diseases etc. AI can perform a huge number of tasks over a shorter period of time.

REFERENCES

[1] Mohammad, S.M. (2020). *Artificial intelligence in information technology*, Retrieved from https://papers.ssrn.com/sol3/papers.cfm?abstract_id=3625444.
[2] Mehta, N., Devarakonda, M.V. (2018). Machine learning, natural language programming, and electronic health records: the next step in the artificial intelligence journey? *J Allergy Clin Immunol* 141:2019_21. https://doi.org/10.1016/j.jaci.2018.02.025e1.
[3] Yu, K.H., Beam, A.L., Kohane, I.S. (2018). Artificial intelligence in healthcare. *Nat Biomed Eng* 2:719–31. https://doi.org/10.1038/s41551-018-0305-z.

[4] Șerban, O., Thapen, N., Maginnis, B., Hankin, C., Foot, V. (2018). Real-time processing of social media with SENTINEL: a syndromic surveillance system incorporating deep learning for health classification. *Inf Process Manag.* 56:1166–1184.

[5] Rajkomar, A., Oren, E., Chen, K., Dai, A.M., Hajaj, N., Hardt, M., Liu, P.J., Liu, X., Marcus, J., Sun, M. (2018). Scalable and accurate deep learning with electronic health records. *NPJ Digit Med.* 1(1):18.

[6] Istepanian, R.S.H., Al-Anzi, T. (2018). m-Health 2.0: new perspectives on mobile health, machine learning and big data analytics. *Methods* 151:34–40.

[7] Bi, W.L., Hosny, A., Schabath, M.B., Giger, M.L., Birkbak, N.J., Mehrtash, A., Allison, T., Arnaout, O., Abbosh, C., Dunn, I.F., et al. (2019). Artificial intelligence in cancer imaging: clinical challenges and applications. *CA Cancer J Clin.* 69:127–157.

[8] Kamel Boulos, N.M.N., Peng, G., Vopham, T. (2019). An overview of GeoAI applications in health and healthcare. *Int J Health Geogr.* 23(6):143–165.

[9] Shaban-Nejad, A., Michalowski, M., Buckeridge, D.L. *Health intelligence: how artificial intelligence transforms population and personalized health.* London: Nature Publishing Group; 2018.

[10] Davis, M.M., Shanley, T.P. (2017). The missing -omes: proposing social and environmental nomenclature in precision medicine. *Clin Transl Sci.* 10(2):64–66.

[11] Topol, E.J. (2019). High-performance medicine: the convergence of human and artificial intelligence. *Nat Med.* 25(1):44–56.

[12] Vo Pham, T., Hart, J.E., Laden, F., Chiang, Y.Y. (2018). Emerging trends in geospatial artificial intelligence (geoAI): potential applications for environmental epidemiology. *Environ Health.* 17(1):40.

[13] Tran, B.X., Vu, G.T., Ha, G.H., Vuong, Q.-H., Ho, M.-T., Vuong, T.-T. (2019). Global evolution of research in artificial intelligence in health and medicine: a bibliometric study. *J Clin Med.* 8(3):360.

[14] Connelly, T.M., Malik, Z., Sehgal, R., Byrnes, G., Coffey, J.C., Peirce, C. (2020). The 100 most influential manuscripts in robotic surgery: a bibliometric analysis. *J Robot Surg.* 14(1):155–165.

[15] Guo, Y., Hao, Z., Zhao, S., Gong, J., Yang, F. (2020). Artificial intelligence in health care: bibliometric analysis. *J Med Internet Res.* 22(7):e18228.

[16] Choudhury, A., Asan, O. (2020). Role of artificial intelligence in patient safety outcomes: systematic literature review. *JMIR Med Inform.* 8(7):e18599.

[17] Karim, F, Majumdar, S, Darabi, H, Harford, S. (2019). Multivariate LSTM-FCNs for time series classification. *Neural Netw.* 116:237–245.

[18] Jing, Y, Bian, Y, Hu, Z, Wang, L, Sean Xie, ZQ (2018). Deep learning for drug design: an artificial intelligence paradigm for drug discovery in the big data era. *AAPS J.* 20:1–10.

19 Digital and Smart Agriculture

Components, Challenges, and Limitations

Fariha Haroon

Kalindi College, University of Delhi, New Delhi, India

Nafisur Rahman

School of Engineering Sciences and Technology, Jamia Hamdard, New Delhi, India

19.1 INTRODUCTION

According to the Food and Agriculture Organization of the United Nations, agriculture currently consumes 38% of the earth's land area. As the population continues to grow, there is less space for both human and animal habitats, as well as for plant life. For example, in India, a country with one of the highest agricultural outputs in the world, the majority of the population relies on subsistence agriculture. This leads to the inefficient use of resources such as water and fertilizers, and makes the output of crops dependent on unpredictable weather patterns. In addition, a large portion of post-harvest food in India is lost or wasted due to poor infrastructure and extreme weather events. To address these issues, it is necessary to implement technology such as data analysis, wireless sensors, and artificial intelligence in order to improve farm operations and establish storage and cold chains. This will not only help to reduce losses in agriculture, but also allow farmers to produce goods in a way that is more environmentally sustainable. Figure 19.1 represents a smart farming system that utilizes advanced technologies and monitoring devices to optimize crop growth, increase yield, and improve overall efficiency in the farming industry. The system consists of two main sections: an agriculture system and a technology system. The agriculture system is designed to improve crop growth and yield by monitoring the field conditions, weather, soil moisture and temperature, etc. The field is equipped with monitoring sensors and image sensors that are used to regularly check the condition of the field and detect any abnormal conditions that may affect the crop growth. These sensors detect the presence of pests and diseases, measure the soil moisture and temperature, and track the crop growth. Drones are also used to map the field and

DOI: 10.1201/9781003363606-19

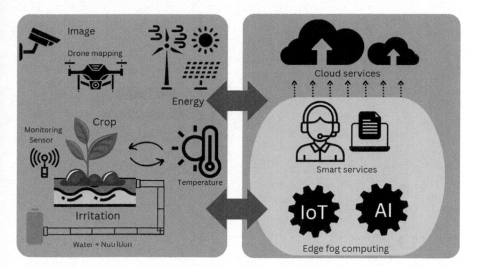

FIGURE 19.1   Smart farming system.

detect any potential threats from wild animals or damage caused by natural disasters. The system also includes an automatic water and nutrition system that ensures that the crops receive the necessary resources for optimal growth. A power generator is also included to supply electricity to the various systems that require it.

The technology system is responsible for collecting and analysing data from the agriculture system. The system uses IoT and AI technologies to monitor and study the data, which is then used to provide smart services such as crop prediction and yield optimization. IoT devices such as sensors and cameras are used to collect data from the field, and AI algorithms are used to analyse the data and make predictions about the crop growth and yield. The system also utilizes cloud computing to store and process the data. The smart services provided by the technology system include precision agriculture, crop health monitoring, weather forecasting, soil analysis, and yield prediction. These services help the farmers to make informed decisions about the crop management, irrigation, fertilization, and harvesting.

In Figure 19.2, a survey conducted in 2020 that shows the highest adoption rate of Internet of Things technology in the agricultural sector was in agricultural processing, while the pre-harvest stage had a low adoption rate due to low farmer incomes and large-scale tenant farming. However, organized sectors such as warehousing and processing saw higher adoption rates [1]. Overall, it is clear that implementing modern technology in the agricultural sector can help to improve efficiency and reduce losses, leading to more sustainable and successful farming practices. By collecting and analysing data, farmers can adapt to changing conditions and plan for the future, ultimately helping to feed the growing population in a more environmentally responsible.

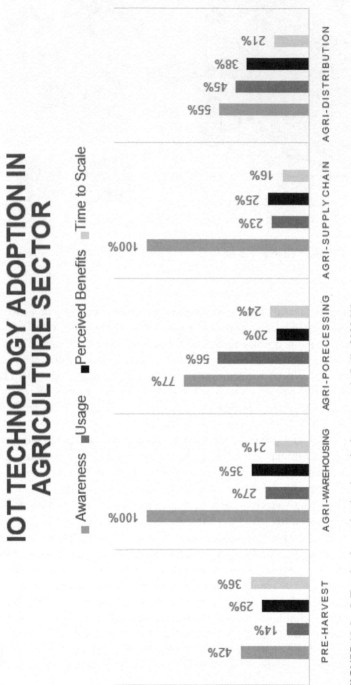

FIGURE 19.2 IoT technology adoption in agriculture sector in India 2020 [1].

19.2 SMART AGRICULTURE-ENABLING TECHNOLOGIES

Of late, technological advancements and proliferation have been rapid. The following sub-sections have discussed some of the technologies enabling Smart Agriculture.

19.2.1 IOT AND WSNs

Internet of Things (IoT) describes physical objects (or groups of objects) with technologies that transfer the data from one device to another over the Internet or communication network. We can see examples of IoT in our everyday life—from kitchen appliances in our homes to transport and metropolitan cities. Innovative projects in cities are using many sensors to understand and manage the environment in a big area. This is being done on a large scale to improve the overall quality of the region. A sensor is explained as an input device that detects and measures from the physical environment and later provides an output (signal) concerning a specific physical quantity. Wireless sensor networks (WSNs) have the power of distributed communication, computing, and sensing features without any physical connection. The combination of IoT and WSNs can increase the overall quantity and quality of goods with an IoT-based intelligent farming system. The application of IoT in agriculture ranges from temperature monitoring to livestock farming to soil moisture monitoring.

19.2.2 CLOUD COMPUTING

Cloud computing refers to the practice of storing and accessing data and software over the internet, rather than on a local hard drive. This method enables users to access and utilize data without the need to maintain and operate physical servers or data centres. Cloud computing comes in three different forms: Software as a Service (SaaS), Platform as a Service (PaaS), and Infrastructure as a Service (IaaS). Each of these types of cloud computing offers varying levels of control, flexibility, and management, allowing users to choose the most appropriate services for their specific requirements. Mobile computing refers to the use of portable devices such as smartphones and tablets to access and process information. These devices are typically connected to the internet and allow users to access data and applications from anywhere at any time. Mobile computing and cloud computing often work together, with mobile devices accessing and processing data stored in the cloud.

19.2.3 DATA MINING

Data mining is the computational process of analysing many datasets, and information to identify trends and patterns. Meaningful patterns can help predict possible outcomes. It involves methods such as machine learning algorithms, statistics, and database systems. Data mining has enhanced the process of organizational decision-making by providing valuable insights through careful examination of data.

19.2.4 Artificial Intelligence

Artificial intelligence (AI) is the simulation of human intelligence in machines programmed to have thinking and intelligence like those of humans. Using these technologies, AI can train computers to accomplish specific tasks by processing large amounts of datasets and recognizing patterns with the help of Data mining and analysis. AI technology has the potential to reduce human effort by automating tasks through the use of robots and drones. Machine learning (ML) is a specific field within artificial intelligence (AI) that utilizes statistical techniques to enable machines to learn from data. AI, on the other hand, aims to replicate human intelligence in machines, particularly computer systems, through the ability to learn, reason, and adapt.

19.3 THE IMPACT OF IOT ON AGRICULTURE

In recent years, technological advancements have been occurring at a rapid pace. One area that has seen significant growth is Smart Agriculture, which is enabled by a variety of technologies such as the Internet of Things (IoT). IoT-based smart agriculture products are designed to assist farmers in monitoring crop fields by utilizing sensors, software, and modules. This allows farmers and other stakeholders to easily monitor field conditions from anywhere, through real-time remote monitoring capabilities (Figure 19.3). Predictions estimate that the agricultural industry will experience a

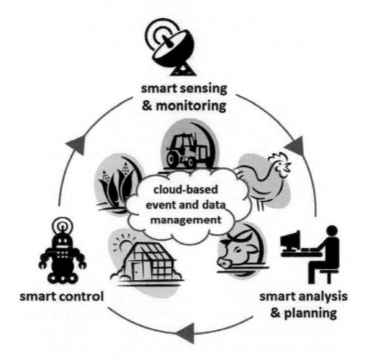

FIGURE 19.3 Smart farming cycle [3].

20% compound annual growth rate (CAGR) as a result of IoT system installations, with the number of connected agricultural devices increasing from 13 million in 2014 to 225 million by 2024 [2].

The goals of the commonly used applications involving IoT in agriculture are:

i. Climate and Weather Monitoring: The selection of suitable crops is dependent on the study of weather and climatic conditions, as well as the ability of the crops to thrive at specific temperatures.

ii. Drone Monitoring: Ground and aerial drones are utilized to evaluate crop health, perform monitoring, planting, spraying, and field analysis, in order to optimize crop yields.

iii. Greenhouse Automation: The production of various crops is facilitated through the manipulation of the local environmental conditions in which the plants are grown. These conditions are adjusted according to the specific requirements of the plants, such as temperature, light, moisture, and nutrients. This allows farmers to cultivate crops throughout the year, regardless of the season.

iv. Data Analysis: The use of precision farming techniques allows for the analysis of soil conditions and other relevant parameters, resulting in increased operational efficiency and improved crop yields.

19.4 SMART SENSORS' APPLICATIONS IN AGRICULTURE

Smart Sensors help detect, monitor, and maintain the physical factors of agricultural land. These sensors play a vital role in monitoring and storing data through IoT for different industrial processes. The processes like collecting, measuring, and transmitting data and centralizing cloud computing platforms, wherever data is collected and analysed for investigating the pattern. This collected data can be monitored at any time by decision-makers. Smart sensors include amplifiers, transducers, analog filters, excitation controls, and compensation sensors. Agostino has described the advances in smart sensors and IoT, assessing weather, monitoring crops, using robots for tasks like harvesting and weeding, and utilizing drones. This enhances decision-making and increases efficiency [2]. Another research has demonstrated the effectiveness of using WSNs for the automatic monitoring of insect pests in agricultural fields [4]. By utilizing WSNs, farmers are able to detect infestations early and are notified of their location, reducing the need for labour-intensive manual inspections of the entire field. Similarly, another paper investigated diseases in crops with the help of Image Processing and IoT [5]. The study evaluates the productivity of farmland by integrating Image Processing and IoT in agriculture (Figure 19.4). By using Image Processing techniques such as K-Means Clustering, Pre-processing, Bilateral Filtering, and Segmentation, the report is able to train a network to detect diseases or pests present in the crops. By using these images and algorithms, the study is able to identify and mitigate damage caused by these factors.

In [6] a new interdigital sensor has been developed for the detection of water temperature, nitrate, phosphate, and pH levels. The sensor's performance has been evaluated using Electrochemical Impedance Spectroscopy (EIS) to measure various temperatures,

FIGURE 19.4   Smart sensor for agriculture.

pH levels, nitrate and phosphate concentrations. In Figure 19.5, the application of smart sensors, field tasks like soil health monitoring, smart irrigation systems, leaf disease identification, crop yield, post-harvesting activities, competent animal husbandry, communication protocol, and emerging future techniques are used. The sensors are subdivided to check the monitoring and level of sub-components essential for crop growth.

Smart irrigation systems are adequate for low water stress-level countries. It occurs when demands for freshwater transcend the available amount, affecting mostly Northern Africa and Western and Central Asia. Table 19.1 presents a variety of remote sensing applications and their respective pros and cons.

Limitations of Sensors:

   i. Sensor node devices have a relatively simple operation which makes them easy to deploy, but also leaves them susceptible to security breaches as they often lack robust security systems [12].
   ii. Smart sensors consist of both actuators and sensors, making them more complex than traditional sensors.
  iii. They can be costly, particularly those with advanced software, hardware tools, high-resolution cameras, and thermal cameras [12].

19.5   COMPUTING IN SMART AGRICULTURE

Farmers and agriculture experts can employ computing techniques in agriculture to gather data from sources such as soil sensors, satellite imagery, and weather stations, providing farmers with valuable information that can be utilized to improve crop management decisions. Cloud analytics has the ability to analyze the production

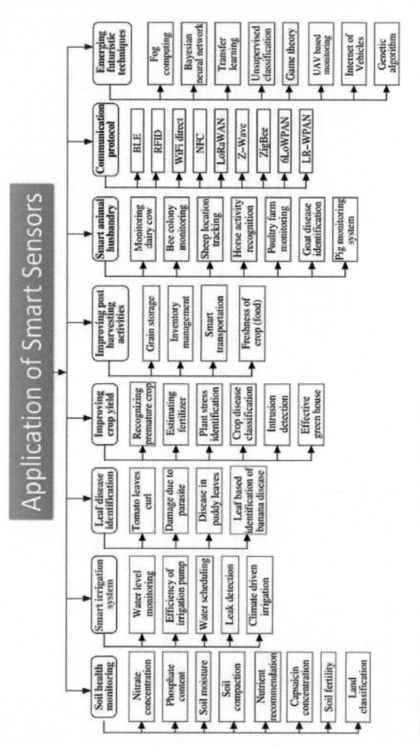

FIGURE 19.5 Different smart sensor applications in agriculture [4].

TABLE 19.1

Remote Sensing Applications and Their Contributions and Limitations

Ref No.	Type	Applications	Pros & Cons
[7]	RFID (Radio-Frequency Identification)Motion-sensing based camera, Distance sensors.	Monitoring livestock drinking behaviour, water quality and consumption.	The system can monitor each drinking event in terms of animal identification, water consumption, drinking water behaviour, and quality. On the other hand, it's implemented in remote grazing site so it's not clear how well it would work on other locations or climates.
[8]	Ardunio Mega 2560, Rain drop sensors, Humidity Sensor, etc.	Forecasting weather on agricultural lands, Harvests, temperature control, humidity control, etc.	The system uses IoT and WSN technologies in smart farming with this hybrid SSOA and MA method. The system can be affected by various factors such as lack of data, missing data, or sensor malfunction.
[9]	PySEBAL (Python-based Surface Energy Balance Algorithm for Land)	Investigating the potential soil physical and chemical properties and plot characteristics affecting the variability of irrigation performance in rice across the KVIS (Kholongchhu Irrigation System, Bhutan)	The study uses two model approaches, random forest-based and linear mixed models, to investigate the factors affecting irrigation performance in rice. It did not achieve good performance in predicting CWP, indicating that additional observational data might be needed to improve our understanding of the key constraints of irrigation performance in the KVIS.
[10]	Small commercial drone and Digital Camera	Implementing an autonomous robot for weeding by laser technology. Providing convenient information to the artificial intelligence system so that it can be properly trained.	The study uses an open source and easily usable machine learning tool that can distinguish with extreme precision the areas where the crop, weeds, a mix of both, or bare soil are present. The study was focused on a two-weed dominant-species scenario that permitted the validation of the method in a controlled environment (experimental plot), so it's not clear how well the findings would apply to other species or in different environments.
[11]	UAV night-time thermal cameras and UAV daytime RGB cameras	Automated counting of wild cranes for wildlife management and population monitoring	Accurate counting of cranes, with an Overall Accuracy (OA) of 91.47% for thermal images and 94.51% for RGB images. Capable of counting in inaccessible areas, at night, and without fear of human interference. Algorithm specifically developed for counting cranes and may not be directly applicable to other species without modification

environment. Though the adoption of cloud computing took some time to gain momentum, Japan is currently the leading adopter, followed by China and the United States [13].

19.5.1 Cloud Computing Models

The Cloud Computing model is divided into three service models which can satisfy the unique requirements of business sectors: SaaS (Software as a Service), PaaS (Platform as a Service), and IaaS (Infrastructure as a Service) (Figure 19.6).

SaaS (Software as a service): Services provided by the software provider and not your company comes under the SaaS category. Services are provided without buying/downloading and installing specific machines. They offer applications that can be accessed directly on the web over a network and on-demand basis. End users use it.

PaaS (Platform as a service): Platform service is halfway between infrastructure and software. It provides the computing platform for developing and designing with minimum redundancy, implemented by application developers. It includes platforms like operating systems, databases, web servers, and language execution environments for software deployment.

IaaS (Infrastructure as a service): This model includes a virtual platform for IT administrators, which requires an operating environment and application deployed. Examples of IaaS are Microsoft Azure, Google Computer Engine, and Amazon Web Services (AWS). The services charge in a pay-per-use model.

Limitations of Cloud Computing:
i. A slow internet connection is one significant concern in rural areas. Satellite and image sensors have gigabytes of image data that can take Up-to days due to less-than-average internet speed. With a low-speed connection, the purpose of cloud computing would fail. Therefore, a stable internet connection is needed.
ii. Another concern is security and privacy. Without proper maintenance and oversight, there is a risk of data breaches as data transmitted from IoT systems to the cloud involves multiple devices. Entrusting sensitive data to a third party can be challenging.
iii. Lack of awareness regarding the latest technology. With rapid technological advancements, farmers need to educate about the ongoing trends. Necessary training is essential for farmers as they opt for hit-and-trial technology methods rather than a systematic approach. This results in significant consequences for the future of farming.
iv. Conflict in different country laws. In the 20th century, there are still countries with no cloud service. Due to this, organizations have to look for service providers outside the country.

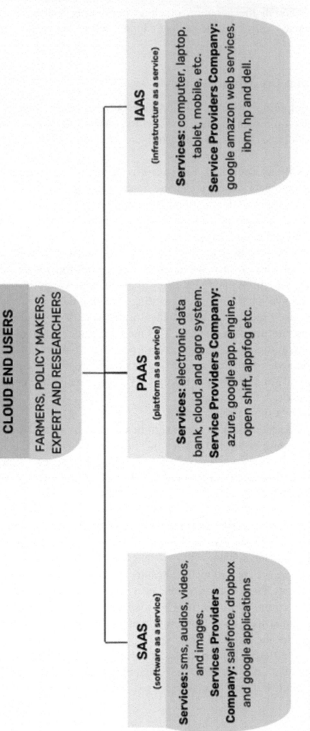

FIGURE 19.6   Cloud service models helping the agricultural stakeholders.

19.6 ARTIFICIAL INTELLIGENCE IN SMART AGRICULTURE

The traditional methods employed in farming are not as effective with a growing population and unpredictable weather, and it needs the application of machine intelligence. AI will boost the overall harvest quality and accuracy. AI-powered sensor devices can be integrated with agriculture robots, autonomous platforms, machines, or weather stations for direct deployment in fields. The Random Forest Algorithm is used to predict crop yields by analyzing sensor data. This approach has been designed to predict the future yields with high accuracy from large datasets. Machine learning (ML) is a technique that falls under the artificial intelligence (AI) umbrella. It learns features and tasks directly from the data provided by field sensors. Deep learning (DL) is a subset of ML in which data goes through multiple non-linear transformations to gain insights and produce an output [14]. Here data science is used to visualize the data and find a meaningful pattern. The ML technique learns features and tasks directly from the data given by the field sensors. Data values were input by various sensors. It predicts the future with high accuracy for a large dataset. ML is a subset of AI. The ML technique learns features and tasks directly from data given by the field sensors. DL is a subset of machine learning in which data goes through multiple numbers of non-linear transformations to obtain an output [15]. This study seeks to do climate forecasting using artificial neural networks to aid in the cultivation of certain crops, such as carrots, apples, grapes, and tomatoes, as well as helping the development of agribusiness in the Caxias Sul region and throughout Brazil. The network architecture used in the study by forwarding propagation of artificial neural networks. Inputs run through Neural Networks that have hidden layers [16]. In this paper, a smart agriculture system based on deep reinforcement learning (Figure 19.7). The deep reinforcement learning models make smart decisions to accommodate the

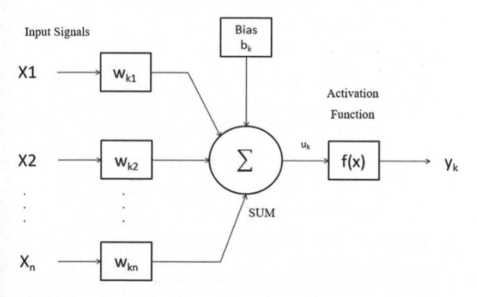

FIGURE 19.7 Structure of an artificial neuron.

environment to adapt to the crops' growth. It includes four layers: the agricultural data collection layer, edge computing layer, agricultural data transmission layer, and cloud computing layer.

According to [17], analyzing unstructured data in machine learning is difficult. Deep learning is a more suitable approach for this type of data analysis as compared to traditional machine learning. It is more versatile as it can handle a variety of data formats, and it can also be used to uncover relationships across interdisciplinary domains.

19.7   CONCLUSION

This literature review aims to examine the current state of research on the integration of Internet of Things (IoT), cloud computing, and artificial intelligence (AI) in smart farming. As the global population continues to grow and food demand increases, it is crucial to explore ways to optimize agricultural production and reduce food waste. The review first evaluates the significance of IoT in agriculture and its ability to improve productivity and efficiency in comparison to traditional methods. The utilization of smart sensors and cloud computing in rural areas is also discussed, along with the challenges and limitations faced in these environments. Additionally, the role of AI, DL, and ML learning in the agriculture sector is examined, specifically with regard to crop growth prediction and decision-making for farmers. The review also explores the use of remote sensing applications and their potential contributions and limitations to the field of smart farming.

It is important to note that the full potential of digital farming can only be realized through proper planning and management by relevant governing bodies and mass awareness promotion. This literature review highlights the ongoing research and developments in this field, and serves as a foundation for future research and implementation of IoT, cloud computing, and AI in smart farming.

Challenges in Adopting AI:

i. Expensive technology requires much testing and updating to achieve accurate results.
ii. Technology adoption is lengthy for farmers as it requires proper infrastructure to work.
iii. A lack of familiarity and understanding of emerging trends in AI is prevalent in rural areas where the adoption of smart agriculture technology is not as widespread.
iv. The increased adoption of technology in agriculture also increases the risk of privacy and security threats. Cyberattacks and data breaches can cause significant issues for farmers. Unfortunately, many farms lack the necessary protections against these types of threats [18].

REFERENCES

[1] "India: IoT Adoption in Agricultural Sector 2020 | Statista." https://www.statista.com/statistics/1234515/india-iot-adoption-in-agricultural-sector/ (accessed Jan. 28, 2023).

[2] "The Future of IoT in Agriculture – 4i Platform blog." https://4iplatform.com/blog/the-future-of-iot-in-agriculture/ (accessed Jan. 28, 2023).

[3] S. Wolfert, D. Goense, and C. A. G. Sorensen, "A Future Internet Collaboration Platform for Safe and Healthy Food from Farm to Fork," *2014 Annual SRII Global Conference*, pp. 266–273, 2014, doi: 10.1109/SRII.2014.47.

[4] R. Kumar, R. Mishra, H. P. Gupta, and T. Dutta, "Smart Sensing for Agriculture: Applications, Advancements, and Challenges," *IEEE Consumer Electronics Magazine*, vol. 10, no. 4, pp. 51–56, Jul. 2021, doi: 10.1109/MCE.2021.3049623.

[5] S. Liberata Ullo, G. R. Sinha, M. Bacco, A. Gotta, P. Cassarà, and J. I. Agbinya, "Advances in IoT and Smart Sensors for Remote Sensing and Agriculture Applications," *Remote Sensing 2021*, vol. 13, p. 2585, vol. 13, no. 13, p. 2585, Jul. 2021, doi: 10.3390/RS13132585.

[6] K. U. Singh et al., "An Artificial Neural Network-Based Pest Identification and Control in Smart Agriculture Using Wireless Sensor Networks," *Journal of Food Quality*, vol. 2022, 2022, doi: 10.1155/2022/5801206.

[7] W. Tang, A. Biglari, R. Ebarb, T. Pickett, S. Smallidge, and M. Ward, "A Smart Sensing System of Water Quality and Intake Monitoring for Livestock and Wild Animals," *Sensors*, vol. 21, Page 2885, vol. 21, no. 8, p. 2885, Apr. 2021, doi: 10.3390/S210 82885.

[8] S. Priya and A. Professor, "Weather Prediction Based on Wireless Sensor Network and Internet of Things with Analysis using Hybrid SSOA with MA," 2022, doi: 10.21203/rs.3.rs-911875/v1.

[9] A. Sawadogo, E. R. Dossou-Yovo, L. Kouadio, S. J. Zwart, F. Traoré, and K. S. Gündoğdu, "Assessing the Biophysical Factors Affecting Irrigation Performance in Rice Cultivation Using Remote Sensing Derived Information," *Agricultural Water Management*, vol. 278, p. 108124, Mar. 2023, doi: 10.1016/J.AGWAT.2022.108124.

[10] M. Vieri et al., "A New Procedure for Combining UAV-Based Imagery and Machine Learning in Precision Agriculture," *Sustainability 2023*, vol. 15, p. 998, vol. 15, no. 2, p. 998, Jan. 2023, doi: 10.3390/SU15020998.

[11] A. Chen, M. Jacob, G. Shoshani, and M. Charter, "Using Computer Vision, Image Analysis and UAVs for the Automatic Recognition and Counting of Common Cranes (Grus Grus)," *Journal of Environmental Management*, vol. 328, p. 116948, Feb. 2023, doi: 10.1016/J.JENVMAN.2022.116948.

[12] "Sensor Networks: The Advantages and Disadvantages You Need To Know – Total Phase Blog." https://www.totalphase.com/blog/2019/04/sensor-networks-the-advantages-and-disadvantages-you-need-to-know/ (accessed Jan. 28, 2023).

[13] "The New Age: Cloud Computing in Agriculture – SourceTrace Systems." https://www.sourcetrace.com/blog/cloud-computing-agriculture/ (accessed Jan. 28, 2023).

[14] "Artificial Intelligence, Machine learning, deep learning and data science – What's the difference? | by Oluebube Princess Egbuna | Facebook Developer Circles Lagos | Medium." https://medium.com/fbdevclagos/artificial-intelligence-machine-learning-deep-learning-and-data-science-whats-the-difference-e82f9e7094a (accessed Jan. 28, 2023).

[15] L. de Carvalho Borella, M. Rodrigues de Carvalho Borella, and L. Luís Corso, "Climate Analysis Using Neural Networks as Supporting to the Agriculture Análise Climática utilizando redes neurais como apoio à agricultura", doi: 10.1590/1806-9649-2022v29e06.

[16] F. Bu and X. Wang, "A Smart Agriculture IoT System Based On Deep Reinforcement Learning," *Future Generation Computer Systems*, vol. 99, pp. 500–507, Oct. 2019, doi: 10.1016/J.FUTURE.2019.04.041.

[17] A. Rai, N. N. Das, and R. P. Singh, *Smart Agriculture: Emerging Pedagogies of Deep Learning, Machine Learning and Internet of Things*. 1967. 2023. [Online]. Available: https://www.routledge.com/Smart-Agriculture-Emerging-Pedagogies-of-Deep-Learning-Machine-Learning/Patel-Rai-Das-Singh/p/book/9780367535803 (accessed Jan. 28)

[18] "AI in Agriculture: Challenges, Benefits, and Use Cases – Intellias." https://intellias.com/artificial-intelligence-in-agriculture/ (accessed Feb. 3, 2023).